WITHDRAWN

Maria do Mar Pereira's work is a compelling and timely feminist ethnography of academic life that explores processes of academic valuation – how do academics determine what constitutes 'proper' knowledge? Pereira turns particular attention to women's, gender, and feminist studies' scholarship and asks how work produced in the field gets imagined as proper knowledge – or as improper knowledge – and how this status is shaped by the institutionalization of the field, the corporatization of the university, the increased precarity of the academic job market, and the dictates of the 'performative university' which promises scholars in the field recognition and legibility so long as they comply with the demands of productivity and hierarchy that mark the new university. Pereira's book is essential reading for feminist scholars invested in understanding the place of the field in the university, and interested in exploring how the university and its dictates and demands has shaped feminist knowledge production.

Jennifer Christine Nash is Associate Professor of African American Studies and Gender & Sexuality Studies at Northwestern University, Australia

This is a brilliant and original book, brimming with ideas, insights and integrity. Maria do Mar Pereira has given us both a nuanced engagement with contemporary Women's, Gender and Feminist Studies, and a compelling ethnography of academia as it becomes disfigured by brutal regimes of performativity. Her intelligence and intellectual generosity shine through on every page. A hugely important contribution.

Rosalind Gill is Professor of Social and Cultural Analysis at City University London, UK

The book describes a fascinating, longitudinal, ethnographic study rich in detail about feminist scholars' perceptions, work tensions and feelings, as well as accurately describing the complex and contradictory values and epistemic conditions in which contemporary gender studies exists in the academy. The discussion about the extent to which 21st century academics work in circumstances that both legitimate long hours and over-production of outputs will be of great interest to anyone trying to understand how modern universities operate. This eminently accessible and important study should also be compulsory reading for all university senior managers.

Professor Rosemary Deem, OBE, PhD, AcSocSci, FSRHE, VP Education, Royal Holloway University of London, UK

Power, Knowledge and Feminist Scholarship

Feminist scholarship is sometimes dismissed as not quite 'proper' knowledge – it's too political or subjective, many argue. But what are the boundaries of 'proper' knowledge? Who defines them, and how are they changing? How do feminists negotiate them? And how does this boundary-work affect women's and gender studies, and its scholars' and students' lives?

These are the questions tackled by this ground-breaking ethnography of academia inspired by feminist epistemology, Foucault, and science and technology studies. Drawing on data collected over a decade in Portugal and the UK, US and Scandinavia, this title explores different spaces of academic work and sociability, considering both official discourse and 'corridor talk'. It links epistemic negotiations to the shifting political economy of academic labour, and situates the smallest (but fiercest) departmental negotiations within global relations of unequal academic exchange. Through these links, this timely volume also raises urgent questions about the current state and status of gender studies and the mood of contemporary academia. Indeed, its sobering, yet uplifting, discussion of that mood offers fresh insight into what it means to produce feminist work within neoliberal cultures of academic performativity, demanding increasing productivity.

As the first book to analyse how academics talk (publicly or in off-the-record humour) about feminist scholarship, Power, Knowledge and Feminist Scholarship is essential reading for scholars and students in gender studies, LGBTQ studies, post-colonial studies, STS, sociology and education.

Maria do Mar Pereira is Assistant Professor in Sociology at the University of Warwick (UK) and Deputy Director of Warwick's Centre for the Study of Women and Gender.

Transformations: Thinking Through Feminism

Edited by
Maureen McNeil, *Institute of Women's Studies, Lancaster University*
Lynne Pearce, *Department of English, Lancaster University*

For a full list of titles in this series, please visit www.routledge.com

Other books in the series include:

Arab, Muslim, Woman
Voice and Vision in Postcolonial Literature and Film
Lindsey Moore

Secrecy and Silence in the Research Process
Feminist Reflections
Róisín Ryan-Flood and Rosalind Gill

Working with Affect in Feminist Readings
Disturbing Differences
Marianne Liljeström and Susanna Paasonen

Feminism, Culture and Embodied Practice
The Rhetoric's of Comparison
Carolyn Pedwell

Gender, Sexuality and Reproduction in Evolutionary Narratives
Venla Oikkonen

Feminism's Queer Temporalities
Sam McBean

Irish Feminist Futures
Claire Bracken

Power, Knowledge and Feminist Scholarship
An Ethnography of Academia
Maria do Mar Pereira

Power, Knowledge and Feminist Scholarship

An Ethnography of Academia

Maria do Mar Pereira

Routledge
Taylor & Francis Group

LONDON AND NEW YORK

First published 2017
by Routledge
2 Park Square, Milton Park, Abingdon, Oxon OX14 4RN

and by Routledge
711 Third Avenue, New York, NY 10017

Routledge is an imprint of the Taylor & Francis Group, an informa business

British Library Cataloguing-in-Publication Data
A catalogue record for this book is available from the British Library

Library of Congress Cataloging-in-Publication Data
Names: Pereira, Maria do Mar, author.
Title: Power, knowledge and feminist scholarship : an ethnography
   of academia / Maria do Mar Pereira.
Description: 1 Edition. | New York : Routledge, [2017] | Includes
   bibliographical references and index.
Identifiers: LCCN 2016030451 | ISBN 9781138911499 (hardback) |
   ISBN 9781315692623 (eBook)
Subjects: LCSH: Women's studies. | Women college teachers. |
   Women college students. | Feminism and education.
Classification: LCC HQ1180 .P464 2017 | DDC 305.4—dc23
LC record available at https://lccn.loc.gov/2016030451

ISBN: 978-1-138-91149-9 (hbk)
ISBN: 978-1-315-69262-3 (ebk)

Typeset in Times New Roman
by Apex CoVantage, LLC

Cover image is an artwork by Helena Almeida.

Ao Lucas,
inimaginável quando comecei a escrever este livro,
irresistível enquanto tentava acabá-lo,
inspirador todos os dias

À comunidade (entendida de forma abrangente e inclusiva)
de Estudos sobre as Mulheres, de Género e Feministas em Portugal,
pelo longo e árduo trabalho diário de criação de conhecimento transformador,
de um campo novo, e de um clima académico diferente

Contents

List of figures   xi
List of abbreviations   xii
Acknowledgements   xiii
Notes on the presentation of material   xvii

Introduction   1

1   An outsider within? The position and status of
    WGFS in academia   28

2   Pushing and pulling the boundaries of knowledge:
    A feminist theory of epistemic status   44

3   WGFS in the performative university (Part I):
    The epistemic status of WGFS in times of paradoxical
    change   69

4   WGFS is proper knowledge, but . . .: The splitting of
    feminist scholarship   95

5   Putting WGFS on the map(s): The boundary-work
    of WGFS scholars   120

6   The importance of being foreign and modern: The
    geopolitics of the epistemic status of WGFS   148

7   WGFS in the performative university (Part II):
    The mood of academia and its impact on our knowledge
    and our lives   179

Conclusion: Negotiating the boundaries of proper
knowledge and of work in the (not quite fully)
performative university   201

Index   225

Figures

1 Comic Strip from *Piled Higher and Deeper* by Jorge Cham
   (www.phdcomics.com)   44
2 Map, *Portugal Is Not a Small Country*, Henrique Galvão (1934)   60

Abbreviations

APEM	*Associação Portuguesa de Estudos sobre as Mulheres* (Portuguese Women's Studies Association)
ATHENA	Advanced Thematic Network in Activities in Women's Studies in Europe
BP	Bologna Process
CIG	*Comissão para a Cidadania e Igualdade de Género* (Governmental Commission for Citizenship and Gender Equality)
CIDM	*Comissão para a Igualdade e para os Direitos das Mulheres* (Governmental Commission for Equality and Women's Rights)
CIEG	Centro Interdisciplinar de Estudos de Género (Interdisciplinary Centre for Gender Studies)
ERC	European Research Council
FCT	*Fundação para a Ciência e Tecnologia* (Portuguese Foundation for Science and Technology) – Portugal's national research council
HE	Higher Education
HEFCE	Higher Education Funding Council for England
LGBTQ	Lesbian, Gay, Bisexual, Trans* and Queer
OED	Oxford English Dictionary
PG	Postgraduate
REF	Research Excellence Framework – the UK's national research evaluation exercise
SciELO	Scientific Electronic Library Online
SSH	Social Sciences and Humanities
STS	Science and Technology Studies
UG	Undergraduate
WGFS	Women's, Gender, Feminist Studies

Acknowledgements

Conducting the research presented in this book was a long process of learning about the production of academic knowledge, both as I analysed how my participants do it and as I became a 'proper' academic myself. But some of the most important insights I gained into knowledge production didn't come from the field work notes I wrote or the books I read. I've been extremely fortunate to be surrounded by fantastic academics, activists, relatives and friends who've taught me that knowledge production is a collective process, and one that's fuelled as much by reading, writing and debate, as by shared food, laughter, silliness and care. I want to thank them here, in the full knowledge, however, that a decade-long project, like this one, spanning several life-stages, countries, institutions and modes of employment, generates more relationships of exchange and support, and heavier debts of gratitude, than I can do justice to in these pages.

It was through the teaching and writing of Portuguese WGFS scholars that I first discovered that it's possible to think critically about power and knowledge, and that everything changes when you do so. Since then, the Portuguese WGFS community has offered ongoing encouragement and invaluable spaces of intergenerational and interdisciplinary collaboration which have transformed and broadened my thinking. As if this wasn't enough, Portuguese WGFS scholars were extremely generous with their time, patience and information as I bothered them with requests for interviews and observation. The least I can do is dedicate this book to them.

Clare Hemmings guided the initial, and formative, stages of this project with her trademark brilliance, attention to detail, dexterity and wit. Even after many years of benefitting from it, I remain stunned by her exceptional ability to ask small questions that make the biggest difference. Long after their 'official task' was completed, Mary Evans and Maureen McNeil have continued to engage generously, supportively and challengingly with my work, and I feel grateful and honoured for the opportunities they've created for me. In particular, it has been a privilege to see my work chosen to integrate the Routledge *Transformations* series, not just because I get to feature alongside many inspiring colleagues, but more importantly because Maureen, Lynne Pearce, Emily Briggs and Elena Chiu are the most delightfully efficient, patient, amusing and encouraging team of editors one could ever hope for.

I want to acknowledge the immense inspiration, support and insight I have gained throughout the research and writing process from mentors, teachers, colleagues and readers across several countries and institutions: Kerstin Alnebratt, Lígia Amâncio, Emma-Louise Anderson, Tobias Axelsson, Ana Brandão, Maria João Cunha, Mafalda Dâmaso, Kathy Davis, Sara de Jong, Rosemary Deem, Daša Duhaček, Virgínia Ferreira, Deborah Finding, Rosalind Gill, Jin Haritaworn, Marsha Henry, Sally Hines, Aggie Hirst, Liisa Husu, Teresa Joaquim, Hazel Johnstone, Gunnel Karlsson, Biljana Kašić, Nina Lykke, Chinwe Madubuike, Sofia Neves, Conceição Nogueira, Carolyn Pedwell, Maud Perrier, Diane Perrons, Fiona Philip, Rui Ferreira Pinto, Aggeliki Sifaki, Bev Skeggs, Manuela Tavares, Anália Torres, Miguel Vale de Almeida, Iris Van Der Tuin, Isabel Ventura, Robyn Wiegman, Carolyn Williams, Rebekah Wilson, Veronika Wöhrer, the participants in the 'Lost (and Found) in Translation' (2007–2009) project at LSE, my colleagues in GEXcel, ATHENA, ATGENDER, WeAVE and the ATHENA sub-group 'Travelling Concepts: Interdisciplinarity', the delegates who commented on my papers in conferences, and peer reviewers at Routledge and different journals. The project also benefitted from the support of colleagues in the LSE and Warwick libraries and the Biblioteca Madalena Barbosa (CIG), and from the astoundingly efficient publishing and copyediting expertise of Tina Cottone and Anna Potter. Yara Richter, caught in the Foucauldian web before she even knew it existed, was an extraordinary research assistant in the final stage of research.

In the last months of writing, as I became more care-ful – gaining new caring responsibilities – but also more care-less (in Lynch's (2010) sense) – with myself – a wonderful group of adults (and children) worked tirelessly to take care of, and entertain, me and my family. Thank you, Alice Mah, Colin Stephen and Lucian; Mia Hutchinson, Nate Tkacz and Ernest and Lena; Natasha Marhia and Siouxdhan, Maya and Ishaan; Charlotte Panesar and Kirpa; Laura Lynas and Billy; Georgina Olsen and Austin; Rachael Leslie and Niamh and Reuben; Melissa Koulter and Caiden; Rachel Smith and Jake; Charlotte Thomas and Joseph; and Cecilia Ghidotti. It really wouldn't have been possible to write this book without the staff at ABC Nursery (particularly Claire Robertson, Lydia Tift, Michelle Howarth and Nabila Bibi), whose commitment to their work, devotion to the children, patience for new parent blunders, magic skills (e.g. to transform shaving foam into Arctic landscapes) and absolutely priceless banter have made our day time and time again.

One reason why I am desperate to finish this book is that I cannot wait to get back to daily work with colleagues and students. UG and PG students, and teaching and research assistants, at LSE, the University of Leeds and the University of Warwick have kept me stimulated, amused and on my toes . . . and some kept me alone so I could think, even though they needed my supervision to advance their own thinking; a special thanks to Liz Ablett, Eleanor Broadbent, Anna Colgan, Joanna Cuttell, Inês Gomes, Demet Gülçiçek, Ruth Pearce, Freya Potter, Alexa Santos and Jey Saung. It has been an absolute privilege and an endless joy to work with a collegial group of brilliant minds at the Department of Sociology of the University of Warwick. I am grateful to them all. Some colleagues – Darani Anand, Claire Blencowe, Gemma Hearnden, Amy Hinterberger, Cath Lambert, Alice Mah, Goldie Osuri, Florian Reiche, Leon Sealey-Huggins, Simone Varriale, John Solomos, Ros Williams and Caroline Wright – have worked particularly hard to remind me every day that there's much more to university life than work; in doing so, they have inspired many of the ideas I develop here (and preserved my sanity and good humour along the way). No one has done so more imaginatively than Hannah Jones, Lynne Pettinger and Nickie Charles, who use (respectively) exquisite crafts, devious questioning techniques and well-timed no-nonsense emails to teach me valuable lessons in the feminist politics of work. Emily Henderson was there at the loneliest times to cook the food, ask the questions and make the points I needed to move my thinking along. Natasha Marhia met me on the day this project started, and came to witness the moment it ended; her stunningly insightful feedback, unending wisdom, devoted companionship and chocolate creations sustained me along the way.

My work and life have been changed, over and over again, by intellectual debates, joint research endeavours, activist work, epiphany-inducing conversations, cohabitation (for one night or several years!), networks of exchange of parenting advice, and general shenanigans with Angeliki Alvanoudi, Kristin Aune, Serena Bassi, Gwendolyn Beetham, Marina Franchi, Manuela Galetto, Mónica García Quesada, Sabine Grenz, Zhang Hui, Patrizia Kokot-Blamey, Tarang Kumar, Mia Liinason, Sam Lyle, Sveva Magaraggia, Chris Rossdale, Amy Russell, Christina Scharff, Greg Taylor, Lena Wånggren and Caroline Willemen. O mesmo agradecimento também se aplica a vocês, com a dose extra de saudades que a língua portuguesa me deixa acrescentar: Liliana Azevedo, Rosa Azevedo, Almerinda Bento, Ana Caetano, Salomé Coelho, Ana Costa, Nelson Vieira da Cunha, Inês Espírito Santo, Joana Henriques, Nuno Lima, Cláudia Lopes, Rui Lopes, Sofia Martinho, João Manuel de Oliveira, Tiago Romeu, Inês Sacchetti, Ana Cristina Santos, Sofia Almeida Santos e Ricardo Silva. A Diana Pais continua a ser o meu musical americano.

Para começar este projeto, tive de me afastar da minha família. Ao fazê-lo, ganhei – e até co-criei – novos membros da família, mas isso só tornou ainda mais custoso estar tão longe da Lina Lampreia, Abílio Mata, Ana Carolina, Matilde, Francisca e Eduardo Mata, Sebastião Ribeiro, Henrique e Leonor Fernandes, Mariana, Francisco e Catarina Ramos, Daniel Silva, Lourdes, Maria João, Lucília e António Mata, d@s 'amarel@s' da família Mata (Clara, Zé Ribeiro, João Paulo, Albano, Zé Goes e João), da Maria Ana e Beatriz Barata, Cristina Costa, Judy Dean, e especialmente da Isabel Matta, Lucília Mata, Rogério Balsemão e Martin Dean. E um dia, de repente, fez-se luz nas West Midlands quando a Violeta Pereira e o Pedro Alexandre vieram dar sentido (e 'nonsense') à vida aqui. Faz-se luz e sentido também cada vez que a Paulina Mata e o Jorge Lampreia tomam conta de mim, de todas as formas possíveis, e às vezes impossíveis.

Jonathan Dean fills my life with comfort, but makes sure I never get too settled in my usual intellectual and political comfort zones. I am ever more amazed by, and grateful for, the limitless insight and happiness that he generates through these 'logics of articulation' of love, friendship, team-work, politics and knowledge. E depois há o Lucas, a pessoa que contribuiu mais direta e insistentemente para atrasar a produção deste livro, interromper a escrita (com distrações e, especialmente, com diarreias) e sabotar a minha produtividade académica. É em parte por isso mesmo que ele merece um dos maiores agradecimentos do mundo.

The fieldwork and writing for this book were enabled, and generously supported, by a grant from the *Fundação para a Ciência e Tecnologia* (SFRH/BD/27439/2006, 2006–2010); a research fellowship awarded by GEXcel (Centre for Excellence in Gender Research, 2011); research exchanges through the GenderAct network, funded by the *Riksbanken Jubileumsfonds* (2011–2013); and a research leave funded by a University of Warwick Academic Returners Fellowship (2015–2016). This support is greatly appreciated. Such funding opportunities and support structures do not, of course, emerge from thin air: securing and managing them requires immense labour which often remains invisible. Therefore, I want to acknowledge the work of the WGFS scholars who led the funding bids for GEXcel and GenderAct, and the commitment of Sandra Beaufoy, whose tireless work for gender equality at Warwick contributed to the game-changing creation of the Academic Returners Fellowship.

I am also grateful for the permission to incorporate here excerpts from material previously published elsewhere. Parts of chapter 3 were included in 'Higher Education Cutbacks and the Reshaping of Epistemic Hierarchies: an Ethnographic Study of the Case of Feminist Scholarship', *Sociology* (2015), 49 (2), 287–304. Chapter 4 is a significantly revised and expanded version of ' "Feminist Theory is Proper Knowledge, But . . .": The Status of Feminist Scholarship in the Academy', *Feminist Theory* (2012), 13 (3), 283–303. A shorter version of chapter 6 was published as 'The Importance of Being "Modern" and Foreign: Feminism and the Epistemic Status of Nations', *Signs: Journal of Women in Culture and Society* (2014), 39 (3), 627–657. Chapter 7 and the conclusion contain very short snippets from 'Struggling within and beyond the Performative University: Articulating Activism and Work in an "Academia Without Walls" ', *Women's Studies International Forum* (2016), 54, 100–110. I also want to thank Jorge Cham (www.phdcomics.com) for permission to reprint the comic strip that opens chapter 2, and Helena Almeida and Módulo – Centro Difusor de Arte for generously allowing me to use in the book's cover reproductions of pieces from Helena Almeida's *Pintura Habitada* series (1976).

Notes on the presentation of material

I use the following symbols when presenting fieldwork material:

> "*Italicised in double quotation marks*": speech recorded and transcribed verbatim
> "Non-italicised in double quotation marks": speech reconstituted from fieldnotes
> <text>: word or phrase originally uttered in English
> (. . .): omitted speech
> [text]: additional information

All fieldwork material is originally in Portuguese and has been translated by me, except where otherwise indicated.

When attributing quotes to research participants, I use 'senior scholar' to refer to scholars who at the time of fieldwork held full-time, paid academic positions and had completed their PhDs at least five years previously. I use 'junior scholar' to refer to scholars who did not hold full-time, paid academic positions and/or did not have PhDs or had completed a PhD within the preceding 5 years.

An asterisk after a page number – for example (Caetano, 2008: 24*) – indicates that the referenced text is not originally in English and the quote has been translated by me.

Introduction

This book has been 10 years in the making, which means that for over a decade I have been asked by colleagues, friends, students, taxi drivers what it is about. I quickly learned that memorising a one-sentence description – the so-called 'elevator pitch' – is key, and soon lost count of how many times I used mine. 'I'm analysing the discourses that circulate in academia about the extent to which women's and gender studies can produce [cue finger-dance[1]] "proper" scientific knowledge, and how feminist academics negotiate those discourses'. Women's, gender, feminist studies (WGFS) scholars[2] from different generations and locations often responded with a sigh, knowing smile, rolling of the eyes, raising of the eyebrows, vigorous nod or sudden jolt to attention; they were clearly familiar with those discourses and negotiations. Many recounted personal experiences in detail, others hinted at stories left untold – 'argh, if you knew the things I've heard in my university!' or 'if I received [insert relevant currency here] every time I'm told that gender studies is too ideological to count as a real academic field. . .'.

These reactions, and much of the international literature on WGFS' institutionalisation, show that the experience of encountering claims that 'WGFS is not quite proper academic knowledge' is shared by many scholars (although it takes very different forms across countries, disciplines, institutions, periods). It also shows that this experience can have significant impacts. In my case, the frequency and stifling effects of those encounters while studying Sociology as an undergraduate student in Lisbon in the early 2000s would eventually become the main impetus for the decision to leave Portugal and continue studying elsewhere. It would also trigger a desire to study these negotiations of WGFS' *epistemic status*. I define this as the *degree to which, and terms in which, a knowledge claim, or entire field, is recognised as fulfilling the requisite criteria to be considered credible and relevant knowledge, however those criteria are defined in specific spaces, communities and moments.* Academics within and outside WGFS are involved in negotiations of epistemic status every day and are well-versed in their language and rituals. Nevertheless, at the centre of these (wearingly) familiar negotiations we can find complex processes and relationships that raise challenging questions about power, inequality and the production and legitimation of knowledge. These questions demand close examination, both using the valuable analytical tools created by feminist and critical scholars who have long problematised epistemic practice, and also developing new tools to make sense of the complex manifestations of these negotiations in times of intense academic and social change.

That is the collective project to which I contribute with this book, a feminist ethnography of academia. It examines several sites of everyday academic work and sociability to explore how academics demarcate the boundaries of 'proper' knowledge, and how WGFS scholarship gets positioned in relation to those boundaries. I conceptualise academic practice as shaped by ongoing struggles over the definition of, and the power to define, what can count as 'proper' knowledge, and should therefore be accepted, funded or certified as such. I draw on long-term fieldwork in Portugal, and participant observation in the UK, US, Sweden, and at international academic conferences throughout the world, and I ask: How is WGFS spoken about in daily academic interactions? To what extent, and in what conditions, is its epistemic status recognised? How does WGFS' epistemic status shape, and get shaped through, the institutionalisation of the field? How are all these relations affected by broader processes of local and international academic change, such as funding cutbacks, the marketisation and metricisation of higher education (HE), or the intensification, extensification and casualisation of academic labour? By asking these questions, I hope to show that understandings of what counts as 'proper' knowledge 'are not the tranquil locus on the basis of which other questions (. . .) may be posed, but that they themselves pose a whole cluster of questions' (Foucault, 2006 [1969]: 28–29).

The epistemic status of WGFS as a problem

One of the most far-reaching and influential contributions of feminist scholarship is the demonstration that scientific activities, products and institutions are constituted by, and constitutive of, relations of power. Feminists operationalise that insight in different ways (Code, 2006; Crasnow *et al.*, 2015), but they share the view that scientificity is not an inherent property of claims, disciplines or individuals, which is susceptible to 'objective' identification and renders them epistemically superior. They see 'scientific', 'proper', 'academic', 'scholarly' or 'authoritative'[3] as 'words of containment, demarcation' (Walsh, 1995: 91) that limit both the forms of knowledge perceived to be accurate and worthy of consideration, and the types of people recognised as credible knowledge producers (Amâncio, 2005; Collins, 1990; Haraway, 1990; Harding, 1991; Kilomba, 2007; Nogueira, 2001). Haraway argues that 'politics and ethics ground struggles for the contests over what may count as rational knowledge (. . .) [whether] [t]hat is admitted or not' (1990: 193). For her and other scholars, the classification of something as scientific is not just an epistemic act but also, and crucially, a political one. The stakes in that classification are high: as Harding puts it, 'whoever gets to define what counts as (. . .) scientific (. . .) also gets a powerful role in shaping the picture of the world that results from scientific research' (1991: 40).

Conceptualising scientificity through this lens renders the epistemic status of WGFS a problem, in two ways. It is a problem in the sense that the field's epistemic status is not a given; it is, rather, a complex object that can be empirically analysed, a construction that one can deconstruct. It is a problem also because epistemic status affects local conditions and possibilities for WGFS research and study, and the forms of circulation of WGFS scholarship. It has been demonstrated that the idea that WGFS is not quite proper knowledge can have a detrimental impact on student engagement and on the career prospects, professional opportunities, and well-being of emerging and established WGFS scholars (Griffin, 2005; Jenkins and Keane, 2014; Marchbank and Letherby, 2006; Morley, 1998; Stanley, 1997). Discussing the institutionalisation of WGFS in Italy, Barazzetti *et al.* explain that:

> [t]he general lack of attention to (or open boycotting of) women's and gender studies on the part of the academic world (. . .) has limited the opportunities of offering (. . .) [WGFS] knowledge to students; (. . .) reduced the ability to do research and theoretical work in this field; (. . .) blocked the growth of new energies and new skills and discouraged those already existent. It has belittled the worth of these studies in students' eyes; and in particular it has blocked comparison, growth and experimenting with new tools and ways of teaching.
>
> (2002: 201)

WGFS is certainly not the only field whose ability to produce proper knowledge is questioned; numerous others, within and outside the social sciences and humanities (SSH), have been at the centre of struggles over epistemic status in the distant and recent past.[4] Nevertheless, the fact that WGFS has generally been framed explicitly as a project of critique of mainstream knowledge production makes negotiations of epistemic status a particularly salient dimension of its institutionalisation. Indeed, claims about epistemic status are one of the means through which those feminist critiques are discounted. The notion that WGFS is not at all, or not entirely, 'epistemologically worthwhile' (Ezequiel, 1999, cited in Le Feuvre and Andriocci, 2002: 261) has been used as justification to dismiss feminist scholars as not qualified to make credible claims about the nature and norms of knowledge production. Because it undermines those efforts of feminist critique, the epistemic belittling of WGFS needs to be problematised. And yet, we must be careful not to presume that WGFS is always and only marginalised in negotiations of epistemic status. It is worth examining feminist academics' 'own entanglements in the power-knowledge tango' and 'to look more carefully at (. . .) patterns [of power] within and around feminism' (McNeil, 1993: 168). As I show in the following chapters, power does not operate in linear or straightforward ways in demarcations of the boundaries of proper knowledge, and feminist scholars have contradictory investments in those demarcations. Because epistemic status has such significant, but complex, effects, it is crucial to research its negotiation.

Conducting that research requires travelling across, and creating bridges between, different bodies of literature. Feminist epistemology and other critical theorisations of the politics of knowledge production are invaluable and inescapable, but shed relatively little light on how epistemic categories are actually invoked and understood in everyday, located academic practice. To find insight on this, it is productive to turn to Science and Technology Studies (STS), and the vast literature on the institutionalisation of WGFS, which offer detailed studies of the micro- and macro-level epistemic negotiations which academics engage in daily. Articulating these different strands of inquiry allows us to explore epistemological questions empirically, or rather, to observe how the questions about the nature of knowledge raised by feminist epistemologists and other theorists play out at the level of the daily academic practices problematised by STS and by research on HE and the institutionalisation of WGFS. In chapter 1 I review the institutionalisation literature; in chapter 2 I show how I have combined feminist epistemology, STS and Foucault to produce a theory of epistemic status.

WGFS' status in times of change: Linking the local and the global, the epistemic and the economic

I put that theory to work in an ethnography of academia, focusing primarily (though not exclusively) on Portugal. Portugal is a productive case study in many ways. WGFS emerged relatively 'late'[5] there but, as I explain in chapter 3, the turn of the 21st century saw a consolidation of the institutionalisation of the field, against a backdrop of not only profound local and global transformation in academia, but also major national political, social and economic upheaval. As a range of so-called 'neoliberal' trends, partly legitimated by a rhetoric of 'austerity' – reduction in state funding for universities, intensification of academic labour, marketisation and metricisation of scientific practice, individual and institutional reorientation towards profitability, or multiplication and complexification of auditing regimes – crept gradually into the Portuguese SSH, and eventually became the over-arching and defining *modus operandi*, negotiations of the epistemic status of WGFS have been intense and undergone significant and complex changes. My initial fieldwork (2008/2009) was carried out when these processes were just beginning and certainly already on scholars' radar; but nothing could have prepared them (or me!) for the state of affairs they described in the follow-up interviews, conducted in 2015/2016, immediately after the fall of the right-wing government that drove through many of those changes in the intervening years.

Although this particular playing out of governmental decisions and (mis)fortunes is specific to Portugal, the story I tell here is certainly not just a *local* or *national* one. As scholars have shown for other countries in the (semi-)periphery of the global academic order (see chapter 6), many of the changes which have recently been implemented locally (e.g. new research evaluation criteria) are inspired by, imported from, and oriented to other countries, particularly the

US and the UK (Aavik *et al.*, 2015; Mountz *et al.*, 2015). The Higher Education Funding Council for England (HEFCE), for example, regularly provides equivalent official bodies in other countries (from Europe to Asia) advice and support on setting up REF-like exercises there, and a proposal to internationalise the UK REF is being considered (HEFCE, 2014; Matthews, 2014). As a result of this, both the political economy and the epistemic status of academic knowledge is increasingly negotiated across, and through, national boundaries. Publishing in anglophone journals, for example, becomes an ever more important – if not obligatory – means for strengthening the local standing of a scholar or institution. This, of course, bolsters those journals' global centrality, influence and impact factor, reinforcing their status as a site of proper knowledge. The story of contemporary academia is, thus, one where the local and global, the centre and periphery, influence and constitute each other (Sousa Santos, 2005). Therefore, my located ethnography of negotiations of WGFS produces insight not just about a specific country, but also about the countries it frames as benchmark, model and aspiration, or those it seeks to distance itself from, or compete with. More broadly, it sheds light on the structure and impacts of global geopolitical academic hierarchies.

By focusing on the Portuguese context during this period, the book therefore offers rare longitudinal insight into the effects on *local* WGFS of the rapid but dramatic *transnational* transformations that have swept academic communities throughout Europe (Liinason and Grenz, 2016) and beyond (Davies and O'Callaghan, 2014; Nash and Owens, 2015). This insight is vital because it situates issues of *epistemology* within the concrete but changing *political economy* of academic labour, two levels of inquiry often addressed separately. Articulating epistemology with political economy, local with global, enables us to better understand the complex relations between contemporary transnational regimes of academic governance, processes of macro- and micro-level change in academic institutions, and the epistemic categories that academics use every day. At this moment in time, WGFS looks very different throughout the world and faces distinct challenges in each local context. Whereas in some places it has become increasingly respected (as is, arguably, the case in Portugal), in others it currently finds itself under fierce attack; in some it has even become the object of moral panics beyond the academy, as political and religious figures in France, Italy, Poland, Brazil and elsewhere denounce 'gender ideology' as a foreign 'pseudo-science' (Grabowska, 2016) threatening national identity, values and traditions, and undermining the 'so called "natural ordering of society"' (Fiore and Habed, 2016). We must, of course, remain attentive to the local specificities of the triumphs, trials and tribulations of WGFS. . . . But linking local with global, and epistemology with political economy, will add to, and help us go beyond, strictly national debates about contemporary WGFS, hopefully generating new forms of transnational insight and solidarity, better equipped to engage watchfully and critically with current academic and political changes and to pro-actively resist their more pernicious effects on WGFS (and beyond).

Speaking of 'science' and 'women's, gender, feminist studies'

At the centre of this project are the categories of science and scientificity, terms defined in varying ways. Because I aim to examine precisely those processes of definition, I leave the terms open and do not provide my own *a priori* definition; it is, nevertheless, important to situate my use of them. As Harding notes,

> Anglo-American conventions (. . .) [restrict] the term 'science' in its central or paradigmatic meaning to the natural sciences, in contrast to the European practice of seeing as equally deserving of the label 'scientific knowledge-seeking' those modes of systematic (. . .) inquiry that are favored in the social sciences and even in humanities and arts.

(1991: 306)

Indeed, in many countries and languages in continental Europe, Latin America and elsewhere (see, for example, Petersen, 2003 on Danish), the categories of 'science' and 'scientific' are used to refer also to the SSH[6] and their use does not necessarily presume or signify an acclamation of positivist notions of science and objectivity. Consider, for example, Braidotti's definition of WGFS: '[w]omen's studies is a field of *scientific* and pedagogical activity devoted to improving the status of women (. . .). Women's studies is a *critical project* in so far as it examines *how science perpetuates forms of* (. . .) *exclusion*' (2000: 33, my emphases). This illustrates one of the book's key arguments: it is crucial to locate demarcations of scientificity, because 'situation and place are constitutive, if not determinative, of how problems are defined, evidence recognized, read, and interpreted: thus, (. . .) place [is] not merely context or backdrop' (Code, 2006: 161). Because much of my empirical material was collected in non-anglophone sites, I use the category 'science' to refer very broadly to academic or scholarly forms of knowledge production, however this may be defined contextually – which is precisely the object of my analysis. Adopting this broader definition also has another important effect: it contributes to disrupt the problematic tendency within STS scholarship to equate studies of scientific practice with studies of the natural or 'hard' sciences, an equation which several feminists have denounced and resisted (Mayer, 2009; Petersen, 2003; Whelan, 2001).

I use the label *women's, gender, feminist studies* or WGFS to speak of the field[7] of research and teaching on women and gender and/or conducted from a feminist perspective, a decision that also requires elucidation, as the field's name has been a fiercely and intensely debated issue (see chapter 1; Braidotti, 2002; Hemmings, 2006). In Portugal, for example, there is even debate about whether that debate is actually a debate! Portuguese scholars use different terms and there is some published discussion on their relative merits (Ferreira, 2001, 2004; Macedo, 2000; Magalhães, 2001). Referring to this, Ferreira notes that '[t]he issue [of naming] is, evidently, complex and continues to be polemical' (2001: 22*). However, in the very same 2001 issue of the WGFS journal *ex aequo*, Magalhães explains that some of the WGFS scholars she interviewed saw it 'as a debate that is already cold' (2001: 46*). One of my interviewees described the current situation as one where disagreement about naming persists, but because scholars have realised that a consensus will never be reached, they continue using their different names independently and naming has ceased to be the object of active debate. To reflect this, APEM (the Portuguese Women's Studies Association) has used the formulation *Estudos sobre as Mulheres/Estudos Feministas/Estudos de Género* (Women's Studies/Feminist Studies/Gender Studies) when referring to the field (Pinto, 2009). This is one reason why I initially chose to speak of WGFS when referring to the field in Portugal. Since I started this research and began presenting on it in Portugal, some colleagues have begun using my condensed formulation to name the field (for example, Tavares, 2015; Torres *et al.*, 2015), and a couple have identified the creation of that name as one of my project's main contributions to Portuguese WGFS. At this level, the field itself has been shaped – although only on a small scale – by the research on it, and WGFS (or EMGF in Portuguese) is now a term with actual community currency, rather than just my analytic shorthand.

I use the term WGFS also to keep the boundaries of my object as open as possible. I am interested in examining the status both of scholarship explicitly framed as belonging to WGFS, and of research that focuses on WGFS themes or takes up WGFS perspectives but is presented as grounded in a particular mainstream[8] discipline. I am also keen to explore the sometimes fraught relationship between those who study gender or women from feminist perspectives, and those who study gender or women but explicitly distance themselves from feminism. Indeed, the boundaries between these different categories are sometimes extremely fuzzy, namely because – as I will show – many scholars describe their work, frame their relationship to WGFS, and name the field differently depending on the context in which, and audience for whom, they speak. In this sense, one can argue – as I do in chapter 1 – that naming decisions are a key element and tool of negotiations of epistemic status, rather than a pre-existing basis for them. Therefore, I use WGFS as a broad umbrella term with contested meanings and changing boundaries. I do not presume an overlap, equivalence or necessary articulation between *women*, *gender*, and *feminism*, and I do not demarcate *a priori* what is WGFS scholarship and who is a WGFS scholar. When identifying interviewees and speakers throughout the book as 'WGFS' or 'non-WGFS' scholars, I draw on their own (sometimes shifting) self-categorisation as affirmed in their overall work, in that particular presentation or in the interview.

An ethnography of academia

Doing research on one's peers is not something that scholars often do. For Wisniewski, the relative lack of ethnographies of HE (as opposed to primary and secondary education) is a form of 'collective "averted gaze"' from the inner workings of academia (2000: 5). Sheehan notes that studying other academics is considered 'bad taste' (1993a: 255) and Butterwick and Dawson describe it as 'one of the greatest taboos' (2005: 52). Friese argues that this is because '[a]cademics don't like to be made into objects. They like to be the subjects who turn others into objects' (2001: 288). In a powerful illustration of the difficulty of conducting such work, Williams and Klemmer start an article on ethnographies of academia with a box offering the following text: 'This space is where I would have liked to present a complete ethnography of [an STS seminar]. (. . .) But some of my colleagues told me that studying them would be problematic' (1997: 165). And yet, academic communities make excellent objects of study.

Even in the simplest academic interaction, there is often much happening. Sitting in a campus café, a group of young scholars discuss the papers they hope to present at the upcoming conference of a national sociological association; one advises another not to submit her abstract to the gender strand because interventions there are too political and unsociological. After the public viva for a doctoral thesis, the examiners meet privately to discuss whether the feminist qualitative methodology used is rigorous enough to make the thesis acceptable scholarship. At a well-attended book launch, a feminist scholar argues that being attentive to contemporary women's studies research will allow mainstream social scientists to produce better knowledge. A lecturer tells an undergraduate class that feminist critiques played an invaluable role in the development of a field, but were not always sufficiently rigorous; two students dispute this. These scenes, all of them true descriptions of real-life events, can be understood as instances of negotiation of the epistemic status of WGFS. But how might one observe and analyse situations like these, both hyper-visible – feminist and other scholars have been reflecting on them for decades, as I discuss in chapter 1 – and invisible – because they are so frequent and mundane, 'because [they are] too much on the surface of things' (Foucault, 1989 [1969]: 58). What methods can be used (and with what effects, possibilities and limitations) to explore this hyper-visible and invisible boundary-work? And what happens when one researches the researchers? These are important questions which I analyse at length elsewhere (Pereira, 2011, 2013) but unfortunately cannot do full justice to here. What I offer, instead, is a brief characterisation of my fieldwork, flagging up some of the complex challenges of managing power, positionality and perspective in fieldwork with, and about, fellow scholars.

I would argue that boundary-work over WGFS can best be analysed through *feminist discursive ethnography*; in other words, through a *feminist ethnography* that focuses on *discourse*. Ethnography is especially suited to a study of 'local culture-in-the-making' (Franklin, 1995: 179) and 'knowledge-in-the-making' (Beaulieu, 2010: 454), and to a conceptualisation of objects as 'accomplishments' rather than facts (Pollner and Emerson, 2007: 125). As I explain in chapter 1, engaging with the *ongoing-ness* and *everyday-ness* of negotiations of epistemic status is a key aim of this project, because those are dimensions hinted at, but not explored, in the literature on the institutionalisation of WGFS. Using ethnography to analyse how WGFS' epistemic status is accomplished is, thus, an epistemic game-changer because it flips the questions we can ask and things we can see. Defining ethnography is, however, more complicated than the lines opening this paragraph might make it seem. Ethnography itself is an object of intense contestation (Atkinson *et al.*, 2007; Riles, 2006) and boundary-work over what constitutes proper ethnography is ancient and ongoing. One axis of boundary-work relates to the fact that ethnography has been central to the affirmation and demarcation of disciplinary identity in anthropology and other fields, serving as 'a valued object of a professional culture', with a 'heavy symbolic, identity-defining load' (Marcus, 2009: 4–5). But ethnography is the object of boundary-work not only because it is highly valued, but also because it has relatively little value. Indeed, ethnographic work is often dismissed as not quite scientific by quantitative scholars or scholars outside the social sciences (Forsythe, 2001; Monahan and Fisher, 2010), and so ethnographers are regularly involved in negotiations over whether their method lies on the 'right' side of boundaries.

My ethnography is focused on discourse. Due to their daunting diversity, analyses of discourse also do not lend themselves to one uniting and stable description (Nogueira, 2001). I adopt a critical discursive approach that is centrally (albeit not exclusively) inspired by Foucault. The author's recurring assertion that his proposals 'are not intended as methodological imperatives' (1978 [1976]: 78) have led scholars to argue that Foucault's methodological contributions should be seen as flexible strategies (Ferguson, 1991; Tamboukou and Ball, 2003).[9] I find Foucault's notion of *genealogy* – developed in *Discipline and Punish* (1979 [1975]) and his later work – particularly productive and flexible, as it is presented both as a methodological device and a mode of critical engagement with the power-effects of scientificity. According to Foucault, genealogy focuses on 'the discourse-power axis or, if you like, the discursive practice-clash of power axis' (2003 [1976]: 178). It requires not just undertaking a 'meticulous rediscovery of struggles', but also 'mak[ing] use of that knowledge in contemporary tactics' (2003 [1976]: 8). Foucault defines those tactics as follows:

> [Genealogy] is a way of playing local, discontinuous, disqualified, or nonlegitimized knowledges off against the (. . .) theoretical instance that claims to be able to filter them, organize them into a hierarchy (. . .) in the name of a true body of knowledge, in the name of the rights of a science that is in the hands of the few.
>
> (2003 [1976]: 9)

Therefore, for Foucault, genealogies of struggles over scientificity are 'theoretico-political' (1991 [1980]: 76) acts that can contribute to disrupting the normalisation of the truth- and power-effects of the category of the scientific. Genealogies can do this because they help to 'dereif[y] contemporary practices and objects, robbing them of their traditional ahistorical, foundationalistic legitimations' (Fraser, 1996: 19) and thus they question the apparent inevitability and legitimacy of the disqualification of particular knowledges.

It is in that vein that I approach negotiations of epistemic status here. Much like Petersen (2003) did in her own analysis of scientific boundary-work, I adopt a Foucauldian understanding of discourse 'as practices that systematically form the objects [and subjects] of which they speak' (2006 [1969]: 54). With Foucault, I conceptualise discursive practices as producing a 'delimitation of a field of objects, the definition of a *legitimate perspective for the agent of the knowledge*, and the *fixing of norms for the elaboration of concepts and theories*' (1977 [1971]: 199, my emphases). I am also persuaded by his argument that we need to focus not just on the 'formation' of discourses 'but [also] the effects in the real to which they are linked' (1991 [1980]: 85), and hence I seek to situate discourses about epistemic status within the broader political economy of contemporary academic practice. In attempting to do this, I have found it useful to articulate Foucault's perspective with other strands of discourse analysis. Of particular relevance is research which problematises the discursive strategies and repertoires used by scientists when making claims about their, and others', work (Gilbert and Mulkay, 1984; Lee and Roth, 2004; Potter, 1996; Potter and Mulkay, 1985). Therefore, I understand 'discourse' both in the broader Foucauldian sense, and in the narrower sense given to it within that body of STS research, which frames discourse as specific instances of speech or text.

In my use of 'ethnography (. . .) with discourse analysis components (. . .) [as a method] furnish[ing] the optics for viewing the process of knowledge production as "constructive" rather than descriptive' (Knorr-Cetina, 1995: 141), I am also inspired by the ethnographic tradition developed in STS, particularly following Latour and Woolgar's (1986 [1979]) and Knorr-Cetina's (1983, 1995) influential studies in laboratories. Mine is not, however, a 'typical' STS ethnography. Much of the methodological STS literature (Hess, 2007: 239 is one example) presumes that its objects are the natural and techno-sciences. Therefore, conventional STS methods are not always suited to research on practices and communities not concentrated in laboratories or analogous settings, as is the case with the SSH (Beaulieu, 2010). Several feminist scholars have denounced the relative marginalisation of the SSH as research objects in STS and argued that it reinforces a hierarchical demarcation of 'soft' and 'hard' sciences (Červinková *et al.*, 2007; Mayer, 2009; Petersen, 2003). Whelan describes this as in itself an instance of boundary-work (and devaluing of WGFS): '[p]hysics is the apex of the natural sciences; studies of physics represent the apex of STS. Feminists who study the soft sciences are, by extension, relatively unskilled labourers doing inconsequential namby-pamby work. Here we have an extraordinary piece of boundary-work' (2001: 557). The 'lack of observable laboratories' in the SSH has led researchers to 'become imaginative as [to] where to find our research subjects/objects' (Červinková *et al.*, 2007: 6). It has taken ethnographers of the SSH – including myself – to offices, libraries, classes, the internet, canteens, conferences, journals and funding agencies to conduct fieldwork (Beaulieu, 2010; Mair *et al.*, 2013; Petersen, 2003).

My own project is primarily based on full-time ethnographic fieldwork in Portugal over one year in 2008/2009, supported by a second round of interviews with some of the original interviewees in 2015/2016. This is supplemented by *ad hoc* observation of daily academic practice in UK (2006–2016), Sweden (2011) and Portugal (2006–2016), and of presentations and debates at dozens of international academic conferences, and meetings of international WGFS networks and associations, in the US and Europe (2006–2016). The main fieldwork period included participant observation in over 50 public, semi-public and closed academic events, including undergraduate and postgraduate teaching,[10] meetings of scholarly associations and conference organising committees, PhD vivas,[11] book/journal launches and, of course, many small and large conferences. Several authors have drawn attention to the importance of conferences as ceremonials (Egri, 1992) whose role goes beyond that of exchange of knowledge. They are also sites for professional socialisation and collective identity formation (Bell and King, 2010; Egri, 1992), for the exercise of evaluation and regulation of academic work (Bell and King, 2010; Ford and Harding, 2008; Henderson, 2015, 2016), and for (re)production and legitimation of academic hierarchies (Friese, 2001) and broader forms of inequality and discrimination, namely in relation to gender, class and race (Bell and King, 2010; Ford and Harding, 2009; Gillies and Alldred, 2007; Henderson, 2015, 2016; Hey, 2003). I tried to attend all WGFS events to which I had access and as many major non-WGFS events as possible.[12] In most conference observations, it was not possible to make my presence as a researcher known to all delegates. For this and other reasons, it was impossible to secure consent for all material collected, as other ethnographers of academia also found (Henderson, 2016; Petersen, 2003). Hurdley notes that as academics we often share gossip and may 'repeat all [we] saw and heard; yet [our] sight and hearing bec[o]me dangerous senses once [we] assume the role of researcher' of other researchers (2010: 518); I discuss the 'dangerous' position of the ethnographer of academia below and in Pereira (2013).

I also conducted interviews. The first round, in 2008/2009, included 36 semi-structured interviews with scholars, students and other individuals in diverse positions vis-à-vis WGFS, in a range of disciplines, a variety of institutions from across the country and at distinct levels of seniority. As part of the interview, I sometimes read out excerpts of one or more of the interviewee's publications and asked them to comment on it, a technique that provided extremely valuable insight on their changing epistemic positions, the negotiations involved in writing collaborative pieces, and how academics adjust to different audiences when writing about WGFS. Observing offices and interactions before/during interviews provided additional insight into the status of WGFS. In one case, I interviewed a scholar in the office she shared with two non-WGFS male colleagues, who walked in and out several times, not acknowledging our presence and speaking loudly. She said this was a frequent occurrence: *"they act as if I'm invisible"*. The second round of interviews was, however, conducted over telephone or Skype. These took place in 2015/2016 and were follow-up interviews with 12 of the original research participants.[13]

The interviews and all informal conversations during fieldwork have dual status as empirical material. They provided considerable information about the historical and institutional context of the processes I was observing, as well as crucial insight into what happened in less public, but influential, spaces that I could not access, such as corridor talk[14] and meetings. However, interviewees' answers were not transparent accounts of 'real' facts. Participants' stories in interviews did not always match the versions of those same stories I heard them tell in other situations, or the stories told by other interviewees about the same event or interaction. Some interviewees narrated the development of Portuguese WGFS in ways that highlighted the pioneering character of their own interventions and downplayed the relevance or scientificity of others' initiatives. Much like others have observed in studies with scientists (Gilbert and Mulkay, 1984; Lee and Roth, 2004; Potter and Mulkay, 1985), some participants more or less explicitly presented themselves as a certain type of knowledge producer: one who is generating quality scholarship and doing the proper or best kind of WGFS.

Therefore, interviews are themselves sites of boundary-work and of negotiation of the relative epistemic status of disciplines, theories and traditions in WGFS, and of participants' position vis-à-vis me as a colleague, former student or fellow feminist. This does not mean that interviews are too subjective, misleading or staged and therefore not reliable (Monahan and Fisher, 2010; Petersen, 2003); they are no more staged than the conferences or classes I observed. Rather, it means that they are themselves valuable additional material through which to analyse the constant work of managing epistemic status. I therefore engage with interviews also as discourse to analyse, rather than just as sources of (always partial, contextual and mediated) information about WGFS in Portugal. In other words, and following Henwood's lead, I approach interview talk both as a *topic* – i.e. as 'episodes of situated interaction and talk' (2007: 271) that can be analysed to examine the boundary-work they do – and as a *resource* – providing useful information about 'processes and realities located beyond the interview as a specific text and context' (2007: 272).

It might go without saying that the material presented here has been subjected to several processes of translation – from coffee-break to notebook, spoken to written word, Portuguese to English. Indeed, this is considered so evident that it is often left unsaid, with researchers frequently 'forgetting (or even denying) the mediation of the researcher as translator, . . . [and] act[ing] "as if" our informants spoke the same language as our readers' (Poblete, 2009: 632). As Natasha Marhia, Christina Scharff and I (Pereira *et al.*, 2009) have observed, when language difference *is* acknowledged, it is usually in technical and brief terms, and the implications of translation for the process of knowledge production are rarely recognised (see also Temple, 2005). In this book, I examine interviewees' words, but the words on the page are both the result of their choices and of decisions I made when translating. In previous drafts, I experimented with strategies for 'foreignising' translation (Venuti, 1998), e.g. including terms in the original language to regularly 'reveal the translation to be in fact a translation, distinct from the text it replaces' (Venuti, 1998: 11–12). However, this resulted in a very unwieldy text, and at times overpowered the substantive analysis of excerpts. Therefore, I have opted to fully translate quotes, but include occasional endnotes both to explore elements that are not representable in English and to render visible the irreducibility of the 'original' to its constructed and situated translation.

Protecting anonymity is extremely important, but extraordinarily difficult, in a project focusing on relatively high-profile individuals within a small community, who can easily be identified. To address this, no pseudonyms are used (so that quotes from the same interview cannot be linked) and identifiable information not directly relevant to the analysis – such as the interviewee's discipline, research theme or gender – is omitted or changed. This is common practice in research with academics (Kapusta-Pofahl, 2008; Platt, 1976; Wiles *et al.*, 2006). I also anonymise claims made publicly because the aim is not to 'point at any particular individuals as idiosyncratic social actors' (Lewis, 2008: 687). As Butler has noted, 'link[ing] individuals to (. . .) views runs the risk of deflecting attention from the meaning and effect [of views] (. . .) to the pettier politics of who said what' (1998: 33). Therefore, I provide accounts which are often vaguer and less 'thick' than I would have liked; to use Kapusta-Pofahl's words, juggling anonymity and analytical richness has been 'a delicate dance' (2008: 40).

According to Wiles *et al.*, '[s]tudies conducted by academic[s] (. . .) of their peers raise specific ethical issues that are not *distinct* from those inherent in all research' but pose complicated challenges (2006: 284, original emphasis), particularly, I would argue, vis-à-vis ethics, power and positionality. Červinková *et al.* identify two key challenges: (a) ethnographers of the SSH are part of the community they study, and so when 'studying the "familiar" (. . .) social scientists are also situated in the field in terms of epistemic, thematic and personal proximities/distances' (2007: 2); (b) fieldwork often 'does not have clear boundaries and expands in temporal, spatial and social terms beyond the defined sites under study' (2007: 2; see also Downey *et al.*, 1997). Beaulieu argues that these challenges make these studies ' "busy" ethnographies' (2010: 463), forcing the ethnographer to 'simultaneously attend to multiple kinds of accountability' and engage in 'a kind of hyper-reflexivity that requires both skill and intensive work' (2010: 460–461). This, as Sheehan notes, can at times cause 'almost paralysing' anxiety (1993b: 75) and place the researcher 'on tenterhooks [especially] during the writing up process' (1993b: 85).

This was, indeed, a 'busy', and sometimes, paralysing study in at least two ways. On the one hand, it is extraordinarily hard to shift our 'attention (. . .) from the substance (. . .) of scholars' products to how those products are made: to the relatively backgrounded, taken-for-granted practices of knowledge production', as Lederman (2006: 483), Petersen (2003) and Henderson (2016) also attempted to do. When I began fieldwork, negotiations of epistemic status seemed to be both present everywhere and extraordinarily hard to observe, as I examine in Pereira (2011, 2013) using the metaphor of a 'frame'. The amount of information to be processed and the degree of alertness required were so unexpectedly overwhelming[15] that for several months after completing the primary fieldwork, I still found it daunting to attend conferences.

My ethnography was 'busy' also because, like other ethnographers of the SSH, I am an insider of the community I studied. Although I have never held a formal academic position in Portugal, I am a Portuguese feminist scholar who has for many years participated in Portuguese WGFS. In the past, I was taught by some participants; I had also collaborated with others in academic or activist initiatives. Being an insider offered considerable advantages both in access to, and in feeling at ease within,[16] my fieldwork sites. However, my insiderness was not a stable given, but something I was often tested on and called to demonstrate. Indeed, I was not the only one doing the observing in my fieldwork, as I discuss elsewhere (Pereira, 2011, 2013). My participants are, of course, co-experts in my field.[17] Authors argue that it is sometimes difficult to explain research aims to participants 'without sending [them] to graduate school' (Smith, 1979 cited in Murphy and Dingwall, 2007: 342). In this case, the participants *are* the graduate school, and can fully understand, and even query, my analysis. They raised many questions about the quality and suitability of my methods and theories – in other words, about the extent to which I was producing knowledge properly. Therefore, I too was doing boundary-work in interviews and through 'pragmatic performances of disciplinary competence' (Pels, 2000: 164) trying to position myself as the right kind of researcher.

But my participants and I did not just have an occupation in common; with many I also shared a commitment to feminism and the strengthening of WGFS. Researchers of the SSH and technosciences have often found that participants were resistant and even hostile (Forsythe, 2001; Mayer, 2009; Neal, 1995; Sheehan, 1993b; Wöhrer, 2008). The scholars I approached, however, were almost always enormously interested in, and supportive of, my research, as well as extremely generous with time, patience and information. I was often told that *"the research you are doing is very important"* (email from participant), relevant or useful. Although encouraging and gratifying, this support generated its own challenges. Participants were what I call a *vigilant* community. They were 'watchful; steadily on the alert; attentively or closely observant' (*Oxford English Dictionary*), both of the phenomena I was examining – which, as co-experts, they have also reflected on, often for many years – and of the claims I produced about those phenomena and their/our community. They are also *vigilant* in the sense that they sometimes position themselves as a 'guardian or keeper' (OED) concerned with a field which they understand to be in some, or many, ways vulnerable. This vigilance manifested itself in different forms, as I examine elsewhere (Pereira, 2011, 2013), and confirmed that one inhabits a 'strange and precarious place' when researching peers, 'walking a touchy tightrope between discretion, loyalty, and [critical] distance' (Friese, 2001: 307).

That tightrope is touchy also, and especially, because scholars disagree on what type of analysis of WGFS' status would most productively contribute to improve its situation. Indeed, trying to identify what might be most 'relevant' and useful for such a heterogeneous field 'opens up [a big] can of worms' (Evans, 1983: 328). Moreover, my participants are not just on the receiving end of claims about the lesser epistemic status of WGFS, but also actively involved in establishing hierarchies between areas of WGFS or dismissing other WGFS scholars' work; they are both marginalised and marginalising in relation to epistemic demarcations, as I show later. This internal boundary-work must also be considered. But how does one 'write about [a] group in a way that preserve[s] the significance of their work as an important feminist project, while providing an honest and critical account' (Davis, 2010a: 148) of the tensions within it? I have tried to manage this in the pages that follow by making ongoing – but never complete – efforts to shift the analytical angle, namely by mapping power in relation to WGFS from many different perspectives. Through this, I attempted to produce an analysis grounded on, and aiming at, what feminist STS scholars have called 'respectful critique' (Forsythe, 2001; Suchman, 2008), a practice that is not 'disinterested' and external but rather 'deeply implicated' (Suchman, 2008: 152).

That analysis is presented in chapters 3 to 7. I start in chapter 3 by teasing out the significant but contradictory ways in which the emergence of an academic culture of performativity has changed the status of WGFS. The emphasis is on the national (and international) landscape of the political economy of academic work, and on epistemic climates and official and unofficial cultures within institutions. Chapters 4, 5 and 6 are more explicitly and closely focused on discourse. Chapter 4 examines how non-WGFS scholars talk about WGFS scholarship in conferences, classrooms and other public settings, showing how they use different discursive devices (including caricature and humour) to *split* WGFS scholarship in problematic ways. In chapter 5, I foreground WGFS scholars' boundary-work. I examine discourse, once again, but widen the discussion by interrogating the relationship between the content of discourse and its conditions of production and reception. I use that to reflect on whether the conditions are always in place for WGFS scholars' boundary-work to actually work. Chapter 6 zooms out even further by investigating how those local negotiations interact with the global geopolitics of epistemic status, i.e. the relations of power between countries in what concerns their status as sites more or less able to produce proper knowledge. The analysis comes full circle with chapter 7, which returns to issues examined in chapter 3, comparing the 2008/2009 and 2015/2016 interviews, and drawing on that to analyse the contemporary mood of academia and the impact of that mood on WGFS knowledge and on the lives and health of WGFS scholars.

Doing epistemic status in a study of epistemic status

In this research project, I sought to analyse the means and discourses through which academics attempt to position their, or others', scholarship as valuable knowledge. But as I write a book about that, discuss the literature, describe my methodology, analyse empirical material or systematise findings, I too want and need the knowledge claims offered here to be recognised as proper WGFS scholarship. Thinking through this awkward position has been one of the most challenging and confounding aspects of the writing, and demanded rethinking or redrafting of many sections. The most significant example is chapter 1. Initially conceived as a relatively conventional literature review, it offered the familiar story of the well-read researcher who has considered relevant texts and identified a gap in the literature and/or significant problems in others' analyses, and so sets out to correct them or fill the gaps through their own project. This is how academics are usually trained to write literature reviews, but it becomes untenable if we consider the literature review as a discursive and political exercise, rather than just a technical one. As many authors have shown (Forero, 2003; Hemmings, 2011; McCarthy, 2007; Petersen, 2003), this plot line 'imposes an order (. . .) which is linear (. . .) [and whose] function is to ratify (. . .) the contribution which is to come' (Massey, 1994: 218). It rests on a *construction* of gaps and limitations – although it is framed as a *description* of existing ones – which often downplays the originality or nuance of existing work, in order to affirm the necessity and (higher) scholarly value of one's own project. This literature review plot also downplays the collective nature of knowledge production, normalising a conceptualisation of knowledge as an individual, and inherently competitive, achievement. Like Bracke and Bellacasa, I would say that '[a]s academics, (. . .) we are supposed to *show that we know better* than those who came before us. As *feminist* academics we feel we ought to resist this (. . .) because we are aware that we do not know "better than" but "better with/because of" those who came before us' (2004: 309, original emphases).

Thinking about how to review literature differently, I was persuaded by Davis' denouncing of modes of reading and critique guided by a search for 'methodological and normative inconsistencies (. . .) [and a] ferret[ing] out [of] problems, inaccuracies and weaknesses' (2010b: 188; see also Hughes, 2004). I was inspired too by Riles' plea for scholarly debate driven by an ethnographic-like critical empathy.

> Ethnography (. . .) always demands evaluation and critical judgment (. . .); ethnographic empathy has never meant naïve acceptance of what informants say or do. But that judgment takes place in the context of the ethnographer's careful appreciation of the way the subject's problems both are and are not the ethnographer's own. (. . .) The same (. . .) critical appreciation is surely required of the collegial reception of one another's [work].
>
> (2006: 28)

Therefore, rather than framing chapter 1 as a reflection primarily about what is lacking in existing literature vis-à-vis my own research questions, I structured it as a critical discussion of what one might learn from that literature and how it can be used to formulate different or further questions.

Nevertheless, I would argue that one does not remove oneself from, or rid oneself of, investments in the textual production of one's epistemic status simply by attempting, or even succeeding, to write a different kind of plot in one chapter.

This book is filled with claims that attempt to demonstrate that I am producing proper feminist knowledge, and that are 'explicitly and implicitly designed to persuade others [including you, my reader] that [I] know what [I am] talking about and they ought therefore to pay attention to what [I am] saying' (Van Maanen, 2010: 240). This happens, to give a simple and widely recognised example (Hemmings, 2011; Stanley and Wise, 2000), when I quote canonical feminist names or must-be-mentioned areas of debate. It occurs in the two paragraphs above; ostensibly, they offer a critical reflection on how I frame my epistemic status through the literature review, but at the same time they help set me up as a proper feminist author. In explaining that I refused a supposedly problematic literature review plot to produce a discussion which is more *reflexive* and *collaborative*, I show off the fact that my work is guided by two concerns which arguably (and justly so, in my view) constitute two of the most celebrated features of feminist work (Letherby, 2003; Neves and Nogueira, 2005; Stanley and Wise, 2000).

If one is always doing epistemic status (even when trying to disentangle oneself from that doing!), what is the most productive way of engaging with that doing in a book which takes the doing as its object? In an earlier draft, I tried to address this by using regular footnotes to create a partly auto-ethnographic sub-text that interrupted the 'normal' flow of the argument and made visible, and unpacked, the internal workings of my own doing of epistemic status. This strategy – dexterously and very effectively used by Petersen (2003), for example – had the bonus effect of illustrating one of my key findings: that negotiations of epistemic status are constant and pervasive. I wrote a few such footnotes but later removed them and replaced them with this discussion. I did so for two reasons. Firstly, I felt that the footnotes still framed epistemic status as something one does here and there, in containable and identifiable moments, and I wanted to avoid this. It is not an exaggeration to say that considerations about epistemic status more or less directly shape every sentence in scholarly texts. This is especially clear to me as a non-native English speaker, first trained in academic writing in a language and context where the style considered most scholarly is worlds apart from the 'authoritative plain style' favoured in many fields within anglophone academia (Venuti, 1995). As Bennett notes, SSH writing in Portuguese is often elaborate and to some extent literary, involving for example long and

> mellifluous polysyllabic sentence[s]; (. . .) words [a]re often included for their rhythmic pattern or sound, and for the shape they g[i]ve to the phrase. Hence, we frequently find (. . .) [sets of] two adjectives (. . .) that are essentially synonyms. In English, (. . .) where meaning rather than aesthetics governs lexical choices, such duplication is considered redundant.
>
> (2007: 183)[18]

As a keen user of long sentences and double adjectivation myself, I was told several times during my early academic training in the UK that my style was too wordy, rhetorical, not quite properly social scientific. Writing this book has therefore required negotiating epistemic status also at the level of word choice and sentence structure. It has demanded adjusting the writing (although the book still contains many double adjectives!) to make claims acceptable and legible – quite literally – in an English-speaking international academic community, with its specific, albeit heterogeneous, criteria of what constitutes good scholarly writing.

The second, and main, reason why I removed the footnotes is that through valuable discussions with readers of earlier drafts, it became clear that my footnotes worked to buttress, rather than just problematise, the construction of my authority. The meta-commentary about my writing could function textually as an exercise in 'showing off' my critical analysis skills, as one reader put it, and establishing myself as a prime agent and subject of feminist reflexivity (Liinason, 2007). I have found that, as Tamboukou and Ball note, even when authors 'attempt to write "otherwise", their (. . .) "eccentric" texts (. . .) can be read very differently from the theoretical and epistemological claims they espouse' (2003: 17). I was caught in a double bind: the more I attempted to make visible and problematisable the production of my epistemic status, the more I strengthened and masked that production. Indeed, my preoccupation with finding a textual strategy that might resolve this can be seen as a manifestation of a 'wish for rescue through some "more adequate" research methodology' (Lather, 2007: 483). This wish rests on the assumption that using a particular methodology will 'take us to some non-complicitous place of knowing' (Lather, 2007: 483), or a place external to negotiations of epistemic status . . . and I do not think that such a place exists.

I therefore opted to not offer sustained commentary on my own textual negotiation of epistemic status. Instead, I strongly urge you to engage with the book also through that lens, i.e. turning the analytical perspective that I explore in this text towards, or against, the text itself. In addition, I want to invite you to conceptualise my experience of being caught in negotiations of epistemic status less as a delimited methodological and epistemological problem that I have personally struggled with, but rather as one manifestation of a much broader, and very important, issue. As academics, within or outside WGFS, we are constantly involved and invested in negotiations of epistemic status at many levels, from the micro-level details of what we write and who we cite[19] to the long and complex processes of attempting to obtain resources and space within institutions; this book offers one analysis of those negotiations.

Notes

1 'Finger-dance' (Garber, 2003) designates the gesture of clenching fingers to create scare quotes for spoken words, namely to indicate a term is being used critically.
2 I use the term 'scholar' to refer not just to professional academics, but also students and researchers who do not work formally or full-time in academic institutions.
3 I do not include scare quotes for these terms throughout the remainder of the book (as the text would become awkwardly inundated with them) but all uses of these and related terms (including 'modern' in chapter 6) must be read as informed by this sceptical and critical perspective.

4 See, for example, Small (1999) on African-American studies, Ross (1997) on dance and performance studies, and Gieryn (1999) on debates over the scientificity of the social sciences vs. the natural sciences.

5 This is factually true but, as Oliveira (2014, 2015) argues, it is problematic to refer to the 'lateness' or 'delay' of Portuguese WGFS uncritically. These terms represent the history of WGFS in Portugal and in other (semi-)peripheral countries in relation to the temporality of its institutionalisation in countries of the 'centre'. This reinforces the academic hegemony of anglophone WGFS (positioned as the yardstick against which all WGFS is characterised) and frames Portuguese WGFS as marked essentially and always by delay. For a more detailed discussion of these issues, see chapter 6.

6 To give one Portuguese illustration, *Diacrítica*, a humanities journal based at the University of Minho and co-directed by the feminist scholar Ana Gabriela Macedo, is described as a publication on *Ciências da Literatura*, i.e. 'literature sciences'.

7 I use the term 'field' instead of 'discipline' because in many countries, including Portugal, the issue of whether WGFS is, and should be, a discipline is intensely contested (Hemmings, 2006).

8 Like Whelan (2001), I acknowledge that so-called 'mainstream' disciplines or theories may themselves also occupy subordinate epistemic positions. Indeed, SSH research as a whole is seen as less scientific than the natural sciences, and there are hierarchies of status between established fields within the SSH. Therefore, I follow Whelan in using the term not to 'posit (. . .) a hegemonic influence in academia generally', but to indicate that a field does not take a 'more explicitly politically-radical perspective' (2001: 537).

9 This is, however, not a consensual position (see, e.g. Scheurich and McKenzie, 2005). There are many debates about what constitutes the proper interpretation of Foucault. This is habitual practice in discussions about canonical authors but it becomes particularly interesting and ironic when it occurs in relation to Foucault, who argued (in response to criticisms about his use of Nietzsche) that '[t]he only valid tribute to a thought (. . .) is precisely to use it, to deform it, to make it groan and protest' (1980 [1975]: 53–54). Commenting on his own work, he wrote '[t]hese are suggestions for research, ideas, (. . .) instruments; do what you like with them. (. . .) It is none of my business [what you do with them] to the extent that it is not up to me to lay down the law about the use you make of it' (2003 [1976]: 2).

10 I attended over half of the weekly or twice-weekly sessions of 2 UG courses in Lisbon universities over 1 semester, and 1 session each of 11 UG and PG courses (both WGFS and non-WGFS) in 6 institutions throughout the country. I also attended induction or open-day presentations for 3 WGFS or WGFS-related degrees. I had permission from lecturers to observe; in some cases, my presence was announced to students at the beginning of the session, whereas in others lecturers decided to reveal it at the end.

11 PhD vivas in Portugal are public events; those I observed had audiences of over 25 people. I attended 3 vivas: 2 for PhDs in a WGFS programme (the first ever WGFS PhDs awarded in Portugal) and 1 for a PhD thesis in a non-WGFS programme, but grounded in WGFS.

12 I was based in Lisbon, which means fieldwork was disproportionately focused on Lisbon and surrounding regions. However, I travelled regularly to other cities, most often (but not exclusively) Coimbra and Porto, to attend events or carry out 4 institutional visits. These involved visiting an institution for 1–4 days to attend events and classes, conduct interviews, spend time with staff and students, speak to librarians, administrators and other non-teaching staff, and receive guided tours of the institution and WGFS offices or libraries.

13 More participants were contacted; some did not reply, while others were keen to take part, but were not able to schedule a follow-up interview in the timeframe suggested.

14 Rabinow (1986) draws attention to the important role of 'corridor talk' in shaping academic hierarchies and reputations. Hurdley (2010) attempted to do an ethnography of relations between corridor life and informal power networks in universities. Her article provides a compelling account of both the importance of empirically researching those relations, and the enormous methodological and ethical difficulty (impossibility?) of doing so.

15 And like for many other ethnographers (Henderson, 2016; Pring, 2001), toilets were instrumental as sites in which to hide to rest or make notes of coffee-break conversations.

16 This can make a significant difference to the emotional experience of research, as illustrated by the accounts of scholars who describe the crippling impacts of feelings of discomfort and alienation in life or fieldwork in universities (Bailey and Miller, 2015; Gillies and Alldred, 2007; Neal, 1995).

17 In her study with WGFS academics, Wöhrer writes 'I want to call the protagonists of my study "co-researchers" (. . .): [t]hey were not only experts in *their* field, but also experts in *mine*, i.e. in a field, that we *shared* – and we both were aware of this fact' (2009: 1, original emphases). I echo this, but prefer to call participants 'co-experts' rather than 'co-researchers', to acknowledge the fact that they were not directly involved in co-designing or conducting this research.

18 See Bennett (2007) for a fascinating discussion of the relations between the conventions of Portuguese academic writing and the country's social, political and intellectual history.

19 Indeed, managing the politics of citation has been one of the most challenging tasks in the writing of this book. To disrupt the asymmetries I analyse throughout it, I was keen to cite WGFS scholars from a range of countries – including plenty of Portuguese scholars, to advance the 'projection' discussed in chapter 6 – and backgrounds. However, I was severely constrained by my contracted manuscript word limit, itself limited by the publisher's plan to make the book more marketable by providing references after each chapter, making it possible to sell them individually. Several hundred references were culled from the final manuscript in an attempt to meet that limit, and that has made the book less inclusive. This is a good example of how our knowledge production is 'caught' (see 'Conclusion') between epistemic concerns, political commitments, the political economy of academic publishing and the day-to-day practical and instrumental logistics of writing.

References

Aavik, Kadri, *et al.* (2015). *Country Reports (Australia, Czech Republic, Estonia, Germany, Iceland, Netherlands, Norway, Portugal, South Africa, Sweden, Switzerland, UK)*. Multiple Papers Presented at the RINGS Network Conference "Gender in/and the Neoliberal University", Prague.

Amâncio, Lígia (2005). "Reflections on Science as a Gendered Endeavour: Changes and Continuities". *Social Science Information, 44* (1), 65–83.

Atkinson, Paul, *et al.* (2007). "Editorial Introduction" in P. Atkinson, *et al.* (eds.), *Handbook of Ethnography* (pp.1–7). London: Sage.

Bailey, Moya and Miller, Shannon J. (2015). "When Margins Become Centered: Black Queer Women in Front and Outside of the Classroom". *Feminist Formations, 27* (3), 168–188.

Barazzetti, Donatella, *et al.* (2002). "Italy" in G. Griffin (ed.), *Women's Employment, Women's Studies, and Equal Opportunities (1945–2001)* (pp.177–230). Hull: University of Hull.

Beaulieu, Anne (2010). "From Co-Location to Co-Presence: Shifts in the Use of Ethnography for the Study of Knowledge". *Social Studies of Science, 40* (3), 453–470.

Bell, Emma and King, Daniel (2010). "The Elephant in the Room: Critical Management Studies Conferences as a Site of Body Pedagogics". *Management Learning, 41* (4), 429–442.

Bennett, Karen (2007). "Galileo's Revenge: Ways of Construing Knowledge and Translation Strategies in the Era of Globalization". *Social Semiotics, 17* (2), 171–193.

Bracke, Sarah and Bellacasa, María Puig de la (2004). "Building Standpoints" in S. Harding (ed.), *The Feminist Standpoint Theory Reader* (pp.309–316). New York: Routledge.

Braidotti, Rosi (2000). "Key Terms and Issues in the Making of European Women's Studies". *The Making of European Women's Studies, 1,* 23–36.

Braidotti, Rosi (2002). "The Uses and Abuses of the Sex/Gender Distinction in European Feminist Practices" in G. Griffin and R. Braidotti (eds.), *Thinking Differently: A Reader in European Women's Studies* (pp.285–310). London: Zed.

Butler, Judith (1998). "Merely Cultural". *New Left Review, I* (227), 33–44.

Butterwick, Shauna and Dawson, Jane (2005). "Undone Business: Examining the Production of Academic Labour". *Women's Studies International Forum, 28* (1), 51–65.

Červinková, Alice, *et al.* (2007). *Research on Social Sciences and Humanities: Sharing Experiences and Discussing Methodological Approaches.* Retrieved 02/04/2016, from http://homepage.univie.ac.at/katja.mayer/ssh/SSHreport_final.pdf

Code, Lorraine (2006). "Women Knowing/Knowing Women: Critical-Creative Interventions in the Politics of Knowledge" in K. Davis, *et al.* (eds.), *Handbook of Gender and Women's Studies* (pp.146–166). London: Sage.

Collins, Patricia Hill (1990). *Black Feminist Thought: Knowledge, Consciousness, and the Politics of Empowerment.* Boston, MA: Unwin Hyman.

Crasnow, Sharon, *et al.* (2015). "Feminist Perspectives on Science" in E.N. Zalta (ed.), *The Stanford Encyclopedia of Philosophy.* Retrieved 02/04/2016, from http://plato.stanford.edu/

Davies, Helen and O'Callaghan, Claire (eds.) (2014). *Journal of Gender Studies.* Special Issue: "Feminism, Academia, Austerity", *23* (3).

Davis, Kathy (2010a). "Avoiding the 'R-word': Racism in Feminist Collectives" in R. Ryan-Flood and R. Gill (eds.), *Secrecy and Silence in the Research Process: Feminist Reflections* (pp.147–160). Abingdon: Routledge.

Davis, Kathy (2010b). "On Generosity and Critique". *European Journal of Women's Studies, 17* (3), 187–191.

Downey, Gary Lee, *et al.* (1997). "Corridor Talk" in J. Dumit and G.L. Downey (eds.), *Cyborgs & Citadels: Anthropological Interventions in Emerging Sciences and Technologies* (pp.245–264). Santa Fe, NM: School of American Research Press.

Egri, Carolyn (1992). "Academic Conferences as Ceremonials: Opportunities for Organizational Integration and Socialization". *Journal of Management Education, 16* (1), 90–115.

Evans, Mary (1983). "The Teacher's Tale: On Teaching Women's Studies". *Women's Studies International Forum, 6* (3), 325–330.

Ferguson, Kathy E. (1991). "Interpretation and Genealogy in Feminism". *Signs: Journal of Women in Culture and Society, 16* (2), 322–339.

Ferreira, Virgínia (2001). "Estudos sobre as Mulheres em Portugal: A Construção de um Novo Campo Científico". *ex aequo, 5,* 9–25.

Ferreira, Virgínia (2004). *Relações Sociais de Sexo e Segregação do Emprego: Uma Análise da Feminização dos Escritórios em Portugal.* PhD Thesis, Universidade de Coimbra.

Fiore, Elisa and Habed, Adriano (2016). *Organizing against the War on "Gender Ideology": Call for Papers for a Special Section of the Atgender Spring Conference: "Feminist Spaces of Teaching and Learning: Queering Movements, Translations and Dynamics"*. Retrieved 02/04/2016, from http://atgender.eu/files/2015/12/Conference_6.pdf

Ford, Jackie and Harding, Nancy (2008). "Fear and Loathing in Harrogate, or a Study of a Conference". *Organization, 15* (2), 233–250.

Ford, Jackie and Harding, Nancy (2009). "Get Back into that Kitchen, Woman: Management Conferences and the Making of the Female Professional Worker". *Gender, Work and Organization, 17* (5), 503–520.

Forero, Olga Restrepo (2003). *On Writing Review Articles and Constructing Fields of Study*. PhD Thesis, University of York.

Forsythe, Diana (2001). *Studying Those Who Study Us: An Anthropologist in the World of Artificial Intelligence*. Stanford, CA: Stanford University Press.

Foucault, Michel (1977 [1971]). "History of Systems of Thought" in M. Foucault (ed.), *Language, Counter-Memory, Practice: Selected Essays and Interviews* (pp.199–204). Oxford: Blackwell.

Foucault, Michel (1978 [1976]). *The History of Sexuality* (Vol. 1). Harmondsworth: Penguin.

Foucault, Michel (1979 [1975]). *Discipline and Punish: The Birth of the Prison*. Harmondsworth: Penguin.

Foucault, Michel (1980 [1975]). "Prison Talk" in C. Gordon (ed.), *Power-Knowledge: Selected Interviews and Other Writings, 1972–1977* (pp.37–54). Brighton: Harvester Press.

Foucault, Michel (1989 [1969]). "The Archeology of Knowledge" in S. Lotringer (ed.), *Foucault Live: Interviews, 1966–1984* (pp.57–64). New York: Semiotext(e).

Foucault, Michel (1991 [1980]). "Questions of Method" in G. Burchell, *et al.* (eds.), *The Foucault Effect: Studies in Governmentality* (pp.73–86). Chicago, IL: University of Chicago Press.

Foucault, Michel (2003 [1976]). *Society Must be Defended: Lectures at the Collège de France, 1975–76*. New York: Picador.

Foucault, Michel (2006 [1969]). *The Archaeology of Knowledge*. Oxon: Routledge.

Franklin, Sarah (1995). "Science as Culture, Cultures of Science". *Annual Review of Anthropology, 24*, 163–184.

Fraser, Nancy (1996). "Michel Foucault: A 'Young Conservative'?" in S. Hekman (ed.), *Feminist Interpretations of Michel Foucault* (pp.15–38). University Park: Pennsylvania State University Press.

Friese, Heidrun (2001). "Thresholds in the Ambit of Discourse: On the Establishment of Authority at Academic Conferences" in P. Becker and W. Clark (eds.), *Little Tools of Knowledge: Historical Essays on Academic and Bureaucratic Practices* (pp.285–312). Ann Arbor: University of Michigan Press.

Garber, Marjorie B. (2003). *Quotation Marks*. New York: Routledge.

Gieryn, Thomas (1999). *Cultural Boundaries of Science: Credibility on the Line*. Chicago, IL: University of Chicago Press.

Gilbert, G. Nigel and Mulkay, Michael (1984). *Opening Pandora's Box: A Sociological Analysis of Scientists' Discourse*. Cambridge: Cambridge University Press.

Gillies, Val and Alldred, Pam (2007). "Making the Right Connections: 'Knowledge' and Power in Academic Networking" in V. Gillies and H. Lucey (eds.), *Power, Knowledge and the Academy: The Institutional is Political* (pp.105–121). Basingstoke: Palgrave Macmillan.

Grabowska, Magdalena (2016). *Keynote Address*. Paper Presented at the Atgender Spring Conference "Feminist Spaces of Teaching and Learning: Queering Movements, Translations and Dynamics", Utrecht.

Griffin, Gabriele (ed.) (2005). *Doing Women's Studies: Employment Opportunities, Personal Impacts and Social Consequences*. London: Zed.

Haraway, Donna J. (1990). *Simians, Cyborgs, and Women: The Re-Invention of Nature*. London: Free Association.

Harding, Sandra (1991). *Whose Science? Whose Knowledge?: Thinking from Women's Lives*. Milton Keynes: Open University.

HEFCE. (2014). *Views on an International REF Invited*. Retrieved 02/04/2016, from http://www.hefce.ac.uk/news/newsarchive/2014/Name,100798,en.html

Hemmings, Clare (2006). "The Life and Times of Academic Feminism" in K. Davis, *et al.* (eds.), *Handbook of Gender and Women's Studies* (pp.13–34). London: Sage.

Hemmings, Clare (2011). *Why Stories Matter: The Political Grammar of Feminist Theory*. Durham, NC: Duke University Press.

Henderson, Emily F. (2015). "Academic Conferences: Representative and Resistant Sites for Higher Education Research". *Higher Education Research & Development, 34* (5), 914–925.

Henderson, Emily F. (2016). *Eventful Gender: An Ethnographic Exploration of Gender Knowledge Production at International Academic Conferences*. PhD Thesis, UCL Institute of Education.

Henwood, Karen (2007). "Beyond Hypercriticality: Taking Forward Methodological Inquiry and Debate in Discursive and Qualitative Social Psychology". *Discourse Studies, 9* (2), 270–275.

Hess, David (2007). "Ethnography and the Development of Science and Technology Studies" in P. Atkinson, *et al.* (eds.), *Handbook of Ethnography* (pp.234–245). London: Sage.

Hey, Valerie (2003). "Joining the Club? Academia and Working-Class Femininities". *Gender and Education, 15* (3), 319–335.

Hughes, Christina (2004). "Perhaps She Was Having a Bad Hair Day!: Taking Issue with Ungenerous Readings of Feminist Texts". *European Journal of Women's Studies, 11* (1), 103–109.

Hurdley, Rachel (2010). "In the Picture or Off the Wall? Ethical Regulation, Research Habitus, and Unpeopled Ethnography". *Qualitative Inquiry, 16* (6), 517–528.

Jenkins, Fiona and Keane, Helen (eds.) (2014). *Australian Feminist Studies*. Special Issue: "Gendered Excellence in the Social Sciences", *29* (80).

Kapusta-Pofahl, Karen (2008). *Legitimating Czech Gender Studies: Articulating Transnational Feminist Expertise in the "New" Europe*. PhD Thesis, University of Minnesota.

Kilomba, Grada (2007). *Africans in the Academia: Diversity in Adversity*. Retrieved 02/04/2016, from http://www.africavenir.org/nc/news-details/article/africans-in-the-academia-diversity-in-adversity.html

Knorr-Cetina, Karin (1983). "The Ethnographic Study of Scientific Work: Towards a Constructivist Interpretation of Science" in K. Knorr-Cetina and M. Mulkay (eds.), *Science Observed: Perspectives on the Social Study of Science* (pp.115–140). London: Sage.

Knorr-Cetina, Karin (1995). "Laboratory Studies: The Cultural Approach to the Study of Science" in S. Jasanoff, *et al.* (eds.), *Handbook of Science and Technology Studies* (2nd ed) (pp.140–166). London: Sage.

Lather, Patti (2007). "Postmodernism, Post-Structuralism and Post(Critical) Ethnography: Of Ruins, Aporias and Angels" in P. Atkinson, *et al.* (eds.), *Handbook of Ethnography* (pp.477–492). London: Sage.

Latour, Bruno and Woolgar, Steve (1986 [1979]). *Laboratory Life: The Construction of Scientific Facts*. Princeton, NJ: Princeton University Press.

Le Feuvre, Nicky and Andriocci, Muriel (2002). "France" in G. Griffin (ed.), *Women's Employment, Women's Studies, and Equal Opportunities (1945–2001)* (pp.231–291). Hull: University of Hull.

Lederman, Rena (2006). "The Perils of Working at Home: IRB 'Mission Creep' as Context and Content for an Ethnography of Disciplinary Knowledges". *American Ethnologist, 33* (4), 482–491.

Lee, Yew-Jin and Roth, Wolff-Michael (2004). "Making a Scientist: Discursive 'Doing' of Identity and Self-Presentation During Research Interviews". *Forum Qualitative Sozialforschung/Forum Qualitative Social Research, 5* (1), article 12.

Letherby, Gayle (2003). *Feminist Research in Theory and Practice*. Buckingham: Open University Press.

Lewis, Magda (2008). "New Strategies of Control: Academic Freedom and Research Ethics Boards". *Qualitative Inquiry, 14* (5), 684–699.

Liinason, Mia (2007). "Who's the Expert? On Knowledge Seeking as Praxis: A Methodological Approach". *Graduate Journal of Social Science*, 4 (2), 40–60.

Liinason, Mia and Grenz, Sabine (eds.) (2016). *Women's Studies International Forum*. Special Issue: "Women's/Gender Studies and Contemporary Changes in Academic Cultures: European Perspectives", *54*.

Macedo, Ana Gabriela (2000). "Gender–Género; Diferença Sexual; Sexo". *The Making of European Women's Studies, II*, 93.

Magalhães, Maria José (2001). "Dez Anos da APEM: Percorrer as Vozes, Significar os Percursos". *ex aequo, 5*, 27–68.

Mair, Michael, *et al.* (2013). *Social Studies of Social Science: A Working Bibliography*. Southampton: National Centre for Research Methods.

Marchbank, Jen and Letherby, Gayle (2006). "Views and Perspectives of Women's Studies: A Survey of Women and Men Students". *Gender and Education, 18* (2), 157–182.

Marcus, George E. (2009). "Notes Toward an Ethnographic Memoir of Supervising Graduate Research through Anthropology's Decades of Transformation" in J.D. Faubion and G.E. Marcus (eds.), *Fieldwork Is Not What It Used to Be* (pp.1–36). Ithaca, NY: Cornell University Press.

Massey, Doreen (1994). *Space, Place and Gender*. Cambridge: Polity.

Matthews, David (2014). "HEFCE Looks at Overseas Links for Research Excellence". *Times Higher Education*, 10/04/2014, Retrieved 02/04/2016, from https://www.timeshighereducation.com/news/hefce-looks-at-overseas-links-for-research-excellence/2012572.article

Mayer, Katja (2009). "Acting with Social Sciences and Humanities: Session Report". *EASST Review, 28* (1), 7–14.

McCarthy, Jane Ribbens (2007). "Representing Academic Knowledge: The Micro Politics of a Literature Review" in V. Gillies and H. Lucey (eds.), *Power, Knowledge and the Academy: The Institutional Is Political* (pp.122–146). Basingstoke: Palgrave Macmillan.

McNeil, Maureen (1993). "Dancing with Foucault: Feminism and Power-Knowledge" in C. Ramazanoğlu (ed.), *Up Against Foucault* (pp.147–178). London: Routledge.

Monahan, Torin and Fisher, Jill A. (2010). "Benefits of 'Observer Effects': Lessons from the Field". *Qualitative Research, 10* (3), 357–376.

Morley, Louise (1998). *Organising Feminisms: The Micropolitics of the Academy*. New York: St. Martin's Press.

Mountz, Alison, *et al.* (2015). "For Slow Scholarship: A Feminist Politics of Resistance through Collective Action in the Neoliberal University". *ACME, 14* (4), 1235–1259.

Murphy, Elizabeth and Dingwall, Robert (2007). "The Ethics of Ethnography" in P. Atkinson, *et al.* (eds.), *Handbook of Ethnography* (pp.339–351). London: Sage.

Nash, Jennifer and Owens, Emily (eds.) (2015). *Feminist Formations*. Special Issue: "Institutional Feelings: Practicing Women's Studies in the Corporate University", *27* (3).

Neal, Sarah (1995). "Researching Powerful People from a Feminist and Anti-Racist Perspective: A Note on Gender, Collusion and Marginality". *British Educational Research Journal, 21* (4), 517–531.

Neves, Sofia and Nogueira, Conceição (2005). "Metodologias Feministas: A Reflexividade ao Serviço da Investigação nas Ciências Sociais". *Psicologia: Reflexão e Crítica, 18* (3), 408–412.

Nogueira, Conceição (2001). *Um Novo Olhar sobre as Relações Sociais de Género: Feminismo e Perspectivas Críticas na Psicologia Social*. Lisboa: Fundação Calouste Gulbenkian.

Oliveira, João Manuel de (2014). "Hyphenations: The Other Lives of Feminist and Queer Concepts". *Lambda Nordica, 1*, 38–59.

Oliveira, João Manuel de (2015). "Tumultos de Género: os Efeitos de *Gender Trouble* em Portugal". *Periódicus, 3* (1), 6–18.

Pels, Peter (2000). "The Trickster's Dilemma: Ethics and the Technologies of the Anthropological Self" in M. Strathern (ed.), *Audit Cultures: Anthropological Studies in Accountability, Ethics and the Academy* (pp.135–172). London: Routledge.

Pereira, Maria do Mar (2011). *Pushing the Boundaries of Knowledge: An Ethnography of Negotiations of the Epistemic Status of Women's, Gender, Feminist Studies in Portugal*. PhD Thesis, LSE.

Pereira, Maria do Mar (2013). "On Being Invisible and Dangerous: The Challenges of Conducting Ethnographies in/of Academia" in S. Strid and L. Husu (eds.), *Gender Paradoxes in Changing Academic and Scientific Organisation(s) (GEXcel Reports, Vol. XVII)* (pp.191–212). Örebro: University of Örebro.

Pereira, Maria do Mar, *et al.* (2009). "Interrogating Language Difference and Translation in Social Science Research: Towards a Critical and Interdisciplinary Approach". *Graduate Journal of Social Science, 6* (3), 1–12.

Petersen, Eva Bendix (2003). *Academic Boundary Work: The Discursive Constitution of 'Scientificity' Amongst Researchers Within the Social Sciences and Humanities*. PhD Thesis, University of Copenhagen.

Pinto, Teresa (2009). "*ex aequo*: 10 Anos em Revista". *ex aequo, 19*, 63–68.

Platt, Jennifer (1976). *Realities of Social Research: An Empirical Study of British Sociologists*. London: Chatto and Windus.

Poblete, Lorena (2009). "Pretending They Speak French: The Disappearance of the Sociologist as Translator". *Social Science Information, 48* (4), 631–646.

Pollner, Melvin and Emerson, Robert M. (2007). "Ethnomethodology and Ethnography" in P. Atkinson, *et al.* (eds.), *Handbook of Ethnography* (pp.118–135). London: Sage.

Potter, Jonathan (1996). *Representing Reality: Discourse, Rhetoric and Social Construction*. London: Sage.

Potter, Jonathan and Mulkay, Michael (1985). "Scientists' Interview Talk: Interviews as a Technique for Revealing Participants' Interpretative Practices" in M. Brenner, *et al.* (eds.), *The Research Interview: Uses and Approaches* (pp.247–271). London: Academic Press.

Pring, Richard (2001). "The Virtues and Vices of an Educational Researcher". *Journal of Philosophy of Education, 35* (3), 407–421.

Rabinow, Paul (1986). "Representations are Social Facts" in J. Clifford and G.E. Marcus (eds.), *Writing Culture* (pp.234–261). Berkeley: University of California Press.

Riles, Annelise (2006). "Introduction: In Response" in A. Riles (ed.), *Documents: Artifacts of Modern Knowledge* (pp.1–40). Ann Arbor: University of Michigan Press.

Ross, Janice (1997). *The Feminization of Physical Culture: The Introduction of Dance into the American University Curriculum.* PhD Thesis, Stanford University.

Scheurich, James Joseph and McKenzie, Kathryn Bell (2005). "Foucault's Methodologies: Archaeology and Genealogy" in N.K. Denzin and Y.S. Lincoln (eds.), *The Sage Handbook of Qualitative Research* (3rd ed) (pp.841–868). Thousand Oaks, CA: Sage.

Sheehan, Elizabeth A. (1993a). "The Academic As Informant: Methodological and Theoretical issues in the Ethnography of Intellectuals". *Human Organization, 52* (3), 252–259.

Sheehan, Elizabeth A. (1993b). "The Student of Culture and the Ethnography of Irish Intellectuals" in C.B. Brettell (ed.), *When They Read What We Write: The Politics of Ethnography* (pp.75–90). Westport, CT: Bergin & Garvey.

Small, Mario L. (1999). "Departmental Conditions and the Emergence of New Disciplines: Two Cases in the Legitimation of African-American Studies". *Theory and Society, 28* (5), 659–707.

Sousa Santos, Boaventura de (2005). "A Universidade no Século XXI: Para uma Reforma Democrática e Emancipatória da Universidade". *Educação, Sociedade & Culturas, 23,* 137–202.

Stanley, Liz (ed.) (1997). *Knowing Feminisms: On Academic Borders, Territories and Tribes.* London: Sage.

Stanley, Liz and Wise, Sue (2000). "But the Empress Has No Clothes!: Some Awkward Questions About the 'Missing Revolution' in Feminist Theory". *Feminist Theory, 1* (3), 261–288.

Suchman, Lucy (2008). "Feminist STS and the Sciences of the Artificial" in E.J. Hackett, *et al.* (eds.), *The Handbook of Science and Technology Studies* (3rd ed) (pp.139–164). Cambridge, MA: MIT Press.

Tamboukou, Maria and Ball, Stephen J. (2003). "Genealogy and Ethnography: Fruitful Encounters or Dangerous Liaisons?" in M. Tamboukou and S.J. Ball (eds.), *Dangerous Encounters: Genealogy & Ethnography* (pp.1–36). New York: Peter Lang.

Tavares, Manuela (2015). "A Visibilidade dos Estudos sobre as Mulheres, de Género e Feministas (EMGF)" in A. Torres, *et al.* (eds.), *Estudos de Género numa Perspetiva Interdisciplinar* (pp.23–26). Lisboa: Mundos Sociais.

Temple, Bogusia (2005). "Nice and Tidy: Translation and Representation". *Sociological Research Online, 10* (2), article 4.

Torres, Anália, *et al.* (2015). "Introdução" in A. Torres, *et al.* (eds.), *Estudos de Género numa Perspetiva Interdisciplinar* (pp.1–6). Lisboa: Mundos Sociais.

Van Maanen, John (2010). "A Song for My Supper: More Tales of the Field". *Organizational Research Methods, 13* (2), 240–255.

Venuti, Lawrence (1995). *The Translator's Invisibility: A History of Translation.* London: Routledge.

Venuti, Lawrence (1998). *The Scandals of Translation: Towards an Ethics of Difference.* London: Routledge.

Walsh, Val (1995). "Transgression and the Academy: Feminists and Institutionalization" in L. Morley and V. Walsh (eds.), *Feminist Academics: Creative Agents for Change* (pp.86–101). London: Taylor & Francis.

Whelan, Emma (2001). "Politics by Other Means: Feminism and Mainstream Science Studies". *Canadian Journal of Sociology/Cahiers Canadiens de Sociologie, 26* (4), 535–581.

Wiles, Rose, *et al.* (2006). "Researching Researchers: Lessons for Research Ethics". *Qualitative Research, 6* (3), 283–299.

Williams, Sarah and Klemmer, Frederick (1997). "Ethnographic Fetishism or Cyborg Anthropology?" in J. Dumit and G.L. Downey (eds.), *Cyborgs & Citadels: Anthropological Interventions in Emerging Sciences and Technologies* (pp.165–192). Santa Fe, NM: School of American Research Press.

Wisniewski, Richard (2000). "The Averted Gaze". *Anthropology & Education Quarterly, 31* (1), 5–23.

Wöhrer, Veronika (2008). *Too Close to be Welcomed? Methodological Reflections on Researching Social Scientists.* Paper Presented at the Conference "The Politics of Knowing: Research, Institutions and Gender in the Making", Prague.

Wöhrer, Veronika (2009). *Complicity and Ambivalence. Conducting Ethnographic Fieldwork in Gender Studies.* Paper Presented at the Conference "Feminist Research Methods", Stockholm.

Chapter 1

An outsider within?

The position and status of WGFS in academia

Facing a blank page and trying to decide how to start this chapter, I look around for inspiration. I peer at the stack of articles on my desk, copied from national and international WGFS journals. I look through the notes I made at a meeting of a newly-formed international network of WGFS centres. I glance at the pile of books about the past, present and future of WGFS which I found in the university library, somewhere on the dozens of shelves that hold classmarks *HQ1101–2030 Women; Feminism*. Still out of ideas, and feeling a little desperate, I try to remember the tips on writing chapter introductions that 3 WGFS professors taught me many years ago at a doctoral course on feminist academic writing, organised by a network of Nordic WGFS departments with state funding. I am occasionally distracted by the high-pitched sound announcing new email. Through WGFS lists, I receive messages publicising WGFS conferences, a call for submissions for a WGFS encyclopaedia, WGFS doctoral scholarships, and feminist activist and arts initiatives. A few other emails trickle in: one reminds me that my university's WGFS centre is meeting tomorrow to discuss the MA and PhD in WGFS, and another informs me that I still owe my membership fee (sigh) for a WGFS professional association.

Two things are particularly striking in this snapshot of an unexceptional writing moment. On the one hand, it illustrates how institutionalised WGFS has become as a field of teaching, learning and research, both 'on campuses and in cyberspace' (Boxer, 1998: 18). WGFS now has space (in offices and library shelves), professorships and scholarships, specialist degrees and courses, dedicated conferences and publications, physical and online networks, and professional associations. Therefore, WGFS can be described as becoming gradually, though not linearly, institutionalised in two distinct but related senses. Firstly, a more or less large and stable space for it has been, and is being, created or extended within existing institutions, such as the traditional disciplines and the organisations – universities, research centres – where academic work is carried out. Secondly, WGFS has become also an academic institution in itself, one which is more or less (inter)disciplinary (Lykke, 2004) and autonomous, and has its own structures of creation and validation of knowledge and its canonical but contested narratives about what its objects, boundaries, aims and histories are, or should be (Hemmings, 2006, 2011; Pereira, 2013, 2014). Therefore, I understand institutionalisation here as the network of multidimensional processes through which a field is formalised (at many levels: epistemic, organisational, professional, etc.) *as part of* academic structures, and *as an* academic structure, of production, certification and circulation of knowledge.[1] As Nash and Owens note, and as I will also show, 'women's studies [i]s an (inter) discipline with a distinctive and fraught relationship to institutionalization's pleasures, pains, pulls, and perils' (2015: vii).

And yet, the second thing that is striking about my writing anecdote is how profoundly uneven and context-specific the level, format and temporality of the institutionalisation described in it is (Braidotti, 2000; Griffin, 2005a). WGFS is most certainly not institutionalised everywhere; the spaces and resources I identify are not available at present to WGFS scholars in many countries and contexts. I can only take advantage of them myself because I left my country of origin, where some of these resources do not (yet?) exist. I had to move elsewhere, much like hundreds of other 'educational migrants' who every year travel abroad in search of WGFS degrees or jobs (Juhász *et al.*, 2005), though many are increasingly finding their opportunities curtailed by racist migration control policies and institutional cultures (Gutiérrez-Rodríguez, 2016).[2]

There is no doubt that WGFS has grown globally; at certain points in history, and in particular places, that growth was so pronounced that some argued that it 'may not be too far-fetched to suggest that this has been one of the most rapidly expanding analytical fields in the [anglophone] western world during the last twenty years' (McNeil, 1993: 152). But WGFS has not always been growing, and its growth has not happened everywhere at the same time. The WGFS 'boom' which arguably occurred in Portugal in the 2000s (see chapter 3) was contemporaneous with the alleged 'demise' (Griffin, 2009; Oxford, 2008) or, more accurately, the 'contraction' (Lynne Pearce, personal communication, 2016) of the field in the UK in the same period, to compare the two contexts I am most familiar with. Even within the same space *and* time, opposite trends can coexist for different elements of the field. The framing of the 2000s as a period of WGFS contraction in the UK is often based on the significant drop in demand at undergraduate level and the closure of several WGFS UG degree programmes (Griffin, 2009; Marchbank and Letherby, 2006). And yet, at that very same time, many postgraduate degree programmes reported stable or increasing intakes (Hemmings, 2006, 2008) – largely due to the inflow of the aforementioned 'educational migrants' – and WGFS research continued to flourish both as its own field and within other disciplines.

It is, therefore, impossible to tell a linear story of institutionalisation. The field looks and feels very different depending on where one is situated, and it can grow and contract at the same time. Apparently stable achievements, spaces and resources may suddenly or gradually be lost, and distinct temporalities can coexist, overlap and intersect, meaning, for example, that a given text or author can be considered cutting-edge in one location and desperately *passé* somewhere else at the exact same time. WGFS is many things at once. It is the transnational community of knowledge production and debate that we intervene in – albeit with unequal access, ease and status (see chapter 6) – when we participate in international conferences (Henderson, 2016) or publish in international journals. But it is also a constellation of many different and distinctive, even idiosyncratic, local WGFS communities, each with its own debates, trends, buzzwords, celebrities, and institutionalisation challenges. (Though some local WGFS communities, particularly those in the US and UK, are positioned as more universal and less specific than others – see chapter 6.) Those two levels of WGFS – the local and the transnational – do overlap, but they sometimes function in such disparate ways and dissimilar temporalities, that working across the two or moving from one to the other can be a dislocatory and baffling experience.

Processes of institutionalisation of WGFS are uneven, complex, unpredictable and rarely linear; thus, they cannot accurately be described in generalising, ahistorical and unsituated terms. The very diverse local and transnational configurations of those processes have been extensively studied and debated; so much so that they constitute a body of 'literature [which] has (. . .) expanded beyond one individual's capacity to encompass' (Boxer, 1998: xvii). It is an especially complex and heterogeneous body of literature. The tone varies significantly: some texts are more conventionally scholarly research pieces published in peer-reviewed journals or books, many are written in a format more similar to a policy or briefing paper, and others are published outside or 'between the lines' (Fernandes, 2008) of habitual academic outlets, as polemics, interchanges or manifestos. It is a complex body of literature also because there is no agreement in WGFS about what constitutes an ideal or successful institutionalisation. This means that a particular institutionalisation profile may be assessed very differently, 'according to which threads one traces and who is speaking' (Hemmings, 2010: 1). Therefore, accounts of institutionalisation are always disparate and potentially contested.

The institutionalisation literature has another important feature: the aim of many texts is not just to analyse processes of institutionalisation, but also to intervene in, and advance, those processes. Several of the first and biggest studies of institutionalisation – especially the large-scale comparative European studies like SIGMA (Braidotti et al., 1995), GRACE (Zmroczek and Duchen, 1991), the 'Employment and Women's Studies' project (Griffin, 2005b; Silius, 2002) or the 'work-in-progress reports' published in the series *The Making of European Women's Studies*, edited by ATHENA (Braidotti and Vonk, 2000) – explicitly aimed at showing the global disparities in the field's development and demonstrating the need for international support mechanisms that would counteract the particular obstacles found locally and nationally (Braidotti, 2000). Therefore, these texts are agents of institutionalisation, and so they are partly constitutive of the phenomena they examine. In this chapter, I offer a necessarily perfunctory overview of this rich body of literature, discussing it specifically from the perspective of how it engages with, and constitutes, the issue of epistemic status.[3]

What we know about the epistemic status of WGFS

References to the epistemic status of WGFS appear very frequently in the literature on institutionalisation, although not in those terms. Be it under the labels of the 'value of feminist knowledge' (Coate, 1999: 142), its 'prestige' (Lykke, 2000: 79), 'scientific status' (Varikas, 2006: 160), 'intellectual credibility' (Messer-Davidow, 2002: 157), 'academic significan[ce] or acceptab[ility]' (Evans, 1997: 59), 'scientific legitimacy' (Mayorga, 2002: 28) or 'academic respectability' (Brunt *et al.*, 1983: 285), numerous texts written at very different points in time and about distinct contexts allude to whether WGFS' ability to produce proper academic knowledge is recognised. Usually, these references are largely descriptive and extremely brief: in the middle of a wider characterisation of the situation of WGFS in a given location, the authors diagnose the epistemic status of the field in a phrase or sentence.

There are hundreds of examples of this, but I list here just a few. In 1973/1974, Rich wrote that 'women's studies are (like Third World studies) [seen in the US as] a "fad"; (. . .) feminist teachers are "unscholarly," "unprofessional," or "dykes"' (1995: 130). At around the same time, in Australian universities WGFS was being described as '"nothing more" than consciousness raising' (Crowley, 1999: 137). More recent studies in several countries indicate that WGFS scholarship has sometimes or often been described as inferior or inadequate on the basis of epistemic criteria. Writing in the early 2000s, Aparicio notes that the field was seen in Spain as 'particular, interested, or downright discriminatory' (2002: 235) and Kaplan and Grewal explain that in their, and other US universities, it 'is said that Women's Studies has always been less rigorous, too political, too ideological, unlike the other disciplines, which are supposed to be free of ideology, politics, and investment' (2003: 67). Describing experiences in the UK at different points in time, several authors indicate that WGFS has sometimes been perceived as too shallow and trivial (Marchbank and Letherby, 2006), 'not very academically demanding' (Griffin and Hanmer, 2002: 38) and too 'soft' (Stacey *et al.*, 1992: 1), as 'a pollutant in the otherwise hygienic process of knowledge production' (Morley, 1998: 12). As Steinberg succinctly puts it, 'feminist scholarship (. . .) [is] marginalised (. . .) because [it is] seen (. . .) [as] not enough and too much' (1997: 195). In some local and national contexts, this framing of the field can relegate WGFS to 'the bottom of the hierarchy of regard and status of academic disciplines' (Price and Owen, 1998: 185), meaning that WGFS scholars may get dismissed as 'not academically qualified' (Chen, 2004: 245) and even as 'imposter[s] in a university dedicated to the neutral, balanced pursuit of disinterested scholarship' (Boxer, 1998: 161). This seems to be especially the case within disciplines and institutions that 'place a high value on objectivity, neutrality, and the other trappings of positive science' (Williams, 2000: 10).

Through these brief references to epistemic status, we learn that WGFS staff and students have encountered claims about the lower scholarly value of the field in many sites and texts in the past and present: university corridors (Boxer, 1998), staff, supervision and academic board meetings (Coate, 1999; Rogers and Garrett, 2002), job interviews (Robinson, 2003), university newsletters (Armitage and Pedwell, 2005), academic books and articles (Boxer, 1998), conferences and classrooms (Henderson, 2014, 2016; Lykke, 2004), debates within disciplinary and professional associations (Amâncio, 2005; Wilkinson, 1991, 1997) or in families and groups of peers/friends (Marchbank and Letherby, 2006; Price and Owen, 1998). The literature also shows that this perception of the field has negatively impacted WGFS scholars' careers and confidence, and academic communities' support to, and engagement with, WGFS (Barazzetti *et al.*, 2002; Griffin, 2005a; Henderson, 2014; Worell, 2000). Characterising the situation in countries of the former Yugoslavia in the mid-2000s, Kolozova argued that WGFS was not recognised 'as a legitimate academic realm' and indicated that '[t]his status of marginality is reflected through its low position on the scale of power relations, "materialised" through the facts of poor funding [and] invisibility' (2006: 111). In an overview of Spanish gender research written in the early 2000s, Valiente explains that WGFS had a 'very negative image (. . .) among most scholars' and 'many mainstream [social scientists] think that gender is a much less important topic for study than other classical (. . .) issues' (2002: 769). This made 'gender research (. . .) a risky option for scholars, who may be denigrated by others (whether openly or not)' (2002: 769). Similar observations have been made, for example, about France. As Le Feuvre wrote in the early 2000s, 'lecturers who have specialised in women's/gender studies are finding that their career paths are hampered by the nature of their research, which, despite often widespread international recognition, still tends to be branded as militant and therefore (implicitly) as unscientific' (2000: 180).

The field's epistemic status also affects teaching, in a range of ways: from the nature of student engagements with the field to the claims that non-WGFS scholars make about WGFS in their teaching. According to Griffin (2005a: 100), in Finland and Italy in the mid-2000s WGFS was generally perceived as not conforming to 'an ideal of objective, uninvested knowledge' and this would 'make some students (. . .) decide not to take the subject for fear of damaging their subsequent career' (see also Barazzetti *et al.*, 2002). Webber analysed 'the kind of knowledges that students [in a Canadian university] understand to be legitimate knowledge or real knowledge' and found 'a tension between students' notions of an imagined "ideal professor" and the actuality of feminist faculty as knowledgeable' (2005: 181), a tension which led many students to perceive WGFS teaching as not legitimate (Bauer, 1990; Marchbank and Letherby, 2006; Titus, 2000). Foster *et al.* (2013) note that in politics and international relations departments in British universities WGFS themes and theories are still often considered trivial and thus left out of, or given little (and sometimes dismissive) attention in, lectures, curricula and textbooks (see also Rowley and Shepherd, 2012).[4] This, it is argued, reinforces its secondary epistemic status in students' eyes.

In some studies, especially micro-level analyses of processes of institutionali-sation, authors go further in their engagement with WGFS' epistemic status, ana-lysing it in more detail and thereby providing insight into how status is negotiated in those processes. These discussions demonstrate, for example, that the epistemic status of WGFS is negotiated in articulation with other struggles over epistemic status. According to Messer-Davidow (2002), the boundaries of sociology in the US were shaped by 'strategies of scientization'[5] deployed by its early practition-ers to increase its status as a scientific discipline. This 'scientization' hindered the recognition of the epistemic value of feminist work, because it was seen to disrupt the boundary between sociological and social discourse, a boundary which was foundational to the discipline's identity in the US. In these sorts of accounts, epistemic status is conceptualised in a more dynamic manner, as something that individuals and groups (attempt to) change. According to the literature, WGFS scholars use several strategies to shape the status of the field as a whole and/or of their particular courses or centres. In her study of the institutionalisation of WGFS in Taiwan, Chen indicates that many academics involved in setting up the first WGFS centres 'chose not to closely align with the local women's movement' in order to increase 'academic receptivity and accumulate cultural and symbolic capital for women's studies in academia' (2004: 236). They also 'strategically used objective and quantitative methodologies to carry out gender research in pursuit of academic credibility' (2004: 67). These strategies proved effective in creating space for the field, but were heavily critiqued by scholars who considered that WGFS should always be centrally and unashamedly political.

The literature also notes that scholars have tried to prove in their institutions that WGFS is a valid scholarly endeavour by highlighting that it is recognised by reputable external (academic or non-academic) organisations such as scholarly publishers (Brunt et al., 1983) or international funding bodies (Aparicio, 2002; Duhaček, 2004). Braidotti writes that in European countries, both those where WGFS is 'under-developed' and those that have 'well-endowed programmes', European Commission support has been experienced as 'a form of international recognition and therefore of scientific legitimation' (2000: 34). In some contexts, governmental support is described as influencing not just the material conditions for WGFS research and teaching, but also academic and public perceptions of the field's credibility. Suaréz and Suaréz explain that a governmental initiative to create a dedicated funding programme for WGFS research 'was crucial not only for the development of further activities but also as a way of normalizing the scientific status of Women's Studies' in Spain (2002: 449). In a case study of insti-tutionalisation that vividly illustrates how categories of scientificity are shaped by broader social and political processes, Zimmermann reports that during the period of state socialism in Central and Eastern Europe 'gender, if discussed at all, was a legitimate subject (. . .) exclusively within the context of class analysis. (. . .) [The] academic culture systematically disqualified gender as an independent cat-egory of analysis' (2007: 10). The situation changed when governments in many of these countries began providing support to WGFS as part of a strategy for, and symbol of, the liberalisation, democratisation and 'EU-ization' of their HE. This 'political recognition of the relevance of gender (. . .) in education' positioned 'the legitimacy of women's and gender studies [as being] in principle at least no longer in question' (2007: 19).

Names have also been shown to play an important part in negotiations of epistemic status. Coate describes the creation in 1975 of a WGFS UG course within the sociology department of an elite British university. It was approved on the condition that it was not called 'Women's Studies', but 'Social Analysis of Sex Roles', to be more compatible with the department's 'serious academic purpose'. Coate asks, 'why was the Social Analysis of Sex Roles acceptable whereas women's studies would not have been? Presumably feminist knowledge could be given space as long as it was not perceived to be oppositional or biased' (1999: 153–154) or, in other words, as long as it was described in terms considered properly academic. The importance of naming as a form of enactment and management of epistemic status is also evident in discussions within WGFS about the name of the field, one of the most contentious objects of debate vis-à-vis the institutionalisation of WGFS (Hemmings, 2006; Pereira, 2013). Scholars' arguments about the value of names are based not just on the conceptual connotations and theoretical implications of those names, but also on the epistemic status work that naming strategies are assumed to do. For example, authors critical of the move towards 'gender studies' argue that it is often adopted to 'aim at greater objectivity by suggesting a higher level of scientific precision' (Braidotti, 2002: 285), 'add an aura of "complexity" to what might otherwise be seen as a narrow or restricted field' (Evans, 1991: 73) and align the field with 'a masculine construction of knowledge that feminists have been fighting against for centuries' (Klein, 1991: 81). These arguments describe a particular name as potentially signalling a conceptualisation of knowledge that does not fulfil at least some criteria considered to be important values of proper WGFS knowledge.

Discussions of the epistemic status of distinct names often focus on comparisons between 'women's studies' and 'gender studies', or their equivalents in foreign languages, when they exist (Braidotti, 2002). In these comparisons, 'women's studies' frequently appears as the term associated in the wider academic community with bias, partiality or lack of objectivity, whereas 'gender studies' is seen as 'less threatening' and 'more academically acceptable' (Zmroczek and Duchen, 1991: 18) (see also Costa, 2006; Pereira, 2013). However, these terms do not have those same connotations everywhere. In Taiwan, the name 'gender studies' has been perceived as too politically radical and incompatible with dominant academic paradigms, due to its association with sexuality and queer studies (Chen, 2004). Góngora explains that unlike other contexts where 'gender is considered as a term that fits in with the social scientific language (. . .), in Chile, both feminism and gender [were seen] as ideologically threatening terms' (2002: 53). Discussing the titles of the first WGFS courses in the US, Boxer explains that '[t]he term *women's studies* was preferred, not least because it sounded more "objective" and more comprehensive than *feminist studies*' (1998: 14, original emphases).

These examples show that the same name can been used to denote very differ-ent positions vis-à-vis scientificity. In Portugal, for instance, some scholars prefer *estudos sobre as mulheres* (literally, studies about women) because they consider that is the term best placed to uphold a politically-engaged analytical stance (*ex aequo* Editorial Board, 1999; Ferreira, 2006). However, others who also prefer that term explicitly distance themselves from such a stance: Nizza da Silva, for instance, writes 'women's studies, although they may contribute to the transfor-mation of women's roles (. . .) are not aimed at struggle, (. . .) or at denouncing. Their aim is, rather, to create new themes, directing analytical attention to spaces of knowledge which have not yet been explored' (1998: 7*; see also Silva and Tavares, 2001). This leads Abranches to suggest that

> [t]he argument powerfully developed by Mary Evans (1982) that Women's Studies *is* Feminist Studies, does not really apply to our [Portuguese] con-text, where (. . .) much that went (and still goes) under the label of Women's Studies sticks to traditional canonical approaches and in no way challenges patriarchical (sic) thought (. . .), let alone proposes "a radical change in the theoretical organization of the universe" (Evans, 1982:19).
>
> (1998: 8–9, original emphasis)[6]

The name *estudos de género* (studies of gender) is also used heterogeneously. It appears in many texts as a term symbolising an explicitly critical perspective, both vis-à-vis existing scholarship and broader social inequalities (for example Araújo, 2002; Nogueira, 2001; Oliveira and Amâncio, 2006). But several scholars argue (in texts and their interviews with me) that this coexists with a trend within and outside academia to use 'gender studies' or 'gender analysis' to refer to uncritical research that does not engage with feminist theory (see chapter 4; Amâncio, 2003; Joaquim, 2005; Magalhães, 2001).

These examples from across the world show that the meaning and status of a name are relative: they vary in space and time, and depend on what a particular name is compared to. We must therefore avoid generalising and unsituated claims about the implications and value of names, because these claims often replicate very specific anglophone histories, and presuppose that each name has an intrinsic and universal meaning, and entirely predictable linear effects.

Asking more questions about the epistemic status of WGFS

The frequency with which references to epistemic status appear in the literature on institutionalisation – even if almost always only in passing – shows how cen-tral issues of epistemic status are in shaping the conditions of WGFS teaching, learning and research. When woven together, these dispersed references provide important insight into the field's epistemic status; I would systematise that insight as follows. WGFS, like other fields, is evaluated within and outside academia in part on the basis of how 'good' the knowledge it produces is. The dominant criteria used in many academic contexts to assess the quality of knowledge lead to the description and dismissal of WGFS as not entirely scientific. Claims about this supposedly intrinsic epistemic inferiority of WGFS are made in many formal and informal settings, and in some contexts that dismissal is so virulent, frequent and intense that it constitutes a form of intellectual harassment, as Kolodny (1996) designates it. However, the field's epistemic status is not static and may change as institutionalisation unfolds, with several actors and institutions playing a more or less direct and decisive role. Due to all the above, considerations about epistemic status take centre stage when WGFS scholars make located decisions about strategies of institutionalisation or naming. WGFS scholars often do not agree on which strategies are best and have had ongoing debates about the extent to which particular names or institutionalisation profiles enable the production of proper WGFS knowledge. Therefore, negotiations of epistemic status are not just externally imposed struggles that WGFS scholars must engage in as they try to create WGFS space in sometimes inhospitable environments; they are also internal contestations that play a central and generative role in the life of the field.

It is clear, then, that the existing literature already tells us much about the epistemic status of WGFS, and particularly about how central, complex and multidimensional its negotiation is. However, because the primary object of many of those texts is not epistemic status, they often address status only tangentially, and so are often unable to follow the many important lines of questioning they hint at. I started this review by noting that most references to epistemic status are descriptive: we are told that in a country, institution or discipline, WGFS has 'low' status or is seen as 'not academic'. But what is understood by 'academic' in that context, and is that understanding shared by all in that academic community? WGFS' status is low in comparison to what? Do all aspects and contributions of WGFS have (equally) low status? How is that lower status asserted or resisted in distinct sites and situations? Who is involved in those processes? How do the contemporary changes in academic labour, research evaluation systems, and the broader global political economy of scholarly knowledge production shape those processes? To bring together these many particular questions in a more general one: how is the status of WGFS (re)produced and negotiated in daily academic practices in contemporary academia?

We should ask these questions not just because they provide topical new insight, but because the tendency in the literature to describe status in ontological and quantified terms ('the status of WGFS is low') can pose problems. One cannot, and should not, expect all studies of institutionalisation to provide detailed accounts of negotiations of epistemic status, as their objects and aims lie elsewhere. However, because epistemic status is often not conceptualised as an issue in itself, change in the institutional position of WGFS tends to be equated with change to its epistemic status. Institutional change and epistemic status are, of course, connected but the relation between them is not linear or determined *a priori* (Pereira, 2008). As Stanley perceptively notes,

the re/writing of knowledge certainly encompasses the re/making of organisations and institutions; however, it is the converse move that is politically and ethically more ambiguous: a changing institution can change in ways that have little or no epistemological or political consequentiality.

(1997: 10)

Indeed, institutional change and epistemic status may sometimes work in the same direction and feed into each other: e.g. an increase in WGFS publications can help to place it more centrally on the academic agenda and bolster the field's status. However, they sometimes work *against* each other. Low status may limit the success of strategies of institutionalisation – as when a new WGFS course or degree fails to recruit sufficient students because the field is considered less scholarly or relevant (Griffin, 2005b; Hemmings, 2006; Silius, 2002). WGFS may become more regularly mentioned in non-WGFS teaching and conferences, but be described in ways that undermine its status or delimit its relevance. This has been the case when WGFS is integrated in curricula and textbooks but described, explicitly or implicitly, as a secondary and narrower area of study (Abbott, 1991; Pereira, 2012; Rowley and Shepherd, 2012). We must, therefore, foreground the messiness of the links between institutionalisation and recognition, a point also made by Barazzetti and Michel (2000). In a discussion of criteria used to evaluate and compare profiles of WGFS institutionalisation in Europe, they argue that

the main concepts used 'institutionalization', 'recognition' (. . .) and their links (. . .) need to be explored further. Does institutionalization (. . .) necessarily imply recognition? And what kind of recognition is it? Who or what institution is providing this recognition and at what level? (. . .) Is it mainly an academic and scientific recognition that we are looking for? How about the recognition of the usefulness of Women's Studies by the society, especially by certain women's rights organizations, for example?

(2000: 76)

The relation between institutionalisation – in both senses of the term: WGFS' changing presence in institutions and its affirmation as itself an institution – and epistemic status is complex, and we do not understand it entirely well at present. Thus, I join Barazzetti and Michel in arguing that we must study that relation more explicitly and dynamically.

I would argue that references to epistemic status in the literature are often relatively brief also because the low status of WGFS is perceived as something which readers (including those from other contexts) will recognise. That is how I myself framed the opening of this book. This is no doubt a legitimate assumption, and one confirmed by the reactions to my own 'elevator pitch', as I described it. As WGFS students and scholars, many of us have experienced this 'lower' status in our daily lives, and because we have read feminist epistemology, we feel we know *how* and *why* it happens, and with *what effects*. But is it that straightforward? If, as I have noted, patterns of institutionalisation, epistemic criteria, or the status of different names all vary significantly across time and (geographical, institutional, disciplinary) space, and are always relative, then a more focused, located and detailed analysis of negotiations of status is necessary and productive.

Literature on institutionalisation which examines how different actors and strategies shape the field's epistemic status – such as Chen (2004), Coate (1999, 2000), Messer-Davidow (2002) or Wilkinson (1991, 1997) – go some way in interrogating these context-specific genealogies. However, this literature generally adopts a historical perspective and focuses on past processes of institutional change (such as the creation of centres, degrees or sections in professional associations), and therefore is not always able to analyse the 'ongoingness' of these negotiations. Studies like Chen's (2004), Coate's (1999, 2000), Henderson's (2016) and Marchbank and Letherby's (2006) include retrospective accounts of interviewees' experiences of the daily work of affirming the epistemic credentials of the field, and indicate that this daily work is crucial. This suggests, therefore, that it is worthwhile to engage more systematically with an observation of these negotiations *as they happen*, namely in classrooms, conferences and other sites of academic work and sociability. Approaching these issues *ethnographically* is, thus, key to foregrounding that ongoing, laborious nature of negotiations of epistemic status.

In sum, I argue that the existing literature on institutionalisation provides rich insight into WGFS' status, but we must complexify our theoretical and empirical engagement with epistemic status, to better understand its ongoing, multilayered negotiation. Without closer attention to the located negotiations that play out quite differently in academic sites throughout the world every day, WGFS' epistemic status can become flattened as something which just 'is', rather than a dynamic construction, continuously and complexly fought over. At a time of intense micro- and macro-level transformation in universities worldwide, there is, therefore, important ethnographic work to be done in interrogating the changing processes, protagonists and outcomes of negotiations of WGFS' epistemic status. That is the work I pursue in the chapters that follow.

Notes

1 My definition, inspired by Chen (2004: 5), is not consensual. Some authors prefer a narrower definition, where 'institutionalisation' refers specifically to the incorporation of WGFS in academic institutions and is distinguished from 'disciplinisation', understood as the constitution of WGFS as a discipline (Widerberg, 2006).
2 See Spivak (2000) and McRobbie (2009) for a discussion of how the educational migration of young women from the global south to the 'cosmopolitan classroom' (McRobbie, 2009: 167) is constituted by, and constitutive of, broader local and global inequalities.
3 For an overview of other aspects of this literature, see Pereira (2011).
4 However, as disciplines operate with different criteria of epistemic value, the UK situation varies across disciplines. According to Griffin and Hanmer (2002), in sociology, cultural studies and the humanities WGFS has been more regularly (though not always) recognised and integrated in curricula.

5 These 'scientization' strategies involved the organisation of the discipline according to scientific methods or, in Messer-Davidow's words, 'convention-structured objectivity practices' (2002: 36).
6 See also *ex aequo* Editorial Board (1999) and Pinto (2008: 29,62).

References

Abbott, Pamela (1991). "Feminist Perspectives in Sociology: The Challenge to 'Mainstream' Orthodoxy" in J. Aaron and S. Walby (eds.), *Out of the Margins: Women's Studies in the Nineties* (pp.181–190). London: Falmer Press.

Abranches, Graça (1998). *"On What Terms Shall we Join the Procession of Educated Men?" Teaching Feminist Studies at the University of Coimbra*. Coimbra: Centro de Estudos Sociais.

Amâncio, Lígia (2003). "O Género nos Discursos das Ciências Sociais". *Análise Social, XXXVIII* (168), 687–714.

Amâncio, Lígia (2005). "Reflections on Science as a Gendered Endeavour: Changes and Continuities". *Social Science Information, 44* (1), 65–83.

Aparicio, Elena Casado (2002). "Women's Studies in Spain: An Update". *The Making of European Women's Studies, IV*, 230–242.

Araújo, Helena Costa (2002). "Há já Lugar para Algum Mapeamento nos Estudos sobre Género e Educação em Portugal? Uma Tentativa Exploratória". *Investigar em Educação, 1*, 101–146.

Armitage, Faith and Pedwell, Carolyn (2005). *Putting Gender on the Map: The LSE Gender Institute's First Fifteen Years*. London: Gender Institute (LSE).

Barazzetti, Donatella and Michel, Christine (2000). "Reflections on Criteria for Comparisons of Degrees of Institutionalization and on Relevant Typologies". *The Making of European Women's Studies, I*, 74–76.

Barazzetti, Donatella, *et al.* (2002). "Italy" in G. Griffin (ed.), *Women's Employment, Women's Studies, and Equal Opportunities (1945–2001)* (pp.177–230). Hull: University of Hull.Bauer, Dale (1990). "The Other 'F' Word: The Feminist in the Classroom". *College English, 52* (4), 385–396.

Boxer, Marilyn J. (1998). *When Women Ask the Questions: Creating Women's Studies in America*. Baltimore, MD: Johns Hopkins University Press.

Braidotti, Rosi (2000). "Key Terms and Issues in the Making of European Women's Studies". *The Making of European Women's Studies, I*, 23–36.

Braidotti, Rosi (2002). "The Uses and Abuses of the Sex/Gender Distinction in European Feminist Practices" in G. Griffin and R. Braidotti (eds.), *Thinking Differently: A Reader in European Women's Studies* (pp.285–310). London: Zed.

Braidotti, Rosi, *et al.* (eds.) (1995). *National Reports for the SIGMA European Subject Area Evaluation of Women's Studies*. Brussels: European Commission.

Braidotti, Rosi and Vonk, Esther (2000). "Introduction". *The Making of European Women's Studies, I*, 9–11.

Brunt, Rosalind, *et al.* (1983). "Sell-Out or Challenge? The Contradiction of a Masters in Women's Studies". *Women's Studies International Forum, 6* (3), 283–290.

Chen, Peiying (2004). *Acting "Otherwise": The Institutionalization of Women's/Gender Studies in Taiwan Universities*. London: RoutledgeFalmer.

Coate, Kelly (1999). "Feminist Knowledge and the Ivory Tower: A Case Study". *Gender and Education, 11* (2), 141–159.

Coate, Kelly (2000). *The History of Women's Studies as an Academic Subject Area in Higher Education in the UK: 1970–1990.* PhD Thesis, Institute of Education.

Costa, Cláudia de Lima (2006). "Lost (and Found?) in Translation: Feminisms in Hemispheric Dialogue". *Latino Studies, 4* (1/2), 62–78.

Crowley, Helen (1999). "Women's Studies: Between a Rock and a Hard Place or Just Another Cell in the Beehive?". *Feminist Review, 61*, 131–150.

Duhaček, Daša (2004). "The Belgrade Women's Studies Centre: The Next Stage?". *The Making of European Women's Studies, V*, 41–45.

Evans, Mary (1991). "The Problem of Gender for Women's Studies" in J. Aaron and S. Walby (eds.), *Out of the Margins: Women's Studies in the Nineties* (pp.67–74). London: Falmer Press.

Evans, Mary (1997). *Introducing Contemporary Feminist Thought.* Cambridge: Polity.

ex aequo Editorial Board (1999). "Editorial". *ex aequo, 1*, 5–10.

Fernandes, Emília (2008). "Elas por Elas: Corpos Ruidosos, Corpos Silenciados em Contexto Organizacional". *Diacrítica, 22* (3), 87–102.

Ferreira, Virgínia (2006). *L'Usage du Genre au Portugal: En Tant que Catégorie Analytique ou Descriptif?.* Retrieved 02/04/2016, from http://www.univ-paris8.fr/RING/activites/rencontres.euro/ferreira.portugal.html

Foster, Emma, *et al.* (2013). "The Personal Is Not Political: At Least in the UK's Top Politics and IR Departments". *British Journal of Politics and International Relations, 15* (4), 566–585.

Góngora, Jimena Gallardo (2002). "Contradictions in the Institutionalisation Process of Women's and Gender Studies in Chile". *The Making of European Women's Studies, IV*, 47–60.

Griffin, Gabriele (2005a). "The Institutionalization of Women's Studies in Europe" in G. Griffin (ed.), *Doing Women's Studies: Employment Opportunities, Personal Impacts and Social Consequences* (pp.89–110). London: Zed.

Griffin, Gabriele (ed.) (2005b). *Doing Women's Studies: Employment Opportunities, Personal Impacts and Social Consequences.* London: Zed.

Griffin, Gabriele (2009). "The 'Ins' and 'Outs' of Women's/Gender Studies: A Response to the Reports of Its Demise in 2008". *Women's History Review, 18* (3), 485–496.Griffin, Gabriele and Hanmer, Jalna (2002). "The UK" in G. Griffin (ed.), *Women's Employment, Women's Studies, and Equal Opportunities (1945–2001)* (pp.1–68). Hull: University of Hull.

Gutiérrez-Rodríguez, Encarnación (2016). "Sensing Dispossession: Women and Gender Studies Between Institutional Racism and Migration Control Policies in the Neoliberal University". *Women's Studies International Forum, 54*, 167–177.

Hemmings, Clare (2006). "The Life and Times of Academic Feminism" in K. Davis, *et al.* (eds.), *Handbook of Gender and Women's Studies* (pp.13–34). London: Sage.

Hemmings, Clare (2008). "Tuning Problems? Notes on Women's and Gender Studies and the Bologna Process". *European Journal of Women's Studies, 15* (2), 117–127.

Hemmings, Clare (2010). "Editorial: Transforming Academies, Global Genealogies". *Feminist Review, 95*, 1–4.

Hemmings, Clare (2011). *Why Stories Matter: The Political Grammar of Feminist Theory.* Durham, NC: Duke University Press.

Henderson, Emily F. (2014). "Bringing Up Gender: Academic Abjection?". *Pedagogy, Culture & Society, 22* (1), 21–38.

Henderson, Emily F. (2016). *Eventful Gender: An Ethnographic Exploration of Gender Knowledge Production at International Academic Conferences.* PhD Thesis, UCL Institute of Education.

Joaquim, Teresa (2005). *Misplaced Subjects: Women's Studies and Gender in the Portuguese Context.* Retrieved 02/04/2016, from http://www.travellingconcepts.net/joaquim1.html

Juhász, Borbála, *et al.* (2005). "Educational Migration and Gender: Women's Studies Students' Educational Mobility in Europe" in G. Griffin (ed.), *Doing Women's Studies: Employment Opportunities, Personal Impacts and Social Consequences* (pp.168–194). London: Zed.

Kaplan, Caren and Grewal, Inderpal (2003). "Transnational Practices and Interdisciplinary Feminist Scholarship: Refiguring Women's and Gender Studies" in R. Wiegman (ed.), *Women's Studies on its Own* (pp.66–81). Durham, NC: Duke University Press.

Klein, Renate D. (1991). "Passion and Politics in Women's Studies in the 1990s" in J. Aaron and S. Walby (eds.), *Out of the Margins: Women's Studies in the Nineties* (pp.75–89). London: Falmer Press.

Kolodny, Annette (1996). "Paying the Price of Antifeminist Intellectual Harassment" in V.A. Clark, *et al.* (eds.), *Antifeminism in the Academy* (pp.3–34). New York: Routledge.

Kolozova, Katerina (2006). "Gender Studies in the Context of the Balkans: The Perspectives and Experiences of Skopje" in T.-S. Pavlidou (ed.), *Gender Studies: Trends/Tensions in Greece and Other European Countries* (pp.111–116). Thessaloniki: ΕΚΔΟΣΕΙΣ ΖΗΤΗ.

Le Feuvre, Nicky (2000). "Women's and Gender Studies in France". *The Making of European Women's Studies, II,* 172–190.

Lykke, Nina (2000). "Towards an Evaluation of Women's Studies in Relation to the Job Prospects of its Graduates". *The Making of European Women's Studies, I,* 77–79.

Lykke, Nina (2004). "Women's/Gender/Feminist Studies: A Post-Disciplinary Discipline?". *The Making of European Women's Studies, V,* 91–101.

Magalhães, Maria José (2001). "Dez Anos da APEM: Percorrer as Vozes, Significar os Percursos". *ex aequo, 5,* 27–68.

Marchbank, Jen and Letherby, Gayle (2006). "Views and Perspectives of Women's Studies: A Survey of Women and Men Students". *Gender and Education, 18* (2), 157–182.

Mayorga, Cláudia (2002). "Gender, Race and Women's Studies in Brazil". *The Making of European Women's Studies, IV,* 25–36.

McNeil, Maureen (1993). "Dancing with Foucault: Feminism and Power-Knowledge" in C. Ramazanoğlu (ed.), *Up Against Foucault* (pp.147–178). London: Routledge.

McRobbie, Angela (2009). *The Aftermath of Feminism: Gender, Culture and Social Change.* London: Sage.

Messer-Davidow, Ellen (2002). *Disciplining Feminism: From Social Activism to Academic Discourse.* Durham, NC: Duke University Press.

Morley, Louise (1998). *Organising Feminisms: The Micropolitics of the Academy.* New York: St. Martin's Press.

Nash, Jennifer and Owens, Emily (2015). "Institutional Feelings: Practicing Women's Studies in the Corporate University". *Feminist Formations, 27* (3), vii–xi.

Nizza da Silva, Maria Beatriz (1998). "Introdução" in M.B. Nizza da Silva and A. Cova (eds.), *Estudos sobre as Mulheres* (pp.1–21). Lisboa: Universidade Aberta.

Nogueira, Conceição (2001). "Construcionismo Social, Discurso e Género". *Psicologia, XV* (1), 43–65.

Oliveira, João Manuel de and Amâncio, Lígia (2006). "Teorias Feministas e Representações Sociais: Desafios dos Conhecimentos Situados para a Psicologia Social". *Revista
Estudos Feministas, 14* (3), 597–615.

Oxford, Esther (2008). "Last Women Standing". *Times Higher Education.* Retrieved
02/04/2016, from http://www.timeshighereducation.co.uk/story.asp?storycode=400363

Pereira, Maria do Mar (2008). "The Epistemic Status of Women's, Gender, Feminist Studies: Notes for Analysis". *The Making of European Women's Studies, VIII,* 144–156.

Pereira, Maria do Mar (2011). *Pushing the Boundaries of Knowledge: An Ethnography of
Negotiations of the Epistemic Status of Women's, Gender, Feminist Studies in Portugal.*
PhD Thesis, LSE.

Pereira, Maria do Mar (2012). " 'Feminist Theory is Proper Knowledge, But . . .': The Status of Feminist Scholarship in the Academy". *Feminist Theory, 13* (3), 283–303.

Pereira, Maria do Mar (2013). "Women's and Gender Studies" in M. Evans and C. Williams (eds.), *Gender: The Key Concepts* (pp.215–223). London: Routledge.

Pereira, Maria do Mar (2014). "Women's and Gender Studies" in L. Meyer (ed.), *Oxford
Bibliographies – Education.* New York: Oxford University Press.

Pinto, Teresa (2008). *A Formação Profissional das Mulheres no Ensino Industrial Público
(1884–1910): Realidades e Representações.* PhD Thesis, Universidade Aberta.

Price, Marion and Owen, Mairead (1998). "Who Studies Women's Studies?". *Gender and
Education, 10* (2), 185–198.

Rich, Adrienne (1995). *On Lies, Secrets, and Silence: Selected Prose (1966–1978).* New
York: Norton.

Robinson, Jean C. (2003). "From Politics to Professionalism: Cultural Change in Women's
Studies" in R. Wiegman (ed.), *Women's Studies on its Own* (pp.202–210). Durham, NC:
Duke University Press.

Rogers, Mary and Garrett, C. D. (2002). *Who's Afraid of Women's Studies?: Feminisms in
Everyday Life.* Walnut Creek, CA: AltaMira Press.

Rowley, Christina and Shepherd, Laura (2012). "Contemporary Politics: Using the 'F'
Word and Teaching Gender in International Relations" in C. Gormley-Heenan and S.
Lightfoot (eds.), *Teaching Politics and International Relations* (pp.146–161). Hound-
mills: Palgrave Macmillan.

Silius, Harriet (2002). "Comparative Summary" in G. Griffin (ed.), *Women's Employment,
Women's Studies, and Equal Opportunities (1945–2001)* (pp.470–514). Hull: University
of Hull.

Silva, Ana da and Tavares, Teresa Cláudia (2001). "Estudos Culturais, Estudos sobre as
Mulheres e Estudos Culturais sobre as Mulheres". *ex aequo, 5,* 123–147.

Spivak, Gayatri C. (2000). "Thinking Cultural Questions in 'Pure' Literary Terms" in P.
Gilroy, *et al.* (eds.), *Without Guarantees: In Honour of Stuart Hall* (pp.335–357). London: Verso.

Stacey, Jackie, *et al.* (1992). "Working Out: New Directions for Women's Studies" in H.
Hinds, *et al.* (eds.), *Working Out: New Directions for Women's Studies* (pp.1–10). London: Falmer Press.

Stanley, Liz (1997). "Introduction: On Academic Borders, Territories, Tribes and Knowledges" in L. Stanley (ed.), *Knowing Feminisms: On Academic Borders, Territories and
Tribes* (pp.1–17). London: Sage.

Steinberg, Deborah Lynn (1997). "All Roads Lead to . . . Problems with Discipline" in
J.E. Canaan and D. Epstein (eds.), *A Question of Discipline: Pedagogy, Power and the
Teaching of Cultural Studies* (pp.192–215). Oxford: Westview Press.

Suárez, Isabel Carrera and Suárez, Laura Vinuela (2002). "Spain" in G. Griffin (ed.), *Women's Employment, Women's Studies, and Equal Opportunities (1945–2001)* (pp.427–469). Hull: University of Hull.

Titus, Jordan J. (2000). "Engaging Student Resistance to Feminism: 'How Is This Stuff Going to Make Us Better Teachers?'". *Gender and Education, 12* (1), 21–37.

Valiente, Celia (2002). "An Overview of Research on Gender in Spanish Society". *Gender & Society, 16* (6), 767–792.

Varikas, Eleni (2006). "GRACE Report: Women's Studies in Greece 1988". *The Making of European Women's Studies, VII*, 159–163.

Webber, Michelle (2005). "'Don't Be So Feminist': Exploring Student Resistance to Feminist Approaches in a Canadian University". *Women's Studies International Forum, 28* (2/3), 181–194.

Widerberg, Karin (2006). "Disciplinization of Gender Studies. Old Questions, New Answers? Nordic Strategies in the European Context". *NORA: Nordic Journal of Feminist and Gender Research, 14* (2), 131–140.

Wilkinson, Sue (1991). "Why Psychology (Badly) Needs Feminism" in J. Aaron and S. Walby (eds.), *Out of the Margins: Women's Studies in the Nineties* (pp.191–203). London: Falmer Press.

Wilkinson, Sue (1997). "Still Seeking Transformation: Feminist Challenges to Psychology" in L. Stanley (ed.), *Knowing Feminisms: On Academic Borders, Territories and Tribes* (pp.97–108). London: Sage.

Williams, Christine L. (2000). "Preface". *Annals of the American Academy of Political and Social Science, 571*, 8–13.

Worell, Judith (2000). "Feminism in Psychology: Revolution or Evolution?". *Annals of the American Academy of Political and Social Science, 571*, 183–196.

Zimmermann, Susan (2007). "The Institutionalization of Women and Gender Studies in Higher Education in Central and Eastern Europe and the Former Soviet Union: Asymmetric Politics and the Regional-Transnational Configuration". *East Central Europe, 34* (1), 131–160.

Zmroczek, Christine and Duchen, Claire (1991). "What *Are* those Women Up To? Women's Studies and Feminist Research in the European Community" in J. Aaron and S. Walby (eds.), *Out of the Margins: Women's Studies in the Nineties* (pp.11–29). London: Falmer Press.

Chapter 2

Pushing and pulling the boundaries of knowledge

A feminist theory of epistemic status

Figure 1 *Piled Higher and Deeper* by Jorge Cham, www.phdcomics.com (03/09/2007)

Jorge Cham's comics about graduate students' experiences are often described as particularly perceptive accounts of the mundane negotiations that constitute daily life in academia (Coelho, 2009). Indeed, Gerard and Tajel's argument (above) about who is a 'scientist', what data is 'real' or 'made up', whether 'subjective' methods produce 'real' data, or whose PhDs are grounded in proper academic work, is a brief but telling illustration of old and ongoing discussions. Debates about what constitutes scientific research, who can be said to do it (well) and how it is positioned vis-à-vis other forms of knowledge production are both 'well trod ground' (Lather, 2005: 3) and 'seemingly interminable' (Gieryn, 1983: 792). The image above was sent to me by an astro-physicist friend with the message: 'I expect a treatise about this comic strip!'. His half-joking request has been ful-filled, because this chapter is precisely an attempt to problematise theoretically the questions raised by Gerard and Tajel. It begins by very briefly sketching the structure of debates about the so-called 'demarcation problem' and then offers a proposal for a theory of epistemic status, weaving together feminist epistemology, STS, and the work of Michel Foucault.

What, and where, is scientific knowledge?

According to Potter, 'the history of (. . .) philosophy of science is strewn with efforts to find the criteria distinguishing scientific knowledge' (2006: 110), i.e. attempts to determine the essential (both in the sense of intrinsic and necessary) characteristics that make a claim or method scientific, thereby differentiating it from other epistemic products or practices (Laudan, 1983). These attempts frame the demarcation of science from non-science (and of good science from bad science) as a problem to be solved. Indeed, the assumption is that a (re)solution can and should be found for it, even if just partially and/or temporarily, and that such a (re)solution can be established *a priori* through abstract inquiry.

Demarcation is framed in these attempts in essentialist terms, with scientificity understood as being wholly or mostly determined by the properties of a claim. Gieryn defines essentialist approaches to demarcation as arguing that 'the conditions *necessary* for the production of valid and reliable knowledge are *sufficient* to explain why science has emerged historically' as a highly valued epistemic activity (1999: 26, original emphases). These approaches to demarcation are also explicitly normative: science is seen as epistemically privileged in relation to other forms of knowledge production and the aim of demarcation is to define the best set of norms for adequate assessment of the scientificity of claims. This perspective was the dominant mode of formulation of the demarcation problem throughout much of the history of western philosophy of science (Taylor, 1996). The relative consensus on the suitability of an essentialist and normative engagement with demarcation does not mean, however, that classical responses to it were identical: according to Taylor, the demarcation problem has been 'a staple of philosophical controversy for centuries (. . .) [and] has been answered in a host of inconsistent ways' by mainstream philosophers (1996: 9).[1]

Particularly since the second half of the 20th century, this framing of the demarcation problem has been intensely critiqued. Two strands of critique have had a particularly significant impact. One strand arises from the work of scholars committed to sociological, historical and anthropological studies of located practices of scientific work. They have reframed the problem as a practical and empirical one, arguing that demarcation cannot and should not be resolved *a priori* and universally, and must be examined through situated studies of how actual communities demarcate science in specific (con)texts and times (Petersen, 2003). This was one of the driving forces for the development of what is currently usually called science and technology studies (STS), a field more or less loosely bringing together different strands of scholarship about the institutions and practices of science. There is disagreement in STS over the extent to which scientific facts can be said to be constructed (Sismondo, 2008; Whelan, 2001) or the methods best suited to analyse that construction (Bowden, 1995). Nevertheless, different STS scholars share a framing of scientificity not as an inherent feature of claims or epistemic activities, but as the result of historically and culturally specific processes of delimitation of the domain of science. The focus in STS is therefore on 'proliferating, situated, rhetorically-inflected scientificities' (Lather, 2005: 9) and demarcation is not the aim of inquiry, but the object of study.

A different, but sometimes overlapping (Lykke, 2008), strand of critique has been led by scholars engaging with demarcation from feminist, anti-racist, post structuralist and other critical perspectives. What these heterogeneous perspectives share is a belief that, to use Code's words, the 'grounds for granting normative status to scientific activity are by no means self-announcing, and that discovering them is more a sociopolitical project than an exercise in determining formal criteria of rationality detached from particular circumstances' (1995: 233). Science is understood as an exclusionary category with considerable and problematic authority in contemporary western societies,[2] which works to create hierarchies and normalise the epistemic and material domination of a narrow subset of epistemic agents and activities over others. As Foucault – one of the key poststructuralist critics of the political effects of the category of scientific – has argued, '[t]here exists at present a problem which is not without importance for political practice: that of the status, of the conditions of exercise, functioning and institutionalization of scientific discourses' (1991 [1968]: 65).

Feminist epistemologists – such as Linda Alcoff (1993, 2000), Lorraine Code (1991, 1995, 2014), Patricia Hill Collins (1990), Evelyn Fox Keller (1985), Miranda Fricker (2007), Donna Haraway (1990), Sandra Harding (1991, 2006) and Hilary Rose (1994) – have been at the forefront of efforts to denounce the political character of demarcation, and draw attention to how it is shaped by, and shapes, gendered relations of power. A leading and very influential role in these critiques of demarcation of scientificity has also been played by black theorists (Collins, 1990; hooks, 1982; hooks and West, 1991; Kilomba, 2007; Mbembe, 2016)[3] and scholars writing from postcolonial, decolonial and 'southern epistemology' perspectives (Bhambra, 2007; Connell, 2007; Goonatilake, 1993; Mohanty, 1988; Said, 1985; Sandoval, 2000; Sousa Santos, 2007; Stepan and Gilman, 1993), to name just a few of the many contributors to these debates. In a piece examining how 'concepts of knowledge and the idea of what scholarship or science is, are intrinsically linked with power and racial authority' (Kilomba, 2007: §3), Grada Kilomba writes:

> our [Black scholars'] voices – through a system of racism – have been systematically disqualified as valid knowledge. (. . .) As a scholar (. . .) I am commonly told that my work on everyday racism is very interesting, but not really scientific, a remark which illustrates this colonial hierarchy in which Black scholars reside: 'You have a very subjective perspective', 'very personal', 'very emotional', 'very specific', 'Are these objective facts?'. Within such masterful descriptions, the discourses and perspectives of Black scholars remain always at the margins – as deviating, while white discourses occupy the centre. When they speak [it] is scientific, when we speak [it] is unscientific.
>
> (2007: §5–7)

Feminist, black, postcolonial and other critical authors reject the traditional framing of the demarcation problem. They argue that demarcations of scientificity must be conceptualised as one element of the broader, ongoing (re)production of gendered, racialised, classed and eurocentric hegemonies, which define lesser and lacking 'others', both within and outside academia. These authors 'are keenly aware that boundary battles about what to include and exclude [in demarcations of scientificity] are often arbitrary, rarely neutral, and always powerful' (Nader, 1996: 4), and they consider that an examination of these 'battles' is productive and necessary, both theoretically and politically. This reference to 'battles' points to an important narrative and theoretical feature of these strands of critique. As Yeatman notes, '[f]eminist and postcolonial intellectuals are clearly attempting to open up contested epistemological spaces. Theirs is a narrative which is ordered by *metaphors of struggle, contest, forced closure, strategic interventions and contingent opening* of public spaces for epistemological politics' (1994: 191–192, my emphasis).

These two strands of critical intervention multiplied existing formulations of the demarcation problem, in ways that go beyond a straightforward distinction between demarcationist and critical positions.[4] Contemporary literature about the boundaries of science is composed of a range of approaches, focused on different levels of analysis, and combining varying forms and degrees of normativity, foundationalism and empirical grounding. Unfortunately, however, the links and traffic between those approaches are often limited. Keen to explore the potential for a closer articulation between them, I offer a theory of epistemic status that weaves together Lorraine Code's feminist epistemology of *rhetorical spaces* (1995), Michel Foucault's concept of *episteme* – as redefined in his later work (1980 [1977]) – and his theorisation of the truth- and power-effects produced in and through claims to scientificity (2003 [1976]), and Thomas Gieryn's concept of *boundary-work* (1999).

A theory of epistemic status

I want to suggest that negotiations over the demarcation of scientificity can be productively problematised through the concept of *epistemic status*, which I define as the degree to which, and terms in which, a knowledge claim, or entire field, is recognised as fulfilling the requisite criteria to be considered credible and relevant knowledge, however those criteria are defined in specific spaces, communities and moments. The term appears occasionally in the epistemological literature (e.g. Code, 1991: 68; 2006a: 72,270; Fricker, 2007: 133), but is not defined or operationalised and is used interchangeably with other related terms much more widely and frequently deployed. These include *epistemic authority* (Code, 1995, 2006a, 2006b; Fricker, 2007; Gieryn, 1999; Taylor, 1996) and *cognitive authority* (Alcoff and Potter, 1993a; Code, 1991, 1995; Keller and Longino, 1996; Sartori, 1994).

Like the authors who use those terms, I am interested in foregrounding the fact that recognition of a claim as proper knowledge produces respectability, influence and power. But I prefer to speak of *status*, rather than *authority*, because the term has an additional dimension which is particularly useful. According to the OED, one meaning of *status* is a 'condition of things'. I would argue that the daily discursive framing of epistemic status as an intrinsic 'condition of things' plays a central role in demarcation, because it masks the fact that labelling a claim (not) scientific is an arbitrary,[5] contested and political act. Scientificity becomes a powerful device if it is perceived as an intrinsic property of claims, its *status*, rather than something produced in, and through, the eye of the beholder (or funder, or peer-reviewer, or other academic decision-maker). Therefore, I speak of epistemic *status* to foreground the processes through which scientificity (or lack thereof) becomes represented as 'flowing, seemingly, from the exigencies of knowledge rather than the manipulations of power' (May, 1993: 112).

Epistemes and the politics of the scientific statement: A Foucauldian approach

My conceptualisation of epistemic status is partly inspired by Foucault, an author who throughout his career was keen to examine the structure and 'politics of the scientific statement' (1980 [1976]-a: 112). This inquiry took distinct forms at different stages.[6] In his earlier work (1974 [1966], 2006 [1969]), Foucault's perspective, language and aims are more demarcationist. He states, for example, that his archaeological analysis 'accepts the fact of science only in order to ask the question what is it for that science to be a science' (2006 [1969]: 212). This seems to suggest that he refuses an essentialist conceptualisation of scientificity. However, at several points in those earlier works his arguments presume and incorporate the possibility of demarcating certain domains as *being* (rather than just *recognised* as being) more or less scientific.[7] He appears, thus, to be operating at least partly with a notion of scientificity that, although discursively constituted and historically specific, is in some way related to the actual epistemic properties of claims and fields.

In his later work, Foucault's approach becomes more explicitly anti-demarcationist and it is that phase that I draw on.[8] In a 1976 interview, he argues that when analysing the relations between truth and power,

> the problem does not consist in drawing the line between that in a discourse which falls under the category of scientificity or truth, and that which comes under some other category, but in seeing historically how effects of truth are produced within discourses which in themselves are neither true nor false.
>
> (1980 [1976]-b: 118)

For him, focusing on this *production* of *effects* of scientificity requires examining the *episteme* characteristic of a given context. An episteme is the '[strategic] "apparatus" which makes possible the separation, not of the true from the false, but of what may from what may not be characterised as scientific' (1980 [1977]: 197). By describing the study of scientificity as a study of epistemes, Foucault recentres the analysis on acts of categorisation and separation, acts which he argues must be conceptualised as political because they perform a double move of excluding a range of claims from the realm of the acceptable and constituting a domain of authorised discourses. These authorised discourses are invested with the significant 'power-effects that the West has, ever since the Middle Ages, ascribed to (. . .) science and reserved for those who speak a scientific discourse' (2003 [1976]: 10). For Foucault, such power-effects are not by-products of, or external factors to, the making of knowledge claims; they are constitutive aspects of it. Hence, what is at stake for him in analyses of demarcations of scientificity is

the aspiration of power that is inherent in the claim to being a science. The (. . .) questions that have to be asked are: 'What types of knowledge are you trying to disqualify when you say that you are a science? (. . .) What discursive subject, what subject of experience and knowledge are you trying to minorize when you begin to say: "I speak this discourse, I am speaking a scientific discourse and I am a scientist."'

(2003 [1976]: 10)

I find this framework useful because it directs the analytical attention away from the content and structure of knowledge claims, and towards the 'effects of power [that] circulate among scientific statements' (Foucault, 1980 [1976]-a: 112), or in other words, the ways in which those claims are implicated in the production of scientificity as a truth- and power-effect. In addition, this framework foregrounds the fact that power-effects are produced not just in statements which succeed in being recognised as scientific, but in *any* claim to scientificity, whether or not it is recognised as 'true'. This is crucial in a study of the epistemic status of WGFS or other relatively marginal fields, because WGFS does make its own claims to scientificity, even if those claims are not always recognised. This requires, on the one hand, not assuming that WGFS' relation to scientificity is always one of marginalisation and, on the other, including in the analysis an examination of the power-effects of WGFS scholars' own claims to scientificity.

Foucault's concept of episteme helps to conceptualise the historically specific sets of standards used to separate and categorise statements, but his framework seems to me to be implicitly grounded on the understanding that these standards are mobilised relatively homogeneously; i.e. the same set of standards is applied in roughly similar ways to assess the scientificity of all statements in a given context. Although he acknowledges that 'the *episteme* is not a sort of *grand underlying theory*, it is a space of *dispersion*, it is an *open and doubtless indefinitely describable field of relationships*' (1991 [1968]: 55, original emphases), Foucault does not offer instruments with which to interrogate how the sources of statements and the characteristics of those making them affect their recognition as scientific. Therefore, his framework – in and by itself – is not well equipped to address the distinctive position of WGFS vis-à-vis categories of scientificity.

> One problem is that when evidence that has been found uncontroversial when presented in support of non-feminist claims is presented to support feminist claims, the uncontroversial becomes controversial. Critics say: (. . .) [S]houldn't we at least wait until more rigorous investigation has been conducted, and by more objective observers? (. . .) How could women (. . .) be producing facts that anyone should regard as serious challenges to the (. . .) value-free facts that the natural and social sciences have produced? Here one can begin to see a place for a distinctively feminist epistemology. (. . .) [T]hese questioners are not (. . .) posing the kind of request for further displays of evidence (. . .) [which is] characteristic of the usual critical modes within (. . .) disciplines. (. . .) [They are questioning whether] claims produced by women, or by people whose research is heavily motivated by feminist concerns, [are] really deserving of the term 'knowledge'.
>
> (Harding, 1991: 108–109)

In a study of WGFS' epistemic status, we must, indeed, ask how the 'uncontroversial becomes controversial' when the person or group making a knowledge claim is seen as too feminist to be scientifically credible. As Harding indicates, feminist epistemology offers powerful tools with which to ask that question, one which many scholars have reflected on.[9] I focus here on Lorraine Code's work, both because her epistemological theorising can productively be adapted for empirical research, and because she is a welcoming but productively challenging interlocutor for Foucault.[10]

Epistemic status in unequal rhetorical spaces: Code's feminist epistemology 'on the ground'

Code's oeuvre 'claims affinities (. . .) with standpoint theory and postmodernism' (2006b: 160) and can be described as a project aiming to develop a *feminist ecological epistemology*, because it focuses not on 'isolated, discrete propositional knowledge claims', but on the ecology of knowledge production, i.e. the 'situations and interconnections of knowers and knowings' (2006a: 6). In my selective appropriation of Code, I draw on what I consider to be two especially important insights. The first is her argument that we need to develop an 'epistemology of everyday life' (1991) that studies located epistemic practices. This call to locate epistemological 'inquiry "down" on the everyday "ground" where knowledge is made, negotiated, circulated' (2006a: 5–6), and to consider how that 'ground' shapes those processes, makes her work a good framework for ethnographic inquiry. The second insight is her insistence on the importance of developing an 'awareness of the effects of geographical-ecological-material locations and of hierarchical social orders that enable, structure, and/or thwart practices of establishing (. . .) knowledge claims' (Code, 2006a: viii). Following this principle forces us to situate negotiations of epistemic status in the broader relations of power and inequality within which they play out.

Code proposes the concept of *rhetorical spaces* (1995) as a tool for the located study of the 'hierarchical social orders that (. . .) structure' the making of knowledge claims. To think of a space of knowledge production as a rhetorical space means, for Code, to examine it as a 'locatio[n], whose (. . .) territorial imperatives structure and limit the kinds of utterances that can be voiced (. . .) with a reasonable (. . .) expectation of being heard, understood, taken seriously' (1995: ix–x). She considers that in rhetorical spaces 'certain things can be said and others cannot, not because (. . .) they are clearly beside the point, but because of ossified perceptions about what the point is' (1995: 4). This overlaps with Foucault's notion of episteme. However, Code's main focus is not on identifying which statements are acceptable within a given domain (like Foucault), but rather *whose* statements are accepted. For Code, 'it matters who is speaking and where and why, and (. . .) such mattering bears directly on the possibility of knowledge claims (. . .) achieving acknowledgement' (1995: x). According to her, presumption of credibility is distributed unevenly, on the basis of 'systemically engrained structural conceptions about the kinds of people who can reasonably claim the credibility at issue' (1991: 233). Therefore, unlike Foucault, what Code seeks to examine is 'how rhetorical spaces are mapped so as to produce *uneven possibilities* of establishing credibility and being heard' (1995: xv, my emphasis).

Code is especially interested in analysing women's 'positions of minimal epistemic authority', 'women's underclass epistemic status' (1995: xiii) and the structural blocks to the acknowledgement of women's contributions to knowledge. According to her, uneven distributions of epistemic authority are usually unacknowledgedly, but always significantly, gendered as they are grounded on, and reproduce, dichotomies that frame femininity as epistemically unqualified. This, in turn, affects the ways in which feminist scholarship is perceived.

> These dichotomies are frequently invoked as principles of exclusion that function to describe, and dismiss, feminist ventures (. . .): to represent feminist inquiry as 'preoccupied with practical matters,' 'too subjective,' 'overly emotional,' 'value-laden,' 'merely political.' They are at once products of and cooperators in constituting a long history in which women are commonly (. . .) typed and stereotyped as irrational, subjective, incapable of abstract thought, and unable to come to terms with reality.
>
> (1995: 192)

Thinking about epistemic status through this lens highlights an important specificity of negotiations of the status of WGFS. Those negotiations will share many features with other demarcation struggles, but as an explicitly feminised and feminist field, WGFS and its scholars are likely be positioned in distinctive ways within uneven distributions of epistemic authority. Studying the impact of these distributions on negotiations of status is key, and Code's insights help to do so.

My use of Code's work is, nevertheless, not entirely orthodox. I detach a focus on gendered distributions of epistemic status from an analysis specifically of *women's* authority and credibility *qua* women. Unlike Code, I do not study primarily the epistemic status of women as producers of knowledge (although I do address this in chapter 5), but the epistemic status of those making knowledge claims from a WGFS perspective – often women, but not exclusively or necessarily so. It is not just people who are gendered; academic fields are gendered too, with many disciplines being perceived to be unequivocally masculine (and masculinising) or feminine (and feminising). This effect is not limited to gender. Broader structures of inequality that position certain people as less knowledgeable will often also position their lives, experiences or perspectives as less valuable objects of knowledge. This means that entire academic fields – not just WGFS, but also scholarship on 'race' and ethnicity, disability studies, LGBTQ studies or research on/from non-western regions or countries, for example – can become in themselves racialised, sexualised and othered, in epistemically disqualifying ways. This disqualification can stick to, and 'contaminate', all scholars in that field, even those who are male, or white, or heterosexual, or otherwise privileged in relation to those axes of inequality. It is also important to remember that women are an extremely heterogeneous group, differently and unequally positioned in broader structures of inequality of 'race', class, ability, sexuality or geopolitics. Therefore, I do not presume that women always do not have, or have less, credibility in rhetorical spaces because they are women: a woman who is a white North-American mainstream economist may be seen as having stronger grounds for claiming academic credibility in certain rhetorical spaces than a man who is a black Brazilian WGFS scholar, for example. For the purposes of this project, then, Code's focus on women must therefore be extended, complexified and theorised more intersectionally.

This articulation of Code and Foucault is a productive but not entirely satisfying framework for a theory of epistemic status. Both authors foreground the stability of epistemes and rhetorical spaces and have a (more or less) implicit conceptualisation of dominant standards of scientificity as relatively unitary and stable, although subject to historical change and applied in uneven, gendered ways. Both Code and Foucault agree that standards of scientificity do not have an essential, fixed, *a priori* existence outside of their ongoing, located mobilisation, and recognise that actual scientific practices are messy and diverse; however, their theoretical focus is nevertheless on the gradual ossification (to use Code's term) of epistemes and uneven distributions of credibility. To engage with this contextual level more directly, we need to look to the literature in STS.

Epistemic status as boundary-work: Gieryn's cartographical framework

In his historical and sociological studies of debates about scientificity (1983, 1995, 1999), Thomas Gieryn develops a proposal for a theory of scientific boundary-work which has since been taken up by many STS scholars (see Amsler, 2007; Lamont and Molnár, 2002 for overviews; see Petersen, 2003 for a very different genealogy of the concept of scientific boundary-work). I use the concept of boundary-work as it is set out in Gieryn's later writing on boundary-work (1999), which attempts to theorise a 'cartographical' approach to the study of the production of science's and scientists' credibility. This is a text where his initial (1983) focus on boundary-work from a sociology of knowledge perspective centred on scientists' 'professional ideologies' (and the 'strains' and 'interests' they generate) usefully gives way to a more discursive and fluid approach.

According to Gieryn, '[t]he adjudication of competing truths and rival realities is, often enough, accomplished in and through *provisional settlements of the boundaries* of science' (1999: 2, my emphasis). He highlights the variability and inconsistency of definitions of scientificity, noting that 'from episode to episode[11] (. . .) few enduring or transcendent properties of science necessarily appear on any map (or in the same place)' (1999: 5). Therefore, he argues that the boundaries of science 'are shaped (. . .) by the local contingencies of the moment: the adversaries then and there, the stakes, the (. . .) audiences' (1999: 5).[12] He calls, therefore, for an examination of science and scientificity as contingent products of ongoing and discursive processes of boundary-work, i.e. exercises in defining where the boundaries of science lie, which unfold as part of attempts to position a given claim or field within or outside those boundaries. This leads to a conceptualisation of epistemic status – or epistemic authority, as Gieryn prefers to call it[13] – as constituted in and through its local enactment, rather than existing as an 'omnipresent ether' (1999: 15). For Gieryn,

> [e]pistemic authority exists only to the extent that it is claimed by some people (typically in the name of science) but denied to others (which is exactly what boundary-work does). (. . .) [S]cience is (. . .) given particular (. . .) borders and territories (. . .) in order to enhance the credibility of one contestant's claims over those of others (. . .). The epistemic authority of science is in this way, through repeated and endless edging and filling of its boundaries, sustained over lots of local situations and episodic moments.
>
> (1999: 14)

In this framework, the location and shape of the terrain of science is seen as 'local and episodic rather than universal; pragmatic and strategic rather than analytic or legislative; (. . .) constructed rather than essential' (1999: 27). The point of the analysis, then, is to examine how traits of scientificity are selectively invoked and used in contingent struggles over authority and resources. For Gieryn, these processes of demarcation are a mechanism of regulation of scientific practice: '[b]oundary-work becomes a means of social control: as the borders get placed and policed, "scientists" learn where they may not roam without transgressing the boundaries of legitimacy' (1999: 16).

Gieryn's focus on the ongoing work of doing and redoing epistemic status, or in other words, his focus on the *processual* character of demarcations of scientificity, opens several avenues for inquiry. It shows that problematizing a field's epistemic status involves not just asking questions about what its status is – i.e. how the field is usually positioned in relation to structures of distribution of credibility (à la Code) and apparatuses that separate the scientific from the non-scientific (in Foucauldian vein). It also requires asking how the field's status is announced, displayed, performed, accomplished on a daily basis. Although it is not written in explicit dialogue with either Foucault or Code, Gieryn's carto-graphical approach can be seen, I would argue, to usefully pick up Foucault's notion that truth- and power-effects are produced in any claim to scientificity, and Code's claim that epistemic practice must be analysed in context. It experiments with these points in ways that highlight the fact that standards of scientificity are constituted through (rather than just reflected in) located, concrete practices of separating the scientific from the non-scientific. It also creates space for the important interrogation of how different rhetorical and institutional tools are used to enact epistemic status (Petersen, 2003). To cite Lather, scientificity becomes analysable as 'a performance – for example, the textual display of the absence of the author and/or the veneer of scientificity accomplished by the use of math-ematics' (2007: 69).

Gieryn's approach has enormous potential for an analysis of the performative nature of epistemic status but I consider that its potential can more productively be explored if it is used in articulation with other frameworks. He writes that

> the 'epistemic authority of science' exists only in its local and episodic enactment (. . .) but this all happens within structural contexts of available resources, historical precedents, and routinized expectations that enable and constrain the contents of a map and its perceived utility or accuracy in the eyes of users.
>
> (Gieryn, 1999: 12)

Understanding those enabling and constraining contexts is key, and it has been argued that Gieryn's theory is not well equipped to make sense of them (Kinchy and Kleinman, 2003). According to Nader, for example,

> some theorists argue that boundaries [of science] are episodic not fixed (Gieryn, 1995), implying that at any historical moment what is included and excluded may change. Maybe. (. . .) [It is] however (. . .) clear that some boundaries have been fixed for a long time, and that the likelihood of change is directly related to the untying of a discourse that is currently isomorphic with the dominant world political and economic structures of multinational corporations and nation-states.
>
> (1996: 24)

Addressing those under-theorised issues requires, among other things, engaging directly with the macro-level of epistemes which Foucault theorises, and fore-grounding the interactions between distributions of authority and wider social and political inequalities, as Code does. Articulating Gieryn with Code and other feminist epistemologists and black and postcolonial scholars is especially important, because this is an area of significant and problematic weakness in his theory of boundary-work. The protagonists of his accounts of boundary-work are mostly white western men in positions of relative authority – scientists, intellectuals, religious leaders, senators, scientific and educational policy-makers, members of school administrations. In his case studies (1983, 1999), the differential between the 'players', 'contestants', 'agents' (as he calls them) in terms of their opportunities to achieve credibility as authoritative commentators on what is 'proper' knowledge is usually relatively small (although it changes and sometimes increases precisely as a result of that boundary-work). They appear as largely unmarked individuals, differentiated mainly or only by their interests, position in professional hierarchies and/or access to professional resources, as if their other characteristics are irrelevant (or secondary) to the struggles being analysed.

His notion of boundary-work is, therefore, one that lacks engagement with the gendered, racialised, eurocentric or classed nature of epistemic authority. Gieryn does acknowledge this in the last sentence of the introduction to his book, but leaves the work of analysing these issues to other researchers or another time. He writes: 'Some readers will regret the inattention here to issues of identity politics and identity epistemics; struggles for credibility (. . .) are deeply gendered, for example, and play themselves out increasingly on a multicultural terrain of uneven advantage. Lots of work ahead.' (1999: 35). And yet, more than 15 years after those words were published, the boundary-work literature still lacks a systematic consideration of these issues (Pereira, forthcoming). To foreground them, we must reframe Gieryn's notion of boundary-work as (primarily) open and episodic. A theory of boundary-work must recognise the often decisive ways in which broader relations of power produce specific closures and predictable patterns of 'uneven advantage' (Gieryn, 1999: 35) that go beyond the merely contingent and episodic.

Epistemic status and power

Code, Gieryn and Foucault all address power, but theorise its shape, place and role in very different ways. According to Lennon and Whitford, '[f]eminism's most compelling epistemological insight lies in the connections it has made between knowledge and power (. . .), [in] the recognition that legitimation of knowledge-claims is intimately tied to networks of domination and exclusion' (1994: 1). This is the insight at the centre of Code's important claim that 'mapping the rhetorical spaces that legitimate or discredit testimony – that foster or forestall incredulity – seems rather to be a way of *mapping social-political power structures*' (1995: 62, my emphasis). Linda Alcoff, a leading author in epistemology, feminism and critical race theory, makes a similar argument: 'who has the presumption of credibility in their favor, and who is likely to be ignored or disbelieved is partly a function of the hierarchy of political status existent in the society' (1993: 69). What Code and

Alcoff mean here is that the assessment of particular people as less able to produce proper scientific knowledge is reflective of macro-structures of power where
they occupy a subordinate position, and is also in itself a form of subordination.

> It is instructive to examine the implications, for a cognitive agent, of a system-
> atic denigration of her experience, whereby the expertise it might be expected
> to produce is denied the status of knowledge. (. . .) [K]nowledge depends
> upon acknowledgment. Among the most immobilizing manifestations of
> *epistemic oppression* is the *systematic withholding* of such acknowledgment.
> (Code, 1991: 250, my emphases)

The impact of this 'extend[s] far beyond the academy, with widespread social
and political implications' (Code, 1991: xi) and its 'effects in patriarchal societies
are to consign women (and other Others) to positions of the unknown, unknow-
ing and unknowable' (Code, 2006b: 147). Power is framed here as something
exercised by individuals and groups who have access to cognitive authority and
are able to mobilise widely shared beliefs about the (lesser) epistemic capacities
of others to withhold acknowledgement. This can be understood as a structure of
epistemic privilege (Code, 1991: 317) – or 'epistemic discrimination' (Dalmiya
and Alcoff, 1993) and 'epistemic injustice' (Fricker, 2007),[14] to use other authors'
formulations.

This conceptualisation of power draws attention to many issues relevant to an
analysis of WGFS' epistemic status. It shows that concrete instances of boundary-
work generally do not happen in a level-playing field. Indeed, its various participants tend to be located differently in structural hierarchies of credibility and
so their claims about epistemic status do not have equal authority and do not
command the same level of assent. Therefore, to a certain extent, the outcome of
these negotiations – albeit in principle open – is often biased in more or less pronounced ways to the disadvantage of those 'others' who are less easily recognised
as producing proper knowledge. Although I see epistemic status as needing to be
continuously recognised, rather than something owned by particular scholars or
fields, I would argue that certain people and groups are tendentially in a better
position to have their claims to epistemic status accepted as true and justified.
Analysing this aspect of the power dynamics of negotiations of status requires
making visible, and hopefully contributing to disrupt, structural obstacles to the
full recognition of the capacity and right of WGFS scholars to participate actively
and equally in academic debates and in demarcations of proper knowledge.

Negotiations of epistemic status are not just structured by, and constitutive
of, *epistemic* power; *professional* power matters too. This is the perspective
from which Gieryn and other scholars – for example Amsler (2007) and Epstein
(1996) – theorise power in struggles over and about scientificity. Being able to
display or access valued professional resources – e.g. a reputable institutional
affiliation, established contacts with other scholars, influence in academic decision-
making – tends to increase the chances of having one's claims acknowledged as

authoritative. This is both because an association is usually made between credibility and good professional standing, and because 'through control over professional organizations, funding institutions, and journals, [defenders of dominant positions in scientific controversies] can suppress heretical views and even punish those who dare voice them' (Epstein, 1996: 173). The reverse also applies: being recognised as a producer of credible knowledge tends to strengthen one's chances of accessing professional resources. Boundary-work can, thus, be seen as a tool with which to obtain valued professional material and symbolic resources; as Gieryn writes, boundary-work 'happens when there is something valued on the line: material resources, prestige, (. . .) power' (1999: 356). Therefore, studying epistemic status requires considering axes of professional power, examining how they impact on negotiations of status and asking how those negotiations in turn affect WGFS scholars' access to institutions, jobs, funding and decision-making positions.

The tale that I have been telling thus far is one where power works through obstacles and oppression, being used by some to silence and/or constrain others and to obtain, protect or deny valued professional resources. It is an important tale because power has worked in that way vis-à-vis the epistemic status of WGFS, as many reflections on the institutionalisation of WGFS have compellingly shown (Stanley, 1997). It is, however, a partial tale that does not fully account for the complexity of the workings of power in negotiations of epistemic status. An engagement with Foucault's influential thinking on power[15] helpfully complicates this tale. I noted above that Foucault considers that any claim to scientificity can be theorised as a power move, whether or not it is successful. This means that although the playing field may not be level, power in negotiations of epistemic status is not entirely, and only, in the hands of those who succeed in securing credibility. This requires that we acknowledge that, despite often occupying a position of relative epistemic and institutional disadvantage, WGFS scholars too are implicated in the 'aspiration of power that is inherent in the claim to being a science' (2003 [1976]: 10). Reframing power in this fashion allows us to examine the enforcement of norms within WGFS about what is proper knowledge, and WGFS scholars' own practices of dismissing the scholarly value of others' work. As Stanley argues, 'feminisms in the academy do not simply face, confront, receive, these dominant ways of knowing. In a very real sense feminism has been itself a creator and maintainer of intellectual and political borderlands in its own right' (1997: 5). For Stanley, evidence of this can be found in WGFS scholars' 'resistance to dissenting feminist ideas, including (. . .) reactions (. . .) to those *other* Others, the feminists who are not like "us", who are too extreme, too different, neither rigorous nor rational nor acceptable. *We* are not like *that!*' (1997: 8, original emphases).

Considering this extra layer of power is important but insufficient from a Foucauldian perspective. It is not enough to simply add to the analysis the power- and truth-effects of WGFS scholars' own claims to scientificity, because such a position would maintain a conceptualisation of power as eminently repressive, i.e.

working through the inhibiting and silencing of that which it is exercised against. As Foucault has influentially argued, power is not just repressive.

> What makes power hold good (. . .) is simply the fact that it doesn't only weigh on us as a force that says no, but that it traverses and produces things, it *induces pleasure, forms knowledge, produces discourse*. It needs to be considered as a productive network which runs through the whole social body, much more than as a negative instance whose function is repression.
>
> (1980 [1976]-b: 119, my emphasis)

Conceptualising power in this way means acknowledging that negotiations may have generative effects even when the distribution of authority is very uneven and results in institutional and epistemic marginalisation. Standards of epistemic status do not just constrain, interrupt or stifle knowledge production – they also enable and animate it. As Potter puts it, '[o]ne cannot make a contribution to knowledge without public standards that determine what one's community will recognize as knowledge; indeed, it is public standards (. . .) that enable one to organize one's experiences into coherent accounts in the first place' (2006: 49). This means that negotiations of epistemic status are not just imposed on WGFS work, but constitutive of it. In other words, research in WGFS cannot be said to have developed just *despite* its marginalisation, but also in ongoing (critical) dialogue with it. This is not a new insight for those working in WGFS. Many WGFS scholars – writing in different countries and at distinct points in the histories of WGFS – have drawn attention to the potentially generative and even pleasurable effects of epistemic marginality. Stanley notes that 'within some disciplines and institutions there have been successful organisational and intellectual closures against feminist ideas. However, perhaps paradoxically, this has sometimes not only permitted but actively facilitated the development of feminist work' (1997: 8). Evans argues that '[b]eing "on the margins" (. . .) is some assistance (. . .) in that a marginal subject has little to lose from developing a position of dissent rather than collusion' (1997: 56). More recently, Scott explains that '[f]or many of us [US-based feminist scholars of her generation], being embattled was energizing; it elicited strategic and intellectual creativity' (2011: 26). This means, to use Adsit *et al.*'s words, that 'Women's studies' unstable relationship to traditional academic situations and practices (. . .) has also been a profound resource for theory production and research within the discipline. An history of institutional liminality (. . .) has shaped feminist theory' (2015: 28). A Foucauldian theorisation of power as productive enables an analysis of this generative role of negotiations of epistemic status.

The theory of epistemic status that I propose here weaves together these different lenses – a feminist analysis of structures of uneven distribution of epistemic authority, an STS-inspired engagement with professional hierarchies, and a Foucauldian commitment to foregrounding the fluid, productive and generative dimensions of power – and turns them on each other. Foucault once wrote that 'scientific discourse (. . .) is so complex a reality that we not only can, but should, approach it at different levels and with different methods' (1974 [1966]: xiv). I try to do so here by conceptualising epistemic status as, simultaneously, structurally ossified (in gendered, racialised, sexualised ways), institutionally shaped, and open to contingent negotiation. I see the relations of power shaping epistemic status and resulting from it as both fluid and attached to specific knowledge producers; both systematically constraining and continuously productive. Keeping these different approaches at the forefront of inquiry is a challenging exercise in analytical juggling, but one that enables a more nuanced analysis of the epistemic status of WGFS.

Metaphors of epistemic status: Thinking of *maps*, *climates* and *negotiations*

Any theory has its own vocabulary and constellations of metaphors, and mine is no exception. There are terms that appear time and time again in the following chapters, as they are central to my thinking on epistemic status. Many of those terms and metaphors work as shorthands for complex sets of relations. In this section, I unpack three: spatial and cartographical metaphors, the concept of *epistemic climate* and the notion of *negotiation*.

References to *spaces*, *maps* and *boundaries* are frequent in my analysis. They are inspired primarily, but not exclusively, by Gieryn's cartographical framework. Other authors I draw on employ these metaphors to explore academic knowledge production. In her writing on rhetorical *spaces*, Code makes explicit that her 'appeal to spatial metaphors picks up', and tries to take forward, a 'concern with location: with territories, mappings, positioning' (1995: ix). Foucault confesses that the spatial has been an 'obsession for me' (1980 [1976]-a: 69) and argues that 'the formation of discourses (. . .) need[s] to be analysed (. . .) in terms of tactics and strategies of power (. . .) deployed through (. . .) *demarcations*, control of *territories* and *organisation of domains* which could well make up a sort of *geopolitics*' (1980 [1976]-a: 77, my emphases). In the introduction to a stimulating collection of analyses of the relationship between feminism and academic borders, Stanley writes:

> the prior production of symbolic frontiers – those who have knowledge and those who merely experience – has given rise to material organisations and institutions and governing bodies and 'states'. These spatial complexities of knowledge/power give rise to (. . .) problematics: just who are the people [and, I would add, the claims] who 'cross over, pass over, go through the confines of the normal' (. . .)?
>
> (1997: 2)

Like these authors, I find it productive to think of negotiations of epistemic status in spatial and cartographical terms, because this metaphor foregrounds some important aspects. Gieryn identifies three of them. Firstly, he argues that maps of scientificity, like other maps, represent 'boundaries that differentiate this thing from that; borders [that] create spaces with occupants homogeneous and generalized in some respect' (1999: 7). Secondly, like other maps, maps of scientificity 'are drawn to help us find our way around' (1999: 7), so that we know where to go and where to avoid. Thirdly, the features represented in them, and the ways in which they are represented, vary according to what uses and publics the map is designed for.

I would add two more points to that list. Firstly, because maps tend to be '*naturalize[d]* (. . .) [as] a window through which th[e] world [can be] seen . . . *as it really [is]*'[16] (Wood and Fels, 1992: 2, original emphases), they constitute a powerful 'tool to shape, legitimize, and institutionalize certain forms of knowledge and collective spatial imaginations' as the most truthful ones (Leuenberger and Schnell, 2010: 805). This also happens with maps of scientificity: they too are often presented and naturalised as direct descriptions of the condition of things. Secondly, maps serve not only to represent the location of spaces, and what shape they have, but also what their position and shape is *relative* to other spaces. A historical Portuguese example offers a compelling illustration of this.

In 1934, the *Estado Novo*[17] propaganda machine launched a poster (as part of the first Portuguese 'Colonial Exhibition', held that year) showing the Portuguese colonies of the time superimposed on a map of Europe, with a legend comparing

Figure 2 Map: *Portugal Is Not a Small Country*, Henrique Galvão (1934)

the surface size of the Portuguese empire with that of several European countries perceived to be central. The map's aim was to prove that 'Portugal is not a small country', a claim that served as its title. As this map demonstrates, countries can be made to seem big(ger) and more central in and through the drawing of maps. Maps of scientificity can produce similar effects, as I will show in this book.

In referring to an *epistemic climate*, I weave together the work of Code and Foucault. The concept's focus is on the epistemes (Foucault, 1980 [1977]) at work in a particular site or community, and the perspective it foregrounds is, to deploy a term used by Code, 'climatological'. Like Code, 'I am interested in whether the climate where (. . .) proposals are circulated is chilly or friendly. My questions are not merely about whether it is possible to say [something] (. . .), but about the conditions for flourishing' (1995: 4). Through this articulation, I want to soften and flexibilise Foucault's notion of episteme. As I argued above, Foucault's use of it sometimes presumes that the separation of the scientific and non-scientific is stable. Framing that separation through the notion of climate opens the scope both for a conceptualisation of demarcation as having different degrees (i.e. different levels of 'chilliness', allowing distinct types of 'flourishing') and for a more central consideration of forms of short-term, long-term or cyclical climate change (Alcoff, n.d.), as well as the potential existence of distinctive *microclimates* within broader epistemic climates. My conceptualisation of academic communities as having particular climates draws also on another body of literature: research about female academics' professional experiences which describes universities as 'chilly climates' for women (Hall and Sandler, 1982, 1986). A chilly climate is defined there as 'the combined result of practices – each of which may seem relatively inconsequential when taken alone – which cumulatively marginalise women/minorities' (Prentice, 2000: 84). These include 'denying the status and authority of women and minorities through sexist comments (. . .) or "jokes" and 'signalling lesser importance through words, behaviours, tone or gestures which indicate that women and/or minorities do not need to be taken seriously' (2000: 84). I will show in the following chapters that these micropolitical practices are integral components of the regulation of WGFS' epistemic status in the performative university.

The pages of the book are also littered with the term *negotiation*. My penchant for (over-)using it echoes its common use in STS and WGFS to indicate an intersubjective construction and contestation (Knorr-Cetina, 1995: 154) and a sense of process. However, my use goes beyond these habitual meanings and alludes directly to the term's Latin etymology. *Negotiation* is formed by the particle *neg* (translating as 'not'), and *otium* ('leisure' or rest) (Klein, 1967), and so literally means 'there is no rest'. Thinking of epistemic status as something that allows 'no rest' helps to underscore the fact that its production is continuous and never complete, and also that it demands active (boundary-)*work*.[18] Stressing the unrelenting and arduous character of these negotiations is relevant in any analysis of epistemic status, but becomes particularly productive and inescapable when one focuses on knowledge claims, claims-makers and fields who are in precarious epistemic and institutional positions, as is often the case with WGFS. Skeggs, for example, draws attention to the 'enormous amount of daily effort and politicking' (1995: 479) involved in running WGFS centres and explains that 'Women's Studies staff have to be *constantly* clued up to the institutional [and, I would add, epistemic] conditions of being made invisible, being ignored, and, therefore, losing out' (1995: 480, my emphasis). As one of my research participants, a Portuguese senior scholar in WGFS, noted in an interview:

> *"There was a word that you used earlier in a question, and I think that you were very right to choose it, which is the word negotiation. I do feel that if we work in this field of feminism, we have to be negotiating all the time, every day and everywhere. This all requires so much effort."*

It is to the constellation of meanings above, and to these experiences of daily work within and outside academia, that I allude when speaking of the *maps* and *boundary-work* produced in *negotiations* of the *epistemic status* of WGFS within changing *epistemic climates*; those never-ending negotiations are the object of the following chapters.

Notes

1 See Gieryn (1995, 1999), Lather (2005, 2006, 2007) and Taylor (1996) for reviews.
2 According to Code, in 'late-twentieth-century affluent societies (. . .) [there is a] presumption of credibility that immediately accrues to any findings reported with the assurance that they are based on scientific research', especially when produced by the ' "exact sciences" ', which are 'grant[ed] pride of place' in the scientific hierarchy (1995: xii; see also Harding, 1991). Authors have argued that this 'unparalleled authority' (Keller and Longino, 1996: 1) of science has suffered several blows in recent decades, especially as a result of highly mediatised scientific controversies and public questioning of scientific research (e.g. Epstein, 1996; Gonçalves, 2000), a questioning that became especially insistent in 2016, with many political commentators arguing that we are now living in a 'post-truth' age. However, authors disagree in their evaluations of the extent to which these processes have transformed the authority of science (Gieryn, 1999; Shapin, 2008).
3 See Nye (2000) for a critical discussion of forms of dismissal of this body of scholarship as not 'real' philosophy.
4 For example, there are feminist philosophers of science, such as Longino (2002), who recognise the political character of demarcation and are critical of dominant paradigms of scientificity, but maintain a conceptualisation of science as a unique form of epistemic activity, and are thus committed to defining norms for (a more emancipatory) identification of what is scientific. See Potter (2006) for a discussion of different positions on this issue within feminist philosophy of science.
5 By 'arbitrary' I do not mean that this labelling is completely open; rather, it is arbitrary in the sense that it is not 'as necessary (. . .) [and] self-evident' (Foucault, 1991 [1980]: 76) as it is made to seem.
6 As Bertani and Fontana stress, '[i]t is typical of Foucault's approach that until the end of his life, he constantly "reread," resituated, and reinterpreted his early work in the light of his later work' (2003: 275). Therefore, I include the original date of publication in each reference to Foucault to situate it in the timeline of his work.

7 One illustration of this is the following passage:

> Clinical medicine *is certainly not a science*. Not only because it does not comply with the formal criteria, or attain the level of rigour expected of physics, chemistry (. . .); but also because it involves a scarcely organized mass of empirical observations, uncontrolled experiments and results, therapeutic prescriptions, and institutional regulations. And yet *this non-science is not exclusive of science*: in the (. . .) nineteenth century, it established definite relations between such *perfectly constituted sciences* as physiology, chemistry, or microbiology; moreover, it gave rise to (. . .) morbid anatomy, which it would be *presumptuous no doubt to call a false science*. (2006 [1969]: 199, my emphases)

8 For detailed examinations of Foucault's changing conceptualisation of epistemes, see Kusch (1991) and Lather (2006).

9 It is impossible to do justice here to the diversity and depth of feminist work which has problematised the relations between knowledge, power and gender. Alcoff and Potter's (1993b) classic edited book, more recent reviews by Anderson (2009), Code (2006b), Crasnow *et al.* (2015), Potter (2006) and Whelan (2001), are all good places to start or continue exploring these debates.

10 She draws on Foucault in several pieces (Code, 1991, 1995).

11 An example is John Tyndall's (1820–1893) efforts to secure greater public support, government patronage and more lecturing positions for scientists, in a historical context where 'both religion and mechanics competed with Victorian science for cultural authority and (. . .) resources' (Gieryn, 1999: 62). According to Gieryn,

> the set of attributions effective for articulating the boundary between science and religion would not be effective for articulating the boundary between science and mechanics (. . .). Tyndall selected from different characteristics of "science" to build each boundary: scientific knowledge is empirical when contrasted with the metaphysics of religion, but it is theoretically abstract when contrasted with the commonsense, hands-on observations of mechanicians; science is justified by its practical utility when compared to the merely poetic functions of religion, but science is justified by its nobler uses as a source of pure culture (. . .) when compared to engineering.
> (1999: 62)

12 He argues that '[t]he skin and innards of science will vary depending on who draws the map – and against whom, and for whom', but stresses however that 'science and its boundaries on cultural maps are supple and pliable things, like warm putty, but not so elastic that they may stretch endlessly in every direction' (Gieryn, 1999: 21).

13 Gieryn defines it as 'the legitimate power to define, describe, and explain bounded domains of reality' (1999: 1).

14 Fricker defines this as a 'wrong done to someone specifically in their capacity as a knower' (2007: 1).

15 For more on his theorisation of power, see Foucault (1978 [1976], 1980 [1976]-b, 2003 [1976]).

16 And because of this, discussions about maps are themselves sites of scientific boundary-work, as Leuenberger and Schnell note:

> Among the geographic community and the public at large cartographic representations have traditionally enjoyed the prestige of privileged and objectified sources of knowledge. (. . .) Cartography, it seems, is not like psychoanalysis. It does not deal with internal phenomena hardly accessible to direct observation. (. . .) [It is] presumed to be susceptible to the scientific method in a most unproblematic fashion. (2010: 804)

17 *Estado Novo* is the authoritarian regime which existed in Portugal between 1933 and 1974.

18 As Wood and Fels write, 'maps (. . .) work in the other [sense] as well, that is, *toil*, (. . .) *labor*. Maps sweat, they strain, they apply themselves' (1992: 1, original emphases).

References

Adsit, Janelle, *et al.* (2015). "Affective Activism: Answering Institutional Productions of Precarity in the Corporate University". *Feminist Formations, 27* (3), 21–48.

Alcoff, Linda (1993). "How Is Epistemology Political?" in R.S. Gottlieb (ed.), *Radical Philosophy: Tradition, Counter-Tradition, Politics* (pp.65–85). Philadelphia, PA: Temple University Press.

Alcoff, Linda (2000). "On Judging Epistemic Credibility: Is Social Identity Relevant?" in N. Zack (ed.), *Women of Color and Philosophy: A Critical Reader* (pp.235–262). Malden, MA: Blackwell.

Alcoff, Linda. (n.d.). *A Call for Climate Change for Women in Philosophy*. Retrieved 02/04/2016, from http://alcoff.com/articles/call-climate-change-women-philosophy

Alcoff, Linda and Potter, Elizabeth (1993a). "Introduction: When Feminisms Intersect Epistemology" in L. Alcoff and E. Potter (eds.), *Feminist Epistemologies* (pp.1–14). New York: Routledge.

Alcoff, Linda and Potter, Elizabeth (eds.) (1993b). *Feminist Epistemologies*. New York: Routledge.

Amsler, Sarah (2007). *The Politics of Knowledge in Central Asia: Science Between Marx and the Market*. London: Routledge.

Anderson, Elizabeth (2009). "Feminist Epistemology and Philosophy of Science" in E.N. Zalta (ed.), *The Stanford Encyclopedia of Philosophy*. Retrieved 02/04/2016, from http://plato.stanford.edu/

Bertani, Mauro and Fontana, Alessandro (2003). "Situating the Lectures" in M. Foucault (ed.), *Society Must Be Defended: Lectures at the Collège de France, 1975–76* (pp.273–293). New York: Picador.

Bhambra, Gurminder (2007). *Rethinking Modernity: Postcolonialism and the Sociological Imagination*. Basingstoke: Palgrave MacMillan.

Bowden, Gary (1995). "Coming of Age in STS: Some Methodological Musings" in S. Jasanoff, *et al.* (eds.), *Handbook of Science and Technology Studies* (2nd ed) (pp.64–79). London: Sage.

Code, Lorraine (1991). *What Can She Know? Feminist Theory and the Construction of Knowledge*. Ithaca, NY: Cornell University Press.

Code, Lorraine (1995). *Rhetorical Spaces: Essays on Gendered Locations*. New York: Routledge.

Code, Lorraine (2006a). *Ecological Thinking: The Politics of Epistemic Location*. Oxford: Oxford University Press.

Code, Lorraine (2006b). "Women Knowing/Knowing Women: Critical-Creative Interventions in the Politics of Knowledge" in K. Davis, *et al.* (eds.), *Handbook of Gender and Women's Studies* (pp.146–166). London: Sage.

Code, Lorraine (2014). "Ignorance, Injustice and the Politics of Knowledge: Feminist Epistemology Now". *Australian Feminist Studies, 29* (80), 148–160.

Coelho, Sara (2009). *Piled Higher and Deeper: The Everyday Life of a Grad Student*. Retrieved 02/04/2016, from http://www.sciencemag.org/careers/2009/03/piled-higher-and-deeper-everyday-life-grad-student

Collins, Patricia Hill (1990). *Black Feminist Thought: Knowledge, Consciousness, and the Politics of Empowerment*. Boston, MA: Unwin Hyman.

Connell, Raewyn (2007). *Southern Theory: The Global Dynamics of Knowledge in Social Science*. Cambridge: Polity.

Crasnow, Sharon, *et al.* (2015). "Feminist Perspectives on Science" in E.N. Zalta (ed.), *The Stanford Encyclopedia of Philosophy*. Retrieved 02/04/2016, from http://plato.stan ford.edu/

Dalmiya, Vrinda and Alcoff, Linda (1993). "Are 'Old Wives' Tales' Justified?" in L. Alcoff and E. Potter (eds.), *Feminist Epistemologies* (pp.217–244). New York: Routledge.

Epstein, Steven (1996). *Impure Science: AIDS, Activism, and the Politics of Knowledge*. Berkeley: University of California Press.

Evans, Mary (1997). "Negotiating the Frontier: Women and Resistance in the Contemporary Academy" in L. Stanley (ed.), *Knowing Feminisms: On Academic Borders, Territories and Tribes* (pp.46–57). London: Sage.

Foucault, Michel (1974 [1966]). *The Order of Things*. London: Tavistock Publications.

Foucault, Michel (1978 [1976]). *The History of Sexuality* (Vol. 1). Harmondsworth: Penguin.

Foucault, Michel (1980 [1976]-a). "Questions on Geography" in C. Gordon (ed.), *Power-Knowledge: Selected Interviews and Other Writings, 1972–1977* (pp.63–77). Brighton: Harvester Press.

Foucault, Michel (1980 [1976]-b). "Truth and Power" in C. Gordon (ed.), *Power-Knowledge: Selected Interviews and Other Writings, 1972–1977* (pp.109–133). Brighton: Harvester Press.

Foucault, Michel (1980 [1977]). "The Confession of the Flesh" in C. Gordon (ed.), *Power-Knowledge: Selected Interviews and Other Writings, 1972–1977* (pp.194–228). Brighton: Harvester Press.

Foucault, Michel (1991 [1968]). "Politics and the Study of Discourse" in G. Burchell, *et al.* (eds.), *The Foucault Effect: Studies in Governmentality* (pp.53–72). Chicago, IL: University of Chicago Press.

Foucault, Michel (1991 [1980]). "Questions of Method" in G. Burchell, *et al.* (eds.), *The Foucault Effect: Studies in Governmentality* (pp.73–86). Chicago, IL: University of Chicago Press.

Foucault, Michel (2003 [1976]). *Society Must be Defended: Lectures at the Collège de France, 1975–76*. New York: Picador.

Foucault, Michel (2006 [1969]). *The Archaeology of Knowledge*. Oxon: Routledge.

Fricker, Miranda (2007). *Epistemic Injustice: Power and the Ethics of Knowing*. Oxford: Oxford University Press.

Gieryn, Thomas (1983). "Boundary-Work and the Demarcation of Science from Non-Science: Strains and Interests in Professional Ideologies of Scientists". *American Sociological Review, 48* (6), 781–795.

Gieryn, Thomas (1995). "Boundaries of Science" in S. Jasanoff, *et al.* (eds.), *Handbook of Science and Technology Studies* (2nd ed) (pp.393–443). London: Sage.

Gieryn, Thomas (1999). *Cultural Boundaries of Science: Credibility on the Line*. Chicago, IL: University of Chicago Press.

Gonçalves, Maria Eduarda (2000). "The Importance of Being European: The Science and Politics of BSE in Portugal". *Science, Technology & Human Values, 25* (4), 417–448.

Goonatilake, Susantha (1993). "Modern Science and the Periphery: The Characteristics of Dependent Knowledge" in S. Harding (ed.), *The "Racial" Economy of Science: Toward a Democratic Future* (pp.259–274). Bloomington: Indiana University Press.

Hall, Roberta M. and Sandler, Bernice R. (1982). *The Classroom Climate: A Chilly One for Women*. Washington: Association of American Colleges.

Hall, Roberta M. and Sandler, Bernice R. (1986). *The Campus Climate Revisited: Chilly Climate for Women Faculty, Administrators and Graduate Students.* Washington: Association of American Colleges.

Haraway, Donna J. (1990). *Simians, Cyborgs, and Women: The Re-Invention of Nature.* London: Free Association.

Harding, Sandra (1991). *Whose Science? Whose Knowledge? Thinking from Women's Lives.* Milton Keynes: Open University.

Harding, Sandra (2006). *Science and Social Inequality: Feminist and Postcolonial Issues.* Urbana: University of Illinois Press.

hooks, bell (1982). *Ain't I a Woman: Black Women and Feminism.* London: Pluto Press.

hooks, bell and West, Cornel (1991). *Breaking Bread: Insurgent Black Intellectual Life.* Boston, MA: South End Press.

Keller, Evelyn Fox (1985). *Reflections on Gender and Science.* New Haven, CT: Yale University Press.

Keller, Evelyn Fox and Longino, Helen E. (1996). "Introduction" in E.F. Keller and H. Longino (eds.), *Feminism and Science* (pp.1–16). Oxford: Oxford University Press.

Kilomba, Grada (2007). *Africans in the Academia: Diversity in Adversity.* Retrieved 02/04/2016, from http://www.africavenir.org/nc/news-details/article/africans-in-the-academia-diversity-in-adversity.html

Kinchy, Abby and Kleinman, Daniel (2003). "Organizing Credibility: Discursive and Organizational Orthodoxy on the Borders of Ecology and Politics". *Social Studies of Science, 33* (6), 869–896.

Klein, Ernest (1967). *A Comprehensive Etymological Dictionary of the English Language.* London: Elsevier.

Knorr-Cetina, Karin (1995). "Laboratory Studies: The Cultural Approach to the Study of Science" in S. Jasanoff, *et al.* (eds.), *Handbook of Science and Technology Studies* (2nd ed) (pp.140–166). London: Sage.

Kusch, Martin (1991). *Foucault's Strata and Fields: An Investigation into Archaeological and Genealogical Science Studies.* Dordrecht: Kluwer.

Lamont, Michèle and Molnár, Virág (2002). "The Study of Boundaries in the Social Sciences". *Annual Review of Sociology, 28,* 167–195.

Lather, Patti (2005). *Scientism and Scientificity in the Rage for Accountability: A Feminist Deconstruction.* Retrieved 02/04/2016, from http://www.iiqi.org/C4QI/httpdocs/qi2005/papers/lather.pdf

Lather, Patti (2006). "Foucauldian Scientificity: Rethinking the Nexus of Qualitative Research and Educational Policy Analysis". *International Journal of Qualitative Studies in Education, 19* (6), 783–791.

Lather, Patti (2007). *Getting Lost: Feminist Efforts Toward a Double(d) Science.* Albany: State University of New York Press.

Laudan, Larry (1983). "The Demise of the Demarcation Problem" in A. Grünbaum, *et al.* (eds.), *Physics, Philosophy, and Psychoanalysis* (pp.111–128). Dordrecht: D. Reidel.

Lennon, Kathleen and Whitford, Margaret (1994). "Introduction" in K. Lennon and M. Whitford (eds.), *Knowing the Difference: Feminist Perspectives in Epistemology* (pp.1–16). London: Routledge.

Leuenberger, Christine and Schnell, Izhak (2010). "The Politics of Maps: Constructing National Territories in Israel". *Social Studies of Science, 40* (6), 803–842.

Longino, Helen (2002). *The Fate of Knowledge.* Princeton, NJ: Princeton University Press.

Lykke, Nina (2008). "Feminist Cultural Studies of Technoscience: Portrait of an Implosion" in A. Smelik and N. Lykke (eds.), *Bits of Life: Feminism at the Intersections of Media, Bioscience, and Technology* (pp.3–15). Seattle: University of Washington Press.

May, Todd (1993). *Between Genealogy and Epistemology: Psychology, Politics, and Knowledge in the Thought of Michel Foucault*. University Park: Pennsylvania State University Press.

Mbembe, Achille (2016). "Decolonizing the University: New Directions". *Arts and Humanities in Higher Education, 15* (1), 29–45.

Mohanty, Chandra (1988). "Under Western Eyes: Feminist Scholarship and Colonial Discourses". *Feminist Review, 30*, 61–88.

Nader, Laura (1996). "Anthropological Inquiry into Boundaries, Power, and Knowledge" in L. Nader (ed.), *Naked Science: Anthropological Inquiry into Boundaries, Power, and Knowledge* (pp.1–28). London: Routledge.

Nye, Andrea (2000). "It's Not Philosophy!" in U. Narayan and S. Harding (eds.), *Decentering the Center: Philosophy for a Multicultural, Postcolonial, and Feminist World* (pp.101–109). Bloomington: Indiana University Press.

Pereira, Maria do Mar (forthcoming). "Boundary-Work that does not Work: Towards a Feminist Theorisation of the Non-Performativity of Scientific Boundary-Work".

Petersen, Eva Bendix (2003). *Academic Boundary Work: The Discursive Constitution of 'Scientificity' Amongst Researchers Within the Social Sciences and Humanities*. PhD Thesis, University of Copenhagen.

Potter, Elizabeth (2006). *Feminism and Philosophy of Science*. New York: Routledge.

Prentice, Susan L. (2000). "Chilly Climate" in L. Code (ed.), *Encyclopedia of Feminist Theories* (pp.84–85). London: Routledge.

Rose, Hilary (1994). *Love, Power and Knowledge: Towards a Feminist Transformation of the Sciences*. Cambridge: Polity Press.

Said, Edward W. (1985). *Orientalism*. Harmondsworth: Penguin.

Sandoval, Chela (2000). *Methodology of the Oppressed*. Minneapolis: University of Minnesota Press.

Sartori, Diana (1994). "Women's Authority in Science" in K. Lennon and M. Whitford (eds.), *Knowing the Difference: Feminist Perspectives in Epistemology* (pp.110–121). London: Routledge.

Scott, Joan W. (2011). *The Fantasy of Feminist History*. Durham, NC: Duke University Press.

Shapin, Steven (2008). "Science and the Modern World" in E.J. Hackett, *et al.* (eds.), *The Handbook of Science and Technology Studies* (3rd ed) (pp.433–448). Cambridge, MA: MIT Press.

Sismondo, Sergio (2008). "Science and Technology Studies and an Engaged Program" in E.J. Hackett, *et al.* (eds.), *The Handbook of Science and Technology Studies* (3rd ed) (pp.13–32). Cambridge, MA: MIT Press.

Skeggs, Beverley (1995). "Women's Studies in Britain in the 1990s: Entitlement Cultures and Institutional Constraints". *Women's Studies International Forum, 18* (4), 475–485.

Sousa Santos, Boaventura de (ed.) (2007). *Another Knowledge Is Possible: Beyond Northern Epistemologies*. London: Verso.

Stanley, Liz (1997). "Introduction: On Academic Borders, Territories, Tribes and Knowledges" in L. Stanley (ed.), *Knowing Feminisms: On Academic Borders, Territories and Tribes* (pp.1–17). London: Sage.

Stepan, Nancy Leys and Gilman, Sander L. (1993). "Appropriating the Idioms of Science: The Rejection of Scientific Racism" in S. Harding (ed.), *The "Racial" Economy of Science: Toward a Democratic Future* (pp.170–200). Bloomington: Indiana University Press.

Taylor, Charles Alan (1996). *Defining Science: A Rhetoric of Demarcation*. Madison: University of Wisconsin Press.

Whelan, Emma (2001). "Politics by Other Means: Feminism and Mainstream Science Studies". *The Canadian Journal of Sociology/Cahiers Canadiens de Sociologie, 26* (4), 535–581.

Wood, Denis and Fels, John (1992). *The Power of Maps*. London: Routledge.

Yeatman, Anna (1994). "Postmodern Epistemological Positions and Social Science" in K. Lennon and M. Whitford (eds.), *Knowing the Difference: Feminist Perspectives in Epistemology* (pp.187–202). London: Routledge.

Chapter 3

WGFS in the performative university (Part I)

The epistemic status of WGFS in times of paradoxical change

"There are many problems that remain [for WGFS] despite all the enormous recent changes. Sometimes things seem good, sometimes they go into decline. There are many changes, but they go in different directions, sometimes opposite directions, making things easier and harder at the same time."

(Interview, senior WGFS scholar)

In the 21st century, the epistemic status of WGFS has been negotiated in many countries against a backdrop of profound transformation of the institutions, structures, values, practices and conditions of academic work. Although these are often officially framed primarily as transformations of the *political economy* of academia – its systems of funding and allocation of resources, its modes of management and evaluation of performance, or its patterns of employment and structuring of workloads – these transformations are undeniably producing a radical shift also in our understandings of the nature and goal of scholarly practice. Therefore, they are having large-scale and far-reaching impacts also at the *epistemic* level: they reorient research agendas, alter the format of the scholarship we produce, and – crucially – transform what counts as proper knowledge, and who counts as a proper knowledge producer.

These *epistemic* and *political-economic* transformations have, of course, also affected the life of WGFS, and the lives of WGFS scholars, often paradoxically; a key aim of this book is precisely to examine and problematise those complex effects. I do this longitudinally, in a two-part analysis that uses Portugal as a case-study. The analysis draws on, and compares, fieldwork material from two different stages in the development of academic cultures of performativity. This chapter focuses on the situation in 2008/2009, when those cultures were nascent in Portugal, to analyse how their emergence suddenly changed longstanding epistemic categories and hierarchies. I return to these themes in chapter 7, where I use data from 2015/2016 to examine what the epistemic climate looks like now that a culture of performativity has become institutionalised as the dominant and overriding organising principle, and discursive framework, of academic work, not just in Portugal but also in many other countries throughout the world.

The rise of the performative university

It is a truism that universities have undergone profound change in many countries in the last two decades. Within and beyond WGFS, scholars, students, activists and others have filled the pages of journals (Davies and O'Callaghan, 2014; Jenkins and Keane, 2014; Liinason and Grenz, 2016; Nash and Owens, 2015b), books and newspapers, the programmes of conferences and meetings (Aavik *et al.*, 2015), and even the rooms (or tents) of university and street occupations with discussions about the nature and impact of those transnational changes: cutbacks to HE and research funding, increases in tuition-fees, large-scale restructuring of degree programmes, pressure for increased publishing productivity, expansion of audit and quality-control mechanisms, or extensification and casualisation of academic work, to name just a few. Many different terms, with distinct emphases and potentialities, have been used to refer to the model of organisation of universities and production of scholarly knowledge that has emerged internationally – albeit with different local configurations – in the wake of those changes: the 'neoliberal university' (Davies and Petersen, 2005; Gill and Donaghue, 2016; Mountz *et al.*, 2015; Sifaki, 2016), 'academic capitalism' (Münch, 2014; Slaughter and Leslie, 1997), 'entrepreneurial university' (Hark, 2016; Slaughter and Leslie, 1997; Taylor, 2014) or 'corporate university' (Nash and Owens, 2015b), among many others.

When analysing the effects of these changes specifically at the level of *epistemic* climates, categories and hierarchies, I find it productive to refer to the emerging regime as a 'performative university' or an 'academic culture of performativity', drawing on the work of Blackmore and Sachs (2000, 2003) and Ball (2000), themselves inspired by Lyotard (1984). According to Ball,

> Performativity is a technology, a culture and a mode of regulation, or a system of 'terror' in Lyotard's words, that employs judgements, comparisons and displays as means of control, attrition and change. The performances (of individual subjects or organisations) serve as measures of productivity or output, or displays of 'quality' (. . .). They stand for, encapsulate or represent the worth, quality or value of an individual or organisation within a field of judgement. 'An equation between wealth, efficiency, and truth is thus established.' (Lyotard, 1984, p. 46).
>
> (2000: 1)

Academic regimes of performativity rest on two fundamental pillars. One is the reconceptualisation of academic activity as work which must aim to achieve the highest possible levels of productivity and profitability, and whose quality can be assessed on the basis of the number of products produced (whether that be articles, patents or successful – or satisfied – students) and income generated (Burrows, 2012; Leathwood and Read, 2013; Lund, 2012; Morley, 2003; Shore, 2010; Sifaki, 2016; Strathern, 2000). As Buikema and Van der Tuin write in relation to the Dutch context, '[b]oth the competitive mode that tenured staff are entrained in and the flexibility that is asked of the non-tenured are predicated on a running-after-the-money that is mind-boggling' (2013: 311). Commenting on the UK situation, Huws argues that 'we are being forced, over and over again, to go through a dual process which I have called begging and bragging. Even the lucky few in permanent jobs can't escape it' (2006, cited in Gill, 2014: 23).

In order to monitor individuals' and institutions' productivity (and reward or punish them accordingly), it is necessary to design and maintain complex structures of auditing and surveillance (Gill, 2010, 2014; Mountz *et al.*, 2015; Power, 1999; Shore, 2010; Shore and Wright, 2000), which constitute the second pillar of regimes of performativity. These structures are grounded on extremely complex technologies of metricisation and ranking, which enable and legitimate a 'quantified control' of academic labour (Burrows, 2012). An example is the growing importance of citation indices, impact factors and other bibliometric indicators in processes of evaluation of individual and collective academic performance. These metrics become reified: they have 'taken on a life of [their] own; (. . .) [they have] become a rhetorical device with which the neoliberal academy has come to enact "academic value"' (Burrows, 2012: 361). These metrics are represented as merely technical and hence objective instruments, and this representation plays a key role in their institutionalisation and legitimation as key components of governance (and monetisation) of academic practice. These metrics are, in fact, not neutral: they are produced on the basis of largely arbitrary criteria and very particular definitions of what counts as a quality outcome, they exclude a large number of publications and citation forms, and are computed by large companies in a context of near monopoly (Burrows, 2012; Erne, 2007). According to Burrows (2012), systems of quantified control have come to occupy such a central and decisive role in contemporary academic cultures in many countries that they cease to function merely as auditing procedures; they also '*enact* competitive market processes' within academia (2012: 357, original emphasis), thus directly contributing to the marketisation of HE and academic knowledge production. Another effect of these auditing structures and systems of quantified control is that they themselves generate further requirements for intense additional labour, as scholars and institutions are forced to regularly produce reports, portfolios and plans that describe and demonstrate their performance.

This reconceptualisation and restructuring of the university transforms knowledge production. It comes to be more explicitly driven by the need to be, and remain, highly productive in measurable and profitable ways that fit into the indices and criteria used to assess 'quality' and 'excellence' (Morley, 2003). But doing the scholarship, although increasingly crucial, is not enough; as Blackmore and Sachs argue, '[i]n the symbolic systems of market-oriented education systems, it is important to "be seen to be doing something"', namely to 'creat[e] market appeal (. . .) in performative educational institutions competing within education markets' (2003: 143). It becomes necessary, therefore, to produce (as well as teach and disseminate) knowledge in ways that lend themselves well to being used in the individual and institutional performative 'displays of "quality"' (Ball, 2000: 1) and efforts of 'image management' (Blackmore and Sachs, 2003: 143) that academics are increasingly interpellated to participate in. This means that an escalating amount of academics' time is 'spent in the practice of "fabrication", in seeking to link the performativity exercises required by the new educational accountabilities to their core work of teaching, researching and leading in some meaningful way' (Blackmore and Sachs, 2003: 143). As Butterwick exemplifies, 'the performance dossier I have to prepare every year [in a Canadian university] is (. . .) incredibly nerve-wracking and time-consuming. It's as if I spend more time preparing the dossier than doing the work that the dossier is supposed to document. Last week I missed an important publication deadline because the dossier deadline came first' (Butterwick and Dawson, 2005: 54).

Scholars analysing changes in academic cultures from other perspectives, not based on the concept of performativity, have also problematised these transformations in knowledge production. They have argued that profitability has gained prominence as a criterion of evaluation of knowledge, shaping decisions about which areas, topics or modes of inquiry will be integrated and promoted in academic institutions. In one of the earliest in-depth characterisations of this emerging model (which they term 'Mode 2') of conceptualisation of knowledge and governance of science, Gibbons *et al.* claim that

> [in Mode 2] additional criteria [of assessment of scholarship] are added (. . .), incorporat[ing] a diverse range of intellectual interests as well as other social, economic or political ones. To the criterion of intellectual interest (. . .), further questions are posed, such as 'Will the [knowledge] be competitive in the market?' 'Will it be cost effective?'
>
> (1994: 8)

In their discussion of trends of commercialisation of science, Mirowski and Sent offer a vigorous critique of Gibbons *et al.*'s account of 'the new production of knowledge', but they too point to the global strengthening of what they call forms of 'conflation of epistemic efficacy with pecuniary profitability' (2008: 673). Bellacasa echoes this, arguing that in contemporary European universities epistemic credibility is increasingly framed as 'credi(t)bility' (2001: 34) (i.e. the capacity to generate income in/through scholarly practice), and that this seriously threatens production of critical scholarship (see also Buikema and Van der Tuin, 2013).

Taken together, these and other analyses make one thing clear: financial considerations – whether framed in terms of profit, value-for-money, or rationalisation of limited resources – are more than just *external* factors interfering with, or over-riding, epistemic assessments. In present-day western academia, income-generation potential seems to be sometimes operating as an epistemic criterion itself, i.e. as one of the bases on which academic communities judge 'the worth, quality or value of an individual or organisation' (Ball, 2000: 1). As Brenneis observes in his study of peer-review and decision-making processes in

US social science funding panels, securing funding becomes 'the definitive mark of serious scholarly accomplishment', and thus, '[i]n writing money we also write status' (1999: 127). To return to the quote by Lyotard reproduced above, 'an equation between wealth, efficiency, and truth is thus established' (1984: 46); in other words, one's efficiency and income-generation is seen to reflect and reveal one's true worth as a scholar, and the more efficient one is, and the more income one generates, the better one's knowledge production is considered to be.

To better understand the relation between the 'performative university' and issues of epistemic status, it is helpful to consider, the conventional understandings of 'performativity' used in WGFS scholarship (Butler, 1988, 1990; Pereira, 2012; Petersen, 2003). Drawing on those, I would argue that a key characteristic of contemporary academic cultures is that epistemic status becomes more explicitly framed and experienced as *performative*. As I show in the previous chapter, the notion that demarcations of scientificity are performative was already central to Gieryn's (1999) theorisation of those demarcations or Petersen's (2003) empirical analysis of them. However, in the performative university there is an additional urgency, frenzy, insecurity and investment in that demarcation of who is (not) a proper scientist. To have one's epistemic status recognised in the performative university, it is often not enough to have published particular work in the past, or have secured an academic position at a certain point, or possess scholarly experience. It becomes necessary to do and re-do epistemic status every day, to continuously constitute oneself as a proper scholar by recurrently and incessantly producing the products seen to count as appropriate displays of scholarly competence, authority and achievement. There is no end to that process of performativity, no limit to productivity, and no possible completion of one's workload, because individual and institutional epistemic status is much more contingent and conditional on its continued enactment through the visible production of prescribed outputs, measurable in indices and narratable in reports. If you do not publish, you perish. Publishing one (or many articles) is, therefore, not just an *expression* of one's work as an academic, but what (temporarily) *makes* one a proper (recognisable, respectable, hireable, promotable) academic (Alldred and Miller, 2007; Leathwood and Read, 2013; Lund, 2012). This creates 'an "academic ratcheting process" that encourages ever more research' (Blackmore and Sachs, 2000: 1).

But publishing is not the only component of that performativity. In the final 3 months of the writing of this book, I was required to undergo (through my UK institution and 2 Portuguese research centres I am affiliated with) a total of 5 processes of individual review and reporting of my 'achievements', 'plans', 'aspirations' and 'working practices', where I had to display not only my past and future publications, but also my ideas for future research funding capture, my strategies for maximising impact, or my commitment to raising my scholarly profile in social media (in addition, of course, to my plans for teaching, administration and 'collegiality', or service). If I explained that I could not dedicate much time to those review and reporting processes because I was immersed in the actual production of one of those desired outputs (this book!), it was made clear that present production was insufficient in itself and that I must also be able to evidence plans for productivity 'going forward'. To adapt Butler's words, but replacing 'gender' with 'epistemic status', we might say, therefore, that in the performative university, '[epistemic status] is in no way a stable identity or locus of agency from which various acts proceed; rather, it is an identity tenuously constituted in time (. . .) through a stylized repetition of acts' (1988: 519), acts both of (high and income-generating) productivity and of (constant and persuasive) fabrication.

As Morris argues vis-à-vis the performativity of gender, 'performativ[e] [logics] are (. . .) both generative and dissimulating' (1995: 573). Drawing on, and adapting, her words, we might say that 'people mistake the acts [of productivity] for the essence [of epistemic status] and, in the process, come to believe that they are mandatory'. Therefore, the 'effect, if not th[e] purpose, [of academic cultures of performativity] is to compel certain kinds of behavior' (Morris, 1995: 573), including, crucially, a commitment to the productive, competitive and incessant work of displaying oneself as a 'proper' academic. This raises several questions: How does that emerging culture of performativity shape WGFS' epistemic status? How does it affect the longstanding epistemic categories, boundaries and hierarchies discussed in previous chapters? What effects does it have on epistemic climates? These are the questions I examine now, drawing on my initial fieldwork in Portugal, conducted in 2008/2009, when performative culture was emerging and becoming institutionalised in Portuguese academia.

Plus ça change . . .: Academic performativity and the transformation of public discourse about WGFS

WGFS emerged in Portugal relatively 'late' (when compared to the US and northern Europe),[1] but throughout the past three decades it has achieved a distinctive, if precarious, presence in Portuguese academia. Much like in other countries, institutionalisation 'has not been easy or linear' (Joaquim, 2004: 88*) and its 'story [is one] of conflicting evolution' (Amâncio, 2005: 75), characterised by 'numerous advancements and regressions, convergences and ruptures' (Ferreira, 2001: 15*). I chart that institutionalisation in detail elsewhere (Pereira, 2011, 2013; see also Ramalho, 2009); in this chapter, I focus on the particular issue of how the emergence of academic cultures of performativity affected WGFS' epistemic status.

Until the early 2000s the dismissal and denigration of WGFS in Portugal was pervasive, public, intense, and sometimes verbally or institutionally violent (Abranches, 1998; Amâncio, 2003b; Ferreira, 2001; Joaquim, 2007; Magalhães, 2001; Pinto, 2007; Tavares, 2011). This was a time when the broader socio-political context was more profoundly anti-feminist and the dominant epistemic climate more rigidly focused on upholding traditional principles of scientificity. Upholding such principles was important in the 1980s–1990s because many SSH fields were very recent,[2] and their epistemic value was not yet widely recognised. SSH scholars were therefore concerned both with legitimating their emerging fields in the eyes of institutions, funders and public, namely by adopting methods considered more scientific, and with demarcating their identity vis-à-vis competing disciplines (Amâncio, 2002; Carreira da Silva, 2016; Magalhães, 2001; Oliveira, 2015). As Messer-Davidow (2002) also found in her study of WGFS' emergence in the US (see chapter 1), this made those fields very resistant to interdisciplinary and critical projects like WGFS. Describing this earlier period, many of the senior Portuguese WGFS scholars I interviewed spoke of *"traumatic"* PhD vivas, stalled careers, receiving *"silence treatments"* or being openly denigrated by colleagues, who sometimes saw them as traitors to their home discipline.

However, the situation began to shift in the 2000s. In my 2008/2009 interviews, many interviewees spoke of the noughties, and particularly their second half, as a decade characterised (though not everywhere) by change. One senior scholar described experiencing *"almost a feeling of vertigo, everything is changing very fast"*. Another noted that *"there's an environment of more acceptance, visibility and growth [of WGFS] now. It's an environment that's only 5 or 6 years old"*. According to several interviewees, by the end of the 2000s it had become less acceptable to openly dismiss WGFS as a *"worthless field"*, *"incapable of producing proper knowledge"*, statements which had been painfully common for many years, and which I myself often encountered as an UG student in Portugal in the early 2000s. The published literature echoes this assessment: Alvarez, for example, speaks of a 'growing and unquestionable receptivity for, and interest, in' the field (2008: 17*). One interviewee, a senior academic, argued that the epistemic climate had changed,[3] and that this affected discourses about WGFS: *"the style here [in her institution] is to not make that explicit, it doesn't look good anymore, so the official discourse now is 'hierarchies don't make sense, all fields are good'"*. Confirming these accounts, during my 2008/2009 fieldwork I observed almost no public instances of unequivocal negation of the epistemic status of WGFS – though this does not mean that WGFS had full epistemic recognition (as I will discuss in the next section and chapter 4), or that it was equally recognised across disciplines and institutions (for a detailed discussion see Pereira, 2011).

Interviewees identified several factors which contributed to this epistemic climate change and to greater public recognition of WGFS. By that time, many SSH were more established and thus there was less pressure to demonstrate scientificity by choosing only more positivist theories, methods and topics. Another important factor was the increasing contact between Portuguese and international academics (see chapter 6 and Carreira da Silva, 2016); one senior WGFS scholar offered this account of the impact of internationalisation:

> *"When my [non-WGFS] colleagues started seeing research on gender in foreign mainstream journals, that really helped legitimate my work – I couldn't be that crazy after all, if gender also appeared in these foreign journals, right? When people began to have more access to international journal databases, and more recently to B-On,[4] and more frequently attending foreign conferences, things changed. The increased recognition of gender studies is*

connected to the opening of Portuguese science to international debates. It's impossible to separate the two."

Moreover, at the end of the noughties there was arguably more openness to gender equality discourse within and outside academia (Pereira, 2010) and a growing acceptance of feminism, which had become increasingly consolidated and visible, namely through the significant mobilisation around two referenda on abortion in 1998 and 2007 (Santos, 2010; Tavares, 2011). Research in the 1990s/early 2000s had found 'strong prejudices against feminism' (Amâncio and Oliveira, 2006: 38) in the general public, and media discourse that was either indifferent to feminism or portrayed it as unfashionable and undesirable (Amâncio, 2000, 2002). Studies conducted in the late 2000s show that feminism retained a tendentially negative reputation in many contexts but had become less frequently, publicly and intensely repudiated in the media and among young people (Martins *et al.*, 2009; Tavares, 2011).

The interviews show, however, that the key driving force in the transformation of epistemic climates vis-à-vis WGFS was the emergence of an academic culture of performativity, and the fact that WGFS was seen as capable of yielding institutional and financial benefits in that culture, at a time when such benefits were sorely needed. In the late 1990s, when FCT (the national research council) and CIDM (the governmental gender equality commission) launched a dedicated funding programme for research on gender and equality policies, the Editorial Board of the WGFS journal *ex aequo* noted that there are ' "eminent" [Portuguese] professors who (. . .) have never been interested in [WGFS]. But as soon as such issues begin to attract funding, they are ready to reorient their concerns and interests' (1999: 8). These 'reorientations' became more frequent in the 2000s, as universities sought to respond to growing cutbacks.

In the 2000s, successive centre-right and centre-left governments reduced funding for HE[5] and pressured universities to expand and diversify their income sources (Amaral and Neave, 2012; Graça, 2009; Mineiro, 2015).[6] Moreover, the HE funding system was transformed: it became more clearly 'performance-based', with 'the attraction capacity of each course/institution' in the student 'market' being considered a marker of quality (MCTES, 2006: 73) to be financially rewarded by the state. All this happened against the broader backdrop of the international implementation of the Bologna Process,[7] with its increased focus on 'marketisation' (Amaral and Neave, 2012; Antunes, 2006; Mineiro, 2015). The adjustment of Portuguese HE to the BP led to the splitting of most existing 4- or 5-year UG degrees with state-subsidised and capped tuition-fees[8] into 3-year 1st Cycle (BA/BSc) degrees (still capped and subsidised) and 2-year 2nd Cycle (MA/MSc) degrees, usually offered at higher, non-capped fees (MCTES, 2006). This made universities very keen to create new 2nd Cycle degrees taught by existing staff as an attempt to increase revenue; in some institutions WGFS offered one attractive avenue for this.

"I've been thinking of creating an MA Gender and Sexuality. I'd had the idea before, and when Bologna started conditions became more favourable, because they started requesting products, products, and we [WGFS scholars]

have something to offer there. (. . .) In the past, there would've been resist-
ance, but now the logic's different, there's no problem, as long as we frame it
as: 'look, we have this, it'll cost zero and can get students'."

Interview, senior WGFS scholar

Interviewees from two other universities reported that heads of department who for decades dismissed their WGFS course proposals because WGFS was *"too subjective"*, *"narrow"* and *"political"*, had recently approached them spontaneously to encourage creation of WGFS courses, as part of university-wide efforts to increase tuition-fee revenue.

The increased emphasis on market competitiveness – not just as goal, but also as condition of survival – affected WGFS. It was something that many interviewees were concerned about, not least because it had made logics of competition more salient within WGFS, according to some of them. In this changed landscape, WGFS scholars were, in a sense, competitors for what was a growing, but still comparatively small, 'market' of students interested in taking WGFS. During a conference coffee-break, one junior scholar described the situation in the following terms: "Bologna has led to much rivalry and competitiveness between institutions. It's a huge problem, and I'm very worried. The different [WGFS] institutions and degrees have their backs turned to each other. It's a sort of 'save your own skin!' climate." This 'rivalry' was not new[9] but, according to 6 interviewees, it grew amidst these broader changes, making it more difficult to organise collectively to promote WGFS' institutionalisation.

However, the increased competition also produced benefits and openings for WGFS. Four interviewees explained that heightened competitiveness between institutions gave WGFS scholars additional leverage in local negotiations over status and resources. It also dissuaded colleagues from publicly dismissing WGFS, as such dismissals become riskier when institutions are trying hard to attract a wide range of students and frame themselves as (more) open and up-to-date (than their competitors).

"Bologna introduced the law of supply/demand in academia, so now things
are different. It's no longer the [male] Professor Thinking-Head deciding
what students do, because students can choose, and pay for their choices.
(. . .) And because funding's more dependent on student numbers, and stu-
dents get to choose their courses, (. . .) that disrupts the old, established
power of the professor who thinks he's king. (. . .) Ten years ago, they'd dis-
courage students from working on gender or choosing us [WGFS scholars]
as supervisors, and students would be afraid and obey. (. . .) They can't do
that now. Last year, one professor told a student not to choose me for supervi-
sor, and she replied "I want her. Otherwise, I'll do my degree in [the Univer-
sity of] Minho instead!" (. . .) If it's a choice between her doing a feminist
dissertation with me or taking her money to Minho, they'd rather have her

here. So Bologna is, in the end, neoliberalism within science, and has many disadvantages, but at this level it helps feminist work a lot."

Interview, senior WGFS scholar

This and other examples show that the emergence of an academic culture of performativity eroded the traditional absolute epistemic and institutional power of the male 'Professor-king' and *"help[ed] feminist work"*. In this changed environment of 'market-oriented education', academic decisions have to be guided, as we saw earlier, by the need to 'creat[e] market appeal (. . .) [to better] compet[e] within education markets' (Blackmore and Sachs, 2003: 143). Explicit sexism, public anti-WGFS discourse and old-school academic conservatism can drive away students (and the valued income they bring) and undermine that market appeal, and thus they become a liability. To return to an earlier interview quote *"the style here is to not make that explicit, it doesn't look good anymore"* . . . and looking good certainly matters in the performative university.

As academic decision-making became more concerned with market value and public appeal (rather than just epistemic quality as defined – traditionally very narrowly – by the (male) *"Professor Thinking-Head"*), the experiences and status of individual WGFS scholars also changed. In an analysis of the position of Australian WGFS amidst partly similar HE marketisation trends, Baird notes that '[i]f individual women (. . .) [and WGFS] programmes can compete in market terms, then their gender or ideological bent will not necessarily count against them. It may even contribute to the institutional brand' (2010: 122). Several interviewees reported that a comparable trend was noticeable in Portugal. Mechanisms of research assessment and allocation of research funding have also become increasingly based on 'performance indicators', a key element of which is scholars' and centres' productivity (MCTES, 2006; Santos Pereira, 2004). In this context, many WGFS scholars began to find that if their WGFS work led to publications and/or grants, and thereby contributed positively to the institution's ratings and revenue, they would encounter fewer challenges to that work and it would stop being publicly framed as epistemically deficient. In an interview, a senior WGFS scholar working in a mainstream social science department provided the following account of those changes:

"One way of trying to increase space for feminist work in [Portuguese] academia presently (. . .) is by publishing lots and having a big CV, because then institutions look at you differently, they want to keep you and support your work, because you produce a lot and that's very important for research centres, as it guarantees more funding. Then they no longer worry about you being feminist, it makes no difference if you're working from a feminist perspective, as long as you produce and keep producing."

Much like Morley observed in her study with feminist scholars in Sweden, UK and Greece, for Portuguese WGFS scholars 'research [became] a type of crucifix to Dracula, so long as it resulted in publications [and funding], the academy was indifferent to the political standpoint' (1998: 179).

What is crucial about this change in the status of WGFS is, of course, that it is conditional: WGFS is recognised as proper knowledge *if* it leads to publications, and *as long as* scholars *"produce and keep producing"*. One might say, then, that in Portugal (and other countries) WGFS exists in a state of *conditional institutionalisation* in the contemporary performative university. When I conducted this first round of interviews in 2008/2009, this was creating a paradoxical situation whereby WGFS' survival and expansion demanded active participation in systems of research evaluation and funding which many WGFS scholars considered profoundly problematic, and which exacerbated rivalry between WGFS groups. The situation was further complicated by the fact that consistently performing highly never fully guaranteed that WGFS' epistemic value would be recognised, as one senior WGFS scholar explained in an interview:

> *"Some gender scholars have been forced (. . .) to use the typical strategy of showing they can do things according to institutional rules. So they dress well, they're very careful, (. . .) produce lots, try to legitimate their work through hegemonic parameters, (. . .) etc., while all along (. . .) not knowing that colleagues in their discipline or department go to conferences, and other more or less public spaces, and say that gender research is silly and worthless, and not serious social science."*

To fully understand negotiations of epistemic status in the performative university, we must therefore also examine this parallel dismissive discourse in *"conferences, and other more or less public spaces"*.

... *Plus c'est la même chose:* The status of WGFS in university 'corridor talk'

As a culture of performativity became institutionalised, the public climate in Portuguese academia shifted, with many participants reporting an increasing openness to WGFS. But this public climate of openness does not always match what happens in university 'corridor life' (Hurdley, 2010). A senior WGFS scholar highlighted this when describing her non-WGFS colleagues' reactions to a WGFS degree proposal discussed in a meeting of the university's scientific committee.

> *"I know that some [committee members] (. . .) don't agree with having a WGFS degree, they don't think it's serious knowledge. But because it's politically correct to support equality, they said nothing in the meeting. (. . .) Also, we could draw on European funding and other subsidies, so there's a certain acceptability that has to do with that. It's a modern and current theme, it links to things happening in Europe, so that's convenient for the institution as well. (. . .) So they went along with it and didn't object, but I know some think it's*

ridiculous. They say so outside the meetings, and there's a lot of sniggering about it in corridors."

Many others recounted that in less public interactions (in classrooms, meetings, etc.) WGFS is still frequently framed as a field of less value and credibility. In all institutions where I conducted interviews, the public climate of recognition of WGFS coexists with a regular questioning of its epistemic status in semi-public and informal settings. Dismissals of WGFS are still very much present as a form of *corridor talk*, in Downey *et al.*'s sense: they are 'the unsaid, but frequently said anyway (though not to everyone)' (1997: 245).

Interviewees reported hearing colleagues regularly describe WGFS as *"Sociology for girls"*, *"silly"*, *"pointless"*, *"not worth reading"*, *"a bunch of whiny feminists and gay men trying to pass off ideology as research"*, and *"devoid of any scientific value"*. I mentioned in the previous section that I did not observe instances of full and unequivocal public dismissal of WGFS during fieldwork, but this does not mean that dismissive comments were absent from fieldwork sites. Sometimes such comments were made, but backstage. For example, over celebratory drinks after a PhD viva, one examiner, a senior WGFS scholar, told me that I would be shocked if I knew what another examiner had said about WGFS in their closed meeting; his comments there were at odds with his WGFS-friendly stance in the public viva. In a conference coffee-break, I overheard junior and senior male sociologists jokingly say that the only reason men would want to attend the gender strands would be to "check out the female sociologists".

Both students and staff explained in interviews that informal claims about the lesser scientificity of WGFS are often made in humorous tone, creating what one participant called a *"culture of teasing"* around WGFS or what Henriques and Pinto describe as 'the ironic halo with which [WGFS] themes are approached' in Portugal (2002: 30*).

> *"Colleagues will sometimes make teasing remarks.* [imitates dismissive laughter] *Feminism's seen as something (. . .) ridiculous, even in the etymological sense of the term, something that's laughable, that doesn't have academic quality."*
>
> Interview, senior scholar

> *"They make jokes about the [WGFS] degree all the time. There's always a little joke; obviously anyone who's read Freud knows what that means. There have been meetings where I got really annoyed, and said 'well, it's good this degree exists, otherwise you'd have nothing to laugh about, you'd have no fun at all, at least this way you can make jokes'. I'm sick and tired of it."*
>
> Interview, senior scholar

> *"Whenever I invite gender people to speak in seminars, one colleague says 'here comes another of your feminist friends. I wonder if she shaved?'[10] (. . .)*

He describes this as just a joke, nothing to take seriously, just innocent teas-
ing, (. . .) but there really is a culture of teasing vis-à-vis this field, which
shows they attribute less importance and value to it. It's not outright hostility,
but it portrays the field as less important than other fields, which are never
the butt of jokes."

Interview, junior scholar

The last interviewee notes that this (frequently sexist and heteronormative) teasing is often described as *"nothing to take seriously"*. This is a key feature of that culture of teasing, and one that plays an important role. Billig notes that the disclaimer that one is 'just joking' makes it possible to voice problem-atic or offensive claims, while sidestepping criticism and accountability. 'A "friendly tease" seems to deny hostility. (. . .) The rhetoric (. . .) can be used to dissipate the negatives, like an air-spray freshening up a bathroom. (. . .) [It is a] "Tease-Spray". Just squirt on your own humorous talk, and (. . .) nasty, critical names will become undetectable' (2005: 25). This cross-institutional culture of (so-called innocent) teasing means that even when it is formally institutionalised as an equal field, WGFS can be invested with a halo of unsci-entificity, lack of credibility and ridiculousness that positions it as an 'other' vis-à-vis allegedly more credible fields.[11] I examine the discursive production of this halo in the next chapter, through an analysis of non-WGFS scholars' public claims about WGFS.

That halo of unscientificity around WGFS provides an excellent illustration of important points made by Stanley almost 20 years ago. In the Portuguese context, the rise of the performative university led to greater acceptance of WGFS; as Stanley argues, 'academic mainstreams (. . .) change over time, and (. . .) academic reproduction involves (. . .) incorporation of that which was formerly Other' (1997b: 202). Nevertheless, even when the 'other' is incor-porated, it can still be othered. That means that WGFS scholars can reside as 'outsiders, "Other" to the academy. (. . .) [They are] inside but marked off, different and, although within, not within in the same way that "real" insiders are' (1997a: 6). I would argue, then, that the emergence of the performative university has produced a complex combination of dynamics of integration and dismissal of WGFS. To use Nash and Owens' words, we could describe WGFS – in Portugal and other contexts – as residing in an 'in-between space inside and outside of institutional legitimacy' (2015a: viii). In some sites, times and dimensions of academic practice, it *"makes no difference if you're working from a feminist perspective"*, namely if one *"produces and keeps producing"* and one's very productive work *"makes a difference"* to student numbers and institutional ratings and revenue. Yet, a spectre of dismissal is often present, because in some (not always predictable) instances, the feminist character of one's work continues to be singled out – more or less openly, in serious or 'just teasing' terms – as making a difference to whether that work can count as proper knowledge.

The hard and precarious work
of maintaining WGFS

Because WGFS' recognition is to a certain extent conditional, and because the threat of dismissal of WGFS in everyday interaction is real (if spectral), maintaining WGFS is especially hard and precarious work. In Portugal, as in many other countries, WGFS may be increasingly valued, but it is not generally considered a *fundamental* and *indispensable* component of education and research in the SSH. It is not seen as a field which *must* be present, but one that *can* be present if, when, and as long as that presence has benefits for the institution. As one senior scholar put it, the field *"is tolerated, but not acclaimed"*. This means that achievements in the institutionalisation of WGFS can, and do, become undone:

> *"We [research group interested in WGFS] are trying to open paths for gender studies (. . .), but those paths are never conquered. The space for gender is never fully conquered. (. . .) It's a space that's won, but never completely. (. . .) We've gradually been able to expand our work, and that's a victory, but we always have to think of how to defend and sustain that space."*
>
> Interview, senior WGFS scholar

> *"I can't quite tell if [WGFS] is really implanted here at the university. If I start thinking about it, I'd say it isn't, because yes, we have an MA programme, it's true, but it's a struggle to maintain it as student numbers are very low sometimes, and so each year we never know if we'll recruit enough to be allowed to continue. I don't know what will eventually happen."*
>
> Interview, senior WGFS scholar

This scholar's concerns about her programme's future were justified, because after this interview the MA programme did indeed close. This is not uncommon: in the past two decades, other degrees and courses have opened and then sometimes had to close temporarily or permanently. Therefore, securing WGFS teaching space – as an autonomous degree programme or an optional course within other programmes – is an always potentially temporary achievement, and one which requires intense work and negotiation to maintain.

This situation is both a cause and result of the fact that in this national context, as in many other countries, WGFS exists in a state that I have called *individualised institutionalisation*. In each institution that has some form of WGFS teaching and research, WGFS exists because a particular scholar, or extremely small group of scholars, has made initiatives to advance it. WGFS' presence is attached to, and contingent on, the presence and work of those individuals, as there are no dedicated WGFS chairs or positions which are independent of those scholars and the fixed-term research projects they secure funding for. Moreover, and as Tavares notes, 'the prestige [that non-WGFS scholars] recognise in particular examples of [WGFS] work is seen as individual prestige, attached to a particular researcher, rather than a sign of the epistemic status of the field' (2015: 24–25*). Therefore, WGFS is not vulnerable just to the fluctuations of 'demand' in the so-called 'student market' or the vagaries of priority-setting by research funders. It is also vulnerable to the life circumstances of WGFS scholars, and so can disappear in situations of, for example, research or parental leave, a move to another institution, retirement, or illness.

> *"And now [after a long period of struggle] issues of gender and feminism are a natural thing in my department, well, I mean, they're '[name of interviewee]'s things', that's how they're framed. (. . .) So institutionally, I can say that I now have perfect acceptance, I can do what I like. But integration, that's the part I'm not sure of, I think we'll only be able to tell if gender's properly integrated here when I leave, you know? There's no guarantee that when I leave some day, it won't die, because there's no group here, it's just me. (. . .) Here [in Portugal] a lot of it [WGFS] is done by isolated people, (. . .) if the person's there, it'll get done, if they're not, it'll disappear. If they retire or move, well, that's it!"*

The individualised nature of WGFS' institutionalisation is heightened in Portugal by the fact that since the early 2000s, due to the HE funding cutbacks mentioned above and the structure of Portuguese scientific careers (Amâncio, 2003a; MCTES, 2006; Pereira, 2011), many universities have not been able to regularly hire new permanent staff, including people to replace those leaving or retiring. As a result, there is an alarming absence of avenues for integration of junior scholars into academic careers (MCTES, 2006), a situation that takes on a specific configuration in Portugal, but shares some features with the regimes of structural casualisation of (junior) academic labour found elsewhere (Adsit *et al.*, 2015; Arrigoitia *et al.*, 2015; Sifaki, 2016). My more senior interviewees spoke extremely highly of the growing number of doctoral/postdoctoral researchers in WGFS since the mid-2000s, but expressed grave concern that the extremely limited employment opportunities would not allow this *"possibility of a future for the field"*, as one scholar described it, to be realised. Without tenured academic jobs, these emerging scholars might have to leave the country (as I did) or abandon academia, and so there is a high risk that this momentum, and individuals, will be at least partly lost. One senior WGFS scholar cautioned:

> *"There are more new/young[12] people [in WGFS]. But my big fear is that institutions won't be able to integrate them. (. . .) We're not in a time of growth, and people are getting old and will eventually retire, (. . .) and the new/young people, as active as they may be, have no institutional power whatsoever! And that's my biggest fear. (. . .) No one can get an academic job anywhere."*

The work of maintaining WGFS in this landscape of *conditional* and *individualised institutionalisation* is described by almost all interviewees, and in several published texts (Ferreira, 2001; Magalhães, 2001), as generating enormous pressure, strain and 'suffering' (Joaquim, 2009: 145). This was mentioned several times during an annual general meeting of the WGFS association APEM, when members discussed the present state and future prospects of WGFS in Portugal.

> *"We know we're going to hear our institutions telling us that we need to be competent, but we're very competent, we're competent all the time, and we're tired of being competent!"*
>
> Senior WGFS scholar

> *"If there's no intervention from the government [to push for recognition of WGFS], we cannot keep doing this thing that wears us down. This effort of saying and doing the same every day . . . it's really exhausting, isn't it? We always have to be checking things, monitoring them to see if we're being included."*
>
> Senior WGFS scholar

Similar feelings were also described in interviews.

> *"We managed to little by little get ahead in the battle for more space for [name of discipline] research on gender here at the university because we're so dynamic (. . .), we won't let the balls drop, (. . .) we spend our life inventing and doing things. We've won some battles, but this continuous fighting is absolutely exhausting."*
>
> Senior scholar in a social science discipline, with WGFS expertise

This interviewee's reference to battles is not unique or uncommon: bellic metaphors are recurrent in interviewees' accounts. Negotiations of epistemic status and institutionalisation are described as a *"fight"*, *"struggle"*, *"combat"*. One senior scholar recounted being subjected to great *"violence"* as a junior academic and explained that once she had recovered, she was able to rejoin the *"frontline"* in the struggle for institutionalising WGFS.

This is not language used, and feelings experienced, only by Portuguese WGFS academics.[13] Several empirical studies – such as Morley's (1998: 163–164) – or personal accounts of institutional experiences – for example, Skeggs (1995, 2008) – describe similar feelings of anxiety and exhaustion caused by the ongoing (boundary-)work of negotiating the state and status of WGFS in more or less chilly climates. Recounting a recent discussion about the future of WGFS conducted on a US-based international mailing list, Alison Piepmeier notes that '[o]ne thing that struck me was that, throughout the discussion, the language of battle was used' (2012: 119). She draws on a review of US WGFS literature to show that 'this kind of expression isn't confined to online discussions': 'from the origins of the field to the present day, (. . .) WGS practitioners (. . .) present themselves as fighters and the discipline of WGS under fire – besieged' (Piepmeier, 2012: 120).

This pressure and stress experienced daily by both WGFS staff and students is real and constitutes one of the gravest and most damaging outcomes of the full or partial dismissal of WGFS as not quite proper knowledge. However, and as Morley suggests, it is important to avoid 'depict[ing] feminists in the academy as micropolitical martyrs – Christ-like figures being tested by adversity to rise triumphantly at the end. This reifies power relations by reinforcing the reductive victim/oppressor binary' (1998: 190). These accounts of pressure or stress are descriptions of actual experiences, but they do more than just describe experiences. There are other dimensions and implications of those narratives that must be considered. Much like Piepmeier, I would argue that 'the besiegement narrative serves a number of functions for WGS faculty and administrators, functions that are practical as well as ideological' and, I would add, epistemic (2012: 124). Piepmeier examines how '[t]his narrative serves as a tool for heightening marginality, [for] intellectual and generational claim staking, and [for] absolution' (2012: 124). I want to suggest that it also has another effect, closely related to the three that Piepmeier identifies. The claim that WGFS is involved in an ongoing struggle (if not battle or war) with precarious achievements, can function also as a basis for demarcating epistemic status, and doing exclusionary boundary-work, *within* WGFS.

In 5 interviews, WGFS academics referred to the need to *protect* the precarious epistemic status of WGFS as a justification for dissuading or excluding particular scholars or forms of scholarship.

> "I supervised a [PhD] student who wanted to use critical approaches. I had solidarity for what she wanted to do, but my concern was 'You really must use conventional methodologies, otherwise they won't let you pass!'. There were moments of tension, because she'd say 'But I don't want to use them, I think they're epistemologically problematic!', and I was scared to death, and tried to convince her, because I was worried she'd have a hard time in the viva. (. . .) I was really terrified. I had gone through so many things myself, I didn't want a student of mine going through similar things, you know? So we had some tension over that, and the student, bless her, ended up partially changing her research design to satisfy my requests."
>
> Senior WGFS scholar

> "Because of the overly ideological nature of some gender research, when I think of who to invite to [guest teach on] these seminars [of a WGFS course for non-WGFS students], my big concern is bringing people who mix a bit of this ideological dimension, which is important for the defence of feminist principles, but can show solid academic work, do you understand? So I don't invite overly ideological people because it might reinforce stereotypes that students already have, and it would also contradict what I want to do with these seminars."
>
> Senior scholar in a social science discipline, with WGFS expertise

"There are things that profoundly irritate me, because they're like the field shooting itself in the foot. If we go to a conference to announce (. . .) that society is sexist and so we should create radical movements to defend women with marches and things, honestly, it's just shooting ourselves in the foot, you know? Of course we must do that too, but (. . .) Some types of attitudes, well, I think they damage our field."

Junior scholar in a social science discipline, with WGFS expertise

I would argue, then, that discourses of struggle and precariousness are well-founded accounts of the institutional and epistemic position of Portuguese WGFS, but they are not just that. They also provide a legitimating rationale for demarcating the scholars, and types of scholarship, who are allowed to speak for, and as, WGFS in specific spaces. As Chen notes in relation to Taiwan, WGFS academics monitor each other very closely; too closely sometimes, she argues (2004: 246). Alluding to the precariousness of WGFS' status allows scholars to explicitly and implicitly justify that monitoring as reasonable and even necessary. If WGFS is in such a precarious situation, then it becomes understandable and legitimate to want to distance oneself from 'the feminists who are not like "us", who are too extreme, too different, neither rigorous nor rational nor acceptable' (Stanley, 1997a: 8). In other words, if the status of WGFS is always at risk, then it makes sense to always want to protect it, not just from those outside it, but also from those within who are seen to jeopardise it because they do not produce knowledge in the proper way. The precariousness of the epistemic status of a field can therefore place its scholars in a dual position vis-à-vis power in boundary-work: they are on the receiving end of refusals to give more space to the field, and at the same time they may be able to draw on those refusals to justify their own refusals to give more space to particular scholarship within the field. In the next chapter, I examine some examples of these internal demarcations, and reflect on their implications for the epistemic status of WGFS.

The paradoxical status of WGFS in the performative university

Researchers of academia argue that the concept of *paradox* is a helpful tool in that research, because it renders visible the ways in which seemingly contradictory practices might not just coexist, but be mutually constitutive (Hark, 2016; Hey, 2004; Van den Brink and Stobbe, 2009). The relation between academic cultures of performativity and epistemic climates and hierarchies is one dimension of academic life where it is certainly appropriate to speak of paradoxes. In Portugal, the emergence of a culture of performativity has produced both unprecedented openings and major hazards for WGFS. The combined effect of significant cutbacks and the emergence of a performative and competitive academic culture (where institutions need to pro-actively, carefully and regularly 'display' their quality and 'up-to-dateness' to attract funding and students) has helped expand space for WGFS in a community that was for long openly hostile to such critical, interdisciplinary fields. Because many Portuguese WGFS scholars are highly performing, well-networked academics with good track-records of securing funding, and WGFS courses/degrees attract students, university administrations have become more supportive of WGFS. This recognition that WGFS has performative potential, and thus brings *financial* and *institutional* value seems to be dissuading many scholars from publicly questioning its *epistemic* value. This is a phenomenon also observed elsewhere. Crowley talks of the 'pragmatics of popularity' when explaining that in several countries it was WGFS' success in attracting students that resulted in '[t]he early hostility towards the venture of Women's Studies in universities g[iving] way to a begrudging acknowledgement' (1999: 137). Campbell notes that 'the introduction of a market principle [in UK HE], which is, of course, appalling in many ways, none the less meant that there was room for manoeuvre for some [WGFS] initiatives, because those initiatives were popular, were consumer-led' (1992: 14). Skeggs reaffirms this, also drawing on the language of paradoxes to observe that '[p]aradoxically, the market led economy for higher education has led to a rapid expansion of Women's Studies courses [in the UK in the early 1990s]' (1995: 479). She adds that the institution of the Research Assessment Exercises in the UK in the early 1990s '(paradoxically) gave women's studies (in some places) greater legitimacy as the phenomenal rate of publications was made apparent' (Skeggs, 2008: 680), much like what has happened in Portugal from the mid-2000s. She notes, however, that this market orientation has made WGFS more vulnerable to market volatility, with drops in student demand or profitability often leading to cuts or extinction (see also Hemmings, 2006; Morley, 1998).

Indeed, these changes in the status of WGFS in Portugal are only *partial, conditional* and *contingent*. They are *partial* because the thawing of the longstanding 'chilliness' towards WGFS is often superficial and does not necessarily represent an actual transformation of academics' views of epistemic hierarchies. It is here that the metaphor of 'climates' becomes especially useful. In this case, it allows us to problematise corridor talk (and other non-public academic interactions, such as meetings) as a site and practice with its own epistemic microclimate, a climate that remains especially 'chilly' for WGFS, even as the broader climate changes. As Prentice (2000) notes, it is the accumulation of many microlevel practices of teasing and dismissal (each of which, on its own, might appear innocent and inconsequential) which produces chilly climates. Drawing on that insight, then, we can conceptualise these instances of corridor talk as an identifiable, distinctive epistemic microclimate, rather than just random, isolated comments by a few individual 'bad apples' who personally disapprove of WGFS. The changes in attitude towards WGFS are also *conditional*, because they depend on (over-)compliance with an academic governance model which demands very high levels of competitive productivity. Finally, they are *contingent* on continued income-generation, and thus WGFS is often precarious and vulnerable to fluctuation in 'student demand' and funding priorities. At the time of my first round of fieldwork (2008/2009), some WGFS programme coordinators reported that they were beginning to have difficulty maintaining levels of student recruitment, and worried that this might jeopardise their programme's sustainability, worries that in many cases have been confirmed, as I found in the 2015/2016 fieldwork and discuss in chapter 7.

How might we, then, make sense of the paradoxical status of WGFS in the performative university? I began this chapter by speaking of 'profound transformation of the institutions, structures, values, practices and conditions of academic work'. But is that transformation really so profound and straightforward? What seems to make those processes of change especially effective is the fact that they are partly buttressed by elements of continuity. As performative academic cultures become institutionalised, epistemic climates and hierarchies are reshaped in significant ways. However, longstanding hierarchies still affect scholars' unofficial assessments of others' work and are regularly invoked in 'corridor talk' and behind the closed doors of meetings where important decisions get made. The spectral – but unmistakable – presence of these 'old' attitudes creates a constant threat of potential epistemic disqualification for scholars from traditionally marginalised fields; this means that compliance with 'new' modes of governance – with their emphasis on productivity, profitability and fabrication – becomes even more important for them. This creates a special, and especially thorny, dilemma for WGFS. The reshaping of epistemic hierarchies has in some instances created opportunities for WGFS, but at the expense of compliance with mechanisms that clash with key principles of WGFS. In the performative university, if WGFS scholars are 'ideal functionaries' (Evans, 2004) they have a good chance of being able to create and sustain space for WGFS work . . . but in so doing they reproduce a system which significantly erodes their (and others') working conditions (Davies and Petersen, 2005; Gill, 2014; Sifaki, 2016), is detrimental to scholars' and students' well-being (Butterwick and Dawson, 2005; Gill, 2010; Gill and Donaghue, 2016), and makes it extremely difficult to maintain the time-intensive intra- and extra-academic political engagement often seen as a hallmark of WGFS (Pereira, 2016; Sprague and Laube, 2009). I problematise this dilemma, and unpack its epistemic, physical and emotional effects, in chapter 7, which constitutes part II of my discussion of the life of WGFS, and the lives of WGFS scholars, in the performative university.

Notes

1 As I discuss in chapter 3, I feel uncomfortable using the term 'late' because it frames the history of Portuguese WGFS, and WGFS in other (semi-)peripheral countries, in relation to the temporality of its institutionalisation in countries of the 'centre', thus reinforcing the academic hegemony of anglophone scholarship. For a more detailed discussion of that hegemony and its effects on the epistemic status of WGFS, see chapter 6.
2 They had been banned by the *Estado Novo* dictatorship (1933–1974) on the grounds that they were revolutionary (Carreira da Silva, 2016).
3 For a detailed analysis of the broader epistemic climate in the Portuguese SSH at that time, see Pereira (2011).

4 *B-On* (www.b-on.pt) is a state-funded digital platform launched in 2004, providing Portuguese universities with full-text access to international journals.

5 In 2000, Portuguese universities received governmental funding of 4247€ per student; by 2008 this had decreased to 3610€ (both adjusted to 2007 prices), a loss of 15% (Cerdeira, 2008). For a comparison of these trends in OECD countries, see Santiago *et al.*, who note that 'only a few countries – the Czech Republic, Hungary, Poland, Portugal, Sweden and UK – experienced a decline in the expenditure per student on T[ertiary] E[ducation] I[nstitution]s between 1995 and 2004' (2008: 153).

6 The percentage of universities' income that came from the state budget decreased in that period from 92.5% in 2000 to 65% in 2008 (Cabrito, 2011).

7 The Bologna Process, established in 1999, is a transnational process of educational reform seeking to create a European HE Area, namely by standardising degrees and promoting mobility.

8 Until 2002, public universities charged the same tuition-fee for all UG degrees; its annual value was equivalent to the monthly minimum wage – in 2002, it was 325€/year. From 2003, institutions were allowed to set their own fees, within a government-defined range increasing every year (450–850€/year in 2013; 630–1063€/year in 2016/2017). In 2003, most institutions aligned fees with the maximum value to cope with funding cuts. Recently, several have opted to not increase fees annually on the basis that in the 'austerity' context many families cannot afford further increases (Amaral and Neave, 2012).

9 According to several interviewees, Portuguese WGFS has always been somewhat fragmented, with limited circulation of information (namely about events) between WGFS sites and, in some cases, distant (or even tense) relationships between individuals or groups (Pereira, 2011, 2013).

10 See Gannon *et al.* (2015) for an analysis of other examples of joking references to 'hairy-legged feminists' in academic 'corridor talk'.

11 See Marchbank and Letherby (2006: 163) for a discussion of students' experiences of 'teasing and denigration when they "c[o]me out" as women's studies students' in English universities.

12 The interviewee uses the term "*gente nova*", which can mean new or young people.

13 They are also not the only feelings described by my interviewees. Walsh notes that '[t]o live out the paradox and complexities of women's presence in the academy is hard, often lonely, and bad for our health. So what keeps us there?'. Trying to answer that question, she highlights that WGFS academics 'take pleasure in the knowledge that working together to transform traditional ways of teaching and (. . .) knowledge production, creates an excitement which sustains hope, energy and affection' (1995: 96). Similarly, working in WGFS has also given my interviewees significant pleasure. Their accounts of pleasure provide rich material with which to interrogate, among other issues, the 'paradoxes of pleasure' (Hey, 2004) that characterise feminist academics' experiences, but I am unfortunately unable to explore those accounts in detail here.

References

Aavik, Kadri, *et al.* (2015). *Country Reports (Australia, Czech Republic, Estonia, Germany, Iceland, Netherlands, Norway, Portugal, South Africa, Sweden, Switzerland, UK)*. Multiple Papers Presented at the RINGS Network Conference "Gender in/and the Neoliberal University", Prague.

Abranches, Graça (1998). *"On What Terms Shall we Join the Procession of Educated Men?" Teaching Feminist Studies at the University of Coimbra*. Coimbra: Centro de Estudos Sociais.

Adsit, Janelle, *et al.* (2015). "Affective Activism: Answering Institutional Productions of Precarity in the Corporate University". *Feminist Formations, 27* (3), 21–48.

Alldred, Pam and Miller, Tina (2007). "Measuring What's Valued or Valuing What's Measured? Knowledge Production and the Research Assessment Exercise" in V. Gillies and H. Lucey (eds.), *Power, Knowledge and the Academy: The Institutional Is Political* (pp.147–167). Basingstoke: Palgrave Macmillan.

Alvarez, Teresa (2008). "Las Mujeres en la Historia Enseñada en Portugal: Avances y resistencias de la Investigación a la Enseñanza" in *Actas del Congresso "Mundos de Mujeres"* (pp.16–20). Madrid: Universidad Complutense de Madrid.

Amâncio, Lígia (2000). "Contributos para a História de um Movimento Social Inexistente: A Representação Social da Feminista" in *Actas do III Congresso Português de Sociologia (CD-ROM)*. Oeiras: Celta & APS.

Amâncio, Lígia (2002). "O Género na Psicologia Social em Portugal". *ex aequo, 6,* 55–75.

Amâncio, Lígia (2003a). "Gender and Science in Portugal". *Portuguese Journal of Social Science, 1* (3), 185–198.

Amâncio, Lígia (2003b). "O Género nos Discursos das Ciências Sociais". *Análise Social, XXXVIII* (168), 687–714.

Amâncio, Lígia (2005). "Reflections on Science as a Gendered Endeavour: Changes and Continuities". *Social Science Information, 44* (1), 65–83.

Amâncio, Lígia and Oliveira, João Manuel de (2006). "Men as Individuals, Women as a Sexed Category: Implications of Symbolic Asymmetry for Feminist Practice and Feminist Psychology". *Feminism & Psychology, 16* (1), 36–44.

Amaral, Alberto and Neave, Guy (eds.) (2012). *Higher Education in Portugal 1974–2009: A Nation, a Generation*. Dordrecht: Springer.

Antunes, Fátima (2006). "Governação e Espaço Europeu de Educação: Regulação da Educação e Visões para o Projecto 'Europa'". *Revista Crítica de Ciências Sociais, 75,* 63–93.

Arrigoitia, Melissa Fernández, *et al.* (2015). "Women's Studies and Contingency: Between Exploitation and Resistance". *Feminist Formations, 27* (3), 81–113.

Baird, Barbara (2010). "Ambivalent Optimism: Women's and Gender Studies in Australian Universities". *Feminist Review, 95,* 111–126.

Ball, Stephen J. (2000). "Performativities and Fabrications in the Education Economy: Towards the Performative Society?". *The Australian Educational Researcher, 27* (2), 1–23.

Bellacasa, María Puig de la (2001). "Beyond Nostalgia and Celebration: Contexts for Academic Women's Studies in Contemporary Universities" in N. Lykke, *et al.* (eds.), *Women's Studies: From Institutional Innovations to New Job Qualifications* (pp.25–45). Utrecht: ATHENA.

Billig, Michael (2005). *Laughter and Ridicule: Towards a Social Critique of Humour*. London: Sage.

Blackmore, Jill and Sachs, Judyth (2000). "Paradoxes of Leadership and Management in Higher Education in Times of Change: Some Australian Reflections". *International Journal of Leadership in Education, 3* (1), 1–16.

Blackmore, Jill and Sachs, Judyth (2003). "Managing Equity Work in the Performative University". *Australian Feminist Studies, 18* (41), 141–162.

Brenneis, Donald (1999). "New Lexicon, Old Language: Negotiating the «Global» at the National Science Foundation" in G.E. Marcus (ed.), *Critical Anthropology Now* (pp.123–146). Santa Fe, NM: School of American Research Press.

Buikema, Rosemarie and Van der Tuin, Iris (2013). "Doing the Document: Gender Studies at the Corporatized University in Europe". *European Journal of Women's Studies, 20* (3), 309–316.

Burrows, Roger (2012). "Living with the H-Index? Metric Assemblages in the Contemporary Academy". *The Sociological Review, 60* (2), 355–372.

Butler, Judith (1988). "Performative Acts and Gender Constitution: An Essay in Phenomenology and Feminist Theory". *Theatre Journal, 40* (4), 519–531.

Butler, Judith (1990). *Gender Trouble: Feminism and the Subversion of Identity.* New York: Routledge.

Butterwick, Shauna and Dawson, Jane (2005). "Undone Business: Examining the Production of Academic Labour". *Women's Studies International Forum, 28* (1), 51–65.

Cabrito, Belmiro Gil (2011). "O Ensino Superior em Portugal: Percursos Contraditórios". *Educativa, 14* (2), 209–227.

Campbell, Beatrix (1992). "Feminist Politics after Thatcher" in H. Hinds, *et al.* (eds.), *Working Out: New Directions for Women's Studies* (pp.13–17). London: Falmer Press.

Carreira da Silva, Filipe (2016). *Sociology in Portugal: A Short History.* Basingstoke: Palgrave Macmillan.

Cerdeira, Luísa (2008). *O Financiamento do Ensino Superior Português: a Partilha de Custos.* PhD Thesis, Universidade de Lisboa.

Chen, Peiying (2004). *Acting "Otherwise": The Institutionalization of Women's/Gender Studies in Taiwan Universities.* London: RoutledgeFalmer.

Crowley, Helen (1999). "Women's Studies: Between a Rock and a Hard Place or Just Another Cell in the Beehive?". *Feminist Review, 61*, 131–150.

Davies, Bronwyn and Petersen, Eva Bendix (2005). "Neo-Liberal Discourse in the Academy: The Forestalling of (Collective) Resistance". *LATISS: Learning and Teaching in the Social Sciences, 2* (2), 77–98.

Davies, Helen and O'Callaghan, Claire (eds.) (2014). *Journal of Gender Studies.* Special Issue: "Feminism, Academia, Austerity", *23* (3).

Downey, Gary Lee, *et al.* (1997). "Corridor Talk" in J. Dumit and G.L. Downey (eds.), *Cyborgs & Citadels: Anthropological Interventions in Emerging Sciences and Technologies* (pp.245–264). Santa Fe, NM: School of American Research Press.

Erne, Roland (2007). "On the Use and Abuse of Bibliometric Performance Indicators". *European Political Science, 6* (3), 306–314.

Evans, Mary (2004). *Killing Thinking: The Death of the Universities.* London: Continuum.

ex aequo Editorial Board (1999). "Editorial". *ex aequo, 1*, 5–10.

Ferreira, Virgínia (2001). "Estudos sobre as Mulheres em Portugal: A Construção de um Novo Campo Científico". *ex aequo, 5*, 9–25.

Gannon, Susanne, *et al.* (2015). "Uneven Relationalities, Collective Biography, and Sisterly Affect in Neoliberal Universities". *Feminist Formations, 27* (3), 189–216.

Gibbons, Michael, *et al.* (1994). *The New Production of Knowledge: The Dynamics of Science and Research in Contemporary Societies.* London: Sage.

Gieryn, Thomas (1999). *Cultural Boundaries of Science: Credibility on the Line.* Chicago: University of Chicago Press.

Gill, Rosalind (2010). "Breaking the Silence: The Hidden Injuries of the Neoliberal University" in R. Ryan-Flood and R. Gill (eds.), *Secrecy and Silence in the Research Process: Feminist Reflections* (pp.228–244). Abingdon: Routledge.

Gill, Rosalind (2014). "Academics, Cultural Workers and Critical Labour Studies". *Journal of Cultural Economy, 7* (1), 12–30.

Gill, Rosalind and Donaghue, Ngaire (2016). "Resilience, Apps and Reluctant Individualism: Technologies of Self in the Neoliberal Academy". *Women's Studies International Forum, 54*, 91–99.

Graça, Vasco (2009). "Sobre o Financiamento da Educação: Condicionantes Globais e Realidades Nacionais". *Revista Lusófona de Educação, 13*, 49–80.

Hark, Sabine (2016). "Contending Directions: Gender Studies in the Entrepreneurial University". *Women's Studies International Forum, 54*, 84–90.

Hemmings, Clare (2006). "The Life and Times of Academic Feminism" in K. Davis, *et al.* (eds.), *Handbook of Gender and Women's Studies* (pp.13–34). London: Sage.

Henriques, Fernanda and Pinto, Teresa (2002). "Educação e Género: Dos Anos 70 ao Final do Século XX". *ex aequo, 6*, 11–54.

Hey, Valerie (2004). "Perverse Pleasures: Identity Work and the Paradoxes of Greedy Institutions". *Journal of International Women's Studies, 5* (3), 33–43.

Hurdley, Rachel (2010). "In the Picture or Off the Wall? Ethical Regulation, Research Habitus, and Unpeopled Ethnography". *Qualitative Inquiry, 16* (6), 517–528.

Jenkins, Fiona and Keane, Helen (eds.) (2014). *Australian Feminist Studies*. Special Issue: "Gendered Excellence in the Social Sciences", *29* (80).

Joaquim, Teresa (2004). "*ex aequo*: Contributo Decisivo para um Campo de Estudos em Portugal". *Revista Estudos Feministas, 12* (3), 88–93.

Joaquim, Teresa (2007). "Feminismos, Estudos sobre as Mulheres, ou 'Para Onde Vai Este Barco?'" in L. Amâncio, *et al.* (eds.), *O Longo Caminho das Mulheres* (pp.203–216). Lisboa: Dom Quixote.

Joaquim, Teresa (2009). "Women's Studies: A 'Misplaced Subject'?". *The Making of European Women's Studies, IX*, 142–143.

Leathwood, Carole and Read, Barbara (2013). "Research Policy and Academic Performativity: Compliance, Contestation and Complicity". *Studies in Higher Education, 38* (8), 1162–1174.

Liinason, Mia and Grenz, Sabine (eds.) (2016). *Women's Studies International Forum*. Special Issue: "Women's/Gender Studies and Contemporary Changes in Academic Cultures: European Perspectives", *54*.

Lund, Rebecca (2012). "Publishing to Become an 'Ideal Academic': An Institutional Ethnography and a Feminist Critique". *Scandinavian Journal of Management, 28* (3), 218–228.

Lyotard, Jean-François (1984). *The Postmodern Condition: A Report on Knowledge*. Manchester: Manchester University Press.

Magalhães, Maria José (2001). "Dez Anos da APEM: Percorrer as Vozes, Significar os Percursos". *ex aequo, 5*, 27–68.

Marchbank, Jen and Letherby, Gayle (2006). "Views and Perspectives of Women's Studies: A Survey of Women and Men Students". *Gender and Education, 18* (2), 157–182.

Martins, Carla, *et al.* (2009). "The F-Word in Congress: News Media and a Portuguese Feminist Event". *Média & Jornalismo, 14*, 55–68.

MCTES, (Ministério da Ciência, Tecnologia e Ensino Superior) (2006). *Tertiary Education in Portugal: Background Report*. Lisboa: MCTES.

Messer-Davidow, Ellen (2002). *Disciplining Feminism: From Social Activism to Academic Discourse*. Durham, NC: Duke University Press.

Mineiro, João (2015). *O Campo Universitário Português: Transformações e Disputas entre 1988–2015*. MSc Dissertation, ISCTE-IUL.

Mirowski, Philip and Sent, Esther-Mirjam (2008). "The Commercialization of Science and the Response of STS" in E.J. Hackett, *et al.* (eds.), *The Handbook of Science and Technology Studies* (3rd ed) (pp.635–689). Cambridge, MA: MIT Press.

Morley, Louise (1998). *Organising Feminisms: The Micropolitics of the Academy*. New York: St. Martin's Press.

Morley, Louise (2003). *Quality and Power in Higher Education*. Buckingham: Open University Press.

Morris, Rosalind (1995). "All Made Up: Performance Theory and the New Anthropology of Sex and Gender". *Annual Review of Anthropology, 24*, 567–592.

Mountz, Alison, *et al.* (2015). "For Slow Scholarship: A Feminist Politics of Resistance through Collective Action in the Neoliberal University". *ACME, 14* (4), 1235–1259.

Münch, Richard (2014). *Academic Capitalism: Universities in the Global Struggle for Excellence*. New York: Routledge.

Nash, Jennifer and Owens, Emily (2015a). "Institutional Feelings: Practicing Women's Studies in the Corporate University". *Feminist Formations, 27* (3), vii–xi.

Nash, Jennifer and Owens, Emily (eds.) (2015b). *Feminist Formations*. Special Issue: "Institutional Feelings: Practicing Women's Studies in the Corporate University", *27* (3).

Oliveira, João Manuel de (2015). "Tumultos de Género: os Efeitos de *Gender Trouble* em Portugal". *Periódicus, 3* (1), 6–18.

Pereira, Maria do Mar (2010). "Os Discursos de Género: Mudança e Continuidade nas Narrativas sobre Diferenças, Semelhanças e (Des)Igualdade entre Mulheres e Homens" in K. Wall, *et al.* (eds.), *A Vida Familiar no Masculino* (pp.225–264). Lisboa: CITE.

Pereira, Maria do Mar (2011). *Pushing the Boundaries of Knowledge: An Ethnography of Negotiations of the Epistemic Status of Women's, Gender, Feminist Studies in Portugal*. PhD Thesis, LSE.

Pereira, Maria do Mar (2012). *Fazendo Género no Recreio: A Negociação do Género em Espaço Escolar*. Lisboa: Imprensa de Ciências Sociais.

Pereira, Maria do Mar (2013). "A Institucionalização dos Estudos sobre as Mulheres, de Género e Feministas em Portugal no Século XXI: Conquistas, Desafios e Paradoxos". *Faces de Eva, 30*, 37–53.

Pereira, Maria do Mar (2016). "Struggling Within and Beyond the Performative University: Articulating Activism and Work in an 'Academia Without Walls'". *Women's Studies International Forum, 54*, 100–110.

Petersen, Eva Bendix (2003). *Academic Boundary Work: The Discursive Constitution of 'Scientificity' Amongst Researchers Within the Social Sciences and Humanities*. PhD Thesis, University of Copenhagen.

Piepmeier, Alison (2012). "Besiegement" in C. Orr, *et al.* (eds.), *Rethinking Women's and Gender Studies* (pp.119–134). New York: Routledge.

Pinto, Teresa (2007). "História das Mulheres e do Género: Uma Progressiva Presença Institucional de Dúbia Legitimação Académica". *ex aequo, 16*, 141–166.

Power, Michael (1999). *The Audit Society: Rituals of Verification*. Oxford: Oxford University Press.

Prentice, Susan L. (2000). "Chilly Climate" in L. Code (ed.), *Encyclopedia of Feminist Theories* (pp.84–85). London: Routledge.

Ramalho, Maria Irene (2009). "SIGMA National Report: Portugal (1995)". *The Making of European Women's Studies, IX*, 119–136.

Santiago, Paulo, *et al.* (2008). *Tertiary Education for the Knowledge Society*. Paris: OECD.

Santos, Ana Cristina (2010). "Portugal" in S. Roseneil (ed.), *Changing Cultural Discourses about Intimate Life: The Demands and Actions of Women's Movements and Other Movements for Gender and Sexual Equality and Change* (pp.184–287). London: FEMCIT.

Santos Pereira, Tiago (2004). "Processos de Governação da Ciência: O Debate em Torno do Modelo de Financiamento das Unidades de Investigação em Portugal". *Revista Crítica de Ciências Sociais, 70*, 5–32.

Shore, Cris (2010). "Beyond the Multiversity: Neoliberalism and the Rise of the Schizophrenic University". *Social Anthropology/Anthropologie Sociale, 18* (1), 15–29.

Shore, Cris and Wright, Susan (2000). "Coercive Accountability: The Rise of Audit Culture in Higher Education" in M. Strathern (ed.), *Audit Cultures: Anthropological Studies in Accountability, Ethics and the Academy* (pp.57–89). London: Routledge.

Sifaki, Aggeliki (2016). "Which Side Are We On? Feminist Studies in the Time of Neoliberalism or Neoliberal Feminist Studies?". *Women's Studies International Forum, 54*, 111–118.

Skeggs, Beverley (1995). "Women's Studies in Britain in the 1990s: Entitlement Cultures and Institutional Constraints". *Women's Studies International Forum, 18* (4), 475–485.

Skeggs, Beverley (2008). "The Dirty History of Feminism and Sociology: Or the War of Conceptual Attrition". *The Sociological Review, 56* (4), 670–690.

Slaughter, Sheila and Leslie, Larry L. (1997). *Academic Capitalism: Politics, Policies, and the Entrepreneurial University*. Baltimore, MD: Johns Hopkins University Press.

Sprague, Joey and Laube, Heather (2009). "Institutional Barriers to Doing Public Sociology: Experiences of Feminists in the Academy". *The American Sociologist, 40* (4), 249–271.

Stanley, Liz (1997a). "Introduction: On Academic Borders, Territories, Tribes and Knowledges" in L. Stanley (ed.), *Knowing Feminisms: On Academic Borders, Territories and Tribes* (pp.1–17). London: Sage.

Stanley, Liz (1997b). "Knowing Feminisms and Passing Women: A Conclusion" in L. Stanley (ed.), *Knowing Feminisms: On Academic Borders, Territories and Tribes* (pp.197–204). London: Sage.

Strathern, Marilyn (2000). "Introduction: New Accountabilities" in M. Strathern (ed.), *Audit Cultures: Anthropological Studies in Accountability, Ethics and the Academy* (pp.1–18). London: Routledge.

Tavares, Manuela (2011). *Feminismos em Portugal*. Lisboa: Texto.

Tavares, Manuela (2015). "A Visibilidade dos Estudos sobre as Mulheres, de Género e Feministas (EMGF)" in A. Torres, *et al.* (eds.), *Estudos de Género numa Perspetiva Interdisciplinar* (pp.23–26). Lisboa: Mundos Sociais.

Taylor, Yvette (ed.) (2014). *The Entrepreneurial University: Engaging Publics, Intersecting Impacts*. Basingstoke: Palgrave Macmillan.

Van den Brink, Marieke and Stobbe, Lineke (2009). "Doing Gender in Academic Education: The Paradox of Visibility". *Gender, Work and Organization, 16* (4), 451–470.

Walsh, Val (1995). "Transgression and the Academy: Feminists and Institutionalization" in L. Morley and V. Walsh (eds.), *Feminist Academics: Creative Agents for Change* (pp.86–101). London: Taylor & Francis.

Chapter 4

WGFS is proper knowledge, but . . .

The splitting of feminist scholarship

> [I offer the metaphor of] the academy harbouring feminism: building it up and replenishing it in some ways, yes; but at the same time given to running it dry, keeping it within walls, seeing to its overall containment.
>
> (Campbell, 1992: 2; cited in McNeil, 1993: 167)

For many WGFS scholars throughout the world, WGFS is a project of both cumulative and critical intervention in the academy: its aim is not just to generate more and/or better knowledge but also, and centrally, to question and transform dominant standards, frameworks and institutions of academic knowledge production. We often see these aims as closely articulated and resolutely inextricable. For one of my interviewees, a junior WGFS researcher, *"the critical and intellectual dimensions of feminist work are completely connected, I just can't separate them"*. Portuguese feminist scholar Sofia Neves echoes this, arguing that 'it is epistemologically impossible to detach [the concept of] gender from feminist [critiques]' (2012: 15*). However creating a separation between these two dimensions of WGFS work seems to be not only possible, but a frequent and defining feature of mainstream academic engagement with, and claims about, that work. Accounts from several countries note that many non-WGFS scholars recognise the relevance and value of some analytical insights of WGFS, but bypass or reject its epistemological, theoretical, methodological and political critique of mainstream academic knowledge. As one senior WGFS scholar I interviewed explained, *"I have several [non-WGFS] colleagues who often say: 'studying women and gender is fine, but doing it in a feminist way is too ideological and that's not acceptable'"*.

This bifurcation of WGFS work has troubled scholars worldwide (for example, Boxer, 1998 on the US; Chen, 2004 on Taiwan; Gerhard, 2004 on Germany; Pereira, C., 2000 on Nigeria), for several decades (Acker, 1989; Stacey and Thorne, 1985 are two examples of earlier discussions). In 1982, Mary Evans noted that among UK-based non-WGFS academics it was

> assumed that 'discovering' women as a subject for academic study does not lead to any significant problems for traditional disciplines and methods of

inquiry. (. . .) [A]cademics merely have to get out their existing guide books on how to study, catalogue and index the social world and proceed in the accepted way.

(1982: 63)

Over 20 years later, Evans argued that 'feminism has achieved at least *partial* academic recognition' (2003: 15, my emphasis) in contemporary mainstream social theory, but noted that 'the impact of confronting the academic world with the very radical challenge to the taken for granted construction of the human subject as male has yet to be fully understood' (2003: 100). Ten years on, Simbürger (2015) arrives at similar findings through her interviews with feminist and non-feminist UK-based sociologists; this leads her to describe social theory as a form of 'selective writing', grounded on the unacknowledged universalising of the particular experiences of white men. Reed (2006) identifies similarities between this partial recognition of feminist theory and the current status of theories of race and ethnicity in the social theory canon. She observes that the work of feminist and black theorists is now seen as a 'critique that can no longer be ignored' but tends to be framed as a 'specialized critique', i.e. 'one whose implications are contained, self-limiting and of insufficient general consequence' (2006: 141). Similar allusions to the partial recognition of WGFS are made very frequently – even if often only in passing – across the literature, indicating that this is a key issue in the understanding of the past and present conditions for teaching, learning, researching and institutionalising WGFS.

But how is this partial recognition materialised in, and produced through, actual academic work? This question has led scholars to empirically examine, for example, how WGFS authors, themes, concepts, analytics and theories are (not) covered in textbooks and curricula (Abbott *et al.*, 2005; Foster *et al.*, 2013; Rowley and Shepherd, 2012),[1] with many authors observing that feminist contributions 'tend to be lumped under the "gender" label and given a couple of lectures or a chapter in a book; "malestream" [research and teaching] can then carry on as normal' (Abbott, 1991: 189). This question has also been the driving force for empirical analyses of whether and how non-WGFS academics (fail to) engage with WGFS scholarship in their writing; in Portugal, such analyses include, for example, Amâncio (2003), Ferreira (2001), Joaquim (2001), Pinto (2008) and Pinto-Coelho and Mota-Ribeiro (2016). Elsewhere, Hawkesworth examined journal articles in political theory, and noted that feminist and critical race theory are 'referred to in the past tense as something that has been transcended, occluded, overcome' (2010: 693). Whelan dissects one example of separation of feminist theory in her analysis of Pickering's (1995) discussion of Haraway's work:

[Haraway's] feminism is mentioned in passing, when Pickering argues that Haraway's politics can be *extricated* from her analysis, of which he approves. But Haraway's feminism isn't just her politics; (. . .) [it] enables her theoretical insights, as she invariably and carefully acknowledges. Pickering is concerned to point out the complex interrelation of all the eclectic elements of scientific work. Yet despite his talk of the 'mangle' of scientific practice, Pickering *neatly separates out* Haraway's *feminism* in an effort to show that we don't have to 'hitch our analyses to particular political projects' (1995:228) – as if political projects aren't part of the mangle.

(2001: 558, my emphases)

Existing discussions have focused mostly on how WGFS scholarship is represented in texts but I want to expand them by examining *ethnographically* how such separations are produced and legitimated in *everyday academic interaction*. Through which discursive strategies is this separation enacted in classrooms, conferences and other sites of academic work and sociability? How and where do non-WGFS scholars place the boundary – or, as I will call it, the *epistemic threshold* – that separates the aspects of WGFS which supposedly are, or not, proper knowledge? How is this partial recognition of WGFS made to appear (and exercise authority) as a reasonable, grounded and true assessment of the intrinsic epistemic status of different aspects of WGFS, rather than a personal and contested position? To tackle these questions, I analyse claims made by non-WGFS scholars when speaking in conferences, lecturing, participating in PhD vivas or interacting with others.

Mainstream scholars' discourses about WGFS

When I asked whether and how Portuguese non-WGFS scholars engage with WGFS scholarship, almost all students and staff I interviewed described this engagement as growing, but selective and partial. They explained that many conceptual contributions of (Portuguese and international) WGFS authors – most notably the formulation of the concept of 'gender' and its framing as a key axis of inequality – have been integrated relatively easily and are now often accepted as relevant (although still frequently absent from, or secondary in, non-WGFS teaching and research). However, the feminist critiques of academic knowledge which ground and frame those conceptual proposals, and are harder to reconcile with mainstream scholarship, are almost entirely overlooked or openly dismissed. Two interviewees described this as follows:

"The concept of gender got in easily and now appears in every text, although those texts don't acknowledge the work carried out by feminist researchers and even the theoretical implications of the concept of gender itself for that [mainstream] work. (. . .) [Gender] enters [non-WGFS scholarship] without reflection, without an understanding of its political implications. (. . .) Everyone thinks they can mention women and men and it's enough to add that, it doesn't demand a change of perspective or critical stance, it does not have implications for how disciplines are constituted, and I think these aspects are the most important work [of WGFS]."

Senior WGFS scholar

"I think at the moment gender's in fashion, and so very easily people say 'I'm doing research and gender is a variable in it'. But in actual fact the gender issues related to feminist theory are not analysed. (. . .) It's seen as very acceptable to affirm gender as something that's important in a piece of research, but feminist issues aren't as easily integrated in mainstream academic discourse, although resistance to them now is less obvious than before."

Junior WGFS scholar

Commenting on this, Teresa Joaquim, a Portuguese feminist philosopher, writes:

The analytical category of gender became more present in Portugal from the 1990s (. . .). It became a 'passe-partout' term, migrating to, and being translated into, many institutional contexts where it is used (. . .) in a way that hides the critique (. . .) [it] implies (. . .). It is an analytical category that has become an important theoretical contribution, but whose source is not recognised – *it is 'cut'* from the field of women's studies, from feminist theories, leading to a depoliticising of the term.

(2004: 89*, my emphasis)[2]

During fieldwork, I observed demarcations of the epistemic status of WGFS that confirm those descriptions. In my participant observation in Portugal of national and international non-WGFS conferences in a range of social science (inter)disciplines, and of non-WGFS UG and PG teaching, I found that non-WGFS scholars rarely referred to WGFS in their interventions. When references were made to it, they were always framed in broadly positive terms, as I discussed in the previous chapter. In some cases, the recognition of WGFS' value was unequivocal, but in the overwhelming majority of instances what was expressed was a positive, but *partial*, *adversative* and *conditional* recognition. The dominant claim was that WGFS can produce, and has produced, credible and relevant contributions to academic knowledge, *but* only *up to* a certain point, or only *some* of its strands, or only *if* done in a certain way. In the sections that follow, I analyse examples of these discourses to examine how boundaries of scientificity are drawn in them and how that boundary-work produces a representation of WGFS as a field that is partly within, and partly outside, the space of proper knowledge, a process that I designate as an *epistemic splitting* of WGFS. I will show that this epistemic splitting is what makes it possible for the concept of gender to *"easily enter"* into the mainstream as proper knowledge (to use the words of the interviewee quoted above), while part or all of its *"theoretical and political implications"* are left outside.

WGFS produces proper knowledge . . . but only when done in a certain way

My first encounter with *adversative* claims about WGFS – i.e. propositions that express opposition or discrepancy through a 'but' or equivalent adversative conjunction – happened on the second day of fieldwork, at a national conference for one social science discipline. During the coffee-break, I drank a glass of milk and mingled before heading to a session on gender. I chatted with an older delegate I did not know; after a few minutes of conference small-talk, she asked what field I specialise in, and I said "gender". "Gender?!", she replied, "but I hope it's none of that esoteric stuff one often finds in that field, hey?! Gender, but properly, with your feet firmly on the ground". I smiled politely and asked, "Esoteric stuff? What do you mean?". She responded matter-of-factly: "Oh, you know, there are things in that field that are driven by faith and dogma, not by science. They're like a religion, and a religion like that is as bad as other religions". She talked excitedly about a French acquaintance "who's researching gender in very interesting ways". I nodded and she continued, taking on a disapproving tone: "But some people in her department do the most absurd research on gender". "Really?", I asked. "Well, I'm sure you've seen some of that very political work on gender! In my opinion, studying gender's great, just as long as it doesn't become esoteric and political. One must analyse things with, you know." She stopped talking, as if the sentence was complete. I looked at her in silence, waiting for her to finish. "One must analyse things with impartiality. No, that feminist stuff is too much". She smiled and asked if I enjoyed working in the UK.

This scene shows that epistemic boundary-work can begin suddenly and when you least expect it. More importantly, it illustrates that some non-WGFS academics' reactions to references to gender are framed very saliently on the basis of a distinction between research about gender with "feet firmly on the ground" that can produce credible knowledge, and research that is too dogmatic and political, "like a religion", and therefore academically unacceptable and best avoided. Another noteworthy feature of this exchange is the delegate's framing of WGFS' potential for unscientific excess as a commonly recognised characteristic of the field, one she seems to assume that I (someone she had only just met) will find as problematic as she does. She describes the potential "absurd[ity]" of WGFS matter-of-factly, as a relatively straightforward and uncontroversial fact: she does not have to provide examples, or even complete all sentences. As the Portuguese saying goes, 'for someone who understands you well, half a word [in this case, half a sentence] is enough'. The tone is not directly confrontational, and she does not question my decision to specialise in gender. The claim is that WGFS has a valuable place and can be "very interesting", but it just needs to be more observant of the crucial epistemic threshold that is seen to separate scientific knowledge from religion, politics and partiality.

References to this idea that WGFS produces interesting knowledge but sometimes strays, or risks straying, too far beyond the boundaries of the academically acceptable were made in several fieldwork sites. They were almost always very brief references, made as part of broader discussions of other topics, as in these two examples from a conference and a classroom. In an interdisciplinary non-WGFS conference, a presenter spoke about critical approaches to law. He briefly mentioned feminist critiques of legal theory, explaining that "they were important, but went too far and were too romantic and simplistic because they assumed this was the only problem of law". Here, the affirmation of the simplicity and homogeneity of feminist critiques works to position WGFS as relevant or interesting but only up to a certain point. Elsewhere, I attended a PG non-WGFS course taught by a senior non-WGFS academic. At one point, the class discussed the merits and weaknesses of interdisciplinarity. The lecturer gave examples of fields in which interdisciplinarity has been especially encouraged. He indicated WGFS, among other fields, and named two well-known Portuguese WGFS scholars.

> "These authors have produced research that's very rich from the point of view of the interdisciplinary bridges it establishes. That's particularly interesting if it's done consistently, which is the case with these two scholars, but is not always the case in gender studies, sometimes it's taken too far, resulting in superficial research."

The cited WGFS scholars are described as having satisfied the required conditions for the production of good research; they, thus, reside on the 'right' side of the epistemic threshold. However, the field of WGFS as a whole is portrayed as not always respectful of that threshold, which means it is partly within and partly outside the boundaries of proper knowledge.

Fleeting claims like these made up the bulk of the references to WGFS made by non-WGFS scholars during my fieldwork. However, I want to focus my analysis on the less frequent cases of longer discussion of WGFS to explore in more depth the complexity of the boundary-work being performed and its collective and negotiated character. I begin by examining an exchange in a seminar for a PG non-WGFS social science course, taught by a senior non-WGFS scholar to non-WGFS students. As the extract is very long, I analyse a section at a time, to better highlight the gradually shifting, and more or less subtle, boundary-marking enacted in it.

> *"(Male) Student: as a social researcher, is it riskier for me to study a reality close to me, that I'm a part of, (. . .) or one that's foreign to me, almost the opposite of my life? (. . .)*
>
> *Lecturer: That's been a debate since forever in the social sciences. Put simply, it touches on the epistemic privilege of the outsider or the insider (. . .). There are good arguments for the merits of one or the other. (. . .)* [He describes some arguments.] *The epistemic privilege of the outsider was an argument developed in the 19th and mid-20th century. The epistemic privilege of the insider also has good earlier traditions, but has been more defended for example in cultural studies and feminist studies. [These fields claim that] being inside (. . .) allows for an analytical sensitivity that outsiders can't have. You'll find arguments in all these different traditions, none is simplistic in relation to this, I think, sometimes they're even very sophisticated, although not always very consistent. (. . .) But it's an ongoing issue."*

Note that he starts by describing feminism (and cultural studies) as offering valuable arguments, explicitly stating that they are not simplistic. Feminist scholarship seems to be described here as one among a range of relevant traditions to be considered. He continued:

> *"Lecturer: I don't have an answer, but I'd like to draw attention to two, three points. (. . .) I feel that the traditional arguments for the epistemic privilege of the outsider and the feminist and cultural studies arguments for the privilege of the insider when taken up completely are too absolute and somewhat caricatural. But each one does make some pertinent points. So what I'd probably have to do is transport with me what's valuable in each one, and then channel that to a subtler process of epistemological control. (. . .) A statement like 'I'm an insider and therefore my perspective will be better' demonstrates a completely inappropriate social determinism, and contemporary social sciences, with their sophistication, wouldn't subscribe to this. They wouldn't subscribe (. . .) to the claim that (. . .) because I'm white or black, man or woman, etc, (. . .) I have epistemic privilege and guarantees of producing better knowledge than my colleague who has another social status, right?"*

Here his position begins to slowly shift. These different traditions are still described as useful, but no longer framed as non-simplistic or sophisticated: when taken too literally and fully, they are *"somewhat caricatural"* and deterministic in a *"completely inappropriate"*, outdated way. They are therefore not entirely compatible with what seems to be his position (and the position discursively framed as most desirable): that of *"contemporary social sciences, with their sophistication"*, which use a more balanced and *"subtler"* articulation of the best of both traditions.

He then continues the discussion, focusing specifically on feminist work.

> *"Lecturer: Anyway, there are people who defend this, but I'm not convinced. [laughs] I admit there are some arguments. For example, you might say that the problems of inequality and abusive domination that women have been subjected to have been analysed mostly by female researchers. That's statistically true. (. . .) But does this mean more epistemic privilege or quality? I have the biggest doubts. I think what it means is more personal interest in the theme, right?*
>
> [Some students start talking simultaneously, making it difficult to understand what they say]
>
> *(Female) Student: But for example with the issue of women, if we talk about a theme like domestic violence, maybe a domestic violence victim will feel more comfortable talking to a woman.*
>
> *Lecturer: But think for example of research on Early Childhood. [laughs] (. . .) What would we do then? [laughs. some students laugh, tone becomes humorous] Do we get a child and take it with us to do the research?* [he

laughs, several students laugh] *I don't want to waste too much time on this, but what I want you to see is that when we start to extrapolate a principle like this, in one or two cases it looks appropriate, but when we start generalising it as a methodological principle, it becomes clear that it has feet of clay.* [laughs] *Just the other day I was talking with colleagues and we were joking about that: if we really took that principle seriously, then people wanting to study the financial crash would need to be a CEO for one of those companies!* [lecturer and several students laugh] *[Being an insider] may give access to lots of information, but does it always mean capacity for analytical deciphering of social processes? I have the greatest doubts."*

The lecturer begins this section with an acknowledgement that there are valid arguments for a feminist defence of epistemic privilege, but takes an explicitly sceptical position in relation to that defence (*"I am not convinced", "I have the biggest doubts"*), framing it as an issue of personal interest rather than epistemic quality. When a student questions his scepticism, he offers a humorous analogy. Messer-Davidow observed a similar dynamic in non-WGFS classrooms in the US: '[w]hen the students raised messy normative issues, the professor brought them back to abstract positivism with humorous reminders' (2002: 242). This humorous analogy has a powerful effect. It aligns a feminist position with two research situations positioned – both through the words used and his tone of voice – as nonsensical and ridiculous. The equating of adult female researchers studying other women, with very young children researching their peers,[3] mirrors other uses of caricatural comparisons in claims about the epistemic status of WGFS. Consider, as one among many possible examples, a response written in 1985 by the British Psychological Society Council to a proposal for the creation of a Society Section on the psychology of women,

> [members] questioned whether there is a theoretical or methodological basis to the study of the psychology of women. (. . .) [The conclusion was] the psychology of women as an area of the discipline lacks the necessary cohesion to be the basis of a scientific Section of the Society in the same way we would not expect to have a psychology of animals Section.[4]
>
> (cited in Wilkinson, 1991: 196)

I would argue that the lecturer's caricatural comparisons work to portray a feminist stance as itself also caricatural, an exaggerated position that students should be wary of aligning too closely with. The argument is then remade in a more nuanced and explicit way, when he claims that this position is appropriate in *"one or two cases"* but cannot be generalised, and therefore cannot provide a basis for sound research. His tone is both ironic and ironising, in Potter's sense: 'ironizing discourse (. . .) turns [the object of description] into talk which is motivated, distorted or erroneous in some way' (1996: 107). His use of humour plays an important role by creating an 'ironic halo' (Henriques and Pinto, 2002: 30*) around WGFS: it helps to instantiate the separation between the reasonable and the ridiculous, and between the laughing lecturer and students, on the one hand, and the laughable potential implications of feminist epistemological and methodological principles, on the other. As Carty and Musharbash suggest, '[l]aughter is dangerous. Laughter is a boundary thrown up around those laughing, those sharing the joke. Its role in demarcating difference, of collectively identifying against an Other, is as bound to processes of social *exclusion* as to inclusion. Indeed, the two are one' (2008: 214, original emphasis) The lecturer's next sentences wrap up the discussion.

> *"When we start noticing that a certain theme is studied mostly by researchers with a certain profile, like research about women's issues, I think that as a scientific community we must try to go against that.* [laughs] *There's something there that isn't completely open, completely right."*

Here, he reinforces an affirmation of the need to engage sceptically and selectively with WGFS (and other similar fields). This is done partly by alluding to a scientific 'we', unmarked in terms of the profile of its researchers, which is positioned against a feminist 'them', too dominated by researchers with the same profile and therefore not *"completely open"* and *"right"*. Interestingly enough, this lecturer's own sub-field is very heavily dominated by white middle-class men (a category he also belongs to), but that does not seem to count as a problematic over-representation of *"researchers with a certain profile"*.

Note that in this long excerpt the lecturer never explicitly rejects feminist contributions: he describes himself as completely open to them in principle, but just not entirely persuaded by their demonstrated epistemic merits. There is no direct repudiation, but his discursive framing of WGFS – the highlighting of the distance between feminist principles and contemporary social sciences; the use of analogies and humour to describe feminist insights as laughably extreme and unsuited to application outside *"one or two cases"* – casts feminism as a limited, constraining and partly untenable subject position for a *"sophisticated"* scholar. He acknowledges that these are debated issues, and that others would offer opposing arguments; however, he externalises and objectifies his personal position as widely shared and normal by saying that *"contemporary social sciences (. . .) would not subscribe"* to certain feminist claims and that *"just the other day I was talking with colleagues and we were joking about that"*. Drawing on Potter, I would say that this externalising enables him to represent his own narrative as 'a factual version' (1996: 108), rather than an interested account. In other words, it enables him to 'produce descriptions which will be treated as *mere* descriptions, reports which *tell it how it is'* (1996: 108, original emphases).

When woven together, these discursive moves produce an *epistemic splitting* of WGFS. They separate it into its *"valuable"* bits – which can be, and have been, successfully integrated into a *"subtler"* contemporary social science – and its less epistemically solid dimensions. The latter can, it is argued, be safely and justifiably disregarded because they are too specific to be of broad relevance and general application, or too outdated, biased and deterministic, potentially generating problems that *"as a scientific community we must try to go against"*. The ironisation of feminist principles is not total: they are useful up to a certain point or threshold (which he defines and marks himself) but not beyond it. In his account, WGFS' weaknesses become salient when a feminist position is taken up completely; if adopted partially, selectively and sceptically, those weaknesses are avoided and mainstream social theory is productively enriched.

It is not just the epistemic status of WGFS (or related fields) that is being negotiated in this long excerpt: through it, the lecturer is also enacting *his own* academic credibility. Reed (2006) observes that feminist critiques have been so influential that it becomes harder for non-WGFS academics to justify completely bypassing them. Evans has also noted that 'academics are generally unwilling to put their names to statements that can be interpreted as anything less than objective or considered' (1982: 61). By portraying himself as someone who is open to feminist critiques and who has carefully examined them but concluded, like other social scientists, that they have *"feet of clay"*, he is able to distance himself from the undesirable position of the (male) academic who is unreasonably and biasedly anti-feminist. In that sense, one can say that these forms of selectively partial recognition act as 'procedures of separation that at once establish the position of the discussed and authorize the discourse of the speaker' (Friese, 2001: 308).

My interviews with scholars and students show that this framing of WGFS in non-WGFS teaching contexts is not a one-off case for this lecturer, nor is it an idiosyncratic discourse specific to him. Indeed, all 9 students I interviewed, based in a range of disciplines, levels of study and institutions, described hearing this type of description of WGFS in some of their non-WGFS courses. One MA student in a non-WGFS degree in another university described one such course – an UG social theory course – as follows:

> *"The reading list had two types of references: some were treated like positive pedagogical examples, and others like negative examples. (. . .) [The message seemed to be:] 'we'll show you these bad examples so you can see what you shouldn't do'. It wasn't said as explicitly as this, but it was presented like that. (. . .) The reading list was deceptive because it seemed much more open than usual in the references included. (. . .) It had feminist references, but they were framed in class as negative examples. (. . .) The lecturers would admit the existence of heterodox positions, but immediately describe them as not to be taken entirely seriously."*

According to this student, this resulted in most students not reading or using feminist work (and other non-WGFS critical literature). An MA student at another institution, recounted similar experiences:

> *"In one UG theory course [in a mainstream social science], the lecturer mentioned feminist authors, but used them to demonstrate that there's a risk*

of taking feminist critiques too far. (. . .) My experience of <mainstream>
lecturers' relationship with feminism here [at her current university] and in
[the university where she studied as an UG] is one of devaluing, belittling it,
showing it's not entirely credible, more than a direct and explicit hostility, but
these things tend to be connected."

These ways of speaking about WGFS in non-WGFS classrooms are also not an
exclusively *Portuguese* phenomenon. After completing fieldwork in Portugal,
I observed a set of lectures for an UG social science course in a British university. In one lecture, a non-WGFS lecturer described a range of theories developed
to explain a particular social process. At the very end, he mentioned feminist
approaches. One PowerPoint slide summarised explanations proposed by feminist
scholars; the next had the title 'Maybe, but . . .' and listed two points that framed
those proposals as easily dismissible and of limited applicability. Each point was
introduced with a (sexist and heteronormative) joke that elicited much laughter
from the 600+ students present. The significant commonalities between this UK
example (and other episodes described in the international WGFS literature)[5]
and my observations in Portugal suggest that these forms of boundary-work are
deployed, and intelligible, across (national and disciplinary) borders.

Research on gender is relevant . . . but can be done (better) with non-WGFS theories

In the analysis above, I drew attention to how the lecturer affirmed the possibility
of integrating the *"valuable"* dimensions of WGFS within mainstream social theory, thereby bypassing WGFS' weaknesses. This is a significant discursive move
because it frames WGFS as potentially partly replaceable by non-feminist work.
I therefore want to devote this section to examining other examples of claims that
gender research is important, but is sounder if/when it uses non-WGFS theories
and/or is conducted by non-WGFS scholars.

An interview excerpt provides a vivid illustration of such claims. The interviewee is a non-WGFS scholar who I contacted after hearing him intervene in a
discussion about the current state of social theory, held as part of a national conference in his social science discipline. He mentioned then that he had recently begun
to look at gender (as one among other variables) in a project using mainstream
social theories, and had had some surprises. I was curious to hear more about
those surprises, and arranged an interview. He spent much of our short interview
explaining that he was finding it enjoyable to research gender and confessing that,
to his initial surprise (*"I was a bit naïve before"*, he said), he was learning a huge
amount from that experience and the work of WGFS colleagues. He then added,

"I really admire and support the work of my colleagues who've been studying
gender for many years. But I also often tease them, saying that we need to

develop measures to protect men! Because you're always interested in find-
ing positive things about women. I'm not interested in finding positive OR
negative things about men OR women! (. . .) In my research I've been using
some of the latest social theories. (. . .) They're not new to me. But they've led
to results that my [WGFS] colleagues weren't expecting. (. . .) They couldn't
believe it, but it was true. The data demonstrated it! So I've learned a lot
from gender research, but I think my colleagues who do it would be able to
understand their objects much better if they weren't always so attached to
gender theories and looked at issues also from these broader perspectives."

He speaks of WGFS researchers as colleagues who do relevant and valid work but
are limited, because they are *"always interested"* in finding certain results or asking specific questions. That is not the case with him, or the mainstream theories he
uses to study gender: he is not *"interested"* and focuses exclusively on the data.
Working from this perspective, he is able to generate unexpected insight, fully
supported by data (and therefore *"true"*). This narrative rests on, and produces,
a binary opposition between the more open, impartial and data-driven nature of
his (and other mainstream) work, and the *"always interested"* and less broad –
and hence potentially limiting – stance of WGFS scholars. He also refers to the
fact that he *"always teases"* WGFS colleagues, something framed as normal and
unproblematic; this confirms other interviewees' accounts (as discussed in chapter 3) of the existence of a *"culture of teasing"* of WGFS.

I was also keen to observe how the relationship between mainstream research
and WGFS scholarship was framed in conferences, key sites in which 'academic
authority is negotiated and established performatively' (Friese, 2001: 286; see
also Henderson, 2016). In one case, I observed a senior Portuguese non-WGFS
sociologist present a paper at an international sociology conference. She began
by explaining that she was presenting a theoretical paper which will *"propose*
an articulation of the concepts of gender and class. This implies a confluence of
Marxism and Weberian approaches with feminism."[6] She showed several slides
describing the first two approaches and discussed them at length, briefly mention-
ing criticisms of these frameworks proposed by *"radical feminism in the 70s"*.
There was no slide on feminist approaches, and no post-1970s feminist work was
mentioned. When she finished, a non-Portuguese delegate asked how she planned
to empirically operationalise this theoretical framework, and noted that she was
using *"a very classical definition of gender and class"* and might find it useful to
consider more recent feminist work. In her reply, the presenter acknowledged that
feminist work had made important contributions, but explained that

"We're pretty sure that when thinking about women's position these [classi-
cal] theories of class are still relevant, because when feminism talks about
women, it tends to assume that women are almost the same, are a homoge-
neous unit, but upper-class women don't have the same living conditions as
lower-class women. Maybe upper-class women have better conditions, more

power than lower-class men. That's why we need to conceptualise things through these classical theories."

By highlighting the relevance of feminist critiques of classical frameworks and feminist theories of class, but describing them as simplistic, the presenter simultaneously acknowledges feminist work *and* reaffirms the higher explanatory power and applicability of non-feminist social theories. The latter can be improved by feminism, but ultimately they are the best analytical tools. This narrative did not, however, go undisputed: as was evident also in the lecture example discussed above, audiences can, and do, disrupt framings of WGFS as flawed or limited. Indeed, periods of questions and debate in conferences can offer 'particularly fertile (. . .) settings' for the study of negotiations of academic hierarchies, 'as categories, boundaries and consensus [tend to be] recurrent topics of discussion' (Potter, 1988: 18).

After the presenter's response, the non-Portuguese delegate asked to speak again: *"I think we need to move away from the classical frameworks of class, because they're insufficient to explain how societies are organised now."* She also added that feminists have formulated several frameworks that foreground the multidimensionality of women's class position. In her contribution, this delegate inverts the portrayal of the two sets of theories: classical theories are represented as important but simplistic and outdated, while feminist frameworks are featured as more complex, robust and better suited to an analysis of contemporary societies. When examining this example, the key question to be asked is not which theories are *really* better or more sophisticated, nor whether this particular scholar, is less competent because she is unfamiliar with recent feminist scholarship. Indeed, it is important to note that the very limited (but growing) stock of WGFS publications in libraries or WGFS courses in universities severely constrains Portuguese scholars' opportunities of accessing, and gaining in-depth knowledge of, past or current WGFS scholarship.

The important question is, rather, how dominant modes of describing and evaluating the epistemic status of WGFS act to 'locate and contain it, limit the discussion, [and] control the work's possible reception' (Code, 1995: 10), and how communities and audiences respond to this, reproducing, resisting or reframing those discourses. But even that question is far from straightforward. This episode took place in a disciplinary conference, so one could analyse it differently. As Harding writes, 'appeal to "the ancients" [is] frequently a useful strategy in the face of disbelief. One can appeal to the forces responsible for the origins of modern science itself (. . .) to increase the plausibility of [a] claim' (1991: 115) (see also Acker, 1989). From this perspective, the referencing of the key (male) names of a discipline may be understood as a way of securing space and recognition for WGFS in a context where such research might be devalued, rather than simply dismissing that reference to classical male authors as an instance of marginalisation and containment of feminist contributions. This means that mainstream engagement with WGFS may have plural and contradictory effects.

The uses of, and reactions to, Pierre Bourdieu's *La Domination Masculine* (1998) offer an interesting illustration of those contradictions. The French scholar is a canonical and extremely influential author in Portugal, and one of the most frequently cited names in sociology (Machado, 2009; Madureira Pinto and Pereira, 2007). He dedicated one of his last books – in English, *Masculine Domination* (2001) – to gender. It has been the object of intense debate, with WGFS scholars in France, Portugal and elsewhere denouncing his refusal to cite or recognise the work of feminist authors (Amâncio, 2003; Armengaud and Jasser, 1994; Ferreira, 2001; Mottier, 2002). Witz notes that he describes feminists as having a 'tendency (. . .) to let their politically interested stance get in the way of an appropriately "reflexive analysis" and to produce "bad science"' (2004: 215) (see also Ramalho, 2001), and argues that this allows Bourdieu to position himself as someone who can 'mak[e] a better job of engaging with the problem of masculine domination than feminists have' (2004: 215).

The book, published in Portuguese in 1999, was mentioned (unprompted) by 9 interviewees and in 5 events. Students and junior WGFS academics (who were students when the book was published) described it as an *"unavoidable reference"*, *"a revelation"* with a *"powerful pedagogical effect"*; other interviewees said they have *"a love/hate relationship with it"*; several established WGFS scholars referred to it as *"offensive"* and *"unacceptable"*. According to the latter, the book directly contributed to making gender a credible and worthwhile object of study in Portuguese social science. However, this heightened recognition of gender's relevance comes, they argue, at the expense of the continued invisibility of WGFS scholarship. This is not just because Bourdieu himself does not engage with it (or even adequately acknowledge it), but also because Portuguese non-WGFS scholars now tend to draw heavily (in some cases, exclusively) on Bourdieu when discussing gender. Two interviewees spoke at length about the book's contradictory impact on the status of WGFS:

> *"I was so shocked when I read Bourdieu's book. What he does is invent, in scare quotes, (. . .) what feminists had already enunciated decades ago. However, he didn't include or mention them. But what's curious is that, as soon as it came out, the book became a weapon for me, I used it in all possible occasions. Any occasion would be good to remind colleagues of the book and quote it somehow, to show that my research themes are actually important. (. . .)*
> *MMP: How would you use the book as a weapon?*
> *In all occasions, in chats over lunch, in the university café, (. . .) we often have theoretical debates over coffee and in corridors, and I seize any opportunity."*
>
> Senior WGFS scholar

> *"Since the book's publication, everyone thinks that if a great foreign sociologist takes the time to write a book about [gender], then the issue must have*

some relevance, right? So everyone mentions gender, but by citing Bourdieu, who as we know, does not cite anyone! When Bourdieu wrote about it, the issue got legitimated within the mainstream, because (. . .) he's such an influential figure [in Portugal]. (. . .) So in a way it's good he wrote that book, although from a feminist perspective I found it insulting. It makes me think: does it contribute? Does it bring anything good? We can ask that.

MMP: What would you answer if I asked that?

Like all fundamental questions, it doesn't have an easy answer. I mean, on the one hand it's good, because it positions gender as a problem worthy of analysis. But on the other hand, the linear way in which that incorporation's made, how it makes feminist authors invisible, it leaves everything as it is, it changes nothing."

Senior WGFS scholar

The uses of Bourdieu's book in Portugal, France and other countries show that it can be extremely difficult to assess WGFS' epistemic status at a given moment, or evaluate its changes over time. WGFS insights – like the need to critically analyse 'masculine domination' – are increasingly recognised by mainstream scholars, but with complex and contradictory effects on the actual reception of WGFS work. Is this mainstream engagement beneficial or detrimental? As the last interviewee argued, this question *"doesn't have a linear answer"*. For many student interviewees, Bourdieu's book provided valuable opportunities to read and write about gender in recognised ways within curricula that did not engage with WGFS.[7] Simultaneously, the book has contributed to make it legitimate to study gender *without* WGFS. The book makes WGFS themes visible, but WGFS scholarship invisible. Thus, it has both created space for analyses of WGFS themes, *and* limited the possibilities of claiming that a distinctively *feminist* approach is necessary for such analyses. This shows, therefore, that the epistemic status of WGFS is composed of many different elements – the status of its concepts, theories, analytics, methods, scholars, of WGFS as a field, to name a few – which do not always overlap neatly or change at the same speed. Indeed, the growing recognition of some elements may come at the expense of the recognition of others.

My WGFS produces better knowledge than yours: WGFS scholars splitting WGFS scholarship

I have thus far discussed epistemic splitting as something that non-WGFS scholars do to WGFS. And yet, WGFS scholars are also actively involved and invested in representing WGFS as a field that is partly within and partly outside the space of proper knowledge. The power to dismiss some WGFS scholarship as epistemically deficient 'is not something that is divided between those who have it and hold it exclusively, and those who do not have it and are subject to it' (Foucault, 2003 [1976]: 29). During fieldwork, I heard several WGFS scholars dismissing other WGFS work on the grounds that it strays beyond the threshold of epistemic acceptability, and explicitly distancing themselves from that work.

> *"I say I'm a feminist and colleagues sometimes stare at me, surprised (. . .). They have this reaction because there's a radical feminism (. . .) that's really not appropriate from a social science perspective. (. . .) Or that extremely irritating feminism that says that men are different from women but in a bad way, women are much better because they're caring! (. . .) It's unacceptable, isn't it, because a social scientist can't think in that way! So anything that comes close to this type of discourse, it's obvious that one has to distance oneself, demarcate oneself from it."*
>
> Interview, senior scholar in a social science discipline,
with WGFS expertise

> *"I identify with gender studies but a certain kind of gender studies, not all of it. (. . .) I identify with more conciliatory and less radical positions, let's put it this way. I'm sorry to say this, but there are things that profoundly irritate me. (. . .) For example, the Congresso Feminista[8] was very interesting. (. . .) But some people would get up, speak very loudly and say 'equality for women!' and, really, come on! It wasn't a demonstration, nor a rally for a political party, it was a scientific conference! I think that's definitely going too far!"*
>
> Interview, junior scholar in a social science discipline,
with WGFS expertise

These comments share several features with the statements by non-WGFS scholars analysed in the previous sections. Like the lecturer in the long extract (pp. 100-104), the scholar speaking in the first excerpt above describes the need to *"demarcate oneself"* from other WGFS scholarship as an *"obvious"* one, because certain strands of WGFS are not *"appropriate from a social science perspective"*. The second excerpt draws on the idea that there is a point beyond which one can say that WGFS is *"going too far"* and is not producing or presenting knowledge in a manner suited to an academic conference.

In my fieldwork, WGFS scholars did not make these kinds of claims in public WGFS settings; they were limited to interviews, informal interactions and semi-public sites, such as classrooms. I want to examine one example of their use in teaching, taken from a class on WGFS offered within a non-WGFS course for non-WGFS social science PG students. The lecturer is a senior WGFS scholar and is reviewing gender theories.

> *"Fausto-Sterling estimated that 4% of the population is intersex. Later, she reduced it to 1.728% [laughs] and even admitted this estimate is based on numerous errors and extrapolations, and on cases obviously unknown. If we exclude cases that other experts don't identify as intersex, the final estimate comes down to 0.018 cases per 100 people. My problem with Fausto-Sterling*

is that, although I believe that quantity isn't everything, I find it troubling to draw on exceptions with such limited expression to question theories that cover the remaining 99%. (. . .) To take these cases and argue there are no sexes, there are biological continua, each person is more here or there, I confess this doesn't convince me, especially bearing in mind that as a social scientist, although not a positivist one, I try to find regularities, so this theory is of no use to me at all. Especially considering that if we want to analyse statistics, we don't find intersex people there. [laughs] I find men and women, and don't know if they are trans, or

(Male) Student [interrupting lecturer]: That shows there's a problem with the statistics! [laughs]

[some other students laugh]

Lecturer: No, the problem is that this idea that gender is arbitrary then led to a huge amount of literature in the 90s discussing how many genders there are. (. . .) These gender theories, in the end, lead to an impossibility. Just the other day, I was in a seminar with a colleague who said [changes her tone of voice, taking on a parodying tone] 'gender theory has nothing to do with men and women, it's about a relational model looking at the masculine and feminine, and so it doesn't necessarily have to be about concrete men and women'. [resumes usual tone] This for me makes no sense at all!! One finds texts which argue that it's impossible to define the characteristics of men and women. (. . .) There are other authors who go even further, and this sounds like a bit of a joke, I know, but sometimes one feels like laughing a bit! There are authors who are very serious, they do good research on all sorts of levels, (. . .) but then argue that [takes on an ironic tone] 'we should just talk about people with a vagina and people with a penis'. [several students laugh] [reverts to original tone of voice] *This is not a conceptual alternative I can use!"*

This excerpt includes many of the discursive moves I identified earlier in non-WGFS scholars' claims about WGFS. The lecturer's reference to statistics at the start delimits the applicability and wider relevance of the theory being discussed; this mirrors the non-WGFS lecturer's claim that feminist principles are valid in only *"one or two cases"* but cannot be generalised beyond that. Another feature they share is the use of humour, here reinforced by the description of aspects of other WGFS authors' work as *"a bit of a joke"* (split from the rest of their work, which is *"very serious"*, *"good research"*) and the implicit invitation (widely taken up by students) to laugh because *"sometimes one feels like laughing a bit"*. This account of other scholars' arguments, and the use of active voicing (Potter, 1996) in high-pitched tones to describe their views, positions them as unsophisticated and laughable. As in earlier examples, the lecturer's statement that *"this doesn't convince me"*, announced as a confession, enables a self-presentation as an open-minded, reasonable scholar who has considered the arguments and evidence, but has not been persuaded. This configures a sceptical frame (Potter,

1996) for students' engagement with particular WGFS theories. In this account, WGFS theories are portrayed as having varying degrees of acceptability, with the speaker's own position framed as firmly grounded within the realm of the serious, some positions going a bit too far, and others even further, becoming a *"bit of a joke"*.

As I suggested in the previous section, the issues that for me are key in analysing these discourses are not whether the WGFS scholars making these claims are *really* feminist or whether the particular theories dismissed in these quotes are being described fairly. That is not to say that those issues were not salient for me, both during fieldwork and as I analyse this material. I personally find some of the dismissed theories and authors not only useful, but formative to my thinking. Consequently, these elements of the classes and interviews – as well as the claims by non-WGFS scholars analysed in the previous sections – annoyed me greatly at the time (although I did not admit that to participants). This was because I saw these claims as misleading 'straw-[wo]man' simplifications of strands of WGFS scholarship that I consider *"sophisticated"* (to use the non-WGFS lecturer's terms) and *"serious"* (to quote the WGFS lecturer above). They annoyed me also because they ridiculed my own academic subject position. As Hemmings notes, stories about theories do not just describe and locate schools of thought, but also '*subjects* (. . .) and this (. . .) makes them affectively saturated for both authors and readers. They are not neutral, and do not ask us to remain neutral' (2011: 5, original emphasis).

Nonetheless, like Hemmings or Hughes (2004), I consider it helpful here to 'shift priority away from who said what, away from thinking about' these feminist interventions 'in terms of "good" and "bad" authors' (Hemmings, 2011: 21), and 'take fuller account of the conditions of (. . .) production' (Hughes, 2004: 103) of boundary-work. The protagonists of the examples analysed in this section are all well-respected WGFS scholars with an unequivocal commitment to increasing the space and recognition of WGFS, and who have themselves struggled to be fully recognised in their institutions. Some of them are based in disciplines or departments with epistemic climates hostile to WGFS. A scholar featured in one of the examples above explained in the interview that distancing herself from 'more radical' WGFS scholarship had been, especially at the start of her career, a key tool with which to demonstrate to her mainstream colleagues that her work was proper knowledge. This had allowed her to secure spaces to research and teach WGFS that would have otherwise been denied. She says that she feels ambivalent about this, and has asked herself many times whether it was a productive strategy. Indeed, forms of distancing from other feminists, much like the quoting of Bourdieu analysed above, can both *generate and withhold* epistemic status for WGFS, so the issues here are not straightforward. Moreover, framing other strands of scholarship as incapable of producing valuable knowledge is not by any means an exceptional act. Much of the language and rituals of contemporary academic practice rest and depend on boundary-work that highlights the superior analytical power of one's claims vis-à-vis competing claims.

Therefore, rather than correct or demonise these particular accounts, what I want to do is draw on them to argue that WGFS scholars concerned with the partial recognition of WGFS cannot look only at mainstream claims for the roots and manifestations of those damaging forms of boundary-work. WGFS scholars must also critically analyse our own boundary-work, as individuals and as a community, to examine how it too may reproduce and legitimate a representation of WGFS scholarship as precariously positioned vis-à-vis epistemic thresholds, as always partially 'too far' or 'too much' or 'not enough'. If we want to argue that the claims that non-WGFS scholars make in conferences or classrooms create problematic hierarchies between fields, then we must be prepared to recognise that our own public and semi-public statements about the epistemic status of 'other' WGFS are part of these broader, power-invested demarcations of what counts as proper knowledge.

Unpacking the splitting, and dismissive recognition, of WGFS

Commenting on the dwindling support for, and recognition of, the humanities within and beyond contemporary universities, the literature scholar Graça Capinha asks: 'is it that, in the end, what's made visible is only what reproduces the dominant models of representation and is easily recognisable epistemologically? (. . .) Is what cannot be appropriated and easily translated by the dominant knowledges (. . .) rendered inaudible?' (2008*). In this chapter I have examined those questions vis-à-vis contemporary forms of partial recognition of WGFS. I have done so through an analysis of a particular type of statement – the argument that WGFS can produce proper knowledge *but* only in some conditions. In the non-WGFS sites and events that I observed, these claims were the most frequent form of *speaking* about WGFS (although it was even more frequent for scholars to *not speak* of WGFS at all).

Much leadership literature has drawn attention to the 'power of but' (Van Brocklin, 2010). Thompson calls it the '#1 Killer Phrase of all time: a politically correct, sweet 'n sour, little two-step that gives with one hand as it takes back with the other' (1994: 7). As I have shown, 'yes, but' claims also play an important role in academic discourse. Briefly commenting on its role as a mode of academic criticism, Barcan notes that 'yes, but' functions as a 'logic of blockage' (1995: 92). In Portugal and many other countries, WGFS scholarship is often described publicly in those positive, yet adversarial terms, and this does indeed create blockages. The 'but' at the centre of these adversarial claims enacts, and depends on, the marking of an epistemic threshold, i.e. a discursive boundary that separates proper academic knowledge from knowledge allegedly too outdated, specific, interested. Through this 'yes, but', WGFS is portrayed as straddling that epistemic threshold: some elements of it (people, concepts, analytics, theories, methodological or epistemological principles) are (brought) within, others are (cast) outside. The splitting of WGFS allows non-WGFS scholars to engage selectively with WGFS and 'to protect themselves against any of feminism's difficult questions' (Skeggs, 2008: 681). This is because that splitting provides a supposedly legitimate epistemological rationale for taking into account the WGFS insights which broadly fit mainstream frameworks, while simultaneously rejecting as epistemologically unsound the WGFS critiques of those frameworks.[9] This produces a double move, whereby WGFS' epistemic status is both asserted *and* denied, enabling what I have called a *dismissive recognition* of feminist scholarship. These discursive moves are, thus, one important means through which, to use the words by Campbell (1992) that opened this chapter, WGFS scholarship is simultaneously replenished and contained in many contemporary academic sites.

These modes of epistemic splitting and dismissive recognition have two features that make them particularly effective and persuasive. Firstly, they express *no direct repudiation of WGFS* and no incitements to audiences to steer completely clear of it. Some consideration of WGFS is more or less explicitly encouraged, but positions of partial engagement and full alignment with WGFS are contrasted in ways that frame the former as more desirable and balanced. This does two things. On the one hand, it fits with, and helps to maintain, a public epistemic climate of openness to WGFS which, as discussed in chapter 3, is especially important in the performative university, as it can strengthen institutions' potential 'market value' by allowing them to benefit from the student interest, and the research funding and ratings that WGFS can attract. On the other hand, it validates the credibility of the speaker as a reasonable, informed and open-minded academic who has kept up-to-date with theoretical developments, thoughtfully considered the merits and limitations of WGFS, learned from its valuable arguments, incorporated them . . . and then moved on.

Secondly, the *epistemic threshold* produced in these discourses *can be positioned in many different places*, according to the characteristics of each boundary-work (con)text. Indeed, and as other analysts of scientists' discourses have argued, 'the strength of this justificatory strategy [of using the notion of "bad science" to disqualify others' work] is its in-built flexibility – allowing the discussant to dismiss any scientific enterprise if they can establish a believable process of contamination' (Kerr *et al.*, 1997: 288; Potter, 1988). This flexible positioning of epistemic thresholds enables institutions, communities or individuals to adjust their position vis-à-vis WGFS according to the 'contingencies of the moment: the adversaries then and there, the stakes, the (. . .) audiences' (Gieryn, 1999: 5). The contingency and variability of epistemic thresholds, and the fact that scholars benefit from positioning them in one place rather than another, were nevertheless rarely acknowledged in my fieldwork sites. Claims are externalised and reified, and thus made to appear as widely shared, neutral descriptions of the intrinsic characteristics of the scholarship being discussed.

I see adversative statements as producing these truth- and power-effects (Foucault, 2003 [1976]), but also want to argue that such effects must not be taken as given or straightforward; they are contradictory and cannot be read directly off discourses alone. I highlighted, for example, that referring to WGFS insights without foregrounding WGFS authors can make WGFS disappear, but may also create the conditions for its appearance in a particular classroom or conference. Moreover, a speaker may deploy several strategies to frame claims as persuasive, but this does not mean audiences will automatically identify with the subject positions discursively constituted as most desirable. Not only do students directly question lecturers' narratives, as we have seen, but they may also remain silent in class but later comment on how outdated a lecturer's position is, as I sometimes observed during fieldwork. Analysing public claims about WGFS, as I attempted to do in this chapter, is therefore an important but limited approach to the study of negotiations of epistemic status. It can help identify how discourses are structured so as to 'permit [the] separating out from among all the statements which are possible those that will be acceptable within (. . .) a field of scientificity' (Foucault, 1980 [1977]: 197) but it is less able to explore whether those demarcations of acceptability are themselves accepted. Therefore, we must consider how WGFS scholars engage with these discourses, and how the truth- and power-effects of these claims are shaped by the contexts and conditions in which they are made. I explore these two issues in the next chapters.

Notes

1 As a pre-fieldwork pilot, I analysed a Portuguese UG sociology textbook and found that gender was framed as a relatively simple topic, not requiring much extra reading or specialist theoretical knowledge (unlike class, for example). Mainstream authors (such as Giddens) were framed as protagonists in the theorising of gender, whereas WGFS scholars were mentioned very rarely and subsumed under the general category of 'female authors'. Liinason (2011) and Eagleton (1996) analyse WGFS textbooks and show that comparable forms of erasure and partial recognition also occur *within* the field. Goldstein (2007) describes a textbook author's experiences of writing sections on gender and negotiating their content with publishers.

2 For other Portuguese discussions of this, see Amâncio (2003), Ferreira (2001), Joaquim (2001), Nogueira (2001), Pinto (2008) and Pinto-Coelho and Mota-Ribeiro (2016).

3 It must, however, be noted that many scholars have argued for the epistemological, ethical and political importance of involving children and young people in the designing and doing of research about their lives (Best, 2007). My own research with young people (Pereira, 2012) has demonstrated both the analytical value of this, and the positive impacts it can have on young people's lives.

4 For a similar analogy, see Brunt *et al.*'s (1983) discussion of the equating of WGFS with 'budgerigar studies' in their UK institution.

5 See, for example, Morrison *et al.* (2005) for an analysis of lecturers' use of sexist jokes (and students' reactions to them) in a British university.

6 The presentation and discussion were conducted in English, so all quotes are in speakers' own words.

7 This was also my experience as an UG Sociology student. On one compulsory social theory course, I wanted to write my essay on gender, using feminist theory. I was told by the module convener that this would not be acceptable, because feminist scholarship "isn't real sociological theory, as it is grounded just on the experiences of those in a particular social position". As Bourdieu was a key name in the module's reading list, I used his work as the starting point and framework for my discussion of gender (which also included feminist authors), and as a result I was able to get the essay accepted.

8 A national academic-activist WGFS conference organised in June 2008 by the feminist organisation UMAR.
9 Analysing arguments used by British universities and professional associations in the 1980s to justify not giving space to WGFS, Wilkinson makes a similar point: '[t]he insistence that psychology is "science", that feminism is "politics" (. . .) is an argument that is (. . .) extremely powerful, for it provides mainstream psychologists with legitimate grounds for dismissing feminist research as illegitimate' (1991: 195).

References

Abbott, Pamela (1991). "Feminist Perspectives in Sociology: The Challenge to 'Mainstream' Orthodoxy" in J. Aaron and S. Walby (eds.), *Out of the Margins: Women's Studies in the Nineties* (pp.181–190). London: Falmer Press.

Abbott, Pamela, *et al.* (2005). *Introduction to Sociology: Feminist Perspectives* (3rd ed.). London: Routledge.

Acker, Joan (1989). "Making Gender Visible" in R. Wallace (ed.), *Feminism and Sociological Theory* (pp.65–81). London: Sage.

Amâncio, Lígia (2003). "O Género nos Discursos das Ciências Sociais". *Análise Social, XXXVIII* (168), 687–714.

Armengaud, Françoise and Jasser, Ghaïss (1994). "Une Offensive Majeure Contre les Études Féministes". *Nouvelles Questions Féministes, 15* (4), 7–20.

Barcan, Ruth (1995). "The Global Confessional: Growing up with the Media". *Continuum, 11* (2), 82–94.

Best, Amy L. (ed.) (2007). *Representing Youth: Methodological Issues in Critical Youth Studies*. New York: New York University Press.

Bourdieu, Pierre (1998). *La Domination Masculine*. Paris: Seuil.

Boxer, Marilyn J. (1998). *When Women Ask the Questions: Creating Women's Studies in America*. Baltimore, MD: Johns Hopkins University Press.

Brunt, Rosalind, *et al.* (1983). "Sell-Out or Challenge? The Contradiction of a Masters in Women's Studies". *Women's Studies International Forum, 6* (3), 283–290.

Campbell, Kate (1992). "Introduction: Matters of Theory and Practice – or, We'll Be Coming Out the Harbour" in K. Campbell (ed.), *Critical Feminism: Argument in the Disciplines* (pp.1–24). Buckingham: Open University Press.

Capinha, Graça (2008). *Puzzles e Móbiles: Para uma Dramática da Verdade*. Paper Presented at the Conference "Caminhos de Futuro: Novos Mapas para as Ciências Sociais e Humanas", Coimbra.

Carty, John and Musharbash, Yasmine (2008). "You've *Got* to be Joking: Asserting the Analytical Value of Humour and Laughter in Contemporary Anthropology". *Anthropological Forum, 18* (3), 209–217.

Chen, Peiying (2004). *Acting "Otherwise": The Institutionalization of Women's/Gender Studies in Taiwan Universities*. London: RoutledgeFalmer.

Code, Lorraine (1995). *Rhetorical Spaces: Essays on Gendered Locations*. New York: Routledge.

Eagleton, Mary (1996). "Who's Who and Where's Where: Constructing Feminist Literary Studies". *Feminist Review, 53*, 1–23.

Evans, Mary (1982). "In Praise of Theory: The Case for Women's Studies". *Feminist Review, 10*, 61–74.

Evans, Mary (2003). *Gender and Social Theory*. Buckingham: Open University.

Ferreira, Virgínia (2001). "Estudos sobre as Mulheres em Portugal: A Construção de um Novo Campo Científico". *ex aequo, 5*, 9–25.

Foster, Emma, *et al.* (2013). "The Personal Is Not Political: At Least in the UK's Top Politics and IR Departments". *British Journal of Politics and International Relations, 15* (4), 566–585.

Foucault, Michel (1980 [1977]). "The Confession of the Flesh" in C. Gordon (ed.), *Power-Knowledge: Selected Interviews and Other Writings, 1972–1977* (pp.194–228). Brighton: Harvester Press.

Foucault, Michel (2003 [1976]). *Society Must Be Defended: Lectures at the Collège de France, 1975–76.* New York: Picador.

Friese, Heidrun (2001). "Thresholds in the Ambit of Discourse: On the Establishment of Authority at Academic Conferences" in P. Becker and W. Clark (eds.), *Little Tools of Knowledge: Historical Essays on Academic and Bureaucratic Practices* (pp.285–312). Ann Arbor: University of Michigan Press.

Gerhard, Ute (2004). "'Illegitimate Daughters': The Relationship Between Feminism and Sociology" in B.L. Marshall and A. Witz (eds.), *Engendering the Social: Feminist Encounters with Sociological Theory* (pp.114–136). Maidenhead: Open University Press.

Gieryn, Thomas (1999). *Cultural Boundaries of Science: Credibility on the Line.* Chicago: University of Chicago Press.

Goldstein, Joshua (2007). "Gender in the IR Textbook and Beyond". *International Studies Perspectives, 8* (3), 320–322.

Harding, Sandra (1991). *Whose Science? Whose Knowledge? Thinking from Women's Lives.* Milton Keynes: Open University.

Hawkesworth, Mary (2010). "From Constitutive Outside to the Politics of Extinction: Critical Race Theory, Feminist Theory, and Political Theory". *Political Research Quarterly, 63* (3), 686–696.

Hemmings, Clare (2011). *Why Stories Matter: The Political Grammar of Feminist Theory.* Durham, NC: Duke University Press.

Henderson, Emily F. (2016). *Eventful Gender: An Ethnographic Exploration of Gender Knowledge Production at International Academic Conferences.* PhD Thesis, UCL Institute of Education.

Henriques, Fernanda and Pinto, Teresa (2002). "Educação e Género: Dos Anos 70 ao Final do Século XX". *ex aequo, 6*, 11–54.

Hughes, Christina (2004). "Perhaps She Was Having a Bad Hair Day!: Taking Issue with Ungenerous Readings of Feminist Texts". *European Journal of Women's Studies, 11* (1), 103–109.

Joaquim, Teresa (2001). "Os Estudos sobre as Mulheres em Filosofia". *ex aequo, 5*, 69–83.

Joaquim, Teresa (2004). "*ex aequo*: Contributo Decisivo para um Campo de Estudos em Portugal". *Revista Estudos Feministas, 12* (3), 88–93.

Kerr, Anne, *et al.* (1997). "The New Genetics: Professionals' Discursive Boundaries". *The Sociological Review, 45* (2), 279–303.

Liinason, Mia (2011). *Feminism and the Academy: Exploring the Politics of Institutionalization in Gender Studies in Sweden.* Lund: Media-Tryck Lund.

Machado, Fernando Luís (2009). "Meio Século de Investigação Sociológica em Portugal – uma Interpretação Empiricamente Ilustrada". *Sociologia, 19*, 283–343.

Madureira Pinto, José and Pereira, Virgílio Borges (eds.) (2007). *Pierre Bourdieu: A Teoria da Prática e a Construção da Sociologia em Portugal.* Porto: Afrontamento.

McNeil, Maureen (1993). "Dancing with Foucault: Feminism and Power-Knowledge" in C. Ramazanoğlu (ed.), *Up Against Foucault* (pp.147–178). London: Routledge.

Messer-Davidow, Ellen (2002). *Disciplining Feminism: From Social Activism to Academic Discourse*. Durham, NC: Duke University Press.

Morrison, Zoë, *et al.* (2005). "'Stop Making it Such a Big Issue': Perceptions and Experiences of Gender Inequality by Undergraduates at a British University". *Women's Studies International Forum, 28* (2/3), 150–162.

Mottier, Véronique (2002). "Masculine Domination: Gender and Power in Bourdieu's Writings". *Feminist Theory, 3* (3), 345–359.

Neves, Sofia (2012). "Género e Ciências Sociais . . . ou Quando a Ciência Também é Política . . ." in S. Neves (ed.), *Género e Ciências Sociais* (pp.15–24). Castêlo da Maia: ISMAI.

Nogueira, Conceição (2001). *Um Novo Olhar sobre as Relações Sociais de Género: Feminismo e Perspectivas Críticas na Psicologia Social*. Lisboa: Fundação Calouste Gulbenkian.

Pereira, Charmaine (2000). "Feminist Knowledge". *Seminar, 490,* article 10.

Pereira, Maria do Mar (2012). *Fazendo Género no Recreio: A Negociação do Género em Espaço Escolar*. Lisboa: Imprensa de Ciências Sociais.

Pickering, Andrew (1995). *The Mangle of Practice: Time, Agency, and Science*. Chicago, IL: University of Chicago Press.

Pinto-Coelho, Zara and Mota-Ribeiro, Silvana (2016). "Gender, Sex and Sexuality in Two Open-Access Communication Journals Published in Portugal: A Critical Overview of Current Discursive Practices" in C. Cerqueira, *et al.* (eds.), *Gender in Focus: (New) Trends in Media* (pp.49–66). Braga: CECS.

Pinto, Teresa (2008). *A Formação Profissional das Mulheres no Ensino Industrial Público (1884–1910): Realidades e Representações*. PhD Thesis, Universidade Aberta.

Potter, Jonathan (1988). "Cutting Cakes: A Study of Psychologists' Social Categorisations". *Philosophical Psychology, 1* (1), 17–33.

Potter, Jonathan (1996). *Representing Reality: Discourse, Rhetoric and Social Construction*. London: Sage.

Ramalho, Maria Irene (2001). "Os Estudos sobre as Mulheres e o Saber: Onde se Conclui que o Poético é Feminista". *ex aequo, 5,* 107–122.

Reed, Kate (2006). *New Directions in Social Theory: Race, Gender and the Canon*. London: Sage.

Rowley, Christina and Shepherd, Laura (2012). "Contemporary Politics: Using the 'F' Word and Teaching Gender in International Relations" in C. Gormley-Heenan and S. Lightfoot (eds.), *Teaching Politics and International Relations* (pp.146–161). Houndmills: Palgrave Macmillan.

Simbürger, Elisabeth (2015). "El Género y La Escritura Selectiva de la Teoría Social: Notas para la Reescritura de lo Social". *Cuadernos de Teoría Social, 1* (2), 33–47.

Skeggs, Beverley (2008). "The Dirty History of Feminism and Sociology: Or the War of Conceptual Attrition". *The Sociological Review, 56* (4), 670–690.

Stacey, Judith and Thorne, Barrie (1985). "The Missing Feminist Revolution in Sociology". *Social Problems, 32* (4), 301–316.

Thompson, Charles (1994). *Yes, But . . .: The Top 40 Killer Phrases and How You Can Fight Them*. New York: HarperCollins.

Van Brocklin, Valerie (2010). *Leading with "Yes, and": Losing the Limits of "Yes but"*. Retrieved 02/04/2016, from http://lawofficer.com/2010/01/12/leading-with-yes-and-losing-the-limits-of-yes-but/

Whelan, Emma (2001). "Politics by Other Means: Feminism and Mainstream Science Studies". *The Canadian Journal of Sociology/Cahiers Canadiens de Sociologie, 26* (4), 535–581.

Wilkinson, Sue (1991). "Why Psychology (Badly) Needs Feminism" in J. Aaron and S. Walby (eds.), *Out of the Margins: Women's Studies in the Nineties* (pp.191–203). London: Falmer Press.

Witz, Anne (2004). "Anamnesis and Amnesis in Bourdieu's Work: The Case for a Feminist Anamnesis" in L. Adkins and B. Skeggs (eds.), *Feminism After Bourdieu* (pp.211–223). Oxford: Blackwell.

Chapter 5

Putting WGFS on the map(s)

The boundary-work of WGFS scholars

A place on the map (. . .) is, after all, also a locatable place in history.

(Mohanty, 2003: 111; see also Rich, 1995: 212)

The maps which Adrienne Rich and Chandra Mohanty have in mind in the quote above represent cities, countries and continents. But their argument that a place on the map is a place in history can be stretched to think also of epistemic maps, charting the relative location and value of different forms of knowledge. A place in epistemic maps is, after all, also a place in the histories of scholarly knowledge that get told, and in the institutions that produce and certify that knowledge. It is, then, important to ask: How do WGFS scholars put WGFS on the map of proper knowledge? What maps do they draw to negotiate the epistemic status of WGFS? This chapter answers those questions through an analysis of WGFS scholars' boundary-work in conferences, PhD vivas and other public sites. Rather than frame WGFS scholars as the (sometimes replaced, displaced and misplaced) objects of the boundary-work of others, as in the previous chapter, what I do here is place them centre-stage as active and pro-active epistemic cartographers.

Mapping the maps that WGFS scholars draw

Discussing how feminist critiques of science have contributed to our understanding of the boundaries of scientificity, Gieryn describes 'feminism [as] (. . .) a robust specimen of boundary-work in practice, a project seeking emancipation in part through reconfigurations of science and politics, culture and nature, object and subject, male and female' (1995: 424). He notes that feminist scholars have 'examine[d] two sets of boundaries – gender and knowledge – and [found] compelling evidence for their intimate coevolution; centuries of double-boundary-work have moved whatever counts as science toward the masculine, and whatever counts as feminine away from science' (1995: 420). He argues that critique and disruption of this 'double boundary-work' is central for feminist scholars because it is a way of fighting the exclusion of *women* from science. I would add that boundary-work is intense and unavoidable for feminist scholars for yet another reason: it is a way of reactively or pre-emptively fighting the full or partial exclusion of *WGFS, as a field*, from the space of science.

Gieryn recognises that there exists a wide variety of feminist critiques of science (and admits he cannot do justice to that variety), but he attempts to schematise feminist boundary-work by saying that feminists deploy a two-fold tactic.

> First, the border between science and values is erased, on grounds that (. . .) examinations of scientific *practice* render the separation chimerical. Second, a new cultural territory is staked out that overlays science and politics, which is said to produce knowledge every bit as credible and useful as that coming from science *sans* values.
>
> (1995: 423, original emphases)

This characterisation highlights crucial components of feminist boundary-work: its erasing of boundaries, repositioning of the epistemic territories of science and politics, and reframing of the relative value of those different territories. However, as Gieryn acknowledges, it flattens the considerable diversity and complexity of actual manifestations of WGFS scholars' boundary-work. For example, there are diverse and sometimes opposing positions within WGFS about the extent to which it is possible and desirable to completely erase the border between science and values, or about whether feminists might want to preserve, reframe or abandon existing criteria of scientificity (Anderson, 2009; Crasnow *et al.*, 2015).

It is not surprising, then, that I have seen many different epistemic maps being drawn in my own observation in the past decade of how WGFS scholars speak about the value of WGFS in public academic settings throughout the world. In this section, I draw on material from my fieldwork in Portugal to identify five particularly frequent, but not exhaustive, maps. I examine a couple of examples of each, characterising the boundaries and terrains that they constitute, and analysing the work they do, not just as epistemological and political interventions in debates about the nature of knowledge, but also as tools in institutional struggles for access to valued resources for WGFS.

1. WGFS is closer to proper science

This epistemic map focuses on three key epistemic terrains: WGFS, proper science and mainstream science. It highlights the proximity between WGFS and specific traits of proper science, while at the same time positioning mainstream science as more distant (than WGFS) from those traits. In other words, WGFS is (at least in some respects) more properly scientific than mainstream scholarship. My first example of this map is taken from the intervention of a WGFS scholar in a roundtable on gender and science, part of an open, interdisciplinary seminar series aiming to introduce emerging fields of research to staff and students unfamiliar with them. She began by explaining how she became interested in WGFS, and then said:

> *"I thought what might be best for an audience with your level of knowledge would be to offer some provocations, I hope you won't be angry. [she laughs] The truth is that right now we're physically in a space [a university] where, supposedly, we should always be stimulating curiosity for the world around us, (. . .) and a critical questioning of the given and obvious. (. . .) However, (. . .) I've found that it's only very recently that academia has slowly begun to pay attention to gender. (. . .) It's shocking and shameful that Portuguese science and scientists haven't been curious, haven't been open to new knowledge, to issues raised by scholars studying gender and women's studies, (. . .) scholars who've tried to open new paths and ask new questions."*

She points to valued elements of widely shared understandings of proper science – it is curious, open to new knowledge and engages critically with the world – and argues that mainstream scholars have not been upholding these values, unlike WGFS scholars, who she describes as committed to *"asking new questions"*.

Similar boundary-work can be found in the following excerpt of a lecture by a WGFS scholar. It was the opening lecture of a course for social science UG students, covering issues of gender, among other themes. Although it is an optional course, some students are 'forced' to take it for timetabling reasons and many are surprised by, and sometimes resistant to, its critical content, as the lecturer later explained to me. To tackle this, the lecturer always starts the course with an explanation of why its themes are relevant. In the seminar I observed, this was framed as follows:

> *"Many gender theories we'll discuss are different, and sometimes even go against the things you've been learning in other courses in [name of discipline], and the ways in which you've been learning there. This might be confusing at times, but it's a valuable intellectual experience, because it'll help you understand that science is about critique and debate, NOT uncritical acceptance of concepts as often happens in other courses you're taking. Science isn't a faith, and if it's not a faith we should be able to interrogate things and critique existing knowledge, and that's a characteristic of gender research and also of this course."*

The lecturer calls upon the familiar dichotomy between (critical) science and (uncritical) faith, but unlike in maps drawn by critics of WGFS (as in the 'esoteric' conference coffee-break encounter which opened chapter 4), this dichotomy is used to *affirm*, rather than deny, the scientificity of WGFS. It is WGFS that is critical, and mainstream science that is a faith. Through this map, the course is presented as better equipped (than mainstream courses) to uphold a key principle of scientificity: critical engagement.

In this first map, WGFS is cast as overlapping with proper science, while mainstream science is rigid, dogmatic, closed, uncritical, and therefore less properly scientific than usually recognised. The aim is not to explicitly critique dominant ideals of proper science, but argue that mainstream science, unlike WGFS, has consistently failed to enact them. This map, which was most frequent in events where WGFS scholars addressed non-WGFS audiences, allows WGFS academics to engage with non-WGFS colleagues on the latter's own turf, in that it mobilises mainstream communities' own criteria of epistemic value to affirm the scientificity of WGFS. The implicit or explicit message is that mainstream scholars should be ashamed of their dismissal of WGFS, as it constitutes a failure to enact the very epistemic ideals they proudly uphold.

2. Proper science should be like WGFS

A second type of map also produces an overlap between WGFS and proper knowledge, although that overlap is drawn radically differently. In the map above, WGFS is framed as already residing close to proper science, and the location of proper science is not questioned. However, this second map argues that the space of proper science should *not* be where currently located or, to be more precise, where mainstream scholars argue it is located. On the contrary, proper science should move closer to the space currently occupied by WGFS, or rather, communities should adopt as ideal the alternative epistemic values proposed by, and followed within, WGFS and other critical fields. During fieldwork, I saw these maps being drawn only by scholars who identify explicitly as feminist, in events with feminist audiences and/or taking place in sites where the epistemic climate was one of commitment to situated and politically engaged knowledge production.

One example is a keynote given by a feminist scholar at a large feminist conference, a presentation received with much acclaim and described by many as a timely, rousing speech.

> *"Generally, what's taught in [Portuguese] universities is what's considered true science: science that is objective, unbiased, impartial. But let's deconstruct that: the objective, unbiased and impartial science is an androcentric, heterocentric science, the science of majorities, of privileged classes and groups. (. . .) Knowledge always derives from a social agent, so valuable scientific knowledge is knowledge that has values and beliefs, (. . .) that can be used to benefit people, increase quality of life, equality, social justice."*

This map is also drawn in classrooms. I observed it, for example, in a seminar for a WGFS course, part of a WGFS PG degree. In this seminar, students had to present their plans for the research project they had to conduct for assessment. One student outlines her ideas and says, "I don't know if in my project I should talk about knowledge as situated knowledge". The teacher answers: "in this room, and in this degree, knowledge is always seen as situated, and that's as it should be! However, as you all know, that's not always the case in other departments and disciplines. That's absurd and they would do well to learn from us, and value knowledge that engages openly with its inevitable situatedness!".

Unlike map 1, this map rests on an explicit, wholesale critique of existing ideals of proper science and that critique guides the boundary-work. Also unlike the first type, mainstream science and ideals of proper science are not separated, but described as overlapping, as one and the same territory. However, this territory is cast in very different terms from those that might be used by the academics that occupy it: mainstream science is not objective, unbiased and impartial, but heterocentric, androcentric, etc. This is one feature that map 2 does share with map 1 (and some of the following maps): it aims to demonstrate that the actual practices and outcomes of mainstream science are not what they are usually perceived to be, or what they are generally made to look like.

3. Mainstream science is just like WGFS

In both maps above, what is centrally at stake in WGFS scholars' boundary-work is the distance between WGFS and the current or ideal location of *proper science*. In other situations, however, maps are more explicitly focused on the position of WGFS vis-à-vis *mainstream science*. A third type of map brings those two territories closer, claiming that they overlap much more than mainstream academics tend, or wish, to admit. Both examples of this map are taken from presentations by WGFS academics in national conferences for mainstream social science disciplines. The first is an excerpt of a paper given by a junior scholar.

> *"This research was designed and conducted from a feminist [name of discipline] perspective. I want to make my particular positioning explicit. However, I must add that all [name of discipline] research, and all social science research in general, just like my research, is produced from a particular, partial position, and is in one way or another contaminated by values."*

The scholar describes her work as partial and located, but downplays the distinctiveness of this, to prevent dismissal by her non-WGFS audience. She does so by arguing that this particular feature of her WGFS perspective (often considered incompatible with scientificity) is actually characteristic of all scientific knowledge production, rather than just WGFS.

A similar move is made in the second example, from a presentation by a more senior academic.

> *"I've found feminist methodologies very inspiring when thinking about [name of theme]. One often hears that feminism is ideological. But ideology is present in all knowledge, so it's hard to understand why ideology is a problem vis-à-vis fields like this and not others. (. . .) For example, feminists talk about*

the need to consider experience, and when they do they're often not taken seriously. (. . .) But many other scholars focus on daily life and experience, and nobody thinks of dismissing them by making references to ideology."

This speaker highlights the similarities between WGFS and mainstream science as in the first example. She also shows how dominant discourses about the relative positions of those two territories are based on double standards that disguise those similarities and exaggerate the difference between WGFS and mainstream science. The overall argument in this map is that mainstream science is just as (if not more) subjective, political or partial than WGFS, which means that WGFS cannot legitimately be devalued relative to mainstream science on those grounds. Much like map 1, this map was drawn most often in situations where WGFS academics attempted to demonstrate the epistemic value of WGFS to non-WGFS audiences.

4. WGFS is just like mainstream science

Map 4 also attempts to assert the value of WGFS by reducing its distance from mainstream science. However, it performs that approximation in the opposite direction: instead of saying that mainstream science is just like WGFS, it announces that WGFS is just like mainstream science. This is illustrated in the excerpt below, taken from a public event organised by a WGFS research centre. In this excerpt, one of its founders speaks about the work developed in the centre.

"We believe that women's studies can be done scientifically in all areas because women are everywhere, and so we can analyse their contributions everywhere. Our efforts to carry out these studies produce research findings, it's a field like any other, producing analyses grounded on careful and rigorous research, and through its findings allowing us to learn more about women's lives, and society in general.'

Map 3 focused on the potentially *devalued* features of WGFS, arguing they are also found in mainstream science. The scholar in this extract, by contrast, foregrounds the potentially *valued* features of mainstream science and claims they are also found within WGFS. A junior scholar in a mainstream discipline with WGFS expertise told me in an interview that she uses this map to frame her research.

"I recently wrote a book on gender for a non-academic, non-feminist audience, (. . .) and the introduction says 'this book is based on the results of scientific research, carried out according to scientific principles'. I wrote that because I wanted to show that research on women and gender can be just as rigorous and scientific as any other scientific study. I wanted to avoid the idea that my claims are scientifically empty, ideological, etc. because I think people tend to think of feminists as people who defend ideas that aren't scientifically grounded."

As in map 1 (and unlike maps 2 and 3), this fourth map does not explicitly critique dominant norms of scientificity. Unlike all three earlier maps, it does not deconstruct or disrupt mainstream science: it describes it in terms recognisable to its inhabitants. It is not surprising, therefore, that this map tended to be drawn in claims aimed at non-WGFS audiences, and was most often mobilised by scholars who work on WGFS themes but identify primarily with their home discipline in mainstream SSH and/or who are less inclined to see themselves as *feminist* academics.

5. WGFS can help mainstream science get closer to proper science

This fifth map was the most frequent in the public events I observed. It was deployed both for non-WGFS and WGFS audiences, and both by WGFS scholars and, especially, by non-WGFS scholars expressing support for the field in the presence of WGFS audiences. It consists in defining two separate spaces: mainstream science, framed as more or less fundamentally deficient in some way, and a better science. WGFS is then flagged as that which can enable mainstream science to gradually move closer to, or overlap more fully with, the space of proper science. The latter, it is argued, is currently distant in space and time, but will be more quickly and fully reached if academic communities recognise, support and engage with WGFS scholarship.

In the first example – a fragment of the closing comments by a non-WGFS academic chairing a gender session at a national conference in a social science discipline – WGFS is described as *"pushing"* that mainstream discipline in the *"right direction"*.

> *"I'm extremely pleased I've had the chance to hear about new research [on gender]. It's very enriching for me personally and for [name of discipline] research as a whole, because there's no part of society that we should not study. (. . .) I'm extremely happy that we're becoming more open to these issues, which should encourage us to always move further, in the right direction. So congratulations for this push you're giving to [name of discipline] in these issues which should be part of its object and concern."*

A similar set of ideas was expressed by another senior academic (a scholar in a mainstream social science discipline, with expertise in WGFS) speaking in a parallel session on 'Theories and Methodologies' at the same national conference. It frames gender as a *"border area"* that can help generate new theories, and thereby enable scholars to achieve insights not accessible to them through existing theories.

> *"There are some border areas in which our [name of discipline] theories do not work completely, they don't satisfy us. (. . .) When we move to the micro-scale, for example the topic of gender violence in interpersonal relationships,*

there are several things that our usual theories simply don't allow us to see. It's this confrontation between our old theories and the challenges posed by these border areas, for example gender, that can be truly creative and productive in generating new theories and improving knowledge in our discipline."

Different versions of this map offer a different assessment of the centrality of WGFS in improving mainstream science. In the two examples above, WGFS is described as capable of pushing a discipline forward, opening new research directions, improving analytical tools and thereby expanding mainstream knowledge's reach and explanatory power. In the next excerpt, WGFS is cast in an even more decisive and ambitious role. It does not just correct existing problems; it is the *"territory"* from which to *"refound"* the humanities. The speaker is a non-WGFS scholar who is part of the senior management team of a university which offers a PG WGFS degree, and participated in that capacity in the opening session of a WGFS conference organised through the degree.

"The humanities, which are currently trying to guarantee not only their survival, but also their complete reformulation and, through it, their public legitimation, can find in this field [WGFS], still relatively young in Portugal, the territory, and more precisely, the intersection, on the basis of which they can refound themselves. (. . .) There's no doubt that feminist scholarship is a site of critical reflection and polemical reason, capable of giving back to philosophy its incisiveness, correcting errors of orientation and preventing abuses of power."

This map type combines different features of the maps analysed above. It shares with map 1 (WGFS is closer to proper science) and 2 (proper science should be like WGFS) the positioning of mainstream science as a territory separate and distant from proper science. Like map 4 (WGFS is just like mainstream science), it claims that WGFS and mainstream science have overlapping concerns, aims and epistemic values. Nevertheless, and unlike map 4, this map critiques mainstream knowledge. That critique, however, is not usually as explicit and forceful as map 2: the main message in most manifestations of map 5 is that WGFS helps *improve* mainstream knowledge, but does not inevitably demand a radical restructuring of it.

Working the audience: The contextuality of epistemic maps

I have noted that some maps tend to be drawn by scholars with particular profiles; however, the relations between the content of maps and the people who draw them are not as clear-cut as the previous pages suggest. There are, of course, identifiable differences between scholars in how they understand epistemic territories and boundaries. But maps were often described by interviewees not (just) as an exact expression of their *a priori* epistemological positions, but as contextual constructions. When I asked how they publicly frame their epistemological or theoretical stance, many explained they adapt it, to some extent, to the specific conditions, audiences and aims of a situation.[1]

> *"MMP: When you have to describe your position vis-à-vis the idea of 'science', how do you do it?*
>
> *[laughs] I describe myself differently depending on the context. [laughs] I guess that's what people mean when they talk about the plasticity of identity in contemporary societies! [laughs]"*
>
> Interview, junior scholar in a social science discipline,
with WGFS expertise

The following is an excerpt of an informal post-conference chat between two women (A and B) doing WGFS PG degrees at different universities:

> "A: Unfortunately at the moment a gender studies degree doesn't help get a job. Sometimes, it makes it harder.
>
> B: Absolutely! I applied for a job and thought 'this time, I won't remove my PhD on feminism from my CV!' But what if they ask what we study in the PhD programme?
>
> MMP: How would you describe it if you had to?
>
> B: I'd say that one cannot deny the influence and importance of science. But the science we have is generally produced by those with more resources: men, white, heterosexual, middle-class, and this interferes with findings. What feminist perspectives do is change science to make it better, to correct problems in existing science. That's what I'd say to explain why it's relevant, which is what I need to do, pragmatically. But that's not how I really think. In my writing, I'm much more critical of science.
>
> A: Yes, but that position you're describing is very feminist too. And it's an effective answer for a potential employer."

These and other comments show that when analysing boundary-work we cannot read claims about scientificity as reflections of what someone *really* thinks. This became especially clear when I asked interviewees to comment on some of their own texts or past initiatives. Many confessed they did not fully identify with every aspect of the structure, content or title of all their publications and initiatives, because they had had to reframe their stance or language for specific audiences or according to the epistemic climate in their institution or discipline. In one interview, I asked a senior WGFS scholar to comment on an excerpt from one of her texts, a co-authored piece from the mid-1990s. In the excerpt, the authors reflect on the nature of WGFS knowledge. The scholar read it and said:

> *"I don't agree with this point we make here about how we must avoid promiscuities between science and politics, I definitely wouldn't defend that. I don't remember exactly what happened at the time with that sentence, I think it was a*

concession I made to the other co-authors, who had a different position. Or maybe it had to do with us seeing this text as an attempt to intervene in an academic community that really wasn't at all open to gender, and [framing things in this way was] a strategy to get them to listen, and secure some kind of legitimation."

As Epstein also found in his study of credibility struggles around HIV/AIDS, 'published sources tell only part of the story – sometimes, in their linearity and smoothness, finished documents *conceal* the story' (1996: 355–356, original emphasis). Texts are not transparent accounts of scholars' thinking; in WGFS, they are often tools in boundary-work, as well as products of sometimes difficult boundary-work between an author and others (co-authors, editors, peer-reviewers), as I show later in this chapter. Therefore, boundary-work claims made within WGFS texts need to be situated within, and interpreted in relation to, the institutional, material and epistemic context of their production.

Two maps are better than one: Weaving maps together

I have identified 5 different maps and analysed them separately, as if they could easily be demarcated, and as if they have parallel and independent existences. That is certainly not the case: different epistemic maps are not mutually exclusive or incompatible. Two or more distinct maps can be, and are, woven together in the same space and time to negotiate the status of one object.[2] This was especially explicit in public vivas for WGFS PhD theses, sites where candidates and (some) examiners were not only discussing the value of a particular thesis, but also attempting to demonstrate to other examiners, the chair of the viva, the audience and the institution that a WGFS thesis is worthy of a doctorate.[3] Indeed, the importance of the events as moments of affirmation of the epistemic status of WGFS as a field was explicitly asserted during proceedings. In one viva, an examiner started her intervention by saying:

> *"This is a public event of enormous historical importance. It's a moment of affirmation and celebration of the field. It's simultaneously a scientific act and an act of citizenship, and should prompt us to remember those who have fought for the existence of this field in conditions of marginality and devaluation."*

The boundary-work that happens in a public PhD viva is, therefore, important, and because there is much at stake in it, it is often especially sophisticated. Consider, for example, the comments below, made by an examiner (a senior WGFS scholar) in one such viva.

> *"Before I talk about the thesis, and in order to better situate it, I want to say that feminist research in this field is distinct from traditional research because it doesn't try to be neutral, it's guided by values, connected to issues of power and oriented to social change. This distinction is very important.*

> *This feminist perspective considers that dominant interests (. . .) shape the development of science, and it therefore questions [science's] autonomy and neutrality. Theory is used (. . .) to point to possibilities of emancipation. (. . .) [Research] is always based on reflexivity and constant self-questioning."*

I read this as an attempt to clarify and assert what it means to do feminist research, and through that to demonstrate that the doctoral candidate's own feminist work is appropriately grounded in widely recognised scholarship and respectful of its standards of epistemic value. This is done by drawing a map that, like map 2, foregrounds the *"very important distinction"* between feminist and dominant norms of scientificity, and explicitly critiques the latter. Responding to this examiner, the candidate maintains the distinction between mainstream science and feminist scholarship, but draws a different kind of map.

> *"These [feminist] epistemologies (. . .) say that research can have values, but anyway, this isn't new, (. . .) because scientific research has always had values. If you go and look, values are present even in the most mainstream research. The big difference is that a feminist perspective makes otherwise hidden agendas explicit, it declares them and so makes the research more transparent, less deceptive, more open about itself. (. . .) Using this approach allowed me to obtain much richer and more diverse results than those obtained using traditional research methods."*

Articulating maps 3 (mainstream science is just like WGFS) and 1 (WGFS is closer to proper science), the candidate highlights that using a feminist approach enabled the production of knowledge that better upholds widely valued ideals, such as openness or transparency. Later, the supervisor, another senior WGFS scholar, makes her own comments. She also recognises the distinctiveness of the candidate's feminist perspective but downplays its specifically feminist character and positions the thesis as, above anything else, an example of a *"truly scientific"* attitude.

> *"[Candidate] was guided, throughout the whole process, by a spirit of true scientific curiosity, (. . .) by a desire to pursue scientific knowledge (. . .). It was this determined attitude (. . .) that allowed the thesis to achieve what it did. (. . .) It wasn't guided only by a feminist agenda, or only a critical agenda, but also by an attitude of true search for knowledge, and I want to highlight that here. This is what, to me, makes the academic quality of this thesis."*

When brought together, these maps represent the thesis both as a radically different kind of inquiry and as an exemplar of dominant values of *"true"* scientificity. This is done by alternatively foregrounding and de-emphasising the distances and overlaps between mainstream research, feminist research and proper science. According to these inter-woven maps, the presence of values cannot be used to disqualify this feminist thesis because values are just as present in mainstream research, and so feminist and traditional perspectives are similar in this respect. At the same time, they are also very different in that feminism does not try to hide this and therefore is more likely to produce knowledge with characteristics of scientificity which mainstream science also seeks and values. And yet, the thesis approaches knowledge production in a fundamentally different way because it is socially and politically committed, and *"oriented to social change"* and *"emancipation"*, rather than just the advancement of science; therefore, it draws on, and promotes, an alternative paradigm of scientificity. I would argue that the weaving of these different maps (although probably not consciously planned as such by the speakers) helps increase the robustness of boundary-work. It does so because it positions the thesis, and feminist scholarship as a whole, in a sufficiently multi-dimensional and fluid place to more easily pre-empt, resist and weather different potential forms of dismissal.

Locating, relocating and dislocating spaces of scientificity

As WGFS scholars navigate a changing academic landscape and more or less chilly epistemic (micro)climates, they draw epistemic maps that represent in diverse and dynamic ways the relative position of mainstream science, proper science and WGFS. Scholars select features of those territories to highlight or downplay, and there are many features to choose from as each territory is in itself sizeable and heterogeneous. They draw on that selection to establish overlaps and separations, affinities and incompatibilities. This means that WGFS can appear in turn – or even at the same time – as just like, and better than, mainstream science. It can be described as resolutely distinctive (and therefore original and necessary), or as not *that* different from other knowledge production (and therefore not legitimately dismissible). What is shared by all maps is a commitment to participating in the work of *locating* science. Some maps also take on a more critical approach to dominant conceptualisations of scientificity. They may attempt to *relocate* epistemic territories, as in map 2, which argues that norms of proper science are currently over 'there', but should be moved over 'here', becoming more closely aligned with feminist epistemological principles. They may also try to *dislocate* those territories (as in maps 1 and 3), i.e. demonstrate that mainstream science does not actually look like the map that its scholars draw of it.

These cartographic efforts are structured on the basis of what is intelligible in particular climates, persuasive for specific audiences and hence more likely to produce the desired effects. This is not specific to negotiations of the status of WGFS. It has been identified also as an important part of the life of other critical fields. In a study of the development of two African-American Studies departments in US universities, Small writes

each department's definition of Afro-American Studies can be traced directly to the efforts of its practitioners to attain (. . .) legitimacy. (. . .) [T]he [department] chairs sought diverse resources from constituencies in local institutional, wider academic, and even wider public arenas; to obtain these resources, they defined Black Studies according to [those constituencies'] expectations (. . .) about what constitutes a legitimate endeavor.

(1999: 697)

This kind of boundary-work is not, however, limited to fields that are precarious and marginal, or which see epistemological critique as *raison d'être* and key aim. Scholars across all fields (re)frame their positions depending on context, and as Blakeslee shows in a study of physicists, they 'expen[d] a great deal of energy developing knowledge structures of both their familiar and their unfamiliar audiences that (. . .) assist[ed] them as they planned for and then publicly presented their work.' (2001: 49). One can argue, then, that '[a]udience is (. . .) an integrated, and integral, component of an author's larger rhetorical process' (Blakeslee, 2001: 50). In that sense, maps are not direct expressions of constant epistemic beliefs that scholars hold and transport with them unchanged wherever they go, but rather situated productions (Gieryn, 1999; Mallard *et al.*, 2009). Context and audience play such important roles in boundary-work that a discursive analysis of the content of maps – like the one I provided above – can only produce a very limited account of the work that WGFS scholars' boundary-work does. It is to an analysis of the context of that work that I now turn.

Boundary-work that does not always work: Power, inequality, and the non-performativity of WGFS boundary-work

In trying to analyse what sort of work WGFS scholars' maps do or what type of hierarchies and splits non-WGFS scholars' discourses about WGFS construct, I have implicitly been assuming that maps and discourses actually *do* and *construct* something. But is that always and necessarily the case? Does WGFS scholars' boundary-work always work? Are these scholars always recognised by their interlocutors as authoritative boundary-workers? To answer these questions, we must, to reappropriate words written by Code,

deflect the focus of (. . .) analysis away from single and presumably self-contained prepositional utterances (. . .) and (. . .) move it into textured locations where it matters who is speaking and where and why, and where such mattering bears directly upon the possibility of knowledge claims, moral pronouncements, descriptions of 'reality' achieving acknowledgment, going through.

(1995: x)

Reframing the analysis in this way requires considering the *conditions of production and reception* of epistemic maps. It also demands, crucially, paying closer attention to *who* individual boundary-workers are.

This *who* is extremely important. Indeed, in their classical ethnography of scientific practice, Latour and Woolgar observed that when scientists assess arguments '*who* had made a claim was as important as the claim itself' (1986 [1979]: 164, original emphasis). The empirical literature on scientific boundary-work tells us much about the people who do that work every day, but many aspects of that *who* are severely neglected in this literature. Latour and Woolgar were concerned with how presumptions of credibility were influenced by audiences' views about a scientist's 'social strategy or their psychological make-up' (1986 [1979]: 163). Other literature reflects on boundary-workers' interests, strategies, assumptions, alliances, disciplinary backgrounds, institutional affiliations, positions in professional hierarchies, political stances and even religious beliefs. However, these studies rarely give us equally detailed insight into boundary-workers 'race' and ethnicity, age, class, (dis)ability, or sexuality, for example. In his theory of boundary-work, Gieryn does recognise that 'issues of identity politics and identity epistemics' are crucial (1999: 35), but he does not explicitly integrate them into his theorising, as I discussed in chapter 2.

Wondering about boundary-workers' personal details is not trite prurient prying. One of the most influential contributions of feminist, black and postcolonial thought on science is the assertion that knowledge producers are inescapably embodied creatures, and that in sexist and racist societies that embodiment makes a difference to how others perceive their epistemic and professional capacity. Over the past decades we have built an impressive and inspiring body of work providing undeniable empirical evidence that credibility and epistemic authority are distributed unevenly, on the basis of 'systemically engrained [gendered, racialised, . . .] structural conceptions about the kinds of people who can reasonably claim [it]' (Code, 1991: 233). That empirical research shows there is a clear (albeit not always fully conscious) tendency to imagine and represent the best, most authoritative, knowledge producer as white, male and middle-class (Amâncio, 2005; Hey, 2003; Kilomba, 2007; Mählck, 2013; Søndergaard, 2005). It also demonstrates this can lead to the devaluing, marginalisation and exclusion of women, black scholars and other 'others' in everyday scientific interaction, recruitment, promotion and peer-review (Ahmed, 2012; Barres, 2006; Husu, 2011; Lamont, 2009; Moss-Racusina *et al.*, 2012). When viewed against the backdrop of these theoretical interventions and the empirical research that corroborates them, the lack of sustained attention in boundary-work literature to gender, 'race', class and other so-called 'identity categories' is striking. This section seeks to contribute to the much needed, and long overdue, work of placing those issues at the centre of our thinking on epistemic boundary-work.

It is extremely difficult to ethnographically analyse the extent to which WGFS scholars' boundary-work 'achiev[es] acknowledgment, go[es] through', to return to Code's words (1995: x). The views of audiences cannot be ascertained accurately from faces and comments, and (as I show in chapter 4) some non-WGFS scholars combine public support for WGFS with explicit, but backstage, dismissal or teasing. Moreover, negotiations of epistemic status are ongoing and iterative processes, and their effects cannot be observed immediately or read off singular instances. Furthermore, and as Code highlights, the 'granting and withholding [of] acknowledgment' happens 'within complex and perplexing situations' (1995: xi), and it is impossible to provide an exhaustive overview of all the factors that may shape it. In light of this, what I do here is draw on Portuguese WGFS scholars' descriptions of past instances of negotiation of epistemic status, and analyse their accounts of the effects of a range of factors which, in their view, shaped the possibilities of recognition of their boundary-work.[4] I examine in particular the impact of two sets of issues: what kind of *person* does the boundary-work, and what kind of *academic* they are.

What kind of person does the boundary-work?

As Nash and Owens note, the 'in-between-ness' of WGFS – as a field both 'inside and outside of institutional legitimacy' – is 'felt differently (. . .) by practitioners who occupy different institutional spaces (. . .) and [is] shaped by gender, race, class, sexuality, nation, disability, and other categories of difference' (2015: viii). This resonates with my interviewees' experiences: they often mentioned that the kind of person they are, or are perceived to be, has impacted on the extent to which their affirmations of the value of WGFS are seen as credible. Different aspects of their identity were identified as significant in this regard. Gender was, perhaps unsurprisingly, one of the most frequently mentioned. Research in Portugal shows that women academics' work is often not recognised (and rewarded) to the same degree as that of their male colleagues (Amâncio, 2003, 2005; Gonçalves, 2009). WGFS scholars are not an exception. Women interviewees made several, but usually very brief, references to the fact that, as women, they are sometimes less easily or frequently recognised as credible knowledge producers, and that the lesser status of the field is inextricably linked to the lesser epistemic and social status of those who work in it.[5] 8 scholars (staff and students) mentioned having their WGFS work described dismissively by colleagues as *"women's things"*, or *"girls' sociology"*. One junior scholar with expertise in WGFS working in a mainstream social science spoke of a *"double"* dismissal of WGFS scholars.

> *"In the social sciences in Portugal, objects and fields of study which are associated with women, or have many women in them, tend to be seen as of less interest,[6] (. . .) and the study of gender is connoted with women, and also with gay men. (. . .) In academia there's active discrimination against women and also lots of homophobia. (. . .) So, if being a woman or gay already leads to being more frequently dismissed, then if on top of that you study a field connoted with women, I think there's a double understanding of your work and what you say as something that isn't interesting or worthy of attention."*

One male interviewee, a senior scholar with expertise in WGFS, also spoke at length about the impact of gender on the chances of having one's claims about the epistemic status of WGFS taken seriously.

> *"I'm a man and have a relatively mainstream performance of masculinity, and I think this made all the difference. (. . .) When I became interested in*

gender, and tried to work on it and include it in teaching, etc., I think the fact I'm a man clearly helped immensely, because it means that things I said were seen to have more authority, like I'm somehow less biased and more credible. (. . .) And this made my trajectory much easier, it meant that institutionalising [WGFS] in my department ended up being relatively easy."

As the two quotes above indicate, gender and sexuality[7] (and sexism and homo-phobia) interact with each other in demarcating who counts as credible. According to some interviewees, it is fairly common for people to mock WGFS by claiming – backstage or unofficially – that an interest in WGFS reflects deviance from, or inability to secure, a 'normal' heterosexual (sex) life.

> *"You can't imagine the comments I hear here at the University! I've been asked by colleagues, in a jokey sort of way, if I'm a lesbian, although they know perfectly well I'm married [to a man] and have a baby. And anyway, even if I was a lesbian, why should that be a problem?!"*
>
> Interview, junior scholar in a mainstream social science,
> with expertise in WGFS

One junior scholar was told by a senior (male) colleague that her interest in WGFS produced a 'spectre' of lesbianism that she should pro-actively try to dodge, as it might compromise her academic authority.[8]

> *"These senior colleagues and I were working together and had to publicly present research findings. Because they know I have an interest in gender, all the difficult issues about gender and sexuality were left for me to present. At a meeting, one says to me, and it wasn't even a joke, he was perfectly serious, 'make sure you're careful about your appearance that day, what you wear and look like, because people may think you're a lesbian and not take you seriously.'"*

Many of the women academics I interviewed have male partners, several of whom are also academics and in some situations working in the same department, disci-pline or university. 6 participants explained that the fact that they (or others) were married, and married to men, made a significant difference to their experience of negotiating the status of WGFS, because it made it harder (though not impossible, as we have seen above) for colleagues to openly dismiss their work as the musings of *"sexually frustrated women"* or *"the rants of lesbians"*. Gay male scholars told me that colleagues rarely made comments about their sexuality in their presence, but they knew that privately their WGFS scholarship and boundary-work was more or less regularly dismissed on the basis of their sexuality. This was con-firmed by the account of a senior woman academic I interviewed.

> *"We were organising a conference panel about women and gender, and I sug-gested inviting x [gay male scholar]. The coordinator [a non-WGFS male*

> *scholar] immediately said 'no, no, if you're going to invite a man, it must be a real man'. I just couldn't believe it."*

Age is also described as shaping the extent to which one's work and boundary-work is recognised as relevant; however, that impact takes different forms. Younger interviewees noted that their age made it harder to get their claims about the value of WGFS taken seriously by colleagues and university administrations. At the same time, a few older WGFS scholars told me they were very keen to get junior scholars to speak in lectures and public events (and two of them invited me to do so), partly because they felt their presence helped legitimate WGFS as a field which is topical, fresh, innovative and at the vanguard of knowledge production. According to them, the presence of younger scholars dissuaded students and other audiences from dismissing WGFS as *"outdated knowledge past its expiry date"*. Another aspect of WGFS scholars' lives that also seems to have an impact on their chances of being recognised as credible boundary-workers is the degree and type of their political activity. One senior WGFS scholar described this in an interview as follows:

> *"As long as [the activism] you're doing isn't too significant, no one will say anything. But from the moment you begin participating too much, then you start getting comments about the problems of contamination of science by activism, and anything you say is liable to be dismissed. (. . .) It's worse if your political activity is in less mainstream sectors. (. . .) I know that some people want to be more politically active, but they won't because they're afraid others will dismiss their academic work by saying they only make a certain claim because they're activists of a certain political or ideological orientation."*

According to 4 interviewees, political involvement was broadly seen by non-WGFS colleagues, and also some WGFS scholars, as acceptable but only *"up to a certain point"* or in certain fora. If that border was crossed, it became harder to get their epistemological claims taken seriously, or their scholarship recognised.

No participants explicitly addressed the impact of 'race', ethnicity, class, (dis)ability or gender identity on the success of their boundary-work. Like Portuguese WGFS and Portuguese academia as a whole, my group of interviewees – to the best of my knowledge, all or almost all white, middle-class, cisgender and apparently abled – is relatively homogeneous, and interviewees did not mention or discuss their positions on those axes. Considering that structural inequalities relating to 'race', ethnicity, class, gender identity, and (dis)ability shape access to, and experiences of, careers in Portuguese academia, and that Portuguese science has been argued to contribute to reproduce and legitimate those inequalities (Fontes *et al.*, 2014; Machado *et al.*, 1995; Maeso and Araújo, 2014; Reiter, 2008), I would suggest that this silence says more about the invisibility of these axes of inequality to those who are privileged in relation to them, and less about their actual influence on boundary-work. I now sorely regret my decision to wait for participants to mention particular axes of inequality, and ask them only about those mentioned. This created a situation where interviewees spoke at length about their marginality (more salient and visible to them) but very rarely about their privilege, thus reinforcing the relative invisibility of structural academic inequalities based on 'race', ethnicity, class, ability and gender identity. It would have been analytically valuable, and politically important, to pro-actively open a debate about those axes and interpellate interviewees to consider how they might be privileged in boundary-work.

What kind of academic does the boundary-work?

Research on the institutionalisation of WGFS has shown that attempts to create WGFS degrees and centres tend to be more successful when spearheaded by senior academics in influential positions (Gumport, 2002; Miske, 1995; Westkott, 2003). My own study confirms this. One interviewee, a junior WGFS researcher, directly links position in institutional hierarchies with likelihood of *"being heard"* in negotiations of epistemic status.

> *"Each person in their university tries to show that this field [WGFS] is worthwhile; depending on how important they are, they'll get heard or not. A professor will manage to get this much attention* [marks high point in the air with her hand], *a senior lecturer will get less* [marks lower point], *a lecturer will get even less* [marks even lower point], *a student will find it impossible to convince anyone this field is valuable.'*

A senior scholar provided the following assessment of the doors opened by her seniority:

> *"When we wanted to convince the university to accept our proposal [to launch a WGFS initiative] it was clear my help and presence would be important because I have a very solid reputation, I'm very well respected, have a considerable body of work behind me, and so I could do something others [less senior colleagues] couldn't, I could come and say [laughs] 'well, it's shameful we don't have anything in this area, everyone does work on this, how can we be so outdated, what kind of university are we?'. And they'd listen to me, they had to, because my position here is high. And they did listen."*

Much like maps 1 (WGFS is closer to proper science) and 5 (WGFS can help mainstream science get closer to proper science), this scholar frames the lack of institutional space for WGFS as a shameful deviation from the principles of good science and the features of a leading university, placing WGFS as that which can bring the institution closer to the terrain it seeks to occupy. This appeal to the shame of being *"so outdated"* and failing to do something that *"everyone [else] does work on"* becomes an even more powerful argument in the performative university, where value is closely tied to ability to match and overtake one's 'competitors'. Much more was needed to eventually secure full support – time, the promise of profitability, active lobbying, intense *"pedagogical work"* in educating others about WGFS, for example – but throughout that process this scholar was able to achieve a level of recognition of her boundary-work unavailable to more junior colleagues.

This makes the intervention of senior scholars – be it WGFS experts, or non-WGFS academics who support WGFS and act as epistemic and institutional advocates – particularly decisive in struggles over the position or status of the field. The significance of senior scholars as pioneers, figureheads and defenders of existing achievements is, however, a double-edged sword, because those achievements often become dependent on those scholars' presence and intervention. This makes them quite precarious, as it means they can quickly become undone when individuals retire, move or are no longer able to take part in these negotiations (as discussed in chapters 3 and 7). The reverse also happens, according to interviewees: if a very senior person is explicitly opposed to WGFS, boundary-work efforts, however robust, are less likely to work, and that colleague's departure can suddenly generate a more welcoming climate for WGFS.

The theoretical, methodological and epistemological positions of boundary-workers or those who support them were also identified by interviewees as shaping the chilliness of climates. If an individual is perceived to be unequivocally located in the territory of scientificity, their claims about the features and boundaries of that territory, and what can and should be included in it, are more likely to be treated as credible maps. One interviewee, a senior WGFS scholar, provided a particularly vivid illustration of how the intervention of such individuals can fundamentally change the direction of boundary-work, with direct material results. The story relates to a chapter she had contributed in the late 1990s to a social science textbook. The chapter covered theories about a (non-WGFS) theme in mainstream research, but considered them from a gender perspective.

> *"That textbook was another battle in the war to get gender taken seriously by my colleagues. At one point my chapter was removed from the table of contents without my knowledge. (. . .) We're at a meeting and someone talks about the table of contents, and I look at it and ask 'where's my chapter?!'. Awkward silence around the table, (. . .) someone goes very red and says 'well, we were thinking that there's another chapter about [x], and that's a very similar theme, so there's no point having two chapters on the same theme'. (. . .) I froze completely, I didn't know what to do. And then, by chance, there was a guy there, not an important person in the department and not someone I knew well, but he was the most positivist person you can imagine. (. . .) He says, looking baffled (. . .) 'what do you mean they're the same themes?! [Interviewee] works on [y], [other author] works on [x], they're completely different things, they're different levels of analysis even!'. I was completely*

shocked. [laughs] He was exactly right, and it just solved the issue then and there, because the others went very quiet and didn't have the nerve to dispute it, because if even such a positivist scholar recognised theoretical specificity and value in what I was doing, then that was it! I kept thinking how lucky I was that he was there and intervened! (. . .) They said 'ok, what's the chapter title again? I'll add it here', and the chapter reappeared on the plans, and was in the book."

This negotiation is described as decisively shaped by the profile of the boundary-workers involved, on the one hand, and *"luck"* and *"chance"*, on the other. Other accounts also stressed the interplay between chance and the structurally privileged epistemic status of specific individuals. In this next episode, the stakes are also high: will a feminist PhD thesis in a mainstream social science be accepted by a panel that includes academics who consider feminist work insufficiently scholarly? This description of events was produced by a senior WGFS scholar also on the panel.

"The chair [male non-WGFS scholar in high institutional position] started the examiner meeting by destroying the thesis, saying 'what kind of research is this? What's all this about taking a feminist stance, this isn't serious research! (. . .) It's unacceptable!' (. . .) But [PhD candidate] was so lucky, because after saying all this the chair turns to his left, and it just so happens that the person sitting to his left is [senior male non-WGFS scholar who is open to WGFS]. (. . .) And [the chair] asks him, 'what do you think, Professor?', and he completely deconstructs [the chair's] dismissive speech, gives the opposite opinion and ends by saying, 'I think the thesis should be accepted'. And who's sitting next to him and is the next person to speak? Me, and I say the same. Next to me was someone who was more ambivalent, but didn't want to explicitly contradict the other professor, and so didn't criticise the thesis much. Then the last two examiners spoke, and they were very much against the thesis, but by then there wasn't really much they could do, because we'd already created a favourable climate. If the discussion had started in the opposite direction, with the others going first, [candidate] would've failed. I have absolutely no doubt! Because we wouldn't have been able to turn the situation around! It just so happened that the undecided person was sitting in the middle, and spoke right after us. I was watching it and thinking, 'such a close call, such a narrow squeak!'."

I read this as a compelling illustration of how contingency and structure combine to form epistemic microclimates in concrete situations of decision-making. A collective (more or less consensual) normative framework to assess what can count as proper knowledge is not something that just exists stably in a discipline, institution or country, nor is it the sum total of pre-existing frameworks that individuals might bring with them. This contingent group's framework was shaped by several factors, from the more stable (the relative seniority of examiners or their epistemological stances), to the more contingent (past and present relationships between them or how able and willing they felt to contest each other's maps on that day), and including, crucially in the eyes of the interviewee, the purely fortuitous (where they sat and which order they spoke in).[9] Luck and chance do play a decisive role, but in the context of, and in articulation with, more ossified unequal distributions of authority between individuals, fields or competing epistemic maps, as others have also shown (Lamont, 2009; Mallard *et al.*, 2009).

Because the spectre of dismissal is often hanging over WGFS (even if just unofficially), it is also especially important for boundary-workers to *"cover their backs"* at all times by complying as perfectly as they can with the relevant rules, regulations and other institutional and epistemic requirements.

> *"When we're planning and organising things for the [WGFS degree], we try to make things as consistent and solid as possible, especially because if you're in a more fragile field like this, (. . .) any slippage will be more criticised than in more institutionalised fields. (. . .) So I always have to pay attention to formal issues, obey formal and legal requirements and deadlines, and all that. (. . .) This helps us maintain an image of quality in the work (. . .) we're doing."*
>
> Interview, senior WGFS scholar

To maintain this careful monitoring and zealous compliance, WGFS scholars have to abstain from doing particular things and often have to manage their work in quite risk-averse ways.

> *"Sometimes we're trying to think of a title for a section of the journal, or discussing ideas for the future, and we'll go and look at other [WGFS] journals from other countries. I've noticed other journals, for example 'Revista de Estudos Feministas',[10] will occasionally do more experimental things, like interviews. (. . .) It's harder to do that in Portugal, I don't think something like that would be well received [by mainstream academics]. (. . .) I have the feeling that any minor deviation we may have [from academic journal conventions], any article we publish that doesn't have the required quality, anything like that may get picked up and give the journal a negative reputation. That has happened in the past. They'll automatically say 'ah well, the journal has no credibility'. So I feel we always have to pay close attention to this, and can't experiment much."*
>
> Interview, junior WGFS scholar, member of the editorial
> board of a WGFS journal

This belief that *"any minor deviation (. . .) may get picked up and give [WGFS] a negative reputation"* can also function, as we saw in chapter 3, to trigger and justify some significant boundary-work *within* the field: that which is too "*experimental*" and "*doesn't have the required quality*" may get excluded for the sake of protecting the precarious "*credibility*" of existing WGFS initiatives.

(Over-)Compliance with institutional rules is also important for students who want to engage with WGFS in their non-WGFS degrees. All 6 students I conducted formal interviews with mentioned they had faced resistance from lecturers when trying to include WGFS in UG and PG essays and dissertations. 3 students reported only being allowed to include WGFS insofar as they scrupulously observed all requirements and produced very good, or sometimes even extra, work. In the following excerpt, an MA student in a non-WGFS social science degree describes the experience of engaging with WGFS theories in the assessment for a 3rd year UG course, where students were required to design and carry out a group research project.

> "*We wanted to work on gender and sexuality, which weren't really talked about in the degree. And it was a struggle! It wasn't just that we wanted to work on a devalued theme, it was also that we were working with alternative epistemological protocols! (. . .) It was a process of negotiation, of trying to conquer legitimacy. (. . .) It was as if it was only admissible for us to work on gender if in everything else we were better than other students! We had to be very conscientious in all the formal requisites. (. . .) There was excessive control of what we did. For example, every group had to write a number of reviews of articles or books they were using. We wrote ours, focusing on the literature we were looking at. But then the lecturer told us to write a couple more, about books unconnected to our research but which were more in line with the course's epistemological stance, so we had to write extra reviews. (. . .) There was huge monitoring, much more intense than with the rest of the class, of whether we'd done the research design in a certain way, whether we'd been rigorous when operationalising the theories. (. . .) We had to obey the lecturer's rules extremely closely. Then in the second semester it became easier, because we'd taken the first semester exam and got high marks, and achieved some legitimacy through them.*"

Unsurprisingly, this student told me later that he eventually stopped doing research on gender partly because "*there were just too many barriers*".

Being a(n over-)compliant academic or student can make the difference when trying to promote WGFS. This is demonstrated not just by the examples above, but also by the material discussed in chapter 3: in the performative university, complying with the demand for intense and profitable productivity is one of the most effective strategies for improving the position and status of WGFS. However, managing to consistently fulfil, or even go beyond, all requirements, never fully shields WGFS scholars from epistemic marginalisation, as this senior WGFS scholar explains:

> "*For a long time, (. . .) my [non-WGFS] colleagues denied or ignored the value of my work. (. . .) But after a while, I had accumulated lots of publications and*

contacts, and they realised they (. . .) couldn't throw me away, because (. . .)
I produced a lot, so couldn't be treated with hostility, they had to treat me as
an equal. But there are ways of treating me as an equal while simultaneously
keeping my scientific contribution ignored and marginalised!"

All these experiences show that one's academic standing and institutional position – two of the aspects of boundary-workers' profile that the boundary-work
literature has examined more systematically – do indeed play a significant role
in shaping the content and outcome of boundary-work. However, the force of
entrenched epistemic hierarchies is such that, for example, being a woman, or not
being *"a real man"*, or working on so-called *"feminine"* topics, can be enough to
partly or fully offset the influence of even the highest professional status. Because
the threat of epistemic disqualification is, for some people, always potentially
present, it must be an integral part of the theorising of boundary-work.

Theorising the non-performativity of boundary-work

The claim that scientificity is produced through practices of boundary-work is
based on the belief that boundary-work is performative. Gieryn (1995, 1999)
argues that scientificity is not an essential property of claims, methods or disciplines but an achievement constituted in and through its local, ritualised enactment. Persuaded by this argument, I have conceptualised scientificity in this book
as a discourse in Foucault's terms: a practice 'that systematically form[s] the
objects [and subjects] of which [it] speak[s]' (2006 [1969]: 54). To adapt once
again – as I did in chapter 3 – Butler's well-known description of the performativity of gender (itself also adapted from Nietzsche), we might say that '[t]here is
no [scientificity][11] behind the expressions of [science]; [scientificity] is performatively constituted by the very "expressions" that are said to be its results' (1990:
25). And yet, my fieldwork shows that boundary-work is not always performative. In others words, it does not always succeed in bringing about or forming
'the objects of which [it] speak[s]' (2006 [1969]: 54): reconfigured boundaries
of scientificity or the valuing of a field, for example. WGFS scholars may draw
maps that represent WGFS as proper knowledge; it is not, however, guaranteed
that their claims about the location (or relocation and dislocation) of epistemic
territories will actually do the (boundary-)*work* they are meant to do. I agree with
Rose that '[t]o locate (. . .) science in context (. . .) gives [us] (. . .) the possibility of developing a sharper sense of what might or might not be achieved within
specific (. . .) circumstances' (1994: 53). It becomes important, therefore, to consider the broader social and political context in which scientific boundary-work
unfolds, and ask more explicitly and systematically how that context constrains
its performativity.

When she asked these questions in relation to the performativity of claims of/to
anti-racism made in academics' writing and universities' 'diversity documents',

Sara Ahmed (2004, 2012) argued that such anti-racist claims are ' "unhappy per-formatives", i.e. utterances that would "do something" if the right conditions had been met, but which do not do that thing, as the conditions have not been met' (2004: §50). Ahmed suggests we have been too quick to assume that performative claims actually operate performatively and calls for more attention to the question of whether in an unequal world the conditions are in place to allow some 'sayings' to be able to 'do' what they 'say' (2004: §54). She also encourages us to be wary of conceptualisations of performativity which ' "forge[t]" how performativity depends upon the repetition of conventions and *prior acts of authorization*' (2004: §51, my emphasis). Ahmed's call, although developed in relation to another set of debates and objects, offers a valuable starting point for a retheorising of aca-demic boundary-work. To flesh out the implications of her arguments, it is helpful to (re)turn to an author that inspired Ahmed's own reflection, the philosopher of language J. L. Austin.

In his series of lectures *How to Do Things with Words*, Austin (1975) argues that some claims are performative, but stresses that performativity is not a prop-erty of a claim but an act only accomplished if conditions are favourable. Devot-ing a whole lecture to the theorising of performativity failures, Austin identifies six conditions or rules which 'are necessary for the smooth or "happy" function-ing of a performative' (1975: 14). The second rule is that 'the particular persons and circumstances in a given case must be appropriate for the invocation of the particular procedure invoked' (1975: 15). Austin is thinking here primarily about issues of professional status or procedural authority: 'say, we are not in a position to do the act because (. . .) it is the purser and not the captain who is conducting the ceremony' (1975: 16). Much like STS authors writing on boundary-work, pro-fessional position and status are the issues most salient to Austin when thinking about *who* are 'the particular persons' making performative claims.

The question of whether 'the particular persons' making a claim are 'appro-priate for the invocation of the particular procedure invoked' (Austin, 1975: 15) takes on a very different meaning, and opens other avenues of inquiry, when asked from a feminist or critical race perspective. In contemporary western societies, boundary-work unfolds within a structural context of epistemic injustice (Code, 2014; Fricker, 2007) where credibility is distributed unevenly, on the basis of 'systemically engrained [gendered, racialised, . . .] structural conceptions about the kinds of people who can reasonably claim [it]' (Code, 1991: 233). Therefore, 'particular persons' will structurally and tendentially be seen as more 'appropri-ate' than others 'for the invocation of' (Austin, 1975: 15) claims about the bound-aries of scientificity. There is always a risk, then, that boundary claims made by certain kinds of scholars will be dismissed as performatives not made by 'appro-priate persons' (Austin, 1975: 15), thus breaking one of the rules 'necessary for the smooth or "happy" functioning of a performative' (Austin, 1975: 15).

In light of this, we can say – adapting Ahmed's (2004) words – that in an une-qual world the conditions are not always in place for some scholars' boundary-work to succeed in doing what it says. Therefore, scholars' position within broader structures of social, political and epistemic inequality cannot be treated as an incidental element of boundary-work, relevant and problematisable only in relation to those who are not white, male, straight, able-bodied . . . a sort of spanner thrown into the (boundary-)works by 'other' scholars. Those inequalities are a central, structural and constitutive element of *all* boundary-work. Thus, I want to argue for a theorisation of boundary-work that sees it as *always potentially* performative, but *not always successfully* (or happily) so, and that recognises that its non-performativity is shaped by, and creates, structural inequalities. Gieryn mentions briefly that 'the best-drawn maps (. . .) sometimes fail to secure credibility for one's claims' (1999: 24), but we must theorise that 'failure' of boundary-work differently. It is not something that happens *sometimes*, but rather an *integral* and *constitutive* part of boundary-work in societies structured by 'epistemic discrimination' (Dalmiya and Alcoff, 1993). Indeed, the 'fail[ure] to secure credibility for one's claims' (Gieryn, 1999: 24) is both an effect of longstanding epistemic inequalities and a key agent in their ongoing reproduction and legitimation.

One must be cautious, however, to not conceptualise in an overly circular and deterministic way the relation between the 'success' of boundary-work and the characteristics of boundary-workers. As Code notes, '[i]t is impossible to decide before the fact which specificities and practices will be salient in any epistemic tale' (1995: 158). Epistemic (micro)climates are contextual and diverse; academic negotiations are not just epistemic, but also professional, financial and personal; structural and fortuitous influences interact in often unpredictable ways (Lamont, 2009; Søndergaard, 2005); the intersections between different axes of a scholar's position (in institutions, in contingent groups, in socio-political structures of inequality) are rarely straightforward; and the emergence of academic cultures of performativity is changing and complicating these relations. These are some of the reasons why contemporary boundary-work is so much, and such hard, work . . . and why it is so important that WGFS scholars discuss and reflect on that work.

Notes

1 For a very interesting account of this process see Kokot, who explains that as an interdisciplinary WGFS scholar who has to 'join and converse with different [academic] "cliques"', she must engage in 'a shapeshifting process where the way I talk, think and write about [my] research transforms with and through the respective audience' (2010: 51).
2 See Henderson (2012) for a fascinating analysis of how one scholar does this in a public lecture on gender for a non-WGFS audience at an Italian university.
3 PhD vivas in Portugal are open to the public. Those I observed had audiences of over 25 people, including academics, students and several people from outside academia (usually relatives and friends of the PhD candidate). They are ritualised, formal and rather solemnly hierarchical events, generally chaired by a very senior representative of the host institution, someone in a high position of power in academic and administrative decision-making. Because they constitute occasions for very senior and powerful people from outside the field to witness the epistemic certification of WGFS work,

be exposed to its theories, concepts and findings, and observe that it is a recognised field which attracts relatively large audiences, public PhD vivas can play an important role in the negotiation of WGFS' status and institutional position.

4 I rarely asked interviewees directly whether a particular factor had made a difference in boundary-work. I encouraged them to describe their efforts to institutionalise WGFS, and asked what factors had hindered or helped advance those efforts.

5 See also Joaquim (2007) for a published discussion of this.

6 For a more macro-level analysis of this, see Cunha's study of the gendering of subfields in Portuguese sociology. She found that men are disproportionately represented in 'the classical fields (. . .), which have relatively high status and guarantee a comfortable position in the national sociological community' (2008: 28*), whereas women are the majority in more recent and/or less central subfields, including gender.

7 I did not ask interviewees about their sexuality. Several of the male participants identify as gay and mentioned this spontaneously. None of the women identified themselves explicitly or indirectly as non-heterosexual.

8 Marchbank and Letherby (2006) draw on research in five English universities to analyse student perceptions of the association between WGFS and lesbianism, and its mobilisation in their daily academic interaction.

9 See Mallard *et al.* (2009) and Lamont (2009) for more accounts of how small and heterogeneous groups negotiate epistemic microclimates when assessing scholarship. They too suggest that these negotiations may be 'influenced by respect for the status hierarchy of the institutional affiliation of panelists, their social characteristics, and their gender in particular' (2009: 600).

10 A well-known Brazilian WGFS journal founded in 1992 (http://www.scielo.br/ref/).

11 In the original, 'gender identity'.

References

Ahmed, Sara (2004). "Declarations of Whiteness: The Non-Performativity of Anti-Racism". *Borderlands, 3* (2).

Ahmed, Sara (2012). *On Being Included: Racism and Diversity in Institutional Life*. Durham, NC: Duke University Press.

Amâncio, Lígia (2003). "Gender and Science in Portugal". *Portuguese Journal of Social Science, 1* (3), 185–198.

Amâncio, Lígia (2005). "Reflections on Science as a Gendered Endeavour: Changes and Continuities". *Social Science Information, 44* (1), 65–83.

Anderson, Elizabeth (2009). "Feminist Epistemology and Philosophy of Science" in E.N. Zalta (ed.), *The Stanford Encyclopedia of Philosophy*. Retrieved 02/04/2016, from http://plato.stanford.edu/

Austin, John L. (1975). *How to Do Things with Words* (2nd ed.). London: Oxford University Press.

Barres, Ben (2006). "Does Gender Matter?". *Nature, 442*, 133–136.

Blakeslee, Ann (2001). *Interacting with Audiences: Social Influences on the Production of Scientific Writing*. Mahwah, NJ: Lawrence Erlbaum Associates.

Butler, Judith (1990). *Gender Trouble: Feminism and the Subversion of Identity*. New York: Routledge.

Code, Lorraine (1991). *What Can She Know?: Feminist Theory and the Construction of Knowledge*. Ithaca, NY: Cornell University Press.

Code, Lorraine (1995). *Rhetorical Spaces: Essays on Gendered Locations*. New York: Routledge.

Code, Lorraine (2014). "Ignorance, Injustice and the Politics of Knowledge: Feminist Epistemology Now". *Australian Feminist Studies, 29* (80), 148–160.

Crasnow, Sharon, *et al.* (2015). "Feminist Perspectives on Science" in E.N. Zalta (ed.), *The Stanford Encyclopedia of Philosophy*. Retrieved 02/04/2016, from http://plato.stanford.edu/

Cunha, Sandra Mestre da (2008). *Quem Estuda o Quê em Portugal*. Retrieved 02/04/2016, from http://www.cies.iscte.pt/destaques/documents/CIES-WP51_Cunha_001.pdf

Dalmiya, Vrinda and Alcoff, Linda (1993). "Are 'Old Wives' Tales' Justified?" in L. Alcoff and E. Potter (eds.), *Feminist Epistemologies* (pp.217–244). New York: Routledge.

Epstein, Steven (1996). *Impure Science: AIDS, Activism, and the Politics of Knowledge*. Berkeley: University of California Press.

Fontes, Fernando, *et al.* (2014). "The Emancipation of Disability Studies in Portugal". *Disability & Society, 9* (6), 849–862.

Foucault, Michel (2006 [1969]). *The Archaeology of Knowledge*. Oxon: Routledge.

Fricker, Miranda (2007). *Epistemic Injustice: Power and the Ethics of Knowing*. Oxford: Oxford University Press.

Gieryn, Thomas (1995). "Boundaries of Science" in S. Jasanoff, *et al.* (eds.), *Handbook of Science and Technology Studies* (2nd ed) (pp.393–443). London: Sage.

Gieryn, Thomas (1999). *Cultural Boundaries of Science: Credibility on the Line*. Chicago: University of Chicago Press.

Gonçalves, Maria José (2009). *Meta-Analysis of Gender and Science Research (Portugal)*. Retrieved 02/04/2016, from http://run.unl.pt/handle/10362/4692

Gumport, Patricia (2002). *Academic Pathfinders: Knowledge Creation and Feminist Scholarship*. Westport, CT: Greenwood Press.

Henderson, Emily F. (2012). "'A Key Area of Knowledge Delivered by Someone Knowledgeable': Feminist Expectations and Explorations of a One-off Economics Lecture on Gender". *Journal of International Women's Studies, 13* (6), 44–56.

Hey, Valerie (2003). "Joining the Club? Academia and Working-Class Femininities". *Gender and Education, 15* (3), 319–335.

Husu, Liisa (2011). *Sexism, Support and Survival in Academia*. Helsinki: University of Helsinki Press.

Joaquim, Teresa (2007). "Feminismos, Estudos sobre as Mulheres, ou 'Para Onde Vai Este Barco?'" in L. Amâncio, *et al.* (eds.), *O Longo Caminho das Mulheres* (pp.203–216). Lisboa: Dom Quixote.

Kilomba, Grada (2007). *Africans in the Academia: Diversity in Adversity*. Retrieved 02/04/2016, from http://www.africavenir.org/nc/news-details/article/africans-in-the-academia-diversity-in-adversity.html

Kokot, Patrizia (2010). *Partnership Anatomies: A Comparative Perspective on Career Advancement and the Private Lives of Women Partners in Chartered Accountancy Firms in Germany and the UK*. PhD Thesis, LSE.

Lamont, Michèle (2009). *How Professors Think: Inside the Curious World of Academic Judgment*. Cambridge, MA: Harvard University Press.

Latour, Bruno and Woolgar, Steve (1986 [1979]). *Laboratory Life: The Construction of Scientific Facts*. Princeton, NJ: Princeton University Press.

Machado, Fernando Luís, *et al.* (1995). "Origens Sociais e Estratificação dos Cientistas" in J.C. Jesuíno (ed.), *A Comunidade Científica Portuguesa nos Finais do Século XX* (pp.109–133). Oeiras: Celta.

Maeso, Silvia Rodríguez and Araújo, Marta (2014). "The Politics of (Anti-)Racism: Academic Research and Policy Discourse in Europe" in W.D. Hund and A. Lentin (eds.), *Racism and Sociology* (pp.207–237). Berlin: Lit-Verlag.

Mählck, Paula (2013). "Academic Women with Migrant Background in the Global Knowledge Economy: Bodies, Hierarchies and Resistance". *Women's Studies International Forum, 36*, 65–74.

Mallard, Grégoire, *et al.* (2009). "Fairness as Appropriateness: Negotiating Epistemological Differences in Peer Review". *Science, Technology & Human Values, 34* (5), 573–606.

Marchbank, Jen and Letherby, Gayle (2006). "Views and Perspectives of Women's Studies: A Survey of Women and Men Students". *Gender and Education, 18* (2), 157–182.

Miske, Shirley (1995). *Center in the Margins: The Development of Women's Studies in a Thai University from Three Organizational Perspectives.* PhD Thesis, Michigan State University.

Mohanty, Chandra Talpade (2003). *Feminism without Borders: Decolonizing Theory, Practicing Solidarity.* Durham, NC: Duke University Press.

Moss-Racusina, Corinne, *et al.* (2012). "Science Faculty's Subtle Gender Biases Favour Male Students". *Proceedings of the National Academy of Sciences, 109* (41), 16474–16479.

Nash, Jennifer and Owens, Emily (2015). "Institutional Feelings: Practicing Women's Studies in the Corporate University". *Feminist Formations, 27* (3), vii–xi.

Reiter, Bernd (2008). "The Perils of Empire: Nationhood and Citizenship in Portugal". *Citizenship Studies, 12* (4), 397–412.

Rich, Adrienne (1995). *On Lies, Secrets, and Silence: Selected Prose (1966–1978).* New York: Norton.

Rose, Hilary (1994). *Love, Power and Knowledge: Towards a Feminist Transformation of the Sciences.* Cambridge: Polity Press.

Small, Mario L. (1999). "Departmental Conditions and the Emergence of New Disciplines: Two Cases in the Legitimation of African-American Studies". *Theory and Society, 28* (5), 659–707.

Søndergaard, Dorte Marie (2005). "Making Sense of Gender, Age, Power and Disciplinary Position: Intersecting Discourses in the Academy". *Feminism & Psychology, 15* (2), 189–208.

Westkott, Marcia (2003). "Institutional Success and Political Vulnerability: A Lesson in the Importance of Allies" in R. Wiegman (ed.), *Women's Studies on its Own* (pp.293–311). Durham, NC: Duke University Press.

Chapter 6

The importance of being foreign and modern

The geopolitics of the epistemic status of WGFS

In this book, I have rather forcefully, and I would argue productively, pulled and stretched the concept of map to try to make sense of negotiations of epistemic status.[1] But looking at real, rather than metaphorical, maps can be extremely productive too. The processes analysed in the previous chapters unfold locally, but happen within, and are part of, global networks of academic and political relations across national boundaries. As Amsler notes, 'the drive for scientificity in a field of knowledge (. . .) is embedded within wider histories of modernization, colonization and globalization' (2007: 33). It is crucial, therefore, to explicitly situate negotiations of epistemic status within those global relations and their histories, and engage directly with the *local and global geopolitics* of epistemic status; that is what this chapter tries to do. My interest in interrogating relations between space and epistemic status is not original. It has been argued that the 2000s saw a 'spatial turn' in debates on scientific practice, with scholars becoming more attentive to how geographical location shapes the terms on which, and degree to which, knowledge is recognised as credible. As Gieryn notes '[t]he *where* of science has come under increasing scholarly scrutiny. Geography (. . .) [is] ever more frequently brought in as [a] factor helping to explain the legitimacy of knowledge claims' (2006: 5, original emphasis). Anderson and Adams echo this, indicating that 'debates about what formally constitutes "science" are now focused as much on geography as on (. . .) epistemology' (2008: 184).

What brings geography and epistemology together in this body of literature and my own work is the observation that places, countries and continents have epistemic status – i.e. they are seen to be more or less able to produce proper scholarly knowledge. That literature is also grounded on the insight – a major legacy of postcolonial and feminist theory – that epistemic status is unequally distributed across the globe, with proper scientificity generally being associated with western countries (Akena, 2012; Connell, 2007; Goonatilake, 1993; Harding, 2008; Nader, 1996; Sousa Santos, 2007). Scholars from around the world have offered compelling analyses of how the hegemony of particular western countries in the global academic system,[2] the status of English as its dominant language of communication, and the structure of the academic publishing industry, generate asymmetrical patterns of knowledge circulation and recognition of authors and institutions (Alatas, 2003; Canagarajah, 2002; Connell, 2007; Griffin and Braidotti, 2002; Lykke, 2004; Mbembe, 2016; Meriläinen *et al.*, 2008; Paasi, 2005; Spivak, 1987; Wöhrer, 2016). They argue that because (some) western countries are considered to generate more advanced and 'exportable' knowledge, scholarship produced outside those countries is much less likely to circulate internationally and be read, referenced and taught elsewhere.

These hegemonies and their effects have been much debated in WGFS networks, conferences and journals because, as Cerwonka argues, examining how WGFS knowledge claims travel transnationally and become used locally 'is crucial for understanding the true complexity of power relations within (. . .) women's and gender studies in a global area' (2008: 811). Contributions to those debates have persuasively shown that the privileging and large-scale 'export' of theories from/about western countries has several detrimental effects (Amâncio, 2003; Braidotti, 2000; Griffin and Braidotti, 2002; Rahbari, 2016; Spivak, 1987): it renders our collective canons worryingly exclusionary, skewed and homogeneous (Calvi, 2010; Egeland, 2011; Widerberg, 1998; Wöhrer, 2016), can lead to inaccurate or simplistic analyses of social life and gender relations in other countries (Cerwonka, 2008; Kašić, 2016; Mizielińska and Kulpa, 2011), may stifle the development of autochthonous feminist concepts or theories (Kašić, 2016; Macedo and Amaral, 2002) and discourage authors from producing nationally relevant knowledge and working with local partners/audiences (Stöckelová, 2012). These debates have made it clear that '[i]nternationally, the domination of Anglo-American literature and discourse in women's studies cannot be separated from the history of Western colonialization and imperialism, and, ironically, this domination continues in discourses emerging in the wake of postcolonial globalization' (Egeland, 2011: 236). This is an important insight; it must be considered by all WGFS scholars in their own practice, and remain at the forefront of collective debates about the past, present and future of WGFS.

There is no doubt that the academic hegemony of particular countries constrains the growth, diversity and local relevance of WGFS. And yet, accounts of WGFS' institutionalisation throughout the world describe many situations where that hegemony has produced not (just) *constraints* and *losses*, but (also) *gains, openings* and *opportunities* for WGFS. In a study of WGFS institutionalisation in Taiwan, for example, Chen notes that Taiwanese academics 'invited feminist scholars from other countries to lecture and help raise awareness [in Taiwanese academia] of the significance of women's studies' (2004: 68–69); according to her, this contributed directly to increase acceptance of, and support for, the field. A second example can be found in Petö's (2001) contribution to a debate about the status of 'western [feminist] theory stars'. She notes that such stars can play a crucial positive role in the development of WGFS in countries outside the centre, namely by providing support to local WGFS initiatives under threat. She illustrates this with a reference to an 'international protest [in 2000] by Joan Scott, Judith Butler, Elizabeth Grosz, Elizabeth Minnich, Rosi Braidotti, to name just a few, who immediately [and with some success] stood up with horror to protest against (. . .) [the firing and demotion of faculty in] a gender studies programme' at a university in Hungary (2001: 91).

These gains, openings and opportunities have not received sustained attention within our debates about global academic exchanges in WGFS, as I have begun to argue elsewhere (Pereira, 2014). Therefore, in this chapter I try to analyse them in depth and highlight the complex ways in which they interact with the losses and constraints we have so thoroughly inventoried. My analysis is profoundly influenced by '[w]ork (. . .) that has focused on the epistemological significance of "travel", "translation" and flux for a politicized feminist project' (Bahovec and Hemmings, 2004: 336; see, for example, Costa, 2006; Davis and Evans, 2010; Vasterling *et al.*, 2006 and other publications in the "Travelling Concepts" series). However, rather than focus on how concrete WGFS products, such as books, concepts or theories, circulate between regions (Cerwonka, 2008; Costa, 2006; Davis, 2007; Davis and Evans, 2010; Knapp, 2005), I want to ask how credibility travels, i.e. how the 'authorizing signature' (Mohanty, 1988)[3] of western scholarship is imported/exported across borders.

Problematising the relation between space and epistemic status in this way requires, however, foregrounding a key postcolonial insight: in global relations, space becomes invested with particular meanings partly because it is understood also in terms of time. Mignolo's analyses of colonial history provide compelling demonstrations of the imbrication of space and time. He explains that '[t]oward the end of the nineteenth century, (. . .) spatial boundaries were transformed into chronological ones', through a 'process of converting the savages/cannibals into primitives/Orientals and (. . .) relocating them in a chronological scale as opposed to a geographical distance' (1998: 35). This 'denial of coevalness' provided the basis for 'relocating people in a chronological hierarchy' (1998: 35). The 'foreign' is therefore not just a different space, but also often another time (Mignolo, 1998; Mizielińska and Kulpa, 2011; Sousa Santos, 2009), and 'collective identities are produced as much through temporal boundaries as they are through spatial ones' (Klinke, 2013: 675). Today, certain countries continue to be seen as more 'modern'[4] and 'advanced' than others, and that is one of the reasons why they come to occupy a hegemonic position in the global academic order. Thus, I join Massey in 'insist[ing] on the inseparability of time and space, on their joint constitution through the interrelations between phenomena; on the necessity of thinking in terms of space-time' (1994: 269). In negotiations of epistemic status, *geo*politics are also *chrono*politics.

I unpack the geo- and chronopolitics of epistemic status in WGFS by asking how global academic relations shape, and are shaped by, local boundary-work. I draw on fieldwork in Portugal (whose semi-peripheral condition I discuss in the next section), and use it to examine how WGFS scholars based in countries at the (semi-)periphery of the global academic order engage with the figure(s) of the supposedly more modern academic centre in their local negotiations. I first show how the modern foreign is brought inside Portugal – physically and symbolically – to strengthen the credibility of WGFS claims or initiatives. I then look at the reverse move: how the projection of Portuguese WGFS scholars outside, into the modern foreign, impacts on the conditions of performativity of their boundary-work within Portugal. But discussions of the geopolitics of epistemic status must go beyond the boundaries of academia, and so in the last section I study speeches made by government representatives and other officials, to show how WGFS is used to symbolise the modernity of the nation and its institutions.

Of centres and (semi-)peripheries: The status of the modern foreign in Portugal

> *And here at the western extreme*
> *Of a ragged Europe, I*
> *Want to be European: I want to be European*
> *In some corner of Portugal*
>
> Afonso Duarte (1956*)

Portugal, located 'at the western extreme' of Europe, has been characterised as an in-between space, ambivalently positioned in global hierarchies. Some scholars, most notably Sousa Santos (2009) describe it as a 'semi-peripheral society', occupying both an intermediate and intermediary position between the centre and periphery of the world-system. Others portray Portugal as located in the perimeter of the centre, as a country that is (*estar*) *in* the global centre but is (*ser*)[5] not *of* the centre (Nunes, 2002: 196*).[6] It is a position in some ways similar to that of other countries, particularly of Southern, and Central and Eastern, Europe: consider, for example, the following quotes: 'contemporary Greek selves are fashioned precisely through the exploration of the tensions of *being*, yet at the same time as *not being*, "western" or "European"' (Cowan, 1996: 62, original emphases); 'Central and Eastern Europe is a "contemporary periphery" because it is "European enough" (geographically), "yet not enough advanced" to become "Western" (temporally)' (Mizielińska and Kulpa, 2011: 18).

The signs and symptoms of Portugal's in-betweenness can, according to these and other authors, be found in its position in several social, economic and cultural indicators. In many of them – e.g. demographic rates, consumption practices, female employment – Portugal is close to Northern European countries, whereas in several other indicators – notably educational levels, poverty, the structure of economy and industry – it is closer to so-called peripheral countries (Ferreira, 1999; Machado and Costa, 2000; Sousa Santos, 1994; Vala and Torres, 2006). Consequently, contemporary discourses about Portugal are, as Sousa Santos argues, characterised by 'the coexistence of contradictory representations of very fast change and frozen immobilism' (2009: 5). Indeed, since the fall of *Estado Novo* in 1974, the country has undergone accelerated modernisation in many spheres, including gender equality and sexual/reproductive rights,[7] but in many respects continues to be understood as having a 'modernisation deficit' or 'incomplete modernity' (Machado and Costa, 2000: 15), and lagging behind other western countries. Therefore, Portugal is frequently described in daily and media discourse as residing on the 'tail of Europe', especially when new statistics place it at the bottom of a European ranking for a valued indicator. This coexists with the description of Portugal as the 'face of Europe', a colonial metaphor still in use today. In his intervention in the parliamentary debate on the EU's Lisbon Treaty during my first fieldwork period, Prime-Minister José Sócrates (2008*) stated: 'Portugal and the Portuguese feel at home in Europe, because Europe is its root and destiny. [Portugal] is the face with which Europe stares, as Pessoa said,[8] and it's the place of encounter between Europe and other worlds'.

These statements point to another key dimension of Portugal's ambivalent status as a 'nation in between' (Reiter, 2005: 81; Sousa Santos, 1994): the country's colonial past. Portugal had the longest-lived modern European empire, spanning 5 centuries and continents, but during part of that period 'had a subaltern and subsidiary [position] in (. . .) world economy and geopolitics, namely in relation to the British Empire' (Vale de Almeida, 2008: 2). According to Sousa Santos, 'the intermediate, semi-peripheral matrix of [contemporary] Portuguese culture' has been partly constituted by the fact that 'from the 17th century, the Portuguese (. . .) considered the peoples of its colonies as primitive and savage, and at the same time were themselves (. . .) considered, by Northern European diplomats and scholars, as primitive and savage' (1994: 133*; 2009). The Portuguese were viewed by other colonial powers as too close to colonised populations, 'half-breeds who generate yet more half-breeds' (Vale de Almeida, 2008: 5).

After the 1974 revolution and the dismantling of the colonial empire, attempts were made to distance Portugal from its imperial past, reorient it towards the 'real and fantasmatic' (Joaquim, 2004: 91*) space of Europe, and reposition it as a European nation.[9] Joining the European Economic Community in 1986 was a key political and symbolic milestone. According to Sousa Santos 'integration in the EU has tended to create the credible illusion that Portugal, because it is integrated in the centre, has become central' (1994: 58*). However, that alignment with the 'centre' is very precarious: the Portuguese are still seen as 'non-whites' (Reiter, 2005) or 'not quite white' (Vale de Almeida, 2008) in some contexts, especially countries with large Portuguese immigrant communities, such as Canada, France, Germany, Switzerland and the US. Like other Southern European countries, Portugal is sometimes depicted internationally as very different from, and less developed than, Northern Europe, a depiction which gained renewed visibility in debates about the financial situation in Southern Europe in the crisis of 2007–2010 and the various post-2010 bailouts.[10]

Because Portugal is not unambiguously recognised as fully modern and European, many aspects of public life are driven by a preoccupation with, and investment in, the affirmation of the country's modern Europeanness. Prime-Minister Sócrates' speech above offers one example. This precariousness shares some features with the position of WGFS. Because Portugal is always potentially

vulnerable to being relegated to the 'wrong' side of a boundary, it becomes necessary to continuously demonstrate it is on the 'right' side.

> [The] imagining of Portuguese nationhood is (. . .) set around the necessity to
> demonstrate to the world (. . .) that Portugal is a modern country and indeed
> a truly European one (. . .). [T]he construction of Portuguese nationhood is
> shot through with a palpable collective struggle for recognition. Hard facts
> are not necessarily helpful in this process, so more emphasis is laid on invok-
> ing Portugal's modernity, Europeanness, whiteness and difference from the
> non-European world, especially its distance from those black Portuguese
> who were previously part of the "pluricontinental" nation.
>
> (Reiter, 2008: 407)[11]

Viegas and Costa note that questions of whether 'Portugal [is] a modernised, developed country, or not very much so' (2000: 2) are always present. They are often
posed explicitly, but 'even when they are not announced as such, they are (. . .) in
the background, as a thread, as the backdrop against which problems are raised,
as a yardstick, as an implicit criterion of assessment' (2000: 2).

Academia is one stage where the negotiation of the country's in-betweenness
plays out. Portugal is semi-peripheral in relation to scientific practice (Delicado,
2013; Nunes, 1996), in line with Alatas' definition of the term: '[academic] communities that [are] dependent on ideas originating in the (. . .) centres, but which
themselves exert some influence on peripheral (. . .) communities [in Portugal's
case, its former African colonies, for example] by way of the provision of research
funds, places in their universities (. . .), the funding of international conferences,
and so on' (2003: 606). The scientific products and protagonists of the 'centre'
have an influential role in Portugal, symbolically and institutionally. Analysing
debates about 'mad cow disease' in the 1990s, Gonçalves found a sharp contrast
between Portuguese politicians' 'deference toward foreign research' produced 'in
more advanced countries' and their dismissal of Portuguese scholars' research,
'rejected as unreliable' (2000: 439). Nunes observed that Portuguese scientists
in a cancer research unit commonly referred to 'cultural stereotypes about Portugal and its presumed difference from Northern European countries as a way of
explaining particular instances of failure' (1996: 13).

Portuguese science is also characterised by a 'dependence on transnational links
and experiences for the viability and legitimation of scientific careers' (Nunes, 1996:
1). Having connections to colleagues abroad is explicitly valued and there is a very
strong orientation towards the foreign (Carreira da Silva, 2016). This has resulted,
for instance, in Portugal being one of the European countries with the highest rates
of international collaboration in co-authoring of articles (Patrício, 2010). Changes
in science policy in the past 15 years, and the connected emergence of academic
cultures of performativity, have further increased the centrality and influence of the
modern foreign within national scientific practice. Following the trend also observable across many other (semi-)peripheral countries (see e.g. Stöckelová (2012) on

the Czech Republic, Meriläinen *et al.* (2008) on Finland, Fahlgren *et al.* (2016), on Sweden, and also Aavik *et al.* (2015) and Paasi (2005)), Portuguese mechanisms of research assessment are increasingly centred on international activities as the most valued form of academic work, with international peer-reviewed publications becoming established 'as a primary criterion for evaluation' (Santos Pereira, 2004: 249). These changes have reinforced the importance of the foreign, because it is now *the main, or only*, provider of the publication, funding and training opportunities that individuals need to achieve the expected performance and status, and on which institutions depend for their ratings and resources.

Reflecting on the links between science and semi-peripherality in Portugal, Roque argues that

> one feature that may define [the Portuguese] semi-peripheral condition is the (. . .) public [use] in Portuguese science (. . .) of the rhetoric that there exists a dangerous delay (. . .) [vis-à-vis the foreign], that there is a modern temporality and symbolic geography centred in a point distant from the national space, [providing] the ultimate model which we must try to keep up with at all cost.
>
> (2001: 284*)

My observations during fieldwork in Portugal confirm his characterisation. In events, interviews and informal chats, scholars and students regularly described Portuguese scholarship as 'delayed'.[12] The two examples below are taken from interviews.

> *"In Portugal, there's a huge delay, we know that. This can seem like an exaggeration, but I often say that in almost everything we have a delay of 30 years vis-à-vis other countries! [Laughs] And there's a special delay in the social sciences, which only really developed after 1974. (. . .) We very much need to work with foreign scholars (. . .), they have other ways of addressing problems, and we need that very much, precisely because our country has always had a delay, has always been less advanced in this [WGFS] and we need to catch the train.[13]"*
>
> Junior WGFS scholar

> *"There's so much ignorance [in Portugal] in relation to this [WGFS]! How is it possible that people don't . . . well, it's our delay, isn't it, it's the fact that we're here, in this hole at the end of Europe."*
>
> Senior WGFS scholar

In one WGFS conference, the chair opened the debate after a panel by jokingly saying:

> *"We're already delayed – as usual, one might say – but well, we're very European in some things but on this we're still somewhat delayed, so I'll try to speed things up a bit! [Much laughter from the audience]"*[14]

It is, however, worth complicating this account: although Portugal is systematically described as delayed, that delay is not always portrayed as negative. A claim regularly made in social science events/texts – but rarely present in WGFS – is that Portugal's delay has positive potential, because it allows Portuguese scholars to learn from international colleagues, avoid their past mistakes and maintain an open perspective. These discourses position the perceived subalternity of Portuguese scholarship as an epistemic virtue, a condition that enables production of good knowledge.[15] Consider the following statement:

> The long period of censorship imposed on the field of social sciences (. . .) strengthened the attitudes of receptivity [in Portugal] to various schools and contributions. Therefore *we are in a good position not to make exclusions*, but to summon and select, in a wider sphere, that which appears to be ripe from [international] production.

> (Almeida, J.F.d., 1991: 81)

The description of Portuguese scholarship as more inclusive works to downplay and mask its (many) exclusions, including the devaluing of WGFS scholarship. More generally, these discourses demonstrate that the valuing of foreign knowledge because it is more 'advanced' can coexist with a valuing of the potential benefits of local 'delay'. Hierarchies between local and foreign scholarship are also complicated by the fact that WGFS scholars (in texts, events and 4 interviews) critique forms of national subservience to foreign theories or concepts, which they believe do not always constitute appropriate tools for analysis of Portuguese society (Macedo and Amaral, 2002; Pinto, 2008; see Widerberg, 1998 for similar arguments vis-à-vis Scandinavia). The relation between (semi-) peripheral scholarly communities and global epistemic hierarchies is rarely straightforward.

Invoking the modern foreign

Gieryn notes that 'a familiar feature of scientists' boundary-work [is] drawing independent authority for one's own [claims] by (. . .) attributing authorship *elsewhere*' (1995: 431, original emphasis). Faced with sceptical audiences in conferences, classrooms and other sites, Portuguese WGFS scholars frequently do just that: announce that they are not the author of a claim or the only person studying something, but that it is also said/done abroad.

> *"[Social science discipline] has been developed from men's perspective, treated as universal. (. . .) This has been clearly denounced, and it wasn't me who said this, it's demonstrated in foreign literature."*
> PhD candidate speaking in viva for WGFS thesis
> in mainstream social science

> *"I'd argue it's important to critically reflect on feminism and political institutions in Portugal. It's not an idea that has come from my head: many, many international researchers have raised that question."*
> WGFS scholar presenting at a non-WGFS social science conference

These scholars are locating the source of their claims about the value of WGFS in the more authoritative space of *"foreign literature"*. In chapter 4, I noted that citation of particular foreign authors, notably Bourdieu, is a strategy that WGFS scholars use to get WGFS recognised. However, in the claims above the focus is less on the authorising signature (Mohanty, 1988) of specific individuals, and actual names are not cited. Indeed, many of those WGFS authors' names would not be recognised by a non-WGFS audience and would thus carry little weight as authorising signatures. What is made salient is the fact that those authors are *"foreign"* or *"international"*.

The foreign is also frequently invoked in and through explicit comparisons between the situation in Portugal and abroad.

> *"I congratulate you for having the courage to explicitly adopt a feminist perspective. (. . .) It's a perspective which, although clearly recognised abroad, isn't yet recognised in mainstream [social science discipline] in Portugal. (. . .) Feminist research is (. . .) still a rarity here, although it's widely done and easily recognised in Anglo-Saxon contexts."*
> WGFS scholar, speaking as an examiner in the viva for a WGFS thesis in a mainstream social science

> *"It was only very recently that some women scientists in Portugal began to be able to come out as feminists in universities, (. . .) but in Northern Europe they were able to do this earlier, so they've been able to argue (. . .) for the institutionalisation of gender studies. (. . .) We must learn from the vast experience and success of Nordic countries."*
> Senior WGFS scholar presenting in a non-WGFS humanities conference

> *"This is (. . .) the first project on [WGFS theme] to be carried out in [social science discipline] in Portugal. (. . .) It's a complete gap in Portuguese research. (. . .) This immense gap in Portugal contrasts with a true <boom> in studies about [theme] abroad. (. . .) There's so much work published abroad that it's very difficult to keep up with the literature."*
> Junior scholar presenting in a non-WGFS social science conference

My interviewees explained that such references to the fact that colleagues abroad are prolifically pursuing and widely recognising WGFS scholarship helped make their work seem more substantiated and *"less like an idiosyncrasy of mine"*, as one senior scholar put it. The modern foreign therefore functions as what Gieryn has called as a truth-spot (2002, 2006), i.e. a site that lends credibility to claims. He proposed this concept to analyse how the credibility of claims can partly be 'sustained by locating in some particular place[16] their authors, their making or their message' (2002: 113) because that place has come to be associated with the production of proper knowledge. But the modern foreign is not just a spot or space; it also represents a particular time, as I argued earlier. Gieryn's concept of truth-spots can, and should, therefore be expanded to reflect that fact that geographical location is framed as chronological difference. Thus, we can speak of the modern foreign as a *truth-point*, i.e. a point in space and in time which lends credibility to claims.

WGFS scholars invoke the modern foreign as a truth-point not just when presenting their work, but also when attempting to persuade resistant university administrations to grant support to WGFS.[17] Beleza explains how she used such comparisons to integrate WGFS in Law curricula. She writes, 'the inclusion of [an optional course on] "Women and Law" in the undergraduate degree (. . .) was not peaceful. Pointing to how common its existence is in most American universities was an important argument in getting it accepted in the end' (2002: 81*). In an annual general meeting of APEM (the Portuguese Women's Studies Association) observed during fieldwork, members explicitly suggested drawing on such comparisons as part of APEM's planned strategy to strength WGFS nationally.

> *"What we must tell whoever wins the [upcoming governmental] elections (. . .) to convince them to give more support to gender studies is 'this is all over Europe! Everyone's doing it, everyone! It's no longer acceptable to not have this, it makes us look bad!'. Even if it's just to make sure that Portugal's not seen to be [lagging behind,] on the other side of the moon, they must support the field!"*

When composing a proposal to create a WGFS programme, one senior scholar went further and contacted WGFS colleagues abroad to ask to use their names – very literally 'authorising signatures' in this case – on the proposal.

> *"I said [to the university administration] 'this is shameful, Portugal not having it [WGFS], it exists all over and we don't have it here!'. (. . .) And for the proposal, (. . .) I got consultants from foreign institutions: [names 5 WGFS scholars, based in the US and Northern Europe].*
> *MMP: What was their role?*
> *They were only there to act as guarantees, witnesses in a way. [Laughs] I wrote that these were highly qualified people with dazzling CVs, and that they'd said that if we needed them to write something for us, they would. But they didn't need to, because it was enough to have their names there, and mention what universities and countries they were from, that was powerful enough."*

This scholar's reference to shame points to a key aspect of the logic of these international comparisons. Contrasting Portuguese institutions with well-respected universities abroad with WGFS provision highlights the former's 'backwardness' vis-à-vis the modern foreign. That backwardness is perceived as problematic, not only due to Portugal's preoccupation with its precarious modernity, but also because backwardness is a liability in the performative university, undermining an institution's 'market value' and ongoing performance of quality. Flagging backwardness produces, therefore, forms of shame or embarrassment which help increase support for the field. As one senior WGFS scholar interviewed explains,

> *"One argument we used [when proposing a new WGFS PG degree] was 'look at foreign universities, (. . .) what's done in Spain, France, England, US, and there's nothing here!'. That usually works because what gives consistency and authority to this field is the fact it exists in institutions abroad, right? (. . .) If respected places have it and we don't, that's embarrassing because it shows we're miles away from them."*

This last scholar refers to, among others, France as example and model. Nevertheless, France consistently appears in comparative European studies as a country with low levels of WGFS institutionalisation (Griffin, 2005). Although French WGFS 'production is rich and varied' (Ezekiel, 1994: 21), several authors describe significant micro- and macro-level obstacles to its recognition (Pinto, 2008; Viennot *et al.*, 2000). Discussing WGFS in France, Armengaud and Jasser themselves invoke the foreign – exactly like Portuguese scholars – to demonstrate how shameful the situation is: 'abroad, in the US, in England, [male] social science experts integrate the results of feminist research in their work' (1994: 13*). And yet this claim is not entirely accurate either: many US- and UK-based authors have denounced their non-WGFS colleagues' lack of attention to, and citing of, WGFS in the past and present, as chapter 4 shows. It seems that because particular countries have considerable symbolic weight as sites with more advanced knowledge (and allegedly progressive gender regimes), it is credible and effective to invoke them, even when the WGFS situation in those countries is not actually as impressive as claimed. In that sense, references to the modern foreign are both real and imaginary. They are both descriptions of actual differences in academic systems or WGFS institutionalisation levels (see Griffin, 2005 for a European overview) and plays on existing (sometimes inaccurate) assumptions about what those differences might be, assumptions which are shaped by the global geo- and chronopolitics of epistemic status and gender equality.

Sometimes, the modern foreign is brought into Portugal not just discursively and/or on paper, but also physically. Scholars from the modern foreign can themselves function as 'authorising bodies', i.e. embodied symbols of epistemic status whose presence lends credibility to Portuguese scholars' work.

> *"We want to have foreign speakers at the conference, that's absolutely crucial, because their presence allows us to better confront [the invited representatives of universities], force them to face the contrast between the European and national landscapes [vis-à-vis the institutionalisation of*

WGFS]. Having foreign speakers helps exert pressure to change attitudes [towards WGFS]."

Interview, junior WFS scholar co-organising a WGFS
conference aimed at a non-WGFS audience

"One thing that directly contributed to legitimating our [WGFS] MA programme was the fact we organised several public lectures by foreign speakers (. . .). One colleague knew people abroad and got lots of them to come, and that was good. (. . .) It made our work more credible, the fact we were bringing foreign scholars to the University to speak about feminism."

Interview, senior WGFS scholar

This last interviewee added later that in meeting these visiting scholars she realised that *"in their universities they experience exactly the same problems we have, although we tend to think that our national context is more difficult"*. Indeed, even scholars who fail to secure recognition in their institutions or countries can operate effectively as authorising bodies in Portugal, because they represent a space/ time of higher epistemic and professional value. International WGFS academics' visits to Portugal are, therefore, not just a means of knowledge circulation, but also a key instrument to evidence and strengthen the field's epistemic status locally.

As these quotes illustrate, invocations are often generic: scholars talk about the 'foreign' or 'international' but do not mention specific countries/regions. Where there is explicit naming of locations, the most common are *"European"*, *"Anglo-American"/"Anglo-Saxon"*, US, UK or England, *"Northern Europe"*, *"Nordic countries"*. Two locations beyond these categories are also sometimes (though less frequently) mentioned and play a particularly interesting role. Spain is one of them. Sousa Santos describes Portuguese narratives about Spain as a 'game of mirrors: sometimes highlighting the contrasts, sometimes highlighting the similarities'; the countries are 'counterposed, always against a background of affinity' (1994: 55*). WGFS scholars' discourses mirror this: references to Spain were based both on an affirmation of its proximity and a foregrounding of its difference vis-à-vis WGFS' recognition.[18] For example, a quote analysed above, where a scholar contrasts the *"complete gap"* in Portuguese literature with a *"true <boom>"* abroad, continues as follows:

"There's so much work published abroad (. . .). This production has been more prolific in the US and UK, but even right here next to us, a Spanish anthropologist has just published a book on this theme."

Junior WGFS scholar speaking in a non-WGFS conference

"Only a few Portuguese universities have [WGFS] degrees (. . .) but we go next door to Spain and all universities have PG degrees, sometimes more than one, and research centres (. . .), many since the 1990s! (. . .) In Portugal

we only have general women's studies journals. If we look at, I won't even say the UK or US, all we need is to look at our neighbouring country and Granada, for example, not even one of the main universities, has a journal on women's history, a subtheme of women's studies!"

Junior WGFS scholar speaking in a non-WGFS
humanities conference

As a country closer to Portugal in location, culture and history, Spain can throw into sharper relief the inadequacy of Portuguese academia's levels and modes of engagement with WGFS. It may be little surprise that Portugal is delayed vis-à-vis *"the UK and US"* (it's not *"even [worth] say[ing]"* what the situation is there), but lagging far behind Spain is another matter: it is more significant and shameful, and it more powerfully threatens the affirmation of Portugal's precarious modernity.[19]

The other context is Brazil. In two WGFS interventions in non-WGFS conferences, Brazil was invoked as a close and therefore potentially more shaming example, much like Spain, but it was positioned differently from Spain. Critically drawing on a Portuguese tendency to dismissively represent Brazil as less advanced (McLaughlin, 2009; Reiter, 2005; Vale de Almeida, 2004), WGFS scholars highlighted how *"interesting"* and *"important"* it was to note that WGFS is more institutionalised in Brazil, arguing that this shows Brazil has *'overtaken us'* in academic development.[20] Brazil was invoked not as a traditional symbol of a modern foreign, but demonstration that even countries portrayed in the popular imagination as *less modern* are already *more advanced* than Portugal vis-à-vis WGFS.[21] Invocations of Spain and Brazil show that it is not always the supposedly most modern foreign that lends the most weight in negotiations of epistemic status. In some situations, comparison with regions considered closer in level of 'development' may work equally or more effectively, because they provide supposedly more realistic, and therefore more shameful, reminders of how developed Portugal might feasibly already be regarding WGFS.

Projecting the (semi-)periphery into the centre

Being in the modern foreign was also described as an effective way of contributing to the recognition of WGFS within Portugal. According to several interviewees, having a physical, institutional or intellectual presence abroad made it easier to secure status and space nationally. One senior WGFS scholar explained that upon returning to Portugal after a period in the US,

"Colleagues saw me as very exotic (. . .), in the way I thought and spoke, and the department liked that, it helped make it more modern, so I had no trouble creating my own space here, and they let me work on my [WGFS] stuff. Although, of course, with time I realised there was still a lot of resistance."

Scholars highlighted the importance and impact of joining international academic networks.

> *"MMP: Do you sometimes feel that in [social science discipline] there are themes considered less relevant?*
>
> *"Yes, of course, completely! These ones, women and gender! Absolutely! Oh yes, it's completely like that! But our colleagues have to put up with us because we do so much, often more than them; we're like fleas, we hop about and go everywhere, we're very internationalised, more than they are! We're in touch with foreign colleagues, do things with them. (. . .) We're in [lists international networks and associations], we've had positions in committees in international associations, and so they end up taking us more seriously because we're so active abroad."*
>
> Senior scholar in a social science discipline, with WGFS expertise

Another important strategy is to implant Portuguese WGFS scholars abroad. As I noted in chapter 3, very few positions have opened in Portuguese universities and this has significantly limited opportunities for renewal and expansion of WGFS. 5 interviewees explained that, in such conditions, the most useful thing early-career WGFS scholars could do, for their careers and Portuguese WGFS as a whole, is leave the country.[22]

> *"The intellectual and institutional climate here isn't going to change much in the coming years, so there's no point staying. If they want to work in gender studies in Portugal, younger scholars need to leave. Ideally, do the PhD abroad, spend some time in the US, and publish in foreign journals. All that helps to legitimate you here. This way, when they return they'll be invested with lots of foreign status."*
>
> Interview, senior WGFS scholar

According to this and other interviewees, Portuguese scholars can be *"invested"* with foreign status, i.e. themselves embody and carry the authority of the modern foreign, thus acting within their own country as authorising signatures and bodies. As an early-career Portuguese scholar who completed PhD training in the UK and is working in a UK institution, I myself was frequently interpellated as a colleague whose relation to the foreign could help advance WGFS in Portugal. Having formal links to 'international' scholars strengthens institutional ratings, so adding me officially as a member of Portuguese WGFS research groups helped boost their performance in national assessment exercises. I was encouraged by participants to stay abroad because any interventions from afar would carry significantly more weight. As one senior scholar told me after we finished the interview,

> *"What we need above anything else is for people like you to be abroad, to be honest, because their connection to foreign universities can help increase the credibility of things here. (. . .) If you're abroad, we can call you for PhD*

> *boards, send students for co-supervision, all real advantages when trying to consolidate the field and get it recognised (. . .). A foreign affiliation has more value than any affiliation you could get in Portugal."*

The projection of Portuguese WGFS abroad is important but not easy. Interviewees sometimes struggle to intervene in the modern foreign, partly due to Portugal's image abroad as an academically peripheral country. One interviewee described being treated in a patronising manner by foreign colleagues in European WGFS meetings. Others spoke of established hierarchies between countries in terms of academic relevance and influence, and discussed these hierarchies' impacts on their work.

> *"Power relations between countries are unequal, and (. . .) countries of the centre have other working conditions, namely making their journals [internationally] visible in ways we can't match. I think Portuguese gender studies has to fight very hard. We pay attention to external scholarship and our foreign colleagues make stunning contributions, but it's hard to affirm ourselves internationally, because of language and because our research or case studies are seen as less relevant."*
>
> Senior WGFS scholar in the humanities

> *"I wanted to have more international publications and sent book proposals to loads of foreign publishers. One reviewer wrote, 'well, ok, write it then, it's a pity it's about Portugal though, because it's such an interesting theme and it'd be perfect if it were on another context, but Portugal, blergh'. (. . .) I can only get work published abroad if I make comparative analyses between Portugal and more well-known countries, otherwise they're not interested."*
>
> Junior WGFS researcher in the social sciences

Portuguese scholarship is seen internationally as too narrow and specific, and thus many WGFS scholars felt they were treated abroad as just a 'case study' (Joaquim, 2004), one which only became sufficiently interesting if its 'Portugueseness' was diluted, namely by including other, more central, countries in the analysis or by minimising discussion of the situated context of the research. The latter is something I have had to do many times myself too – in articles, book proposals, and even in this book, which does not include the detailed analysis of Portuguese WGFS' institutionalisation provided elsewhere (Pereira, 2011). This was another level on which I was interpellated as a potentially useful player. Having accessed the modern foreign and its audiences (namely through the book you are reading right now), it was hoped I might contribute to educating foreign scholars about Portuguese WGFS, "because no one knows us abroad, and it might get them more interested", as one junior WGFS scholar told me during a conference coffee-break. This hope – that my internationally-published work and its international readers might do something within local negotiations of epistemic status – shows just how much the doing of this research is inextricably, though unpredictably, involved in the very processes it describes.

Making the (semi-)periphery central and modern through WGFS

The geopolitics of epistemic status are further complicated by the fact that WGFS scholars are not the only people involved and invested in shaping the relation between WGFS and the modern; governmental and institutional representatives also negotiate that relation in their own boundary-work. This means that the relation between WGFS and affirmations of modernity can be problematised from the reverse perspective: not how claims about Portugal's (lack of) modernity are used to display and strengthen the status of WGFS (as examined in the previous sections), but how claims about WGFS are used to display and strengthen the modernity of Portugal.

In many (semi-)peripheral countries, scientific development is regularly framed in public discourse as closely aligned with, and an avenue of, modernisation (Harding, 2008; Shapin, 2008). That has also been the case in Portugal, historically (Brandão, 2012; Gonçalves *et al.*, 1996) and in the present. The official 'guiding document' for science policy at the time of my primary fieldwork, entitled *A Commitment to Science for the Future of Portugal*, states that 'scientific progress[23] is a motor of development and a source of progress' and that it is 'urgent' to 'overcome our scientific and technological delay vis-à-vis the more developed countries' (MCTES, 2006: 3–4*). Women and gender equality have also featured in public discourse, and in universities, in many countries as 'a symbol of [the] "modern"' (Üşür, 2006: 133). Evans argues that in the past and present British universities, for example, have used women as a sign of modernisation (2004: 85,102). She writes that '"[a]llowing" women into universities (. . .) has a twofold impact: it allows universities to appear "modern" and yet at the same time it maintains the *status quo*' (2004: 98, original emphasis). Monteiro's (2010) study of state feminism provides examples of the use of women as markers of modernity in Portugal. One example is the creation in 1970 by *Estado Novo* of a *Working Group for the Definition of a National Policy in Relation to the Woman*. Inquiring into why an anti-feminist fascist regime would establish such a body, Monteiro argues that a contributing factor was the fact that the 'Portuguese state was anxious, at the time, to clean its discredited image vis-à-vis the United Nations as a country still retaining its colonies' (2010: 379*). This move was 'an attempt to offset its bad image', by displaying the 'government's openness to issues of women's condition' and hence its commitment to modernity (2010: 379–380*).

This use of science and of women and gender as symbols of modernity was also evident in the academic events I observed. It is common in Portugal to invite high-ranking governmental and university representatives to speak in conference opening or closing ceremonies, especially when they have funded the event. When participating in WGFS conferences, government representatives often explicitly framed WGFS as a project both demonstrating the present modernity of the nation and enabling its ongoing modernising. In a closing ceremony speech for a WGFS conference, a secretary of state used WGFS to contrast the less advanced Portugal of the past with its present, more modern, incarnation.

> *"As I listened to the previous speaker, (. . .) I was thinking of how far Portuguese society has come, how it has advanced, for us to now have fields like this [WGFS] in universities. When we look back, and (. . .) looking back isn't necessarily an act of nostalgia, it can be an act of critical reflection, (. . .) it's clear just how far we've come and how much we've travelled to get here."*

He then talks at some length about women's rights throughout Portuguese history and concludes by saying:

> *"To stimulate our society to be more open and modern (. . .), we must mobilise and educate. (. . .) To do that, I believe it's very important for universities to be interested in these themes [of WGFS], because these are, after all, the themes of our time and the themes of our modernity. I'm convinced this is why you were all here, and also why [the organisers] held this event. Thank you. [Applause]"*

By framing WGFS as the *"themes of our time and the themes of our modernity"*, this speech positions the country, the institution hosting the event and its audience firmly within the modern, because it is interested in, and supportive of, WGFS. It is not exactly clear who this 'our' refers to, but I interpret it as alluding both to 'our', in the sense of *present, contemporary* time/modernity and 'our', as in *Portuguese* time/modernity, thereby aligning the two and positioning Portugal as a nation of this (modern) time.

These ceremonial claims about WGFS are not made only to affirm the modernity of the nation; WGFS is called upon also to demonstrate that particular institutions are sites of up-to-date and innovative teaching and research. Consider this speech given by a university representative in the opening ceremony for a WGFS conference.

> *"To say that universities must be attentive to the world is to say the obvious. But universities haven't always been attentive to the world. (. . .) That's why all changes (. . .) in our university that reflect that attention are always welcome. The decision to offer [WGFS programmes] in our university is inscribed in that aim because (. . .) it's a field which has much to do with issues that are very old but also very much of our current time. These issues are particularly pressing today – as illustrated by the fact that last year [2007] was the European Year of Equal Opportunities for All. (. . .) That's why we supported this conference from the start (. . .) because the idea was interesting and current, and corresponded to (. . .) the objectives of [university]."*

He describes *"attention to the world"* as a crucial and *"obvious"* concern, but one which many universities have failed to uphold. He then frames this institution's WGFS programme, and the conference itself, as being *"inscribed in that aim"*.[24] The presence of WGFS is, therefore, proof that the institution is engaging with *"the world"*, giving attention to issues *"of our current time"*, and thus more modern than the other universities which have failed to keep up with the times.

A total of 7 interviewees described similar situations of strategic appropriation of WGFS by university administrations.

> *"Gender equality is now a bit of a fashion [governmentally], they've discovered that in political terms it's a goldmine, [because] it's something that used to be less explored and now can be explored, thereby allowing them to show they've done something. (. . .) This is undeniable, in my opinion. (. . .) In academia the same thing's happening, institutions can explore a field that (. . .) has become more visible, exists in other countries and doesn't exist here, and they use that to show they're doing things, they're more modern and innovative than other universities."*
>
> Senior WGFS scholar

One senior scholar explained that her institution often uses her as an *"alibi-expert"*.

> *"MMP: Do you feel your efforts to persuade others of the relevance of women's studies have had results?*
>
> *I don't know if it's my persuading that had results. (. . .) You have to see it's always useful for an institution to have an expert on these matters, a sort of alibi-expert. They'll say 'oh yes, we know all about those issues, we have an expert in our university'. (. . .) I definitely felt that, it was very visible."*

Institutions' use of WGFS scholars/hip 'as alibis, in the name of an (alleged) image of progress and "political correctness", only adopted superficially' (*ex aequo* Editorial Board, 1999: 9*) is also discussed in the literature. Abranches recounts the experiences of WGFS scholars at the University of Coimbra. They faced significant institutional resistance in the 1980s and 1990s, but when the University hosted the SIGMA Conference on Women's Studies in Europe (July 1995), '[i]n his opening speech, and to the astonishment of many quarters, the Rector explicitly mentioned GREF [the university's *Feminist Studies Group*] as a testimony of the University's commitment to Women's Studies' (1998: 12). She argues this was part of 'a strategy of using us [GREF] as a token of the University's up-to-dateness in the academic world market' (1998: 16). Clearly, the notion of, and orientation towards, academic 'market value' was not something that emerged in Portugal only in the 2000s, with the large-scale institutionalisation of cultures of performativity. Even before, WGFS was already being used to symbolise modernity and generate value.

Although these institutions' affirmations of support for WGFS contributed to form a positive epistemic climate and a public culture of openness to WGFS, some interviewees found them potentially problematic. 3 scholars argued that they positioned Portugal or a specific institution as already advanced and equal, masking the resistance still faced by WGFS scholars. In her work on non-performativity discussed in chapter 5, Ahmed argues that 'the claim that saying is doing can bypass th[e] ways in which saying is not sufficient for an action, and can even be a substitute for action' (2004: §51; 2012). Indeed, according to some interviewees, such public (ceremonial or daily) affirmations of support for WGFS deflect attention from the ways in which those same institutions do *not* support WGFS, potentially making it harder to denounce ongoing forms of explicit and implicit dismissal and to demand more support for the field.

WGFS and the epistemic of status of nations

In everyday scholarly life in academically semi-peripheral and peripheral countries, the modern foreign can function as a truth-spot (Gieryn, 2002, 2006) or, as I prefer to call it, a truth-point, i.e. a point in space/time that when invoked produces truth-effects, as Foucault might put it. My choice of the term 'invocation' is not arbitrary. The OED defines it as 'to call on (God, a deity, etc.) (. . .) as a witness; to appeal to for aid or protection (. . .) or in confirmation of something'; 'To utter (a sacred name) in invocation; To call to (a person) to come or to do something'. The modern foreign does actually often function as a sacred name, or as I labelled it, drawing on Mohanty, an authorising signature (or body). Because it may aid or protect them in local struggles, Portuguese WGFS scholars call upon the modern foreign to come (discursively or physically) to witness and confirm the value of WGFS, and to act, using Braidotti's terms, as a 'stamp of approval' (2000: 34; 2002). Invoking the modern foreign is a very old, tried-and-tested strategy. It was already used in Portugal in the late 19th century, according to Roque (2001). In his study of the emergence of Portuguese anthropology, he found that scholars of the period also drew on 'a rhetorical strategy of chrono-demarcation of a Portuguese scientific delay (. . .) and affirmation of the threat of scientific peripheralisation of the national community (vis-à-vis the designated centres of European science)' (2001: 241*). Just like my participants, these 19th century scholars organised visits to, and collaborations with, scholars of the centre to secure status and resources locally. In the performative university of the early 21st century, an alignment with the modern foreign becomes even more important. By symbolising that a university is up-to-date, in the lead and ahead of the (semi-)peripheral curve, such an alignment helps to 'creat[e] market appeal (. . .) [for] educational institutions competing within education markets' (Blackmore and Sachs, 2003: 143).

But WGFS is not just the subject of invocations; it is also an object in the invocations of others. Semi-peripheral countries and institutions are embroiled in their own boundary-work, negotiating the boundaries seen to separate modern from delayed, centre from periphery. As Sousa Santos (1994) and Nunes (1996) argue, this often involves a process of *imagination of the centre*, whereby 'in order to be included among "developed" societies, a country increases the visibility of those features generally associated with "development", and correspondingly decreases the visibility of those associated with "underdevelopment"' (Nunes, 1996: 14–15). In many countries throughout the world, the existence of WGFS can be, and has been, framed nationally and institutionally as a marker of 'development', as a symbol of a 'diverse' and 'inclusive' modernity (Abranches, 1998; Evans, 2004; Ferguson, 2012; Musser, 2015) and as a 'token of academic excellence' (Hark, 2016: 86). Therefore, WGFS gets invoked, and made more visible, in institutions' and countries' own processes of imagination of the centre, sometimes to the detriment of the field itself.

The specific links between global relations of power and local negotiations of authority, and between the epistemic status of WGFS and of nations are very much shaped by a region's particular histories, cultures and politics. In (semi-)peripheral contexts where countries of the centre are acclaimed as academic models of reference and agents of certification of scholarly quality (as in Portugal, Taiwan (Chen, 2004) or the Czech Republic (Stöckelová, 2012)), invocations of the modern foreign are likely to be effective. Nevertheless, the same invocation may have different – even opposite – effects within contexts where the global hegemony of the western centre is disputed, as described in Cerwonka's (2008), Egeland's (2011), Kapusta-Pofahl's (2008), Mizielińska and Kulpa's (2011), and Zimmermann's (2007) reflections on the status of WGFS and queer scholarship in Central and Eastern Europe. Zimmermann argues that the institutionalisation of WGFS in that region has been shaped by 'the geopolitically and economically motivated struggle over the relationship of various countries of the former Soviet Union towards the West' (2007: 159). In this context, association with the modern foreign might be toxic for WGFS; indeed, Zimmermann argues that WGFS was repudiated in some of those countries because it was seen as a '"symbolic marker" of compliant westernization', part of 'a long tradition of using the "women's question" or "progressive women's politics" for the purposes of western political dominance' (2007: 141). An especially recent example of the repudiation of WGFS partly on account of its supposed 'foreign-ness' are the ongoing moral panics in several countries about 'gender ideology'; in Poland, for example, WGFS scholarship has been publicly described by political, religious and academic figures as a foreign 'pseudo-science' which threatens national identity and thus acts as a form of 'terrorism' (Grabowska, 2016).

In countries of the centre, the foreign has less weight as a marker of (higher) epistemic status, but it can still impact on WGFS' status in other guises, namely as a potential source of income. Hemmings notes that in her British university, and in a context of 'institutional thirst for international fees', it was 'the *international* development of the field that finally convinced institutional bureaucrats to support (albeit in minimal terms) a field they otherwise failed to see the national relevance of' (2008: 125, original emphasis). The meanings and value of the foreign will differ across regions, but all these examples demonstrate that it very often plays a key role in epistemic and institutional negotiations over WGFS.

What issues do the complex relations between epistemic status, national identity and the status of the modern foreign raise for WGFS? In a text on WGFS' institutionalisation in Croatia, Kašić challenges WGFS scholars to consider issues of 'location, (. . .) western/eastern, northern/southern cooperation, (. . .) and expectations regarding our roles and status in relation to (. . .) the different stages of women's studies development in [different] countries' (2004: 38). She suggests we must ask 'whether the legitimisation of [WGFS in (semi-)peripheral contexts can] only be achieved through the mediating of recognised and well-respected programs of women's/gender studies from the West and how that influence[s] the efforts and contributions of local feminists and potential collaborations' (2004: 39). I want to close this chapter by engaging with that question. In debates about the relations between WGFS scholarship from different countries, much critical attention has rightly been dedicated to exposing international asymmetries between countries in terms of status and influence. Trying to illustrate this, Griffin and Braidotti (2002) suggest that readers play a game to see how many books they own by, and how many names they know of, feminists from several relatively peripheral European countries; they predict readers will struggle because of the entrenched international inequalities in whose WGFS work gets circulated, read and cited. Portugal is one of the countries they mention, and it is true that many of my interviewees struggle to get their work circulated internationally because Portugal is not perceived to be as epistemically alluring and authoritative as the countries of the centre. Therefore, we must ask what becomes repressed, made invisible and excluded through, and because of, the hegemony of western, anglophone feminism.

But drawing on the analysis offered here, I suggest we must consider both what gets silenced because of these hegemonies, *and* what becomes possible and speakable for WGFS scholars in (semi-)peripheral contexts through the invocation of a hegemonic modern foreign. We must avoid 'model[s] of [western] domination/ imposition and subaltern submission/complicity' which risk 'eras[ing] the process of local appropriation' of foreign ideas (French, 2003: 376; see also Vasterling *et al.*, 2006: 71) and, I would add, of local appropriation of the epistemic status of the foreign. I am not calling for a reframing of these global asymmetries as only or mostly positive – they have undeniable and powerful negative impacts – but, rather, as extremely complicated relationships. I am arguing for a reframing that recognises more explicitly that those asymmetries produce both losses *and* gains for WGFS, and that the two interact with each other. For example, I show that WGFS scholars from (semi-)peripheral countries sometimes emphatically frame their contexts as less advanced, because locally this heightens the persuasiveness of their WGFS claims and demands; and yet, the framing of their countries as academically underdeveloped reproduces and legitimates the very same hierarchies that devalue those scholars' work internationally, and makes it harder for them to see their work published and cited elsewhere (Wöhrer, 2016).

I am sometimes asked whether the small-scale local gains produced by invocations of the modern foreign are worth the risk of reproducing the pernicious academic hegemony of the centre and the heavy losses it imposes. This is an important question, but it cannot, and must not, be answered in a straightforward or abstract way. WGFS is a diverse field with conflicting pressures, demands and aims, and those gains and losses are closely intertwined; thus, answering that question requires much clearer specification. Are the gains worth the risks – *for whom, and at what level?* In the short-term or long-term? Locally or globally? For the development of knowledge, broader political transformation or the strengthening of institutionalisation?

Global academic hegemonies have very different impacts and implications on each of those levels. For example, the asymmetrical canonisation of authors from the centre and the large-scale reliance on their work to analyse gender in (semi-) peripheral contexts makes global WGFS debates profoundly unequal and contributes in the *long-term* to stifle local concept-formation and theory-building, as Macedo and Amaral (2002) persuasively argue vis-à-vis the Portuguese context. And yet, many scholars in the (semi-)periphery, and specifically in present-day Portugal, find that quoting and invoking the centre makes all the difference in the *short-term* when attempting to create WGFS programmes, get a WGFS book published and thus advance the local *institutionalisation* of WGFS.

There are many other examples of complex entanglement. Politically, WGFS scholars' framing of their own (semi-)peripheral contexts as *not yet that* modern (compared to the centre) helps disrupt problematic attempts to portray their own countries/institutions as already modern and equal. On the other hand, this acclamation of the modern foreign as term of reference and foil arguably contributes to normalise its hegemony, not only as a place of proper knowledge but also as *the* site and route of progress. This is by no means a minor issue in a global order where the category of 'egalitarian modernity' is regularly invoked to position western nations as symbols, protectors and enforcers of development, and to enact and justify domestic or international exclusions and violence (Abu-Lughod, 2002; Al-Ali and Pratt, 2009; Puar, 2007). These entanglements are complicated further by the fact that WGFS scholars based in the centre can, and do, benefit from these global hegemonies in many ways: tendentially, their work will be more easily recognised as transnationally relevant and more widely read, they will more frequently be invited to present it abroad, and their degree programmes will be more attractive to WGFS 'educational migrants'. The latter is an especially significant example of how WGFS scholars and programmes in the centre may profit directly from the lesser academic status of the (semi-)periphery and differences between countries in levels of WGFS institutionalisation. Educational migration from the (semi-)periphery to the centre in search of reputable WGFS training from 'world-leading' universities often helps sustain WGFS degree programmes – and, of course, WGFS jobs – in those universities, even in times of falling local demand for WGFS. However, global academic hegemonies also create problems for WGFS scholars in the centre. In my observations at international conferences and my research period in Sweden, I heard one problem in particular flagged many times by colleagues based in the US, UK and Scandinavia. The global geopolitics of WGFS' epistemic status are premised on the framing of particular countries as WGFS success stories. This can complicate the work of WGFS scholars in the centre, because those success stories can be, and have been, harnessed by states and institutions to justify denying support to WGFS initiatives or even closing them down, on the grounds that WGFS is already doing comparably well in that context (Fahlgren *et al.*, 2016; Liinason, 2010, 2011a, 2011b; Zmroczek and Duchen, 1991).

These examples of complex entanglements of losses and gains make one thing clear: how one assesses the impact of global hegemonies on WGFS will depend on the aims one foregrounds and the particular needs of a WGFS community. Those assessments must, thus, be openly and regularly debated, remain attentive to context, and recognise the imbrication of local epistemic-institutional negotiations and the global chrono- and geopolitics of academia. They must also, and crucially, recognise that WGFS scholars (in the centre and (semi-)periphery) have complex, ambivalent and not always fully acknowledged investments in the epistemic and material inequalities of global academic relations. The (semi-) peripherality of a country in global hierarchies, or the (semi-)peripherality of WGFS in academic hierarchies does not mean that WGFS or that country is peripheral or external to the relations of power that constitute certain sites as central. WGFS is always imbricated in global relations of power; working to disrupt and transform those relations requires constant attention to how we, as WGFS scholars, define and invoke the space/time of proper knowledge, as well as a continuing critical engagement with the ways in which WGFS is used by others to imagine nations.

Notes

1 The title of this chapter is inspired by Gonçalves' (2000) article.
2 My use of the concept of 'hegemony' vis-à-vis global academic exchanges draws on Meriläinen *et al.* (2008).
3 Mohanty uses this term in a discussion of how western feminist scholarship creates 'a composite, singular "third-world woman" – an image which appears arbitrarily constructed but nevertheless carries with it the authorizing signature of western humanist discourse' (1988: 62–63).
4 I conceptualise the 'modern' not as a descriptive term, but as a performative and contested category that has been the object of ongoing, exclusionary and very violent boundary-work in the past and present (Bhambra, 2007). I do not place scare quotes around subsequent references to the term for the reasons set out in the introduction, but all uses of it should be understood in that vein.
5 In Portuguese, the verb 'to be' has two formulations. *Ser* is used for intrinsic and stable characteristics (the verb shares its root with 'essence') – e.g. *eu sou Portuguesa*, I'm Portuguese. *Estar* refers to temporary states or current location (it shares a root with 'status') – *eu estou atrasada*, I'm late.
6 A claim that bears a striking and telling resemblance with Wise's (1997) description of WGFS itself as ' "in" but not "of" the academy'. See also Hall's (2002–2003) reflection on the ways in which many 'others' – including himself – get positioned as 'in but not of Europe'.

7 High-profile developments in the past 10 years include the legalisation of abortion following a national referendum (2007), the recognition of same-sex marriage (2010) and adoption by same-sex couples (2015), and the passing of a new gender identity law (2011) (Santos, 2010, 2013; Vale de Almeida, 2012b).

8 He is referring to poet Fernando Pessoa and his *Mensagem* (1934), a poetry collection on the history of Portugal and its colonial empire. Pessoa writes: 'Europe is lying propped upon her elbows:/ From East to West she lies, staring/ (. . .) Out at the West, the future of the past./ The face with which she stares is Portugal' (2007 [1934]: 13).

9 As Griffin and Braidotti highlight, 'it is the countries with a "broken" history (. . .) – that is, countries which went through periods of fascist rule or dictatorship – that are keenest to establish a United Europe because it is through that process that they can acquire a new and unblemished identity' (2002: 11).

10 Participants in these debates sometimes refer to Portugal, Ireland and/or Italy, Greece and Spain as PIGS (or PIIGS); see for example BBC (2010).

11 For a discussion of how the affirmation of Portugal's modernity and Europeanness is enabled by, and leads to, forms of 'othering' of non-white Portuguese citizens and non-European lusophone countries, see for example Araújo and Maeso (2015), Reiter (2005, 2008) or Vale de Almeida (2012a).

12 Similar claims were made by the WGFS scholars interviewed by Magalhães (2001).

13 The expressions 'miss the train' or 'catch the train' are often used in Portugal to refer to the country's position vis-à-vis an imagined train of modernity (for examples see Sousa Santos, 2009: 24,27).

14 Some elements of this comment get lost in translation. In Portuguese, the same word can be used to refer to being backwards/less advanced and being late/behind schedule (*atrasada/o*). The speaker is playing with those multiple meanings: she is alluding simultaneously to the facts that (1) the session is running over, (2) the Portuguese are described as delayed relative to Europe and (3) the Portuguese are seen to often be late. Also, her claim that *we are very European* uses the verb *estar*, so denotes a temporary, not intrinsic position. It is formulated in the feminine plural, so refers explicitly to 'we' as Portuguese feminists or WGFS scholars, rather than Portugal as a whole.

15 I would suggest that these discourses echo problematic aspects of narratives of lusotropicalism and Portuguese exceptionalism (Freyre, 1961). Unfortunately, I cannot pursue here an analysis of what might be termed a discourse of Portuguese *scientific* exceptionalism. For a more detailed, yet still fairly brief, discussion of this, see Pereira (2011).

16 Gieryn focuses on laboratories and fieldwork sites, though I would argue that the notion can be applied also to countries/regions.

17 I have myself used invocations of the modern foreign in Portugal in the past, for example when justifying a focus on WGFS in UG essays, or applying for funding for WGFS research. Consider this excerpt from my application to FCT for funding for this research project in 2006:

> [I will explore] the assumptions about science (. . .) at the core of the discourses produced in negotiations of the scientific status of gender studies. The need for such a discussion is particularly urgent in Portugal, (. . .) [where] social science research is very recent (. . .) in comparison to most other Western countries. (. . .) Conducting this study in a British institution with a well-established gender studies department (a space that does not exist in Portugal) will enable me to ground the study in international debates (. . .), and draw on those debates to reflect on, and contribute to, the development of Portuguese social science and the institutionalisation of Portuguese gender studies.

18 For accounts of WGFS institutionalisation in Spain, see Borderias *et al.* (2002), Griffin (2005) and Suárez and Suárez (2002). For a comparison of the earlier stages of WGFS' institutionalisation in Spain and Portugal, see Cova (1998).

19 Spain also plays a similar role in relation to other aspects of Portuguese life, namely debates about LGBTQ rights. After Spain approved same-sex marriage (2005), a revised law on recognition of parental rights in assisted reproduction (2006) and a new gender identity law (2006), the Portuguese LGBTQ movement and politicians, academics and the media began regularly invoking Spain as a model of what might be possible in Portugal (Santos, 2013). One organisation, ILGA-Portugal, produced posters with the slogan 'Spain 3 – Portugal 0', tapping into a sense of sporting competitiveness with Spain.

Franchi (2015) and Dines and Rigoletto (2012) identified similar discourses in Italy. They note that Spain is invoked in Italian media debate on same-sex partnerships as 'the "ambivalent double of Italy" representing both loss [because Spain has overtaken Italy in LGBTQ rights] and the possibility of social change' (Franchi, 2015: 149). This invocation is powerful because Spain has '[l]ong [been] considered Italy's close – though inferior – cultural cousin' (Dines and Rigoletto, 2012: 479) and thus that 'overtaking' creates 'anxieties (. . .) [vis-à-vis] Italy's perception of its own liminal position in Europe' (2012: 484)

20 For accounts of WGFS institutionalisation in Brazil see Costa (2006) and Mayorga (2002).

21 Portuguese WGFS scholars are, generally, not themselves explicitly dismissive of Brazil; indeed, many express a profound admiration for Brazilian WGFS, frequently attending events or publishing in journals in Brazil, and inviting Brazilian colleagues to Portugal. In the *Congresso Feminista* (a landmark national WGFS conference organised in 2008), for example, the choice of 5 keynotes (Brazilian, Spanish or Latin American scholars/ activists) was guided by 'a logic that's different from common practice. (. . .) The aim is to make visible work from countries like Brazil and Spain, which often gets hidden by the "great" anglo-saxon or francophone theoretical production' (Manuela Tavares, member of the organising committee, cited in Almeida, S.J., 2008*).

22 Portugal has one of the highest rates of brain drain in Europe, with 19.5% of its university-educated nationals working abroad (Cerdeira *et al.*, 2016; Patrício, 2010).

23 These references to science also include the SSH.

24 Another – strikingly similar – example of this discourse can be found in Meirinho (2015), a transcript of a speech given by a member of the administration of another Portuguese university in the opening ceremony of a WGFS conference.

References

Aavik, Kadri, *et al.* (2015). *Country Reports (Australia, Czech Republic, Estonia, Germany, Iceland, Netherlands, Norway, Portugal, South Africa, Sweden, Switzerland, UK).* Multiple Papers Presented at the RINGS Network Conference "Gender in/and the Neoliberal University", Prague.

Abranches, Graça (1998). *"On What Terms Shall We Join the Procession of Educated Men?" Teaching Feminist Studies at the University of Coimbra.* Coimbra: Centro de Estudos Sociais.

Abu-Lughod, Lila (2002). "Do Muslim Women Really Need Saving? Anthropological Reflections on Cultural Relativism and Its Others". *American Anthropologist, 104* (3), 783–790.

Ahmed, Sara (2004). "Declarations of Whiteness: The Non-Performativity of Anti-Racism". *Borderlands, 3* (2).

Ahmed, Sara (2012). *On Being Included: Racism and Diversity in Institutional Life.* Durham, NC: Duke University Press.

Akena, Francis Adyanga (2012). "Critical Analysis of the Production of Western Knowledge and Its Implications for Indigenous Knowledge and Decolonization". *Journal of Black Studies, 43* (6), 599–619.

Al-Ali, Nadje and Pratt, Nicola (2009). *What Kind of Liberation?: Women and the Occupation of Iraq*. Berkeley: University of California Press.

Alatas, Syed Farid (2003). "Academic Dependency and the Global Division of Labour in the Social Sciences". *Current Sociology, 51* (6), 599–613.

Almeida, João Ferreira de (1991). "Social Science" in J. M. Gago (ed.), *Science in Portugal* (pp.75–84). Lisboa: Imprensa Nacional – Casa da Moeda.

Almeida, São José (2008). "Várias Correntes do Feminismo Representadas por Convidadas Estrangeiras em Congresso". *Público*, 24/05/2008, Retrieved 02/04/2016, from http://www.publico.pt/portugal/jornal/varias-correntes-do-feminismo-representadas–por-convidadas-estrangeiras-em-congresso-262292

Amâncio, Lígia (2003). "O Género nos Discursos das Ciências Sociais". *Análise Social, XXXVIII* (168), 687–714.

Amsler, Sarah (2007). *The Politics of Knowledge in Central Asia: Science Between Marx and the Market*. London: Routledge.

Anderson, Warwick and Adams, Vincanne (2008). "Pramoedya's Chickens: Postcolonial Studies of Technoscience" in E. J. Hackett*, et al.* (eds.), *The Handbook of Science and Technology Studies* (3rd ed) (pp.181–204). Cambridge, MA: MIT Press.

Araújo, Marta and Maeso, Silvia Rodríguez (2015). *The Contours of Eurocentrism: Race, History, and Political Texts*. Lanham, MD: Lexington Books.

Armengaud, Françoise and Jasser, Ghaïss (1994). "Une Offensive Majeure Contre les Études Féministes". *Nouvelles Questions Féministes, 15* (4), 7–20.

Bahovec, Eva and Hemmings, Clare (2004). "Teaching Travelling Concepts in Europe". *Feminist Theory, 5* (3), 333–342.

BBC News (2010). *Europe's PIGS*. Retrieved 02/04/2016, from http://news.bbc.co.uk/1/hi/8510603.stm

Beleza, Teresa (2002). "Antígona no Reino de Creonte: o Impacte dos Estudos Feministas no Direito". *ex aequo, 6*, 77–89.

Bhambra, Gurminder (2007). *Rethinking Modernity: Postcolonialism and the Sociological Imagination*. Basingstoke: Palgrave MacMillan.

Blackmore, Jill and Sachs, Judyth (2003). "Managing Equity Work in the Performative University". *Australian Feminist Studies, 18* (41), 141–162.

Borderias, Cristina*, et al.* (2002). "Historical Dossier on the Making of European Women's Studies: Spain". *The Making of European Women's Studies, IV*, 203–242.

Braidotti, Rosi (2000). "Key Terms and Issues in the Making of European Women's Studies". *The Making of European Women's Studies, I*, 23–36.

Braidotti, Rosi (2002). "The Uses and Abuses of the Sex/Gender Distinction in European Feminist Practices" in G. Griffin and R. Braidotti (eds.), *Thinking Differently: A Reader in European Women's Studies* (pp.285–310). London: Zed.

Brandão, Tiago (2012). *A Junta Nacional de Investigação Científica e Tecnológica (1967–1974): Organização da Ciência e Política Científica em Portugal*. PhD Thesis, Universidade Nova de Lisboa.

Calvi, Giulia (2010). "Global Trends: Gender Studies in Europe and the US". *European History Quarterly, 40* (4), 641–655.

Canagarajah, A. Suresh (2002). *A Geopolitics of Academic Writing*. Pittsburgh, PA: University of Pittsburgh Press.

Carreira da Silva, Filipe (2016). *Sociology in Portugal: A Short History*. Basingstoke: Palgrave Macmillan.

Cerdeira, Luísa, *et al.* (2016). "Brain Drain and the Disenchantment of Being a Higher Education Student in Portugal". *Journal of Higher Education Policy and Management, 38* (1), 68–77.

Cerwonka, Allaine (2008). "Traveling Feminist Thought: Difference and Transculturation in Central and Eastern European Feminism". *Signs: Journal of Women in Culture and Society, 33* (4), 809–832.

Chen, Peiying (2004). *Acting "Otherwise": The Institutionalization of Women's/Gender Studies in Taiwan Universities*. London: RoutledgeFalmer.

Connell, Raewyn (2007). *Southern Theory: The Global Dynamics of Knowledge in Social Science*. Cambridge: Polity.

Costa, Cláudia de Lima (2006). "Lost (and Found?) in Translation: Feminisms in Hemispheric Dialogue". *Latino Studies, 4* (1/2), 62–78.

Cova, Anne (1998). "L'Enseignement de L'Histoire des Femmes dans la Péninsule Ibérique" in A.-M. Sohn and F. Thelamon (eds.), *L'Histoire Sans les Femmes: Est-elle Possible?* (pp.313–323). Paris: Perrin.

Cowan, Jane (1996). "Being a Feminist in Contemporary Greece: Similarity and Difference Reconsidered" in N. Charles and F. Hughes-Freeland (eds.), *Practising Feminism: Identity, Difference, Power* (pp.61–85). London: Routledge.

Davis, Kathy (2007). *The Making of "Our Bodies, Ourselves": How Feminism Travels Across Borders*. Durham, NC: Duke University Press.

Davis, Kathy and Evans, Mary (eds.) (2010). *Transatlantic Conversations: Feminism as Traveling Theory*. Farnham: Ashgate.

Delicado, Ana (2013). "At the (Semi-)Periphery: The Development of Science and Technology Studies in Portugal". *Tecnoscienza, 4* (2), 125–148.

Dines, Martin and Rigoletto, Sergio (2012). "Country Cousins: Europeanness, Sexuality and Locality in Contemporary Italian Television". *Modern Italy, 17* (4), 479–491.

Duarte, Afonso (1956). *Obra Poética*. Lisboa: Iniciativas Editoriais.

Egeland, Cathrine (2011). "'There Are No Specific Women Questions': Some Considerations on Feminist Genealogy". *European Journal of Women's Studies, 18* (3), 231–242.

Evans, Mary (2004). *Killing Thinking: The Death of the Universities*. London: Continuum.

ex aequo Editorial Board (1999). "Editorial". *ex aequo, 1*, 5–10.

Ezekiel, Judith (1994). "Pénurie de Ressources ou de Reconnaissances? Les Études Féministes en France". *Nouvelles Questions Féministes, 15* (4), 21–27.

Fahlgren, Siv, *et al.* (2016). "Resisting 'Overing': Teaching and Researching Gender Studies in Sweden". *Women's Studies International Forum, 54*, 119–128.

Ferguson, Roderick (2012). *The Reorder of Things: The University and Its Pedagogies of Minority Difference*. Minneapolis: University of Minnesota Press.

Ferreira, Virgínia (1999). "Os Paradoxos da Situação das Mulheres em Portugal". *Revista Crítica de Ciências Sociais, 52/53*, 199–227.

Franchi, Marina (2015). *Mediated Tensions: Italian Newspapers and the Legal Recognition of De Facto Unions*. PhD Thesis, LSE.

French, John D. (2003). "Translation, Diasporic Dialogue, and the Errors of Pierre Bourdieu and Loïc Wacquant". *Nepantla: Views from South, 4* (2), 375–389.

Freyre, Gilberto (1961). *Portuguese Integration in the Tropics*. Lisboa: Agência Geral do Ultramar.

Gieryn, Thomas (1995). "Boundaries of Science" in S. Jasanoff, *et al.* (eds.), *Handbook of Science and Technology Studies* (2nd ed) (pp.393–443). London: Sage.

Gieryn, Thomas (2002). "Three Truth-Spots". *Journal of History of the Behavioral Sciences, 38* (2), 113–132.

Gieryn, Thomas (2006). "City as Truth-Spot: Laboratories and Field-Sites in Urban Studies". *Social Studies of Science, 36* (1), 5–38.

Gonçalves, Maria Eduarda (2000). "The Importance of Being European: The Science and Politics of BSE in Portugal". *Science, Technology & Human Values, 25* (4), 417–448.

Gonçalves, Maria Eduarda, *et al.* (1996). "Political Images of Science in Portugal". *Public Understanding of Science, 5* (4), 395–410.

Goonatilake, Susantha (1993). "Modern Science and the Periphery: The Characteristics of Dependent Knowledge" in S. Harding (ed.), *The "Racial" Economy of Science: Toward a Democratic Future* (pp.259–274). Bloomington: Indiana University Press.

Grabowska, Magdalena (2016). *Keynote Address.* Paper Presented at the Atgender Spring Conference "Feminist Spaces of Teaching and Learning: Queering Movements, Translations and Dynamics", Utrecht.

Griffin, Gabriele (2005). "The Institutionalization of Women's Studies in Europe" in G. Griffin (ed.), *Doing Women's Studies: Employment Opportunities, Personal Impacts and Social Consequences* (pp.89–110). London: Zed.

Griffin, Gabriele and Braidotti, Rosi (2002). "Introduction: Configuring European Women's Studies" in G. Griffin and R. Braidotti (eds.), *Thinking Differently: A Reader in European Women's Studies* (pp.1–30). London: Zed.

Hall, Stuart (2002–2003). "In But Not of Europe: Europe at Its Myths". *Soundings: Journal of Politics and Culture, 22*, 57–69.

Harding, Sandra (2008). *Sciences from Below: Feminisms, Postcolonialities, and Modernities.* Durham, NC: Duke University Press.

Hark, Sabine (2016). "Contending Directions: Gender Studies in the Entrepreneurial University". *Women's Studies International Forum, 54*, 84–90.

Hemmings, Clare (2008). "Tuning Problems? Notes on Women's and Gender Studies and the Bologna Process". *European Journal of Women's Studies, 15* (2), 117–127.

Joaquim, Teresa (2004). "*ex aequo*: Contributo Decisivo para um Campo de Estudos em Portugal". *Revista Estudos Feministas, 12* (3), 88–93.

Kapusta-Pofahl, Karen (2008). *Legitimating Czech Gender Studies: Articulating Transnational Feminist Expertise in the "New" Europe.* PhD Thesis, University of Minnesota.

Kašić, Biljana (2004). "Women's Studies in Croatia: Between Feminist Sensibility and Critical Responsibility". *The Making of European Women's Studies, V*, 30–40.

Kašić, Biljana (2016). "'Unsettling' Women's Studies, Settling Neoliberal Threats in the Academia: A Feminist Gaze from Croatia". *Women's Studies International Forum, 54*, 129–137.

Klinke, Ian (2013). "Chronopolitics: A Conceptual Matrix". *Progress in Human Geography, 37* (5), 673–690.

Knapp, Gudrun-Axeli (2005). "Race, Class, Gender: Reclaiming Baggage in Fast Travelling Theories". *European Journal of Women's Studies 12* (3), 249–265.

Liinason, Mia (2010). "Institutionalized Knowledge: Notes on the Processes of Inclusion and Exclusion in Gender Studies in Sweden". *NORA: Nordic Journal of Feminist and Gender Research, 18* (1), 38–47.

Liinason, Mia (2011a). "The Construction of Gender Research in Sweden. An Analysis of a Success Story". *SQS – Journal of Queer Studies Finland, 5* (2), 30–43.

Liinason, Mia (2011b). *Feminism and the Academy: Exploring the Politics of Institution-alization in Gender Studies in Sweden*. Lund: Media-Tryck Lund.

Lykke, Nina (2004). "Between Particularism, Universalism and Transversalism. Reflections on the Politics of Location of European Feminist Research and Education". *NORA: Nordic Journal of Feminist and Gender Research, 12* (2), 72–82.

Macedo, Ana Gabriela and Amaral, Ana Luísa (2002). "A Palavra, a Identidade e a Cultura Translativa: Para uma Introdução ao *Dicionário Terminológico de Conceitos da Crítica Feminista*" in M.I. Ramalho and A.S. Ribeiro (eds.), *Entre Ser e Estar: Raízes, Percursos e Discursos de Identidade* (pp.383–408). Porto: Afrontamento.

Machado, Fernando Luís and Costa, António Firmino da (2000). "An Incomplete Modernity: Structural Change and Social Mobility" in J.M.L. Viegas and A.F. Costa (eds.), *Crossroads to Modernity: Contemporary Portuguese Society* (pp.15–40). Oeiras: Celta.

Magalhães, Maria José (2001). "Dez Anos da APEM: Percorrer as Vozes, Significar os Percursos". *ex aequo, 5*, 27–68.

Massey, Doreen (1994). *Space, Place and Gender*. Cambridge: Polity.

Mayorga, Cláudia (2002). "Gender, Race and Women's Studies in Brazil". *The Making of European Women's Studies, IV*, 25–36.

Mbembe, Achille (2016). "Decolonizing the University: New Directions". *Arts and Humanities in Higher Education, 15* (1), 29–45.

McLaughlin, Philippa Pinto (2009). *Brazil and the Brasileira in the Portuguese National Imagination: The Case of the Mothers of Bragança versus the Girls of Brazil*. MSc Dissertation, LSE.

MCTES (Ministério da Ciência, Tecnologia e Ensino Superior) (2006). *Compromisso com a Ciência para o Futuro de Portugal*. Lisboa: MCTES.

Meirinho, Manuel (2015). "Um Novo Projeto Numa Escola de Tradição e Inovação" in A. Torres, *et al.* (eds.), *Estudos de Género numa Perspetiva Interdisciplinar* (pp.128–129). Lisboa: Mundos Sociais.

Meriläinen, Susan, *et al.* (2008). "Hegemonic Academic Practices: Experiences of Publishing from the Periphery". *Organization, 15* (4), 584–597.

Mignolo, Walter (1998). "Globalization, Civilization Processes, and the Relocation of Languages and Cultures" in F. Jameson and M. Myoshi (eds.), *The Cultures of Globalization* (pp.32–53). Durham, NC: Duke University Press.

Mizielińska, Joanna and Kulpa, Robert (2011). " 'Contemporary Peripheries': Queer Studies, Circulation of Knowledge and East/West Divide" in R. Kulpa and J. Mizielińska (eds.), *De-Centring Western Sexualities: Central and Eastern European Perspectives* (pp.11–26). Farnham: Ashgate.

Mohanty, Chandra (1988). "Under Western Eyes: Feminist Scholarship and Colonial Discourses". *Feminist Review, 30*, 61–88.

Monteiro, Rosa (2010). "Feminismo de Estado em Portugal: Algumas Reflexões Exploratórias" in M.J. Magalhães, *et al.* (eds.), *Quem Tem Medo dos Feminismos?* (Vol. I, pp.373–381). Lisboa: Nova Delphi.

Musser, Amber Jamilla (2015). "Specimen Days: Diversity, Labor, and the University". *Feminist Formations, 27* (3), 1–20.

Nader, Laura (ed.) (1996). *Naked Science: Anthropological Inquiry into Boundaries, Power, and Knowledge*. London: Routledge.

Nunes, João Arriscado (1996). *The Transcultural Lab: Articulating Cultural Difference In/ Through Scientific Work*. Coimbra: Centro de Estudos Sociais.

Nunes, João Arriscado (2002). "As Dinâmicas da(s) Ciência(s) no Perímetro do Centro: Uma Cultura Científica de Fronteira?". *Revista Crítica de Ciências Sociais, 63*, 189–198.

Paasi, Anssi (2005). "Globalisation, Academic Capitalism, and the Uneven Geographies of International Journal Publishing Spaces". *Environment and Planning A, 37* (5), 769–789.

Patrício, Maria Teresa (2010). "Science Policy and the Internationalisation of Research in Portugal". *Journal of Studies in International Education, 14* (2), 161–182.

Pereira, Maria do Mar (2011). *Pushing the Boundaries of Knowledge: An Ethnography of Negotiations of the Epistemic Status of Women's, Gender, Feminist Studies in Portugal.* PhD Thesis, LSE.

Pereira, Maria do Mar (2014). "The Importance of Being 'Modern' and Foreign: Feminist Scholarship and the Epistemic Status of Nations". *Signs: Journal of Women in Culture and Society, 39* (3), 627–657.

Pessoa, Fernando (2007 [1934]). *Message.* London: Shearsman Books.

Petö, Andrea (2001). "An Empress in a New-Old Dress". *Feminist Theory, 2* (1), 89–93.

Pinto, Teresa (2008). *A Formação Profissional das Mulheres no Ensino Industrial Público (1884–1910): Realidades e Representações.* PhD Thesis, Universidade Aberta.

Puar, Jasbir (2007). *Terrorist Assemblages: Homonationalism in Queer Times.* Durham, NC: Duke University Press.

Rahbari, Ladan (2016). *The Changing Face of Teaching Gender and Its Position in the Mainstream Academia in Iran.* Paper Presented at the Atgender Spring Conference "Feminist Spaces of Teaching and Learning: Queering Movements, Translations and Dynamics", Utrecht.

Reiter, Bernd (2005). "Portugal: National Pride and Imperial Neurosis". *Race & Class, 47* (1), 79–91.

Reiter, Bernd (2008). "The Perils of Empire: Nationhood and Citizenship in Portugal". *Citizenship Studies, 12* (4), 397–412.

Roque, Ricardo (2001). "Porto-Paris, Ida-e-Volta: Estratégias Nacionais de Autoridade Científica" in J.A. Nunes and M.E. Gonçalves (eds.), *Enteados de Galileu: A Semi-Periferia no Sistema Mundial da Ciência* (pp.247–298). Porto: Afrontamento.

Santos, Ana Cristina (2010). "Portugal" in S. Roseneil (ed.), *Changing Cultural Discourses about Intimate Life: The Demands and Actions of Women's Movements and Other Movements for Gender and Sexual Equality and Change* (pp.184–287). London: FEMCIT.

Santos, Ana Cristina (2013). *Social Movements and Sexual Citizenship in Southern Europe.* Houndmills: Palgrave Macmillan.

Santos Pereira, Tiago (2004). "Science Policy-Making, Democracy, and Changing Knowledge Institutions". *International Social Science Journal, 56* (180), 245–256.

Shapin, Steven (2008). "Science and the Modern World" in E.J. Hackett, *et al.* (eds.), *The Handbook of Science and Technology Studies* (3rd ed) (pp.433–448). Cambridge, MA: MIT Press.

Sócrates, José (2008). *Intervenção do Primeiro-Ministro.* Retrieved 15/07/2010, from http://www.governo.gov.pt/pt/GC17/PrimeiroMinistro/Intervencoes/Pages/20080423_PM_Int_Tratado_Lisboa_AR.aspx

Sousa Santos, Boaventura de (1994). *Pela Mão de Alice: o Social e o Político na Pós-Modernidade.* Porto: Afrontamento.

Sousa Santos, Boaventura de (ed.) (2007). *Another Knowledge Is Possible: Beyond Northern Epistemologies.* London: Verso.

Sousa Santos, Boaventura de (2009). "Portugal: Tales of Being and Not Being". *Portuguese Literary & Cultural Studies, 20,* 1–46.Spivak, Gayatri (1987). *In Other Worlds: Essays in Cultural Politics.* New York: Methuen.

Stöckelová, Tereza (2012). "Immutable Mobiles Derailed: STS, Geopolitics, and Research Assessment". *Science, Technology & Human Values, 37* (2), 286–311.

Suárez, Isabel Carrera and Suárez, Laura Vinuela (2002). "Spain" in G. Griffin (ed.), *Women's Employment, Women's Studies, and Equal Opportunities (1945–2001)* (pp.427–469). Hull: University of Hull.

Üşür, Serpil Sancar (2006). "Women's Studies in Turkish Academic Life" in T.-S. Pavlidou (ed.), *Gender Studies: Trends/Tensions in Greece and Other European Countries* (pp.129–138). Thessaloniki: ΕΚΔΟΣΕΙΣ ΖΗΤΗ.

Vala, Jorge and Torres, Anália (eds.) (2006). *Contextos e Atitudes Sociais na Europa*. Lisboa: Imprensa de Ciências Sociais.

Vale de Almeida, Miguel (2004). *An Earth-Colored Sea: "Race", Culture, and the Politics of Identity in the Postcolonial Portuguese-Speaking World*. New York: Berghahn Books.

Vale de Almeida, Miguel (2008). *"Not Quite White": Portuguese People in the Margins of Lusotropicalism, the Luso-Afro-Brazilian Space, and Lusophony*. Retrieved 02/04/2016, from http://miguelvaledealmeida.net/wp-content/uploads/2008/05/not-quite-white-english.pdf

Vale de Almeida, Miguel (2012a). "'After the Big Sweep': Colonial Narratives and Second Class Citizens in Contemporary Portugal" in S. Kahn, *et al.* (eds.), *The Lusotropical Tempest: Postcolonial Debates in Portuguese* (pp.17–28). Bristol: Seagull/Faiolean.

Vale de Almeida, Miguel (2012b). "Tripping Over History: Same-Sex Marriage in Portugal". *Anthropology Today, 28* (3), 24–27.

Vasterling, Veronica, *et al.* (2006). *Practising Interdisciplinarity in Gender Studies*. York: Raw Nerve Books.

Viegas, José Manuel Leite and Costa, António Firmino da (2000). "Introduction: Overlapping Processes of Social Change" in J.M.L. Viegas and A.F. Costa (eds.), *Crossroads to Modernity: Contemporary Portuguese Society* (pp.1–12). Oeiras: Celta.

Viennot, Elaine, *et al.* (2000). "Historical Dossier on the Making of European Women's Studies: France". *The Making of European Women's Studies, II*, 167–221.

Widerberg, Karin (1998). "Translating Gender". *NORA: Nordic Journal of Feminist and Gender Research, 6* (2), 133–138.

Wise, Sue (1997). "What Are Feminist Academics For?" in L. Stanley (ed.), *Knowing Feminisms: On Academic Borders, Territories and Tribes* (pp.120–131). London: Sage.

Wöhrer, Veronika (2016). "Gender Studies as a Multi-Centred Field? Centres and Peripheries in Academic Gender Research". *Feminist Theory, 17* (3), 323–343.

Zimmermann, Susan (2007). "The Institutionalization of Women and Gender Studies in Higher Education in Central and Eastern Europe and the Former Soviet Union: Asymmetric Politics and the Regional-Transnational Configuration". *East Central Europe, 34* (1), 131–160.

Zmroczek, Christine and Duchen, Claire (1991). "What *Are* Those Women Up To? Women's Studies and Feminist Research in the European Community" in J. Aaron and S. Walby (eds.), *Out of the Margins: Women's Studies in the Nineties* (pp.11–29). London: Falmer Press.

WGFS in the performative university (Part II)

The mood of academia and its impact on our knowledge and our lives

From November 2015 to February 2016 I conducted follow-up interviews with 12 of my original research participants. 7 years had passed since I first sat in their offices, living rooms, or neighbourhood cafés and asked about their experiences of negotiating the epistemic status of WGFS, encounters which produced the interview material analysed in the previous chapters. Those intervening 7 years were a significant and intense time. In the 2008/2009 interviews, the performativisation of academia was unmistakable, and already clearly influential vis-à-vis WGFS, but it was, in many ways, a relatively incipient, partial and haphazard development. By 2015/2016, logics of performativity were arguably the dominant and over-riding organising principle, and discursive framework, of academic work in Portugal and many other semi-peripheral countries (Aavik *et al.*, 2015; Stöckelová, 2012). Neither my participants, nor myself, could have entirely predicted (though some were not far off) how quickly and pervasively the performative academic model would become institutionalised, how deeply embedded it would become in organisational structures, work practices and everyday talk, and how profoundly it would shape individual academics' sense of self and career orientation. Therefore, it seemed justified and productive to interview my participants again, to find out how they interpret these changes, and what impacts they have had on WGFS' institutionalisation, and especially on macro- and micro-level epistemic climates and the status of WGFS within them.

I was keen to explore a number of questions. In a context of advanced performativisation of academic work, had WGFS become more or less established? Is there more space for WGFS work? Is it still mocked in corridor talk? Is it more widely and easily recognised as capable of producing 'proper' knowledge? Have the potential openings for WGFS which I had initially identified actually come to fruition? The follow-up interviews focused on the same issues that had (pre)occupied me several years earlier; the aim was to update, revisit and potentially revise the analysis I had produced, based on the original fieldwork, of the relationship between the political economy of academia and demarcations of what counts as proper knowledge. The new interviews certainly generated plenty of rich material with which to fulfil that aim. And yet, there was something different about (most of) those follow-up interviews, a diffuse but palpable and unmistakeable shift which unsettles the terms of my analysis and reframes the issues at stake, and which has thus led me to question the tone and thrust of some of my original arguments.

Good news and bad news: The landscape of WGFS in times of austerity and performativity

In their description of WGFS' current position and status, these recent interviews share many features with the original ones. Participants' accounts, like any narrative about the institutionalisation and development of WGFS (Hemmings, 2006), are *subjective, situated, disparate* and *contested*. They assess current patterns and trends of institutionalisation differently, often according to their biography (and even their personality, as one senior scholar put it), position in WGFS and their universities, or notions of what counts as proper WGFS. Three different scholars[1] located within the *same* university (albeit in distinct departments) produced narratives as diverse as this:

> "[In the past 7 years] there have been many changes for the best, [. . .] extraordinary changes in terms of our acceptance and recognition. (. . .) [WGFS] is now completely normalised here."

> "As far as I can see, I don't think there have been many changes [since 2008, in the status of WGFS]. (. . .) The [unofficial] teasing of the field continues. (. . .) My research centre doesn't think that 'women's things', as they call them, are relevant AT ALL."

> "As for social and academic openness to, and recognition of, this area of studies . . . I don't think there is any, still! I think that hasn't improved [in the past 7 years]; on the contrary, I think it got worse."

It is possible to find such disparate accounts also because the past 7 years have seen both openings and closures, changes and continuities. A key milestone was the creation of a new research centre, CIEG (Interdisciplinary Centre for Gender Studies). Founded in February 2012 at the University of Lisbon by a team led by the sociologist Anália Torres,[2] it congregates WGFS scholars from across the country and different disciplines. It was evaluated as 'excellent' in the most recent national research evaluation exercise (2013–2015). (This was an unprecedentedly polemical and fiercely criticised exercise[3] which departed significantly from earlier rounds (Deem, 2016), reinforcing performativity by formalising several extraordinarily abrupt and quite radical changes in understandings and measurements of scientific quality, expectations of individual performance, allocation of resources,[4] and relationship between the academic community, evaluators and public funders.[5]) Several participants described CIEG's founding as a breakthrough in Portuguese WGFS, namely because it made more space and resources available for WGFS and brought colleagues from different institutions together through its projects and events, including a very large international congress in May 2016. Other milestones mentioned by several participants included the launch in 2013 by the feminist organisation UMAR of the *Feminist University*, a free and open WGFS university (Ferreira, E. *et al.*, 2015); the creation in 2015 of a stream on 'Gender, sexualities and intersectionality' in CIS (a Psychology research centre within ISCTE-IUL); and the widely publicised (namely in mainstream media) award in 2013 of 2 large European Research Council grants – a Starting Grant (Ana Cristina Santos) and a Consolidator Grant (Sofia Aboim) – to Portuguese academics working on gender and sexuality, the only ERC grants awarded to Portuguese social science scholarship that year.[6] Participants highlighted the latter as

> *"very important because if an international agency like the ERC[7] recognises 2 projects like this as amongst the best in Europe, and awards them such high-profile funding, then that proves these topics are important, and the work that Portuguese gender studies scholars do really is good, maybe even BETTER than work that gets done on conventional topics, which more easily gets seen as valuable scholarship."*

However, not all developments during this period were positive. The fears expressed by participants in the original interviews (see chapter 3) about the precariousness of WGFS degrees, namely due to difficulties in sustaining student recruitment, have been realised, and some of those degrees have since closed. In February 2016, one of the leading WGFS journals, *Faces de Eva*, announced that funding cuts made it impossible to continue to publish a paper version of the journal, and launched a public fund-raising campaign to cover printing costs. Debates within the Editorial Board of *ex aequo*, the other main WGFS journal, about the journal's sustainability have intensified as a result of funding cuts and changes in the requirements set by ScieLO (the international bibliographic database that hosts it), which have become more demanding and harder to meet with the resources available to WGFS scholars. All of these changes occurred against the backdrop of the devastating 'austerity' measures imposed to Portugal as part of the €78 billion bail-out implemented in 2011 by the International Monetary Fund, European Central Bank and European Commission, and implemented primarily by a right-wing government (2011–2015). Austerity brought crippling cutbacks to universities: the state budget for HE suffered a reduction of 25.6% between 2011 and 2013 (Cerdeira, 2012), there was a steep decline of 26.7% (between 2009 and 2015) in the funding allocated to FCT (the national research council), and the number of doctoral and postdoctoral grants awarded by FCT fell by 44.6% (between 2009 and 2015) (FCT, 2015). According to several interviewees, the latter led to the loss of substantial numbers of applicants to, and students in, WGFS PhD programmes.

 This conjuncture has, unsurprisingly, not helped overcome the structural obstacles to WGFS' development and sustainability discussed in the original interviews (see chapter 3). Amidst these severe budget cuts and strict government-imposed constraints on new staff recruitment (even if just to replace departing colleagues), most younger WGFS academics remain precariously employed. WGFS continues to exist in many institutions in a state of individualised institutionalisation, maintained by senior scholars now 7 years closer to retirement, who consider it unlikely they will be replaced by others with commitment to, and expertise in, WGFS. According to one interviewee, this has further deepened the *"divide"* between *"the growing and vibrant research [on gender and sexuality] conducted by increasing numbers of people in quite precarious conditions"* and *"the body of permanent university staff, who do teaching, curriculum design, etc., usually along very disciplinary, traditional lines, with very little, if any, attention to gender and sexuality"*. This *"bicephalous situation"* means that *"there's actually lots of innovation [in WGFS], and lots of people in it, but you just don't see the field (. . .) when you open a university or department website, because those people don't have places in universities"*. For many interviewees, however, a glimmer of hope has risen in the horizon for the first time in many years, following the election of a left-wing coalition government which has promised to reverse many of the most contested recent changes in scientific policy (see endnote 3) and work more actively, and in greater consultation with academics, to support science and HE, and enhance scientific employment opportunities (Ferreira, N., 2016).

I am in the rare and fortunate position of having comparable material from 2 rounds of interviews with the same participants, conducted at 2 key points in the institutionalisation of academic cultures of performativity – one round when such cultures were emerging, the other when they were well established. Therefore, my plan was to use this last chapter to ask whether the trends of restructuring of epistemic categories and hierarchies which I had identified in the late 2000s had become realised more than half a decade later. On the surface level, it looks like they have. As many interviewees noted, being and remaining productive continues to be a key condition for getting WGFS recognised as scholarship of value:

> *"What you produce and how much continues to be the most important thing in how your institution sees you and whether it supports your work; in fact, all that is more important now than ever."*

> *"Institutions love a big grant, like ERC grants – it brings money, acts as an indicator of productivity, and so they can use it to enhance their status. . . . And suddenly, feminist work becomes a star pupil to be publicly celebrated. It gets used as a sign that the institution's excellent because it gets grants – although the merit, of course, belongs exclusively to the researcher – when in that same institution it [feminist work] used to be seen, not that long ago, as inferior and objectionable."*

> *"If we [WGFS scholars] weren't so productive, and indeed more productive than people working on more traditional areas of research, we'd probably be much more discriminated on account of the kind of work we do, you know? That's my feeling – we're not discriminated against for being feminist because our productivity protects us. (. . .) In a productivist academic culture like this, what matters is productivity, not what kind of work you do. That's why I think [name of scholar], for example, has been able to do [initiative x] and hasn't faced as many obstacles as we've encountered in the past, it's*

*because high productivity protects you. (. . .) That doesn't necessarily mean
we're producing what we most enjoy and actually would like to produce. (. . .)
This is a sort of dilemma: we can maintain the field because we produce,
although we don't actually agree with the epistemology at the heart of this
academic logic! But if we'd completely refused to play the game, by now we'd
probably be a dying field, because it'd be discriminated against."*

There is clear evidence that a *"productivist"* culture, as this last interviewee calls
it, has produced opportunities and recognition for WGFS that were unavailable in
the previous more 'traditional' (and more explicitly patriarchal and unashamedly
hierarchical) academic regime, and that this culture has to some extent *'protected'*
WGFS from enduring sexist epistemic discrimination. Even though none of my
interviewees *"actually agree with (. . .) this academic logic"*, that logic does
allow individual scholars, if sufficiently productive and successful, to create space
for WGFS without *"many obstacles"* in institutions that used to consider the field
"inferior" and *"objectionable"*.

All of my earlier analysis (see chapter 3, and Pereira, 2011; 2015) of the impact
of a changing academic political economy on epistemic climates and demarcations
was structured around the concept of 'paradox'. I wanted to avoid simplistically
celebratory or damning diagnoses, and sought instead to foreground complexity
and contradiction, showing that in many performative universities openings and
closures for WGFS not only coexist, but are inextricably linked and mutually constitutive. It is not surprising that I was committed to finding openings and some
cause for optimism, considering that the original analysis was first drafted in 2010,
amidst what seemed like an overwhelming wave of frightening transformations not
just in academia, but especially in society, politics and the economy in Portugal,
the UK and elsewhere in the world. As Emily F. Henderson has noted (personal
communication, 2016), the feminist emphasis on, and constant rehearsing of, the
'doom and gloom of neoliberalism' can unwittingly be problematically paralysing.
Instead, I adopted Goldie Osuri's approach: 'it is perhaps more useful to engage
with the neoliberal present, theorise it, and learn to strategise rather than simply
worry' (2007: 145). Therefore, I tried to complicate that feminist emphasis on
doom, gloom and worry by highlighting some of neoliberalism's openings, in the
hope that debating and understanding them would allow us to resist, subvert and
transform neoliberalism more effectively. I am (partly) a Foucauldian, after all. . . .

I still believe that recognising the performative university's paradoxical openings and 'perverse pleasures' (Hey, 2004) is both epistemically and politically
imperative. And yet, revisiting the original analysis now in light of the second
round of interviews has led me to wonder whether I was not, in fact, too naively
optimistic in one particular, but pivotal, aspect: the implicit (and, I admit, entirely
unreflected) assumption that WGFS is the sum of all its constituent parts, and thus
that openings for *individual* scholars (or research teams) equate to openings for
the *field*. In other words, I presumed that accumulated individual advancement
signifies, represents and enables an advancing WGFS, and thus a collection of
successful and prolific individuals will contribute to the success and proliferation

of WGFS. The problems of this assumption became apparent when I examined the follow-up interviews from a perspective different from the one I had planned – rather than focus on what has been happening in the *epistemic and institutional landscape* of WGFS, we can ask what has happened to the *people* in WGFS.

"Depression" is *"in the air"*: The mood of WGFS in the performative university

At first glance, my interviewees' professional situation did not appear to have changed much in 7 years: almost all were working in the same institution and often the same position. However, one thing was conspicuously different: how they *feel*. From the very first interview I was struck, and often deeply affected, by how utterly drained and profoundly depleted the interviewees seemed to be. Their pressured exhaustion was conspicuous in their tone of voice. In some, it manifested as a frantic anxiety, rushed speaking regularly broken up by self-interruption, as if their sense of being in constant hurry bled into, and fragmented, their thought and speech. Others, however, spoke slowly and gravely, interviews punctuated by tired sighs and despondent pauses, as if they had limited energy with which to think and speak. Their pressured exhaustion was also something they spoke emotively, explicitly and frequently about.

> *"Surviving periods of great constraint, as we've had with austerity in the last years, demands so much psychological energy that after a while you don't have any strength left, because you're facing difficulties on a daily basis. (. . .) 'How will we cope with fewer people? How will we produce more?' (. . .) You're facing those questions EVERY day, and you're left in a state of psychological exhaustion, and you want to give up, because there's no energy left at all. (. . .) I haven't had proper holidays in AGES. [voice raises and becomes more assertive] I CAN'T TAKE IT ANYMORE! [pause] You know that feeling? That feeling of being completely WORN OUT, worn to the bone, NOT EVEN your free time is preserved. [silence] I mean . . . [slows down] I've only had [lists the small number of days off had in the past 18 months]. This is unacceptable. (. . .) It's just devastating, devastating!"*

> *"Yesterday, someone looked at me and said 'you look tired!' [laughs]. Well, sleeping 5 hours a night for months on end doesn't do anyone any good, doesn't do your skin or health any good! And yes, we're tired because all these changes, that is, what does it mean, for example, this pressure, you know, for example, this pressure to generate profit (. . .), you must offer MA degrees, PhD degrees, and that means you have to teach much more. [lists the high number of modules she is running that academic year] (. . .) This is absolutely draining, and at the end the one thing they'll ask you is: 'so, how many articles did you publish?' [silence] 'Well, I didn't publish a single one! That's the way it is!' (. . .) [nervous laughter] [sigh] Oh well! It's . . . [silence] This is all a bit of a sob story."*

"We're just in a state of exhaustion. Enormous exhaustion. Enormous exhaustion, enormous demotivation. (. . .) Well, I guess I've had my rant . . . Poor you! It can't be very pleasant to talk to us [academics] at the moment. [nervous laughter]"

"This brutal imposition [of publication productivity as the aim and measure of academic work] drove everyone to complete madness. (. . .) [speaking quickly] All that people talk about is (. . .) where they've published, and where they'll publish, and how little the other person has published but I published more and so I'm better, I mean, listen, this is a sick climate, ok, and it makes us all ill. It's utter despair to live in these circumstances, it's a desperate life! The days are depressing, you know? [nervous laughter]"

The quotes above hint at some of the causes for this *"state of exhaustion"*. Although some aspects of their concrete manifestation are specific to the contingencies of Portuguese academia, those causes will be familiar to scholars throughout the world working within academic cultures of performativity, as they reflect the trends that characterise those transnational cultures (see chapter 3 and Ball, 2000; Mountz *et al.*, 2015). My interviewees speak of a much increased workload[8] (as a result of heightened expectations of academic performance, failure to replace departing colleagues, and downsizing or extinction of administrative support due to budget cuts, among other factors); a vertiginously expanding audit culture, creating innumerable layers of extra administrative and 'fabrication' (Ball, 2000) work and constant interpellations to describe and evidence performance *"in never-ending reports that take an enormous amount of time to write"*; the implementation of new systems of research evaluation, with much at stake – resources, reputations, relationships, etc. – but with constantly changing regulations and criteria, creating disorientation, uncertainty and a *"loss of trust"* (senior scholar) in those evaluation systems; the reorientation of academic practice towards the constantly increasing production of measurable outputs of a certain (narrow) kind; the escalating pressure to publish only or primarily in English (which is participants' second or even third language); teaching becoming increasingly devalued, but staff being expected to do more of it; the erosion of academic careers, an *"incomparable worsening, compared to 7 years ago, of our working conditions"* (senior scholar), and the widening of the gap between permanent staff and a precarious, often younger, workforce. As a result of, and through, these changes, performativity has arguably become the dominant organising principle of contemporary academic work in Portugal.

The combined effect of those changes has not just produced severe physical and intellectual fatigue, but also affected interviewees' emotional relationship with their work – their passion and motivation to do it, their sense of identification with it, and their perception that it is meaningful and worth the increasing sacrifices.

"In my research centre we have the war, the pressure to publish and the threat that if you don't publish, you're kicked out. It's a completely

*transformed world. . . . This is what we've come to! (. . .) [sigh] I don't know
where we'll end up. All my life I've said that after retiring I would take an
emeritus role and hang around here until I was 70, because why would
I want to go home? To get depressed? I no longer think like that. (. . .) This
place is wearing me down, day by day, and has a destructive effect on me.
I never, ever thought I'd feel like this, but I find myself craving retirement
so all this can stop."*

> *"I must admit I don't let the pressure to publish get to me too much, but
> I can do that because I have a job, and status, and so (. . .) I'm in a comfort-
> able position. But I can't escape the feeling of (. . .) alienation. The aliena-
> tion is what really gets to me, i.e. you're forced to spend a large part of your
> time on evaluations, self-evaluations, verification and evidencing of this or
> that, paperwork, changing rules (. . .), endless surveys, online systems for
> this and that. Do you know what I mean? All the administrative bureaucracy
> of control mechanisms within this <audit culture>, which you're obliged to
> comply with in incredibly tight deadlines, always very last minute, with lots
> of hysterics surrounding it, and that's profoundly alienating stuff, because
> there's no creativity, it doesn't contribute in the least to your growth, thinking,
> articulation with others, nothing! That's what it is, it's alienation, and aliena-
> tion is a draining thing."*

This *"state of exhaustion"* and *"alienation"* is more than just an individual experience. To use the words of participants, taken from excerpts presented above, it is
a *"sick climate"* that *"makes us all ill"*, and determines the collective atmosphere.
Some people are more deeply affected by it than others – depending, for example, on their particular working conditions, temperament or generation[9] – but all
experience its effects. The shared nature of those feelings of physical exhaustion,
intellectual depletion and emotional despondency is compellingly described in
this excerpt:

> *"I'm very critical of the changes in academia in the past years. I think every-
> one is still recovering from this, basically, whack on the head we've received.
> (. . .) It has affected people in the deepest, most intimate core of their being,
> because suddenly what was at stake was an idea of academic merit that didn't
> match what people saw as merit. (. . .) This has really affected people's lives.*
> *MMP: Other people I've interviewed say they notice a certain, how can
> I put it, not depression because that's maybe a very strong word, but a feeling,
> a state of (. . .)*
> *But you can say depression, because in a sense that's exactly what it is.
> (. . .) If we studied the health impact of these changes, (. . .) I think we'd find
> that people's psychological health has been affected, you notice that clearly
> every day all around you (. . .), people are more anxious, depressed, less able
> to deal with frustration, they have physical health problems, chronic pain,*

they need medication to be able to sleep. (. . .) You interact with people and it's clear they're always at the very limit of their strength, the limit of their capacities, they drag themselves. (. . .) People have the constant sense that they're running. Running, running, running, not quite knowing where, you know? Not least because we might be running for one goal today, and then the goalposts shift, and that goal will no longer be valued tomorrow. (. . .) This affects the atmosphere, affects people's desire to be with each other, the exhaustion becomes so deeply entrenched and it's generalised, you can actually feel it in the air all around you."

It is telling that in my intervention in this excerpt, I struggled to find a term to describe the 'thing' that myself and others noticed in Portuguese academia, something diffuse but unmistakable, private but generalised, that *"you can actually feel (. . .) in the air all around you"*. The 'thing' we noticed was certainly a set of feelings, a term which, like Cvetkovich, I conceptualise in an 'intentionally imprecise [way], retaining the ambiguity between feelings as embodied sensations and feelings as psychic or cognitive experiences' (2012: 4). But we tend to understand feelings as individual sensations or experiences located in bodies and minds, rather than *"in the air all around you"*. And yet, the *"depression"* generated by academic cultures of performativity is a collective, communal and contagious feeling.[10] As Cvetkovich (2012) argues, that depression is a 'public feeling', and one that can be considered an 'epidemic' in the 'corporate university', where workers are expected to 'live with (. . .) sometimes impossible conditions' in a culture 'that say[s] that you are only as good as what you produce' (2012: 18–19).

I find it useful to think of these public feelings, both private and collective, both 'embodied' and 'psychic and cognitive' (Cvetkovich, 2012), both material (felt *"in the physical health problems, chronic pain"*, exhaustion) and ethereal (felt *"in the air"*), as a *mood*.[11] As Felski and Fraiman write, 'a focus on mood reframe[s] our perspective' (2012: v): it invites us to transcend and disrupt the binary 'clunky categories often imposed on experience: subjective versus objective, feeling versus thinking, latent versus manifest' (2012: vi) and, as Hemmings (2012) adds, public versus private. To focus on mood is to attempt to describe something unfocused that often escapes description, as in my struggle in the excerpt above to put *"a feeling, a state"* into words. A mood is, as Felski and Fraiman argue, 'ambient, vague, diffuse, hazy, and intangible', it 'lingers, tarries, settles in, accumulates, sticks around', unlike, for example, emotions, which tend to be more intense and transient (2012: v; Hemmings, 2012).

Crucially, moods are shared and collective – they are an 'attunement (. . .), a convergence of collective emotions situated in precise movements and institutions' (Highmore and Taylor, 2014: 10). Because they are both within and beyond us, 'everywhere and nowhere', moods 'bridg[e] and lubricat[e] relations between ostensibly separate entities: self and other' (Felski and Fraiman, 2012: xii). As such, they can connect us to those around us – or at least some of them (Ahmed, 2014) – in intense but elusive ways: 'we are enveloped or assailed by a mood.

Mood is a feeling of I-and-world together' (Felski and Fraiman, 2012: vii). Considering my interest within this project in metaphors of *climate* (see chapter 2), it is interesting and propitious that many authors have argued that '[m]ood is like the weather' (Felski and Fraiman, 2012: v; Highmore and Taylor, 2014: 8), 'existing as an atmosphere' with its 'own pressure systems' (Highmore and Taylor, 2014: 8). We might say, therefore, that alongside the *epistemic climate* and the *(chilly) micro-political climate* analysed in chapter 3, we can also consider mood as a *climate* affecting the life of WGFS, and the lives of WGFS scholars. How, then, is this *"sick climate"*, a mood of physical exhaustion, intellectual depletion and emotional despondency that *"makes us all ill"*, shaping WGFS knowledge?

Producing WGFS knowledge in a *"sick [academic] climate"*

According to my interviewees, several epistemic activities are becoming increasingly difficult, if not impossible, to sustain in the performative university due to the increased time pressures, the relentless productivity expectations and the attendant general mood of exhaustion and alienation. *Reading* was one of those activities:

> *"Obviously in the current conditions I don't have the time to update my knowledge and read what's being written. (. . .) One has to set priorities, and with the pressures I have at the moment, my priority isn't reading other people's work, I just can't do it, there's no chance of fitting it in, as much as it pains me to say this."*

> *"I can't sit and read, I wish I could! But that's the same for all my other colleagues (. . .). If someone sends me something to read 'Oh, read this, I think you'll like it', or 'I've written this, it would be great to get your feedback', complete panic, those are the worst emails, when someone sends me something to read, because, there's just no, there's just no time, there really isn't!"*

> *"There's absolutely, ABSOLUTELY, no time to read. I used to keep a pile of things I wanted to read – I don't even bother doing that systematically now, because I know (. . .) I'll never find time to do that reading."*

This study itself illustrates how sudden and significant the loss of reading time was in the past 7 years. In the introduction, I explained that when I wrote up my initial findings in 2009, my participants felt like a *vigilant* community, vocally and insistently keen to find out what I was writing about them and when they could read it. In 2011, when these academic changes were in full swing, I sent the 31 scholars interviewed a 7-page document with a summary of findings, and asked them to get in touch if they wanted to read the longer analysis; only 3 did so. When arranging the second round of interviews, I re-sent the 7-page summary, and invited participants to read it in advance, so we could discuss it during the interview (emphasising, however, that this was not compulsory). Only 2 of the 12 follow-up interviewees managed to read the document; all others explained, regretfully, that they had been too busy to get the chance to peruse it. As one interviewee put it,

> "The fact that I don't even have time to read a study that's actually about me and our field, and that I'd been so keen to read, tells you all you need to know about how pressured and crazy universities are at the moment. If I can't find time to read studies about me, you can imagine how much time there is to read other research – none at all!"

In just a few years, the academic working conditions changed so significantly that my originally *vigilant* community came to find it increasingly hard to remain 'watchful; (. . .) attentively or closely observant' (OED) of research being published by other WGFS colleagues. Everyone is pressured to write more and more, but has less and less time to read the work that gets written.

Thinking is another activity that interviewees find it increasingly hard to carve time for.

> "To produce at the rate (. . .) and the format [short articles in international journals] that's required, you don't have time to think as much and as deeply, there's less reflection, you have to be much more contained in how far you develop your ideas and analysis, (. . .) and it's hard and extremely alienating to work like that. (. . .) Even when we manage to produce work, we often don't feel very excited about what we've produced, because you know you rushed it, and didn't really have time to think about it properly, and that's demotivating."

> "The conditions to think are so much worse. So much worse! (. . .) When you think, it's always on the basis of immediate need, what you need to do next, and that's it! Lots of stuff falls by the wayside, and everyone's working like this. (. . .) The way I think in my research is just fire-fighting, it isn't anything else. I don't actually think, I just fire-fight."

In a climate where there is little time to *read* and *think*, it is not surprising that scholars find it difficult also to maintain a whole range of other, more collective, activities central to knowledge production and the sustaining of a field. Interviewees explain it is increasingly hard to *organise and attend academic events* and to *meet, and debate with, other colleagues*.

> "I have some interesting event ideas (. . .) but then the exhaustion makes me think 'ouch, no, organising that is too much work. It's too much, I can't face it'."

> "Everyone's tired and busy. (. . .) We'll organise an event, students will come, but who will come from the staff? 2 people? Maybe 3, in exceptional circumstances! Because people just don't have the availability. (. . .) I myself can't attend lots of events I'm interested in."

"People just don't have the conditions to meet, the time to talk to each other, people don't talk! I mean, talk to other people in this field, I'm not even talking about meeting with people in other fields! (. . .) Everyone's so busy, so each person is sitting in their own little corner, focusing on their own little task, and no one discusses anything! A few years ago (. . .) [in the late 2000s] there were lots of events going on and people would go, you'd meet and have conversations. Now, people are buried in their own hole, because they're so tired and overwhelmed. (. . .) And in this climate, you tell me – where is there the space to discuss whatever? Never mind feminist theory – there's no space to discuss any theory at all!"

"We don't talk, we don't do things collectively! (. . .) And that's because of this dispersion and individualisation, this exhaustion, these bureaucratic demands (. . .) and requirements of productivity. Because of them, we don't have the time to meet, and that failure to meet means we don't discuss the knowledge we produce, and that absence of discussion weakens our work. It may look like things are somehow ticking along, but the truth is the lack of meeting and discussion weakens everything we do."

This climate also affects the running and growth of many of the 'institutions' of WGFS. A senior scholar involved in a WGFS degree programme explained:

"It's impossible to arrange a meeting [of the group involved in the programme], it's hellish trying to find 2 hours in a week where 12 people can get together to think collectively about our strategy or the organising of something. (. . .) This makes it incredibly difficult to develop growth strategies, which is something I'd really like to do, because if we don't grow, we die, (. . .) but that's the sort of thing that can't be done by one person, not even 2, it has to be a team, and we struggle to get the team moving, and the reason we struggle is precisely due to the excessive workload that we all have. (. . .) I'd like to create partnerships with institutions abroad, (. . .) and I can't find the time to even begin thinking about it!"

A member of the Board of APEM, the Portuguese Women's Studies Association, noted that APEM's work is also compromised:

"In APEM, we find it hard to do things, events, projects, meetings. . . . We want to, we really, really want to, but we're not able to, we can't cope, we just can't, we're too tired and overloaded, it's very hard, just very hard."

WGFS journals are also affected, as a member of one editorial board explains:

"I'm really worried and sceptical about the journal's future, because it's completely outside the for-profit circuit of the big international academic publishing companies. It survives on occasional and very small funding pots and on the voluntary work of lots of people. And so I think its survival is very

difficult. (. . .) It would help if we were indexed in a big indexing platform, but the amount of work that involves. (. . .) It's just overwhelming, you know? It's labour that's not compatible with voluntary work, the work you do after midnight, which is the only time we have to dedicate to these things!"

In a recent editorial of the WGFS journal *ex aequo*, Virgínia Ferreira, the journal's editor, writes:

> Who will want to continue doing the work of journal editing [and peer review- ing] in these conditions [of academic capitalism]? Are we not giving up that work and leaving it entirely in the hands of the structures of knowledge capi- talism, which will take it upon themselves to exclude anything which can- not be converted into profit? We are confident that this will not be the route chosen by *ex aequo* to tackle the current challenges (. . .) will we be able to survive and resist? Let's, at least, have some hope (. . .) in the meantime, we will continue doing our best,
>
> (2015: 5*)

The kind of interactional, collective and collegial work that these and other WGFS scholars are finding it challenging or impossible to do is not an optional extra or expendable add-on. How can a field (WGFS or any other) survive and thrive if its scholars do not have the necessary conditions – including time, energy, stam- ina, motivation, intellectual vigour and emotional vitality – to read, peer review and debate each other's work, attend events, create partnerships, meet to discuss growth strategies, organise conferences, run professional associations, and man- age journals? It is those activities, structures and organisations that constitute and maintain a field, and that give broader meaning and resonance to the knowledge scholars produce individually. In that sense, WGFS is, in fact, more than just the sum of the actions, outputs and achievements of each individual scholar. It is also, and centrally, this interactional, collective and collegial work they do together, work which is being eroded or becoming impossible in the performative univer- sity, with its fetishising of individual performance and competition, its escalation of requirements of productivity, and its depletion of scholars' bodies, imagination, passion and capacities (Mountz *et al.*, 2015).

In academic cultures of performativity, the hard but often invisible reproductive and collective work of *field-making* is generally not recognised, valued or recom- pensed. For many WGFS scholars, it is something they do ' "between the lines" of academia, in the evenings', in the words of members of the Portuguese WGFS research group NIGEF (University of Minho) (quoted in Fernandes, 2008: 89*). This creates special challenges for WGFS, especially in those countries where it is precariously institutionalised and less well-resourced, and thus requires more alert, ongoing and laborious field-making. The performative university does pro- duce (conditional) openings for (productive) individuals and teams, but at what cost, not just to the health, intellectual, emotional and political vitality, and the personal life of each individual scholar, but also to the invisible but inestimable work of *making* the *field*, and to the quality and intensity of our collective engagement as a community of knowledge producers?

Draining or empowering? Collegial work in individualistic times

As Gill and Donaghue predicted in their analysis of the 'deep crisis [currently] affecting universities' all over the world, what I encountered when I spent some 'time with academics' 7 years after our initial interviews was a group of 'people stretched to breaking point', affected by individual feelings, and a collective mood, of physical exhaustion, intellectual depletion and emotional despondency so significant that it might be described as a 'psychosocial and somatic catastrophe' (2016: 91). Because that catastrophe 'hamper[s] sharing and exchange' (2016: 93), it is having undeniable epistemic consequences. As Davies and Petersen (2005) have argued, the logics of the 'knowledge economy' may actually work to undermine and thwart the production of knowledge. The significant difference in my interviewees' experiences of, and feelings about, their work in the 2 rounds of interviews, separated by 7 years and a process of structural performativisation of academia, fully confirms the fundamental 'irony' that Davies and Petersen argue is at the centre of trends of neo-liberalisation of universities:

> this transformation of universities (. . .) may occlude the very work of producing the innovative knowledge that makes universities the creative hub of the so-called knowledge economy. The new subjects of neo-liberalism ideally transform themselves to produce the products desired (. . .). This focus on end-products may put them at risk of losing the capacity to fulfil (or *even to feel*) the desire to carry out significant, creative or critical intellectual work.
>
> (2005: 78, my emphasis)

It is common to discount these feelings – of exhaustion, alienation, overwhelm – as personal ailments (if not failures) to be discussed in private and managed individually (Gill and Donaghue, 2016; Pereira, 2016). But if this academic culture undermines our capacity to 'fulfil' and 'feel' the desire to produce 'significant, creative or critical' scholarship (Davies and Petersen, 2005: 78) – and also to care for ourselves, our colleagues and our communities beyond the academy (Lynch, 2010; Pereira, 2016) – then we can no longer afford to not confront it collectively. If performative academic cultures recognise epistemic status in productive WGFS work, but produce a WGFS community where so many scholars are too tired and rushed to be able to properly read others' work, peer review, meet, debate, plan, attend events, maintain associations and journals, then we are facing a different beast. The key challenge may no longer be how to negotiate WGFS' epistemic status, but something even more basic and foundational: how to guarantee that we have the working (and living) conditions to be able, individually and collectively, to do 'significant, creative or critical work' in the first place, both within and beyond the performative academy.

Mobilising debate and action on this 'psychosocial and somatic catastrophe' (Gill and Donaghue, 2016: 91) and its effects on WGFS knowledge is urgent. It is especially crucial in those contexts where WGFS exists in a state of individualised institutionalisation (see chapter 3), a situation where both the likelihood and the negative consequences of individual depletion are magnified as there are fewer, if any, other colleagues who can share the work of maintaining WGFS in an institution. Mobilising debate and action on this is, however, extremely and distinctively difficult, because in many ways – and unlike what happens in other challenges faced by WGFS scholars in academia – this 'psychosocial and somatic catastrophe' (Gill and Donaghue, 2016: 91) contains and sows the seeds of its own reproduction.

As Cvetkovich argues, the 'public feeling' of 'depression' that shapes life in contemporary academia 'often keeps people silent, weary, and too numb to really notice the sources of their unhappiness'; it is a 'for[m] of biopower that (. . .) [operates] more insidiously by making people feel small, worthless, hopeless, (. . .) that takes the form of minds and lives gradually shrinking into despair and hopelessness' (2012: 12,13; see also Sifaki, 2016). Exhausted and overwhelmed by their increasing workloads, crushed by incessant and diverse demands, and anxious about how 'behind' they are on their work, academics get swept into an addictive and draining 'cycle of busyness' (Ross, 2015). That cycle (re)produces the feeling that they do not have the time, and especially the energy, to step back from, reflect on, and attempt to change the performative university. In such a situation, the impulse for many academics is to dive even deeper into work to 'catch up' (Pereira, 2016), in search of the elusive feeling of calm, satisfaction and fulfilment which they hope awaits them when the email inbox is finally cleared and the 'to do' list is finally empty. When the inbox or to-do lists are so full, and the body and mind so tired, it can seem impossible to add something else to one's plate – even if that 'something' is an effort to resist the inbox, disrupt the to-do list, care for the body or give the mind a rest. The physical and intellectual depletion and the emotional and political overwhelm are so paralysing that they undermine the capacity to resist and fight the structures that generate them.

This key feature of performative academic cultures – the fact that they reproduce themselves partly through luring cycles of busyness that induce paralysis (Mountz *et al.*, 2015), hopelessness and worthlessness – becomes especially evident if we compare the narratives about exhaustion produced by research participants in 2008/2009 and 2015/2016. In the first round of interviews, many of them told me that they were tired and exhausted of doing what I called (in chapter 3) 'the hard and precarious work of maintaining WGFS'. Yet, if you return to the quotes analysed in that sub-section, you will find that the tiredness that they describe is distinct from the tiredness I found in 2015/2016: it is, narrated in a different language and experienced as a different mood.

"We're tired of being competent!"

"This effort of (. . .) doing the same every day . . . . it's really exhausting (. . .). We always have to be checking things (. . .) to see if we're being included."

*"We won't let the balls drop, (. . .) we spend our life inventing and doing things.
We've won some battles, but this continuous fighting is absolutely exhausting."*

The exhaustion of 2008/2009 was, I would argue, expressed as an outraged, angry and self-asserting feeling shared by an indignant community (note the preference for 'we' as the subject of claims of exhaustion) battling a common opponent or challenge (though not always collaboratively). Although some interviewees recognised they felt drained and disheartened – with one announcing that *"if there's no intervention from the government (. . .), then we cannot keep doing this thing that wears us down"* – there was something energetic, combative and galvanising about the mood. It was punctuated by, and seemed to foster, a confident sense of righteousness, a rousing belief in the need for continued fighting and resistance, and a heartening feeling of collectivity, all of which seemed to animate the speaker and the audiences (including myself). There was no noticeable sense that the oft-cited exhaustion was in any way a symptom of personal weakness or a sign of personal failure; on the contrary, that exhaustion symbolised the scale and ferocity of the opposition to WGFS, highlighted the urgency and value of continued WGFS work, and thus gave scholars (including myself) a renewed and renewing sense of individual and collective purpose.

The exhaustion of 2015/2016 is different in subtle but significant ways. Interviewees recognise that their impossible workloads could not be adequately managed by anyone. However, many of them yearn or strive to be 'better' at managing it, and so there is an implicit sense that their struggles with those workloads constitute, to some extent, an individual limitation and disappointment. The exhaustion of 2015/2016 is, therefore, a more melancholic, self-questioning and paralysing exhaustion, different from the righteous, self-asserting and galvanising exhaustion of 7 years previously. Although interviewees explicitly recognise the shared nature of that exhaustion, they seem to experience it as a much more personal feeling. Others – colleagues, students – are frequently framed as sources of additional demands, work or pressure that threaten to derail one's individual struggle to manage work and fulfil institutional requirements and deadlines. This makes the exhaustion of 2015/2016 also more isolated and isolating, more individualised and individualising, more inward-facing and irritable. In many ways, this different exhaustion confirms the accounts produced by scholars all over the world (Acker and Armenti, 2004; Butterwick and Dawson, 2005; Cvetkovich, 2012; Davis, 2011; Gill, 2014; Gill and Donaghue, 2016; Leathwood and Read, 2013; Mountz *et al.*, 2015; Pereira, 2012, 2016; Reevy and Deason, 2014; Sifaki, 2016; Sparkes, 2007; Wånggren *et al.*, in press) about the emotional, intellectual and physical effects of inhabiting a 'toxic' (Blackmore and Sachs, 2007; Gill, 2010), 'careless' (Lynch, 2010), 'punishing', 'cult'-like and guilt-tripping (Sifaki, 2016) performative academic culture which 'forestall[s] (. . .) (collective) resistance' (Davies and Petersen, 2005). As Amsler writes,

> where the worth of work is judged according to how much surplus (. . .) value
> it generates in competitive commodity markets, all workers are haunted by

perpetual threats of devaluation, exclusion and 'redundancy'. Under these conditions, academics labour to prove that we are not unproductive, unprofitable
and unfit for purpose, often being pressed into competing against or disregard-
ing each other in order to do so. (. . .) [It] is exhausting and divisive labour.

(2014, §3)

Felski and Fraiman argue that mood 'inflects [intellectual work] in subtle and less
subtle ways, informing the questions we ask, the puzzles that intrigue us, the styles
and genres of argument we are drawn to' (2012: vi). It is, indeed, the case that
Portuguese WGFS scholars' current 'intellectual work' is profoundly and indelibly
shaped by the mood of the performative university. But their relationship with, and
mode of orientation to, others is being affected too, confirming Felski and Fraiman's
suggestion that 'mood [also] informs our felt connection *or lack of connection with
others* along with our sense of what things mean and how they matter' (2012: vii,
my emphasis). As Sifaki notes, '[i]n the current landscape of competition-enhanc-
ing managerial decisions, this feeling of shame [when "failing" to fulfil ideals of
academic productivity] cultivates avoidance of connections, as a process of (. . .)
survival' (2016: 116). The collective is draining, rather than energising; what many
interviewees say they crave is leave, silence, holidays, time alone. (Although some
also say they sorely miss past periods when they felt they had time to more regularly
meet and more closely engage with colleagues and students.)

Like many of my participants, when I feel overwhelmed by the 'perpetual
threats of devaluation' and the 'exhausting and divisive' demand (Amsler, 2014)
to always *produce more, better, faster*, I want to turn inwards and away, isolate
myself in order to do the productive work that might (temporarily) acquiesce my
anxiety and silence that demand.[12] This can, of course, be restorative and generative. Indeed, the book you are now holding in your hands (or reading on a
screen) exists only because I made the resolute decision to withdraw from many
networks, projects, roles, activities, spaces and even relationships for several
months in order to write it. Turning inwards and away to focus on one's own ideas
and scholarly work, may, in fact, be extraordinarily pleasurable and empowering
for women and WGFS scholars, so often expected to take care of others in their
institutions and disproportionately saddled with the demanding pastoral work that
universities require but do not reward (Acker and Feuerverger, 1996; Cardozo,
in press; Lynch, 2010; Morley, 2003; Mountz *et al.*, 2015; Wånggren *et al.*, in
press). Investing in our own 'significant, creative [and] critical work' (Davies and
Petersen, 2005: 78) is also, of course, important for the development of the field.

But as I have argued in this chapter, WGFS is more than the sum of each of our
individual outputs and cannot be reduced to them, however excellent and numerous they may be. The *making* and *maintaining* of a field requires that we also turn
towards others and participate in forms of collective and collegial engagement
(reading, listening, attending, reviewing, organising, disagreeing, networking,
running, managing, welcoming, introducing, supporting, mentoring, debating,
meeting, planning) that are less valued in cultures of performativity (Mountz
et al., 2015) and often get sacrificed when time, energy and patience is limited,

as is clearly, and painfully, the case in the performative university. Collective and collegial engagement is crucial not only because it allows us to produce richer knowledge and a stronger field of WGFS, but also, and importantly, because it is the best way to fight 'the neoliberal university's ontology of individualism and ethics of disconnection' (Kašić, 2016) and resist its *"sick climates"* of individual-istic performativity (Liinason and Grenz, 2016; Motta, 2012; Mountz *et al.*, 2015; Wånggren *et al.*, in press). These climates are not only *"making us all ill"*, but also actively preventing us from doing (and even wanting to do) the very things – thinking, connecting with others, resting – that might disrupt and change that cli-mate, and help us recover from the 'deep, affective, somatic crisis [that] threatens to overwhelm us' (Burrows, 2012: 355).

One of feminism's most important lessons is that public sharing and discus-sion of individual experience can disrupt the normalisation of the status quo, enabling the game-changing realisation that 'the problem' is not in the indi-vidual and cannot be solved by individual adaptation (Gill and Donaghue, 2016; Mountz *et al.*, 2015; Pereira, 2012, 2016), but is located instead in unequal structures that can be transformed. The culture and mood of academia has changed dramatically in several countries in recent years, and for many of us these changes have brought absurd workloads, physical exhaustion, intellectual depletion and emotional despondency. As a result, we are often not able to cre-ate the space for encounter and exchange, and the time to step back from the manic rhythm of the everyday and question our working and living conditions. It is precisely that space and time which can help us realise and remember that different academic cultures, and different moods, are possible. Such space and time is, therefore, desperately needed; in the last section of the next, and final, chapter, I discuss how we might expand it.

Notes

1 In this chapter, where I draw only on material from the 12 follow-up interviews, I do not provide interviewee information for any excerpt, for several reasons: there are fewer interviews and the quotes I use discuss quite personal experiences, so I want to minimise the chances of speaker identification; seniority and home discipline are less central in the analysis I provide here (except on one level, which I discuss in an endnote below); the category of 'seniority' now masks more than it clarifies, because 7 years later all follow-up interviewees would count as 'senior scholars' according to my original classification, although between them they have very different positions and number of years of experience.
2 I am a member of the CIEG founding team myself, although I played a less central role in its creation than other colleagues in the team.
3 On the day I wrote this section (February 19, 2016), the new Minister for Science Manuel Heitor, member of a left-wing coalition government elected in October 2015, announced that following the widespread criticism of the 2013–2015 evaluation exer-cise, its period of 'validity' will be significantly shortened (to 2 rather than 5 years) and a new, significantly revised exercise will be completed before the end of 2017. Its specific guiding principles have yet to be announced – they will be defined in the com-ing months by a committee led by Karin Wall, a sociologist known in part for her work

on gender – but are set to include a 'reduction in the importance given to the *quantity* of scientific publications, with greater weight given to the *content* of researchers' work' (Silva, 2016*, my emphases).

4 A quota of 50% was set from the start for the number of research centres who would be successful and receive funding.

5 Unlike previous exercises, run by FCT (the national research council) and using panels that included some national peer reviewers, the 2013–2015 evaluation exercise was contracted out to the European Science Foundation and used panels exclusively composed of international peer reviewers, some of whom have been accused by the Portuguese academic community of knowing little about, and adopting a patronising approach to, Portuguese scholarship (AAVV, 2014; Agência Lusa, 2014; Deem, 2016).

6 Aboim coordinates the research project 'TRANSRIGHTS – Gender Citizenship and Sexual Rights in Europe: Transgender Lives from a Transnational Perspective' and Santos was awarded a grant for 'INTIMATE – Citizenship, Care and Choice: The Micropolitics of Intimacy in Southern Europe'.

7 For a detailed discussion of the profoundly significant role of the 'foreign' as an authorising and legitimating agent, see chapter 6 and Pereira (2014).

8 One participant, a senior scholar, told me she was teaching on 11 semester-long courses (5 of which she convened) that semester. This contravenes the nationally regulated limit of teaching hours for academics, but her institution's paperwork was managed in such a way that this contravention would not be immediately evident to external examiners and the quality assurance agency.

9 Several younger interviewees seemed less profoundly surprised, disrupted and depleted by these changes, in part, I would argue, because their (or 'our', as I am part of that generation myself) formative academic socialisation happened already within this performative culture. Thus, conceptualising their work and organising their career within the terms of that culture seems to come more 'naturally' to them, as some of the older participants also remarked.

10 Recent neuroendocrinological research provides evidence that stress and anxiety are, indeed, contagious (Engert *et al.*, 2014; Max-Planck-Gesellschaft, 2014).

11 I am grateful to Carolyn Pedwell for suggesting this line of enquiry.

12 Although that never happens, of course, because the cycle of performativity never ends. In my current (UK) institution, for example, there was not a single day's rest between the two most recent cycles of the REF (the national research evaluation exercise) (see Deem, 2016); as soon as the 2014 submission was completed, we were immediately interpellated to begin systematically thinking about, and actively working on, the next submission, although it was 6 years away and its specific rules and requirements were (and still are) not yet known.

References

Aavik, Kadri, *et al.* (2015). *Country Reports (Australia, Czech Republic, Estonia, Germany, Iceland, Netherlands, Norway, Portugal, South Africa, Sweden, Switzerland, UK).* Multiple Papers Presented at the RINGS Network Conference "Gender in/and the Neoliberal University", Prague.

AAVV. (2014). "July 2014 Archive". *Blog "De Rerum Natura"*, Retrieved 02/04/2016, from http://dererummundi.blogspot.co.uk/2014_07_01_archive.html

Acker, Sandra and Armenti, Carmen (2004). "Sleepless in Academia". *Gender and Education, 16* (1), 3–24.

Acker, Sandra and Feuerverger, Grace (1996). "Doing Good and Feeling Bad: the Work of Women University Teachers". *Cambridge Journal of Education, 26* (3), 401–422.

Agência Lusa (2014). *Processo de Avaliação da Ciência é "Enormíssimo Erro de Política Pública", diz Reitor de Lisboa*. Retrieved 02/04/2016, from http://portocanal.sapo.pt/noticia/32971/

Ahmed, Sara (2014). "Not in the Mood". *New Formations, 82*, 13–28.

Amsler, Sarah (2014). "For Feminist Consciousness in the Academy". *Politics and Culture, 2014* (1), article 2.

Ball, Stephen J. (2000). "Performativities and Fabrications in the Education Economy: Towards the Performative Society?". *The Australian Educational Researcher, 27* (2), 1–23.

Blackmore, Jill and Sachs, Judyth (2007). *Performing and Reforming Leaders: Gender, Educational Restructuring, and Organizational Change*. Albany: SUNY Press.

Burrows, Roger (2012). "Living with the H-Index? Metric Assemblages in the Contemporary Academy". *The Sociological Review, 60* (2), 355–372.

Butterwick, Shauna and Dawson, Jane (2005). "Undone Business: Examining the Production of Academic Labour". *Women's Studies International Forum, 28* (1), 51–65.

Cardozo, Karen (in press). "Academic Labor: Who Cares?". *Critical Sociology*.

Cerdeira, Luísa (2012). *O Ensino Superior*. Paper Presented at the Conference Orçamento de Estado 2013: Uma Primeira Leitura, Lisboa.

Cvetkovich, Ann (2012). *Depression: A Public Feeling*. Durham, NC: Duke University Press.

Davies, Bronwyn and Petersen, Eva Bendix (2005). "Neo-Liberal Discourse in the Academy: The Forestalling of (Collective) Resistance". *LATISS: Learning and Teaching in the Social Sciences, 2* (2), 77–98.

Davis, Kathy (2011). " 'I'm Just a Girl Who Can't Say No': Some Reflections on Responsibility and Resistance". *European Journal of Women's Studies, 18* (2), 115–117.

Deem, Rosemary (2016). "Recent Research Evaluations in the UK and Portugal: Methodologies, Processes, Controversies and Consequences" in C. Sarrico, *et al.* (eds.), *Global Challenges, National Initiatives, and Institutional Responses: The Transformation of Higher Education* (pp.159–186). Dordrecht: Springer.

Engert, Veronika, *et al.* (2014). "Cortisol Increase in Empathic Stress is Modulated by Emotional Closeness and Observation Modality". *Psychoneuroendocrinology, 45*, 192–201.

FCT. (2015). *Estatísticas*. Retrieved 20/02/2016, from https://www.fct.pt/estatisticas/bolsas/index.phtml.pt

Felski, Rita and Fraiman, Susan (2012). "In the Mood: Introduction". *New Literary History, 43* (3), v–xii.

Fernandes, Emília (2008). "Elas por Elas: Corpos Ruidosos, Corpos Silenciados em Contexto Organizacional". *Diacrítica, 22* (3), 87–102.

Ferreira, Eduarda, *et al.* (eds.) (2015). *Percursos Feministas: Desafiar os Tempos*. Lisboa: Escrytos.

Ferreira, Nicolau (2016). "Nova Direcção da FCT Promete Servir os Cientistas mas Pede Co-Responsabilidade à Comunidade". *Público*, 10/02/2016, Retrieved 19/02/2016, from http://www.publico.pt/ciencia/noticia/novo-presidente-da-fct-promete-servir-a-comunidade-cientifica-mas-exige-responsabilizacao-1722907

Ferreira, Virgínia (2015). "Editorial". *ex aequo, 32*, 5–7.

Gill, Rosalind (2010). "Breaking the Silence: The Hidden Injuries of the Neoliberal University" in R. Ryan-Flood and R. Gill (eds.), *Secrecy and Silence in the Research Process: Feminist Reflections* (pp.228–244). Abingdon: Routledge.

Gill, Rosalind (2014). "Academics, Cultural Workers and Critical Labour Studies". *Journal of Cultural Economy, 7* (1), 12–30.

Gill, Rosalind and Donaghue, Ngaire (2016). "Resilience, Apps and Reluctant Individualism: Technologies of Self in the Neoliberal Academy". *Women's Studies International Forum, 54*, 91–99.

Hemmings, Clare (2006). "The Life and Times of Academic Feminism" in K. Davis, *et al.* (eds.), *Handbook of Gender and Women's Studies* (pp.13–34). London: Sage.

Hemmings, Clare (2012). "In the Mood for Revolution: Emma Goldman's Passion". *New Literary History, 43* (3), 527–545.

Hey, Valerie (2004). "Perverse Pleasures: Identity Work and the Paradoxes of Greedy Institutions". *Journal of International Women's Studies, 5* (3), 33–43.

Highmore, Ben and Taylor, Jenny Bourne (2014). "Introducing Mood Work". *New Formations, 82*, 5–12.

Kašić, Biljana (2016). *Unsettling Women's Studies, Settling Neoliberal Threats in the Academia.* Paper Presented at the Atgender Spring Conference "Feminist Spaces of Teaching and Learning: Queering Movements, Translations and Dynamics", Utrecht.

Leathwood, Carole and Read, Barbara (2013). "Research Policy and Academic Performativity: Compliance, Contestation and Complicity". *Studies in Higher Education, 38* (8), 1162–1174.

Liinason, Mia and Grenz, Sabine (2016). "Women's/Gender Studies and Contemporary Changes in Academic Cultures: European Perspectives". *Women's Studies International Forum, 54*, 79–83.

Lynch, Kathleen (2010). "Carelessness: a Hidden Doxa of Higher Education". *Arts and Humanities in Higher Education, 9* (1), 54–67.

Max-Planck-Gesellschaft (2014). *Your Stress Is My Stress.* Retrieved 02/04/2016, from http://www.eurekalert.org/pub_releases/2014–04/m-ysi043014.php

Morley, Louise (2003). *Quality and Power in Higher Education.* Buckingham: Open University Press.

Motta, Sara (2012). *Beautiful Transgressions: A Radical Feminism for Our Times.* Retrieved 02/04/2016, from https://ceasefiremagazine.co.uk/beautiful-transgressions-1/

Mountz, Alison, *et al.* (2015). "For Slow Scholarship: A Feminist Politics of Resistance through Collective Action in the Neoliberal University". *ACME, 14* (4), 1235–1259.

Osuri, Goldie (2007). "How to Stop Worrying About the Neoliberal Present and Start Engaging With it". *Australian Feminist Studies, 22* (52), 145–147.

Pereira, Maria do Mar (2011). *Pushing the Boundaries of Knowledge: An Ethnography of Negotiations of the Epistemic Status of Women's, Gender, Feminist Studies in Portugal.* PhD Thesis, LSE.

Pereira, Maria do Mar (2012). "Uncomfortable Classrooms: Rethinking the Role of Discomfort in Feminist Teaching". *European Journal of Women's Studies, 19* (1), 128–135.

Pereira, Maria do Mar (2014). "The Importance of Being 'Modern' and Foreign: Feminist Scholarship and the Epistemic Status of Nations". *Signs: Journal of Women in Culture and Society, 39* (3), 627–657.

Pereira, Maria do Mar (2015). "Higher Education Cutbacks and the Reshaping of Epistemic Hierarchies: an Ethnographic Study of the Case of Feminist Scholarship". *Sociology, 49* (2), 287–304.

Pereira, Maria do Mar (2016). "Struggling Within and Beyond the Performative University: Articulating Activism and Work in an 'Academia Without Walls'". *Women's Studies International Forum, 54*, 100–110.

Reevy, Gretchen M. and Deason, Grace (2014). "Predictors of Depression, Stress, and Anxiety Among Non-Tenure Track Faculty". *Frontiers in Psychology, 5* (701), 1–17.

Ross, Annie (2015). "Hitting Refresh in the Modern World: How to Break the Cycle of Busy-Ness". *Huffington Post*, November 20, 2015, Retrieved 02/04/2016, from http://www.huffingtonpost.co.uk/annie-ross/hitting-refresh-in-the-mo_b_8670080.html

Sifaki, Aggeliki (2016). "Which Side Are We On? Feminist Studies in the Time of Neoliberalism or Neoliberal Feminist Studies?". *Women's Studies International Forum, 54*, 111–118.

Silva, Samuel (2016). "Karin Wall Coordena Grupo que vai Definir Regras para Nova Avaliação dos Centros de Investigação". *Público*, February 19, 2016, Retrieved 02/09/2016, from https://www.publico.pt/ciencia/noticia/karin-wall-coordena-grupo-que-vai-definir-regras-para-nova-avaliacao-dos-centros-cientificos-1723857

Sparkes, Andrew C. (2007). "Embodiment, Academics, and the Audit Culture: A Story Seeking Consideration". *Qualitative Research, 7* (4), 521–550.

Stöckelová, Tereza (2012). "Immutable Mobiles Derailed: STS, Geopolitics, and Research Assessment". *Science, Technology & Human Values, 37* (2), 286–311.

Wånggren, Lena, *et al.* (in press). "Feminist Work in Academia and Beyond" in R. Thwaites and A. Pressland (eds.), *Being an Early Career Feminist Academic: Global Perspectives, Experiences and Challenges*. Basingstoke: Palgrave Macmillan.

Conclusion

Negotiating the boundaries of proper knowledge and of work in the (not quite fully) performative university

> [U]niversities would repay the investigation of trained ethnographers. The rich mix of species would be rewarding in itself, as would the contest between the spirit of the university past with the reality of the university present.
>
> (Evans, 2004: ix)

In the contemporary university, WGFS is caught. It is caught in struggles over the power to define what counts as proper knowledge, caught in dynamic demarcations of epistemic boundaries, caught in the 'contest between the spirit of the university past [and] the reality of the university present'. It is caught (and split) by others in their own struggles over the status of disciplines, institutions and even entire countries or regions. But it also gets itself caught and caught up. It is caught, for example, in its own internal demarcations of status. It is caught in paradoxical positions of compliance with, and critique of, emerging academic cultures of performativity. Its scholars are caught up in their own ambivalent personal and collective investments in the 'perverse pleasures' of working in the 'greedy institution' that is academia (Hey, 2004; see also Leathwood and Read, 2013). In the contemporary university, WGFS is caught, in Reddy's sense of being 'embedded in a nexus of relationships that each makes its own demands' (2009: 95). In this book, I have sought to tease out some of the diverse and shifting manifestations of the 'caught' position of WGFS in the contemporary university. This concluding chapter brings them together, to make sense of the 'nexus of relationships' they constitute, and to identify ways in which we might critically negotiate (and in some cases, pro-actively resist) the different demands they make of us.

The push-and-pull of epistemic status

I set out, in this book, to analyse the epistemic status of WGFS, and found that it should not be understood as a stable condition, or a static position in clear hierarchies of disciplines and people. It is, rather, a patterned but contingent outcome of many ongoing and paradoxical movements of approximation/distance. Although each empirical chapter focuses on different issues, to some extent they all describe practices of pushing and pulling of boundaries, and movements towards, and away from, specific objects. In chapter 3, I show that in Portugal WGFS was for many years generally not welcomed, on the grounds that it lay outside the boundaries of scientificity. Yet, as epistemic and sociopolitical climates change, and as WGFS is identified as having financial value, WGFS becomes less frequently and publicly pushed away, and sometimes actively pulled closer. This push-and-pull does not just change over time but also across space: several non-WGFS scholars express support for WGFS in official settings, but distance themselves from it, namely through humour, in corridor talk. Others have identified similar movements of approximation/distance. Červinková and Stöckelová (2008), for example, argue that such movements play an important role in shaping the relations between established disciplines and what they call 'inter/disciplinary hybrids'. In their ethnography in the sociology department of a Czech post-1989 university, they observed that WGFS, one such 'hybrid', is kept 'out/on the margin of "proper" sociology' but 'mobiliz[ed] (. . .) as "sociology" when convenient' (Červinková and Stöckelová, cited in Mayer, 2009: 4). One could argue, then, that the relative positions of, and relations between, fields are not fixed but in flux.

The discourses of partial and dismissive recognition of WGFS analysed in chapter 4 offer another example of this push-and-pull. In their discourses about WGFS, non-WGFS scholars often affirm both an approximation to certain WGFS contributions and a distancing from others. In these claims, closely related dimensions of WGFS are split and pulled apart, with some framed as credible scholarly contributions and others cast away as not quite scientific. But there is much more to negotiations of the epistemic status of WGFS than non-WGFS scholars pushing WGFS around, so to speak. As I explore in chapter 5, WGFS scholars negotiate epistemic status by doing their own pushing and pulling of boundaries, creating approximations, overlaps or separations between WGFS and other epistemic territories. The distances between territories do not remain constant: scholars accentuate or minimise them depending on their aims and audiences. In many situations, WGFS and non-WGFS scholars are pushing and pulling in different or even opposite directions, as chapter 6 demonstrates. To secure support for the field, many WGFS scholars describe Portuguese SSH as delayed and highlight how distant Portugal is from countries of the modern foreign. At the same time, government and university officials use the existence of Portuguese WGFS to demonstrate that the country or institution is already modern.

Thinking of WGFS' epistemic status as sets of movements, and not just as a state of 'low status' as it is often framed (see chapter 1), is key to making sense of the paradoxical position and status of WGFS in many contemporary performative universities. It is paradoxical, in at least four ways: it is characterised both by continuity and change, involves both recognition and dismissal, often forces WGFS scholars to (over-)comply with academic systems they are critical of in order to be able to produce critical scholarship, and particular developments (e.g. mainstream scholars' interest in WGFS themes) may simultaneously strengthen and undermine the field's status. Indeed, and as Morley also demonstrates, '[t]he academy, like any other organization, is full of contradictions – structures are both fixed and volatile, enabling and constraining' (1995: 180). Conceptualising epistemic status as something produced in and through movement, and that is not even across all dimensions of WGFS, allows us to better understand how these paradoxes are produced and maintained, or in other words, how it becomes possible for supposedly opposite trends to coexist in a given space or time.

In some instances, opposite trends coexist in parallel, with different trends happening alongside each other but not necessarily intersecting. This is the case, for example, when different disciplinary or institutional contexts have distinct epistemic climates, and there is recognition of WGFS in some contexts but not others. However, these opposite trends of approximation and distancing often intersect and interact, enabling and buttressing each other; this makes their coexistence particularly important to analyse and challenging to tackle. As I show in chapter 4, non-WGFS scholars' explicit acclamation of some elements of WGFS makes it possible for them to openly dismiss other (more critical) elements with less risk of being considered unreasonable, biased or anti-feminist. Therefore, the recognition of some parts of WGFS helps to legitimate the dismissal of others, and makes that dismissal harder to denounce. This makes that coexistence of opposite trends a key tool in boundary-work. It allows institutions or communities to access some of the benefits that WGFS may yield – namely funds or research ratings (chapters 3 and 7), or the fact that WGFS can function as an 'alibi' symbolising an institution's diversity, modernity and 'up-to-date-ness', and hence increase its 'market value' (chapter 6) – without always fully recognising the epistemic status of WGFS. But WGFS scholars also use this coexistence of movements of approximation and distance to their advantage. It allows them, for example, to invoke elements of mainstream definitions of scientificity to make WGFS credible to audiences very invested in such definitions, while simultaneously developing critiques of those mainstream definitions in other sites (or even in those same sites).

These articulations of continuity and change, recognition and dismissal, are not an exclusively academic phenomenon: they can, and must, be understood as one manifestation of broader patterns of engagement with feminism and gender equality in western countries. In an interview-based study of Portuguese men's discourses about gender (Pereira, 2010), I found that a generalised adoption of an egalitarian rhetoric coexisted with traditional models of unequal division of childcare and household tasks. The interviewees did not frame this as a contradiction; on the contrary, they used affirmations of a personal commitment to gender equality to downplay or legitimate the inequality of their domestic arrangements. I argued there that this offers an example of how the transformation of discourses may signal and effect change, but 'operate also as a mechanism to reinforce continuities' (2010: 260*). Other interview-based studies conducted elsewhere have generated similar findings. Edley and Wetherell's (2001) UK-based research on men's talk about feminism observes that their claims are grounded in a 'Jekyll and Hyde style "binarization" of discourse' (2001: 445) that opposes a 'benign, sane and rational, positive or neutral' feminism (2001: 444) to an extremist and

unreasonable feminism. This 'provides men with some important rhetorical flexibility (. . .); they can be both "pro" and "anti", in favour and against, both supportive and (. . .) critical of feminists' (2001: 451). Much like I have argued here
in relation to non-WGFS scholars, Edley and Wetherell suggest that such combinations of support and criticism allow the interviewees to reject some feminism principles but maintain a 'positioning [of themselves] (. . .) as modern-day,
"reconstructed" [men]' (2001: 445).

These paradoxical combinations can also be found in media and popular
culture. Analysing representations of feminism in UK newspapers *The Guardian* and *The Times*, Dean found 'an explicit or implicit affirmation of a safe,
unthreatening form of feminism via a disavowal of a more radical feminist position' (2010: 391; see also Sheridan *et al.*, 2005 on Australian media). He uses
the 'notion of "domestication" to refer to the process of drawing distinctions
between different manifestations of feminism, some of which are repudiated
at the same time that others are afforded space and legitimated' (2010: 391).
McRobbie (2009) argues that 'contemporary popular culture (. . .) appear[s]
to be engaging in a well-informed and even well-intended response to feminism' (2009: 11). However, it 'positively draws on and invokes feminism as
that which can be taken into account, to suggest that equality is achieved, in
order to install a whole repertoire of new meanings which emphasise that it is
no longer needed' (2009: 12). She also describes processes of separation quite
similar to the epistemic splitting analysed in chapter 4. In those separations, it is
not scientificity that serves as a threshold for separation; it is, for example, girl-
ishness in the film *Bridget Jones* or charges of political correctness that 'play
a kind of boundary-marking function' (2009: 24), separating 'quite reasonable
and acceptable ideas like gender equality (. . .), [from feminist uses of these
ideas, seen as] (. . .) taken too far, abused and turned into something monstrous,
dogmatic and authoritarian' (2009: 37). All this research confirms Massey's
claim that '[i]f there is one thing which has most certainly demonstrated its
flexibility in an age which as a whole is frequently accorded that epithet, it is
sexism' (1994: 212).

I would caution against an overly hasty reading of these studies' conclusions
as applying integrally also to academia[1] or other national contexts,[2] but there are
important overlaps between their analyses and mine. We share one key observa-
tion-engagements with feminism within and outside academia in western countries are negotiated in 'shifting sands', to use Evans' terms: 'monolithic patriarchy
no longer exists in all its glory in universities (though many tattered remnants
remain) and so how to intervene (. . .) becomes a more complicated issue. (. . .)
The old world has shifted and in part disappeared, but what has taken its place is
full of ever changing shifting sands' (1995: 83). We must, therefore, foreground
the 'shiftingness' of contemporary universities in discussions about, or interventions into, the status of WGFS. Much of that 'shiftingness' is produced, of course,
by the increasing performativity of academic cultures.

The (not quite fully) performative university: Performativity, non-performativity and the status of WGFS

The epistemic status of WGFS is always on the move, but it also regularly gets settled and stabilised within material and symbolic hierarchies. One of the hardest things to do when analysing WGFS' epistemic status is tracing the relations between the fluidity of epistemic status and its stabilisation in local decision-making (for example, on whether a thesis, textbook chapter or journal article can be accepted), in institutional structures and epistemic climates. Drawing on interview material, I found that this relation is shaped by many factors, from the more contingent (e.g. who is present at a meeting) to the more structural (national and international HE policy changes), from the local (a department's concerns to increase revenue or ratings) to the global (the geopolitics of epistemic status in an increasingly transnational academic system), and by different configurations of power. The interaction between, and relative weight of, those factors in a particular context is not constant or determinable *a priori*. To quote Code, '[i]t is impossible to decide before the fact which specificities and practices will be salient in any epistemic tale' (1995: 158). Sometimes it is not even possible to establish this after the fact, as Baird illustrates in her analysis of institutional negotiations over a WGFS post in an Australian university: '[a]t the end of the day it was never clear exactly in what ways the relations of power had flowed in order to defeat the proposal to "de-profile" the Women's Studies position. (. . .) We never found out who had spoken to whom, or which conversations had made an impact' (2010: 120). Therefore, although they are identifiably patterned, negotiations of WGFS' epistemic status are always partly unpredictable and ultimately contingent.

One of the factors that has most significantly reshaped those relations recently (in Portugal and several other countries) is the emergence, institutionalisation and transnationalisation of an academic culture of performativity. In the performative university, epistemic capacity and value are often structurally framed not as something that an individual or institution has, but something they must continuously enact and evidence, through regular and profitable production of a defined range of countable and accountable 'outputs'. Productivity and profitability become, in that culture, key drivers, aims and symbols of good academic performance. As one senior Portuguese WGFS scholar put it during a presentation in a WGFS conference, *"the problem that we now have in Portugal (. . .) is that one criterion of scientific validation is funding – that is, what brings in money is good science, what doesn't, isn't"*.

This is another dimension in which the performative university is a paradoxical site of shifting sands. The interpellation to orient individual and institutional academic practice in line with income-generation opportunities and financial concerns is insistent and incessant. As Strathern notes, 'the academy has no problem in being responsive to "the market"' (2000: 11). However, in the public events

I observed, scholars never explicitly acknowledged that they were responsive to, or guided by, the market: they framed their views (namely those on WGFS) as driven by *epistemic*, rather than financial, considerations.[3] Representatives of university administrations did not announce that they supported WGFS in part because it generates funds or increases outputs; they would say, for example, that WGFS is valuable because it helps expand or improve mainstream knowledge (map 5 in the typology of maps offered in chapter 5), or because it allows universities to engage with issues *"of our time"* and thus remain modern and *"attentive to the world"*, to return to discourses analysed in chapter 6. I have suggested, much like other authors, that in contemporary universities there is an increasing 'conflation of epistemic efficacy with pecuniary profitability' (Mirowski and Sent, 2008: 673). And yet, what seems to make that conflation especially powerful – as a mode of governance of HE and science, and as a pillar of cultures of performativity – is the fact that it is not complete or static. In their day-to-day interactions, scholars and administrators frame the relation between epistemic value and pecuniary potential in shifting ways: the two are frequently overlapped, but sometimes they are pushed apart.

Drawing on Gieryn (1999), I would argue that this oscillation in academic discourse between invocation and erasure of the financial plays an important role in maintaining the epistemic status of scientific knowledge. Gieryn notes that '[f]or scientists, the mapping task is to get science close to politics, but not too close' (1995: 435). He argues that scientific boundary-work requires careful management of one's perceived position vis-à-vis non-epistemic interests.

> [Such] interests are attached (to others) or denied (on our side) in order to legitimate our [scientific] map as an accurate rendition, rather than some self-interested distortion. (. . .) [B]oundary-work is compromised if maps (. . .) were shown to be merely self-serving cartographic instrumentalities designed to restore science budgets.
>
> (1999: 356–357)

Investing in the most profitable knowledge can generate resources for institutions subjected to crippling cutbacks and guarantee their sustainability in a performative and competitive environment. In that sense, it is beneficial for universities to insist on profitability as a criterion for academic decision-making. However, a conceptualisation of academic practice that aligns too closely or overlaps too explicitly with a search for profit may be detrimental. If universities are seen to focus on profit, like any other company or business, part of their epistemic distinctiveness vis-à-vis other sectors of society is erased and academics' epistemic authority in society is undermined. This helps explain the paradox that the financial – as a concern, criteria or goal – seems ever-present in everyday life in western universities (Sifaki, 2016), and yet is often absent from scholars' and institutions' public narratives about what drives them.

Publicly admitted or not, the increasing academic orientation towards productivity and profitability has, as I demonstrate here and elsewhere (Pereira, 2015), transformed enduring epistemic categories and hierarchies, producing (to some extent) a dislocation and relocation of boundaries of scientificity. In altering the rules of the 'epistemic game', those transformations have impacted on WGFS and on WGFS scholars. In Portuguese academia, a longstanding epistemically essentialist belief that WGFS is intrinsically less capable of producing proper knowledge has lost ground. In many contexts, it has given way to an (in principle) open willingness to recognise the epistemic status of WGFS, partly on condition that, and insofar as, it *performs* that epistemic status effectively. This can be done, for example, through high productivity, income generation, student attraction potential, good results in audit and evaluation exercises or internationalisation (by projecting the institution or country into the modern foreign, or bringing the authorising bodies, status and funds of the modern foreign within). Because Portuguese WGFS scholars and groups have in the last few years secured impressive achievements on all those counts, they have come to be recognised as capable of *doing* epistemic status, in its emerging performative guise. Consequently, new openings and opportunities – discursive, material, institutional – have emerged for them, but on a contingent and conditional basis, *"as long as [they produce and keep producing"*. As Hark writes in her own discussion of the place of WGFS in the 'entrepreneurial university', 'the paradoxical precondition for [feminist] dissent is participation' in 'the academic "game"'' (2016: 84) of productivity, audit and performativity.

But is the contemporary university, in Portugal and elsewhere, so linearly, fully and unequivocally a *performative* institution? Evidently and absolutely not. Part of the performative university's performance of its academic excellence rests on its ritual presentation of itself as an open, diverse and meritocratic institution (Ahmed, 2012; Blackmore and Sachs, 2007; Ferguson, 2012; Morley, 2003; Sifaki, 2016; Thornton, 2013). Success and status are framed as in principle open to all, as long as they fulfil the performance requirements that allow the institution to enact and enhance its excellence. This condition is, however, profoundly and unevenly exclusionary in itself, because it presumes a particular kind of 'care-less worker' (Lynch, 2010). It demands workers who have no caring responsibilities that might constrain productive capacity – whether care of others or even care of themselves (either because they have a partner who takes care of them or/and because in the name of work they sacrifice rest, exercise and other practices of self-care necessary for physical and emotional well-being). This ideal of the proper academic worker is, of course, deeply gendered. Those high, and increasing, performance requirements demand a rate and type of work that is incompatible with the care work (for students, colleagues, family members, other dependants), emotional labour and administration (of teaching, households, everyday life) that women are disproportionately saddled with in and out of the academy, and socially expected to be fully committed to (Cardozo, in press;

Clegg, 2013; Lynch, 2010; McRobbie, 2016; Mountz *et al.*, 2015; Wånggren *et al.*, in press). In that sense, the performative university is not, and can never be, as open, diverse and meritocratic as it purports to be.

But even when WGFS scholars fulfil those unrealistic and exclusionary productivity requirements and tick all the right performative boxes, they can be dismissed and denigrated – in corridor talk and behind closed doors, in insidious ways often difficult to challenge – and have their scholarly contributions split, 'overed' (Fahlgren *et al.*, 2016) (i.e. framed as anachronistic and no longer necessary), rendered invisible, or replaced and displaced by work on gender by non-WGFS scholars. This occurs because, to return to Evans' words, 'many tattered remnants remain' of the 'old' 'monolithic patriarchy' within the 'new', performative university (1995: 83) or, as Kašić frames it 'the 'neoliberal trend [is] impregnated with the old fashioned order of academic design that counts on (neo)conservatism' (2016: 130). There is enduring institutional sexism and racism (and other forms of inequality) in performative universities (Ahmed, 2012, 2015; Amâncio, 2005; David, 2014; Franklin, 2015; Gutiérrez-Rodríguez, 2016; Husu, 2011; Mählck, 2013; Moss-Racusina *et al.*, 2012; Swan, 2010; Van den Brink, 2010), and this shapes understandings and assessments of academic 'excellence' (Jenkins, 2014, 2015; Jenkins and Keane, 2014). Thus, not all enactments of academic excellence, no matter how productive, are equally likely to be successfully performative. As credibility and epistemic status are distributed in uneven (sexist, racist, classist, colonialist, ableist, cisgenderist) ways, certain scholars are always susceptible to being considered '[in]appropriate persons' for 'the smooth or "happy" functioning of a performative' (Austin, 1975: 15); this potentially renders their claims to performative academic excellence unsuccessful, or non-performative (Ahmed, 2012).

These structural constraints to successful performativity must be explicitly recognised not just in the theorising of boundary-work, as I argue in chapter 5, but also in the literature on the 'performative university'. It is true that in the performative university '[t]he performances (of individual subjects (. . .)) serve as (. . .) displays of "quality"' (. . .) [and] stand for [. . .] the worth (. . .) of [that] individual' (Ball, 2000: 1). Nonetheless, an individual's (or field's) performance, however impressive, will not always and necessarily serve as a display of quality if the individual (or field) is considered intrinsically less worthy. In the performative university, epistemic status is, no doubt, increasingly framed as something one *does* (over and over again, by orientating oneself to an ever-receding horizon of productivity), but it is also, and still, something that one *is* . . . and in an unequal world, some people get to *be* it more than others. Therefore, important as it may be (and I believe it is crucial!) to highlight the very distinctive *performative* nature of contemporary academic cultures, we must not focus so fully on that *new performativity* that we neglect to highlight the *continuing* structural inequalities (namely of gender, 'race', class, [dis]ability, or geopolitics) that produce systematic *non-performativities*.

How, then, do we negotiate the epistemic status of WGFS in the 'shifting sands' of the (not quite fully) performative university? I do not believe it is possible or desirable to find a one-size-fits-all solution for the problem of epistemic status. Considering that local epistemic climates are diverse and contradictory, and that the performativity of WGFS scholars' boundary-work is shaped by several factors and not guaranteed, working out how to negotiate epistemic status must be a matter of ongoing located debate, rather than *a priori* and general pronouncement. Nevertheless, I agree that '*rhetoric pathos*, or the unfortunate trait of posing a problem without making much progress toward its solution' (Hackett *et al.*, 2008: 6, original emphasis) can be frustrating, especially at a time of disturbing transformations and pressing problems. Therefore, I want to offer some recommendations for how WGFS scholars might negotiate the boundaries of knowledge, and the boundaries of work, in (not quite fully) performative universities.

Towards reflexive flexibility in feminist epistemography

First, I want to focus on the epistemic maps that WGFS scholars draw, or their *epistemographic* practices, as I want to call them.[4] In chapter 5, I identified 5 maps drawn particularly frequently by WGFS scholars when negotiating epistemic status. I found there is a close relation between epistemology and epistemography, but they do not necessarily coincide. A scholar's epistemological stance will partly shape how they describe WGFS' epistemic virtues and the extent to which they attempt to relocate or dislocate mainstream understandings of scientificity. Nevertheless, epistemology does not *determine* epistemography. Scholars adapt the maps they draw to their aims and audiences and so will not always be entirely consistent. In a manner reminiscent of map 3 – mainstream science is just like WGFS – we can highlight that this inconsistency is not an exclusive or even distinctive trait of WGFS boundary-work. On the contrary, one of the most frequently observed traits of scientific discourse across disciplines is the contextuality, flexibility and inconsistency of the repertoires that scholars use when demonstrating and evaluating scientificity (Gieryn, 1995, 1999; Gilbert and Mulkay, 1984; Lamont, 2009; Latour and Woolgar, 1986 [1979]; Lee and Roth, 2004; Petersen, 2003). These scholars argue that this inconsistency is not a sign of bad academic practice, but a key feature of scientific discourse allowing scientists to more easily adapt and react to different forms of contestation. Feminist scholars have also drawn attention to this inconsistency. Harding writes: 'scientific rationality certainly is not (. . .) monolithic. (. . .) It has been versatile and flexible enough (. . .) to permit constant reinterpretation of what should count as legitimate objects and processes of scientific research' (1991: 3).

If epistemic hierarchies are not monolithic and get maintained through flexibility, and if non-WGFS scholars frequently legitimate their dismissal of WGFS by flexibly articulating dismissal and recognition, then WGFS scholars can only combat those hierarchies and dismissal by using epistemographic flexibility themselves. Aladjem's Foucauldian-inspired claim that '[i]f power relations assume "multiple forms," resistance must at least be "multiple" and (. . .) localized' (1996:

290) must be applied to negotiations of the epistemic status of WGFS. I have often been asked which of the 5 maps is better or less problematic, or which one WGFS scholars should use in daily interactions. These are unanswerable questions because a map's value depends on what one wants to do and where. Each map has strengths, but might also create obstacles to the institutionalisation of WGFS and/or feminist attempts to transform mainstream scientific values. For example, affirmations that WGFS is closer to proper science (map 1) or WGFS is just like mainstream science (map 4) seem to be relatively effective in persuading non-WGFS audiences; nonetheless, both risk reinforcing the hegemony of mainstream values of scientificity. Map 2's claim that proper science should be like WGFS explicitly disrupts that hegemony, but according to some interviewees cannot always be used with mainstream audiences, as it makes it easier for them to peremptorily dismiss WGFS scholars. Feminist critiques of the idea that there is such a thing as *the* truth (as in map 2) have been crucial in combating exclusions and hierarchies in academic knowledge production, but as Rose notes being able to make '[t]ruth claims still matter[s] when sexual violence or levels of radiation pollution are the stakes' (2001: 118). Therefore, no map is perfectly suited to help achieve all the different aims – epistemic, institutional, political – that WGFS scholars might have when negotiating epistemic status.

There is little use, then, in attempting to find *the* proper or unproblematic WGFS epistemic map. It seems institutionally and analytically more effective to be equipped not with one map, but with an atlas containing diverse maps which can be used to tackle different forms of questioning, splitting or containing the epistemic status of WGFS. We need to continue developing an understanding of the changing dynamics of boundary-work in performative universities, and strengthen practices of *reflexive epistemographic flexibility* in negotiations of epistemic status. By this, I mean being flexible in the maps we draw but articulating that flexibility with ongoing vigilance and critical individual and collective reflection about the impacts of our boundary-work. This reflexive[5] engagement must be grounded on the recognition that maps have complex epistemic and institutional impacts that we do not always fully control, as I argue in chapter 6 with the example of invocations of the modern foreign. It also demands recognition of the fact that WGFS scholars are not just subjected to exclusionary demarcations of scientificity, but are also invested in creating and policing epistemic boundaries, namely within the field itself, as chapters 3–5 explored.

Precisely because of that reason, I would argue that there is one mode of boundary-work that WGFS scholars must never use, even if it might be effective in certain contexts or for particular aims. It is the epistemographic practice of highlighting the (higher) epistemic value of one's WGFS work by directly contrasting it to other strands of WGFS which are framed as not proper knowledge, as going 'too far', as being ridiculous and risible. I analysed examples in chapters 4 and 5. In Portugal, this epistemographic mode appears very rarely in publications but it does emerge in classrooms, and other less public and officially recorded sites. Elsewhere in the world, I and many others have encountered mild or extreme versions of it in texts (Hemmings, 2011; Hughes, 2004), classrooms and conferences (Henderson, 2016). Using other WGFS work as the supposedly non-scholarly, 'extreme' or 'simplistic', foil which highlights the scholarliness of one's own 'balanced', 'sophisticated' and 'acceptable' WGFS work can sometimes secure recognition for WGFS. But this is not enough, in my view, to justify its use because it affirms the epistemic status of particular WGFS scholarship at the expense of a negation of the epistemic status of other WGFS scholarship. Therefore, it re-enacts the common mainstream representation of WGFS as a field that is partly within and partly outside the space of proper knowledge (chapter 4), reinforcing the dominant belief that the scholarly value of WGFS can be recognised insofar as particular aspects of it are repudiated.

It is, then, a form of boundary-work that constrains other WGFS scholars' possibilities for boundary-work and their chances of securing recognition for their claims and support for their initiatives. To argue against the use of this epistemographic mode is not to claim that critiquing other WGFS work is unacceptable. Critique is vital and generative; as Strathern has argued, '[f]eminism lies in the debate itself' (1988: 24). But critique within WGFS must be conducted through fair assessment of the merits and limitations of a knowledge claim or body of work, rather than by relegating it outside the space of proper knowledge and framing it as too ridiculous, extreme or unscholarly to even merit academic space, attention or debate. Framing WGFS scholarship – seriously or humorously – as positioned partly within and partly beyond the boundaries of proper knowledge has been a device used for long in the field's dismissal; WGFS scholars must refuse to replicate it in their own boundary-work.

Because boundary-work has significant impacts, not just within its local context, but also on broader epistemic and material hierarchies between people, fields and even countries, I want to call for more reflexive and accountable attention to feminist epistemography. There is a long feminist tradition of reflection and debate on epistemology, but this related, but separate, issue of epistemography, i.e. how WGFS scholars demarcate spaces of proper knowledge in their academic work and sociability every day, has received less explicit and systematic consideration. Positioned at the intersection of epistemic and institutional processes, different dynamics of power, and micro- and macro-levels of analysis, feminist epistemography raises challenging but valuable questions, as this book demonstrates. Negotiations of epistemic status demand immense and reflexively flexible boundary-work; hopefully, the more we analyse and debate those negotiations, the easier it will be to make them work to the advantage of our diverse feminist interventions in the production of academic knowledge.

Postscript – our knowledge, our bodies, our selves: Resisting work and working for collective resistance

WGFS publications usually end here: a diagnosis of a problem in our knowledge, followed by a call to produce more knowledge, or to produce knowledge differently, in the hope that this might change power in the world or within WGFS.

This book almost ended here too. But my most recent fieldwork (chapter 7) threw a spanner into those plans. That insight into the contemporary *mood* in academia has made it clear that our current challenges are not just, or maybe even primarily, *epistemic*. Producing *more* knowledge is not necessarily the solution at this moment; focusing on *producing more* can even work to normalise and reproduce the *"productivist"* logics that are having such detrimental impacts on the lives, bodies and work of WGFS scholars. In the performative university, there are problems to diagnose not just in relation to *our knowledge*, but also, and crucially, in relation to *our bodies* and *selves*, problems which generally become 'hidden' (Gill, 2010) and sidelined in our formal work although they inescapably shape the lived experience of producing it.

We can no longer ignore that there is a 'psychosocial and somatic catastrophe' in universities (Gill and Donaghue, 2016: 91), a 'deep, affective, somatic crisis [that] threatens to overwhelm us' (Burrows, 2012: 355). We can no longer overlook the fact that depression, exhaustion, alienation are becoming a structural 'epidemic' in an academic culture 'that say[s] that you are only as good as what you produce' (Cvetkovich, 2012: 18–19). In the face of this, we can no longer frame that depression, exhaustion, alienation as private problems to be addressed through personal adaptation (Bellacasa, 2001; Berg and Seeber, 2016; Pereira, 2016), individualised investment in technologies of self (Gill and Donaghue, 2016) and casual, but despairing, conversations by the photocopier, in the departmental staff-room or over conference meals. We can no longer accept as given the increasing workload, heightened monitoring, proliferating audits, escalating expectations of productivity, mounting reorientation towards profitability, expanding privatisation of academic institutions and processes, intensifying casualisation of work, and growing individual and institutional competition. We can no longer treat as incidental to our everyday academic work the fact that those transformations have severely toxic, often irreversible and extremely worrying impacts on our knowledge, bodies and selves. We can no longer do 'business as usual' and try to just 'keep calm and carry on', as the old but – tellingly – suddenly ubiquitous exhortation (Bramall, 2013) goes.

It is urgent that we think and rethink our individual and collective relationship to work, as WGFS scholars. We must maintain inclusive, committed and systematic debate about how WGFS' institutionalisation has relied on, reproduced, normalised and been affected by the casualisation of academic labour (Adsit *et al.*, 2015; Arrigoitia *et al.*, 2015; Bashore *et al.*, 2015; Beetham, 2012, 2013; Wånggren *et al.*, in press), and also about institutionalised WGFS' relationship with para-academic and alternative-academic colleagues, practices, spaces and networks (Mendick, 2016; Wardrop and Withers, 2014). For those of us in the privileged position of holding more stable academic jobs – a position where pressures to enhance one's CV are overwhelming, but do not determine immediate conditions of survival, as with unemployed and precariously employed colleagues (Lopes and Dewan, 2014; Roy, 2010; Wånggren *et al.*, in press; Withers, 2013; Wunker, 2015) – it is crucial to reflect critically on our own investments in work and productivity.

The performative university is a greedy (Hey, 2004) and toxic (Gill, 2010), but tempting (Kašić, 2016) and seductive (Fahlgren *et al.*, 2016) institution. It purportedly offers WGFS scholars the possibility of circumventing and short-circuiting entrenched epistemic inequalities: in performativity cultures, one supposedly no longer needs to be male, white, positivist, or work on certain topics to be the 'appropriate person' (Austin, 1975: 15) to claim epistemic status. Unlike traditional academic regimes, more explicit and aggressive in their sexist repudiation of WGFS, the performative university gives WGFS scholars the promise of – at least partial – recognition and support, *"as long as [they] produce and keep producing"*. This offers an often empowering, if largely illusory, sense of control. The corridor talk may still be sexist, the micro-climates may still be chilly, WGFS scholars' boundary-work may not always be fully performative . . . but if we are productive, *"if we do so much, often more than [our non-WGFS colleagues]"*, then they have to *"put up with us"*. As Hey writes, '[w]e hope that if only we work harder, produce more, publish more, conference more, achieve more, in short "perform more", that we will eventually get "there"' (2001: 80).

Being productive is seductive not just because it gives us more control over the extent to which our WGFS work is recognised, but also because it is easy to reconcile with our existing inclinations, desires, concerns and broader epistemic-political project. According to Gill, 'academics are, in many ways, model neo-liberal subjects (. . .). Neoliberalism found fertile ground in academics whose predispositions to "work hard" and "do well" meshed perfectly with its demands for autonomous, self-motivating, responsibilised subjects' (2010: 241; see also Sifaki, 2016). WGFS scholars' predispositions often mesh even more perfectly with those demands than the average academic's. This is because many see their work (the research, 'service', 'public engagement', 'outreach' and 'impact' work, teaching, support to students) as a vocational form of epistemic-political intervention in, and care for, the world (Alvanoudi, 2009; hooks, 1994), and as a personal commitment and responsibility to a broader project of social change, in many ways constitutive of their sense of self and relations with others. As Beverley Skeggs writes, WGFS is populated by '[women who] never sp[eak] about our work as a job, it [is] a vocation, or a political/moral project' (2008: 680). Moreover, when WGFS is precariously institutionalised employment opportunities tend to be even more limited than in other fields. In those difficult conditions, productivity can become a lifeline for oneself and a responsibility towards others: one senior WGFS scholar I interviewed explained that she does not really need to be as productive as she is, but constantly developing new research bids is the only thing she can do to secure a livelihood for her students and colleagues seeking work in the field. As Davis writes, '[m]ost of us care deeply about our students, our disciplines and the projects we do. We are probably all doing more than we are being paid for, because, after all, we love what we are doing and rightly feel privileged to be allowed to do it' (2011: 116). If our publications and other professional activities have the potential to change society, inspire and help others, give them a job and salary, as well as shape policies, practices and representations, then it seems logical, desirable, beneficial and supremely collegial to seek to produce as much, and as productively, as we possibly can.

And yet, in the performative university this otherwise commendable and fruitful 'predisposition' has problematic implications. Skeggs describes feminist scholars 'affectionately as "driven maniacs", women so devoted to their political and academic work that they often became seriously ill as a result, only to recover and start all over again', and asks 'if we were the perfect workers for capital: accelerating productivity, rarely concerned about labour conditions' (2008: 680). She argues that the institutionalisation of research assessment exercises in the UK fundamentally changed feminist scholarship: it 'increased the individualism and competitive nature of women's studies, both through carrots (the prize and pride of having so many publications) and the shaming and blaming stick of letting colleagues down', it 'decrease[d] time spent on external political activities and increase[d] time writing', and it 'influenced the type of appointments made, developing (. . .) a form of subjectivity attached to personal performance' (Skeggs, 2008: 680); she suggests that 'this is when feminism *in* the academy became feminism *of* the academy' (2008: 680; original emphases).

Skeggs' (2008) reflection seems to confirm Davies' argument that 'it is very risky to buy into (. . .) the language of those who would govern us through the (. . .) the tying of dollar values to each aspect of our work' (2005: 1). When the productivist logic of performativity is deeply entrenched in institutional life, it becomes very easily incorporated as part of academics' sense of self, scholarly work, and relations with others (Davies and Petersen, 2005; Fahlgren *et al.*, 2016; Mountz *et al.*, 2015; Sifaki, 2016). This makes it extraordinarily difficult to 'play the game' of productivity, even if for subversive and emancipatory ends, without internalising and reproducing at least some of the game's assumptions and rules (Fahlgren *et al.*, 2016; Wånggren *et al.*, in press). We often end up unwittingly normalising an ever-receding horizon of productivity and an ableist academic culture which excludes the scholars and students unable to maintain those levels of productivity (Berg and Seeber, 2016; Mountz *et al.*, 2015; Tagore, 2009; Vihlman, 2009). We 'play the game' of academic productivity but often end up 'exhaust[ed], stress[ed], overload[ed], (. . .) anxi[ous]' (Gill, 2010: 229) and 'ontologically insecure: unsure whether we are doing enough, doing the right thing, doing as much as others, or as well as others, constantly looking to improve, to be better, to be excellent' (Ball, 2003: 220). That productivist and individualising ontological insecuritisation becomes part of academia's mood, and hence it affects – i.e. produces effects and affects on us – even if we are critical of it. And precisely because it is such an individualistic, alienating, depleting and anxiety-inducing game, it is extraordinarily difficult (as I show in chapter 7) to 'play the game' of productivity and still have energy and time for the devalued collegial work that constitutes a field's lifeblood – reading, listening, attending, peer reviewing, organising, meeting, supporting, welcoming, mentoring, debating, planning (Mountz *et al.*, 2015).

Alongside all those negative effects and affects, this academic cult(ure) of productivity has given WGFS scholars – individually and collectively – jobs, status, opportunities, power, space for research and teaching, and immensely pleasurable feelings of pride and satisfaction in the things achieved and the recognition received from others. '[T]he question (. . .) [then] is how to deal with challenges that are at once obstructive, destructive even, *and* vitalizing' (2000: 14, original emphasis), to borrow words written by Strathern in a reflection on the impact on anthropology of academic 'audit cultures'. In attempting to answer that question, I have been persuaded and inspired by Kathi Weeks' (2011) critique of work, and call for a 'feminist time movement'.[6] Unpacking the 'forces – including the work ethic – that promote our acceptance of and powerful identification with work' (2011: 12), Weeks argues that we must challenge the contemporary organisation of work and resist the moralisation, sanctification and normalisation of (intense) work. She suggests this can be done through a politics of 'refusal of work – understood as a rejection of work as a necessary center of social existence, moral duty, ontological essence, and time and energy and understood as a practice of "insubordination to the work ethic" (Berardi, 1980, 169)' (Weeks, 2011: 109). Weeks explains that 'the point is not to deny the present necessity of work or to dismiss its many potential utilities and gratifications, but rather to create some space for subjecting its present ideals and realities to more critical scrutiny', in order to 'provide an opportunity to raise questions about those aspects of life that are too often accepted as unalterable' (2011: 171), constitute 'different subjectivities' and open 'paths to alternative futures' (2011: 101).

Within academia, such a politics of refusal of work can be implemented in practice, for example, by more regularly saying 'no', as Davis argues: '[w]e need to work on developing a collective habitus of responsibility and resistance. This would include a commitment to not take on more work than we can do. (. . .) I firmly believe that each of us would profit by a strategy of refusal (saying no to tasks one cannot realistically complete)' (2011: 117). It can also be done by

> letting go of the drive to succeed, or to get the perfect 'balance' in life and work, (. . .) [and] inventing new ways of thinking about work which replaces the logic of the talent led economy with the more commonplace idea of a "good job well done". Often I have thought surely it should be enough to spend a morning teaching, an afternoon doing supervisions and some marking of essays and then go home and switch off and enjoy the children or indeed grandchildren, and help with home-work rather than feeling the need to return late night to the computer and to the completion of yet another peer-reviewed journal article.
>
> (McRobbie, 2016)

The individual and collective process of 'inventing [these] new ways of thinking' requires that we talk about these issues. As Acker and Armenti write, '[g]oing without sleep will not change things but talking about it might' (2004: 21). In all 6 occasions in which I publicly presented these ideas – separate academic events in different countries and with distinct audiences – one or more delegates were moved to tears by the relief of seeing someone formally 'break the silence' and make visible 'the hidden injuries of the neoliberal university', to use Gill's (2010) title. These audience reactions are not unusual. In his article on the embodied experiences of scholars struggling to cope with academic audit cultures, Sparkes includes comments from readers. One reader, an early-career male academic, writes

> [t]he end result of reading [this article] was – I had to lock my door – I cried . . . Maybe, if I'm being honest, perhaps I also cried for myself – which surprised me. I wonder if I'm cut out for this game. How can I survive in it? Do I want to do this? Do I want to be part of this? Am I really any good? And I hope it moves people to some form of action. It has stirred 'something' in me.
> (2007: 541–542)

It is not enough to write about these issues – as we have seen, many academics in the performative university feel that they do not have enough time to read. Therefore, in our everyday practice we must challenge academia's 'culture of speed' (Berg and Seeber, 2016) and resist the (often self-imposed) pressure to use one's working time always and only to do 'productive' things (Mountz *et al.*, 2015). We must create in our institutions supportive environments to 'tal[k] about it' (Acker and Armenti, 2004: 21) and opportunities for us to step back from the hectic pace of the performative university, working and interacting with others in 'slow' ways (Berg and Seeber, 2016; Mountz *et al.*, 2015) in order to 'make a new imagination and calibration of work both desirable and possible' (Mountz *et al.*, 2015: 1249). This might mean, for example, setting up fortnightly or monthly meet-ups over lunch or coffee, where colleagues can reflect on the toxic effects of these working conditions, provide peer support, and discuss strategies of resistance. Pro-actively setting up such meeting spaces – whether physical or virtual – also helps to overcome a key obstacle to collective debate about contemporary changes in academic cultures: the fact that in the 'academia without walls' (Gill, 2010) many academics spend most of their time working within closed walls in isolation. In a culture of isolated and extremely time-pressured work, where we are often too geographically distant or busy to have meaningful conversations even with immediate colleagues, organising these regular conversations keeps the structural nature of these problems in full view and creates the conditions to develop collective responses to them (Mountz *et al.*, 2015).

But, important as they may be, such conversations cannot be limited to these 'safe' informal spaces of 'ranting' (Wånggren *et al.*, in press). In our formal interactions with colleagues, line managers and students, we must regularly highlight the unsustainability of current working practices, verbalise the unachievability of 'normal' expectations of productivity (Mountz *et al.*, 2015), and voice the importance of nurturing a "care-ful" – as opposed to "care-less", in Lynch's (2010) sense – life within and beyond academia. It is easy to dismiss this sort of talk as ineffective, self-centred whining, or as a potentially risky exposure of one's own weakness and incapacity to 'keep up'. However, naming these issues – in PhD supervision, department meetings, annual reviews, conference papers – can

have profoundly transformative effects, because it interrupts the normalisation of ludicrous expectations of productivity and punctures the illusion that this is, and will always inevitably be, the nature of academic work. In so doing, that naming can hopefully 'stir something' in people and 'mov[e] [them] to some form of action' (Sparkes, 2007: 542). As Weeks argues, '[t]his effort to make work at once public and political is (. . .) one way to counter the forces that would naturalize, privatize, individualize, ontologize, and also, thereby, depoliticize it' (2011: 7). We must also, of course, engage in broader collective political action, whether through trade unions, local campaigns in our universities, or national (and international) activist movements beyond academia. We must actively participate in wider efforts to change the conditions and ethic of contemporary work, to resist the marketisation of, and cutbacks to, HE, public services and the welfare state, and to transform the social, political and economic system which produces these (and many other) forms of systematic exploitation.

A practice and politics of refusal of work is not easy to implement and maintain. It is, in many ways, a strategy available only, or primarily, to the privileged, those who already have a job, guaranteed income, the range of opportunities and the status to be able to refuse work without concern for their survival, fear of reprisal or worry about the fall-out. Even those of us who vocally and passionately advocate for it are often very bad at sustaining it ourselves. I, myself, am terrible at saying 'no'; indeed, one colleague was so concerned about this that she recently hand-made for me a felt dice with 'no' written on 5 sides, and 'maybe, roll again' on the 6th, ordering me to use it whenever I receive a request or invitation. As Davis (2011) argues, many other WGFS scholars would benefit from a 'no' dice. Another colleague has for long been encouraging me to set up with her the kind of regular meeting space for denaturalisation and critique of work that I advocate here, but I have been too busy, and anxious about that busy-ness, to carve out proper space and time for it.

This book itself is a product and symbol of my inability to practise what it preaches. My writing is driven by the desire to help change our individual and collective investments in the performative university's standards of productivity and ideals of epistemic status. And yet, I have carefully and strategically planned the timing and form of that writing in order to guarantee that (a) I am 'REF-able' (i.e. recognised as a proper academic within the narrow and problematic terms of the UK's current research assessment exercise), (b) that I can thus pass probation and get promoted, and (c) that I can contribute as productively as possible to the ratings of my department and the WGFS research centres in Portugal and the UK which I am affiliated to. This is an ambivalent entanglement that other authors writing critically (but in 'productive' and 'countable' ways!) about the performative university also acknowledge (Fahlgren et al., 2016; Sifaki, 2016; Wånggren et al., in press).

My writing is also driven by the desire to foster critical reflection on our working practices. And yet, my practices of work on it reproduce the very problems I critique. The book has been written late at night, on weekends, during bank holidays, while on maternity leave, sacrificing sleep, sanity, self-care, and time with, and care for, my family and friends. In order to write it, I withdrew from organising and participating in events and campaigns; I stopped meeting, mentoring and supporting colleagues, students and fellow activists; I rejected invitations to peer review, debate and supervise; and I asked my colleagues to suspend and postpone many of the planning and strategising efforts in our WGFS centre. Throughout the final months of writing, my email had an assertive automatic 'out of office' message asking everyone to leave me alone, a decidedly non-collegial note which many colleagues found amusing and inspiring, and asked to borrow and use themselves to increase their own productivity when writing. I am composing this paragraph on an unusually sunny Sunday morning in March, hoping I can finish this section quickly so I can go downstairs to join my 15-month old baby (whose squeals of delight I sometimes hear through the closed door of my study), and relieve my partner, also an academic, who is anxious to get cracking with the writing of a lecture for tomorrow. I am checking the final proofs for this page in absolute silence at 4.56 am on a dark night in November, desperate to go to bed because I will now only get 2 hours of sleep before the lecture I am due to teach in the morning.

The inconsistency between our current working practices as WGFS academics and many of the political, ethical and epistemic principles we defend is certainly not lost on me. I would argue that it is a telling inconsistency which demonstrates many important things. It demonstrates that these thinking patterns and working practices are deeply entrenched in us, and in the field of WGFS. It demonstrates that it is necessary and urgent to have proper debates about those thinking patterns and working practices, the people they exclude, the things they destroy and the 'perverse pleasures' (Hey, 2004) they generate. It demonstrates that 'rais[ing] questions about th[e]se aspects of [academic] life' (Weeks, 2011: 171), constituting 'different [academic] subjectivities' and opening 'paths to alternative futures' (2011: 101) is not something we can do alone or that we can leave to colleagues who are, for whatever reason, struggling most to fulfil ideals of performativity. It must be a concerted and organised collective effort (in coalitions of stable, casual, unemployed and para- academics, junior and senior staff, colleagues from different disciplines and institutions), it must become an explicit and integral part of the formal and informal culture of WGFS, and we must pro-actively support each other in trying to sustain these efforts in our individual practice.

On a more personal level, I would argue that this inconsistency between working practices and epistemic-political principles demonstrates that it is high time for me to put my practice where my writing is, wrap up this book and (re)turn to my family, friends and academic and activist colleagues. I absolutely cannot wait. As for you . . . why are you still reading? Put the book down now, and go spend the rest of your day being unashamedly and deliciously non-productive. Who knows what might happen if you, and all of us, do it more often?

Notes

1 For example, Edley and Wetherell (2001) identified logics of binarisation, but the academic discourse I observed was not structured in binary terms. The value of WGFS tended to be the framed as a question of degree: some work is clearly scientific, some is too close to the threshold of scientificity, some is very far beyond it.

2 McRobbie argues that UK media discourse suggests feminism 'is no longer needed' (2009: 12), but research on Portuguese media observes that coverage of feminism often highlights the fact that many feminist goals have not yet been achieved, and thus feminism is still necessary (Peça, 2010). That said, many films or texts analysed by McRobbie travel across national borders, and are popular also in Portugal.

3 The situation is different when what is at stake is the closure of WGFS programmes or initiatives. In Portugal and elsewhere, such closures are generally justified publicly on the basis of decline in student recruitment and profitability (Hemmings, 2006).

4 The concept of 'epistemography' is used in some publications, but framed in terms different from those I have defined here. One example is Dear's (2001) proposal that STS research be conducted as a practice of epistemography, which he defines as the description of how 'scientific knowledge was actually made in various disciplines and in various times and places in history' (2001: 129). He uses ' "[e]pistemography" as a term [to] signa[l] that descriptive focus (. . .) [on] developing an empirical understanding of scientific knowledge, in contrast to *epistemology*, which is a prescriptive study of how knowledge can or should be made' (2001: 130–131).

5 I believe that greater reflexive awareness and accountability in epistemographic practice can make a real difference to WGFS scholars' boundary-work. However, reflexivity can only be a tool and starting point; as Liinason argues, treating it as the 'final solution' for all dilemmas in feminist knowledge production can be problematic, because it 'c[an] turn a process of reflexivity into a routine decision, supposedly reflexive and critical, but in practice nothing less than a mechanical matter of routine' (2007: 48).

6 My thinking on this has also been inspired by conversations with Lena Wånggren and the work she has published with other colleagues (Wånggren and Milatovic, 2014; Wånggren *et al.*, in press).

References

Acker, Sandra and Armenti, Carmen (2004). "Sleepless in Academia". *Gender and Education, 16* (1), 3–24.

Adsit, Janelle, *et al.* (2015). "Affective Activism: Answering Institutional Productions of Precarity in the Corporate University". *Feminist Formations, 27* (3), 21–48.

Ahmed, Sara (2012). *On Being Included: Racism and Diversity in Institutional Life*. Durham, NC: Duke University Press.

Ahmed, Sara (2015). "Sexism – A Problem with a Name". *New Formations, 86*, 5–13.

Aladjem, Terry K. (1996). "The Philosopher's Prism: Foucault, Feminism, and Critique" in S. Hekman (ed.), *Feminist Interpretations of Michel Foucault* (pp.283–298). University Park: Pennsylvania State University Press.

Alvanoudi, Angeliki (2009). "Teaching Gender in the Neoliberal University" in D. Gronold, *et al.* (eds.), *Teaching with the Third Wave* (pp.37–54). Utrecht: ATHENA.

Amâncio, Lígia (2005). "Reflections on Science as a Gendered Endeavour: Changes and Continuities". *Social Science Information, 44* (1), 65–83.

Arrigoitia, Melissa Fernández, *et al.* (2015). "Women's Studies and Contingency: Between Exploitation and Resistance". *Feminist Formations, 27* (3), 81–113.

Austin, John L. (1975). *How to Do Things with Words* (2nd ed.). London: Oxford University Press.

Baird, Barbara (2010). "Ambivalent Optimism: Women's and Gender Studies in Australian Universities". *Feminist Review, 95*, 111–126.

Ball, Stephen J. (2000). "Performativities and Fabrications in the Education Economy: Towards the Performative Society?". *The Australian Educational Researcher, 27* (2), 1–23.

Ball, Stephen J. (2003). "The Teacher's Soul and the Terrors of Performativity". *Journal of Educational Policy, 18* (2), 215–228.

Bashore, Katie, *et al.* (2015). "Practicing Institutional Feelings: A Roundtable". *Feminist Formations, 27* (3), 217–236.

Beetham, Gwendolyn (2012). *Emotional Labor and Ethical Hiring Practices in Academia.* Retrieved 12/03/2016, from http://www.insidehighered.com/blogs/university-venus/emotional-labor-and-ethical-hiring-practices-academia

Beetham, Gwendolyn (2013). *Getting (Un)Stuck in the Middle.* Retrieved 12/03/2016, from https://www.insidehighered.com/blogs/university-venus/getting-unstuck-middle

Bellacasa, María Puig de la (2001). "Beyond Nostalgia and Celebration: Contexts for Academic Women's Studies in Contemporary Universities" in N. Lykke, *et al.* (eds.), *Women's Studies: From Institutional Innovations to New Job Qualifications* (pp.25–45). Utrecht: ATHENA.

Berg, Maggie and Seeber, Barbara (2016). *Slow Professor: Challenging the Culture of Speed in the Academy.* Toronto: University of Toronto Press.

Blackmore, Jill and Sachs, Judyth (2007). *Performing and Reforming Leaders: Gender, Educational Restructuring, and Organizational Change.* Albany: SUNY Press.

Bramall, Rebecca (2013). *The Cultural Politics of Austerity: Past and Present in Austere Times.* Basingstoke: Palgrave Macmillan.

Burrows, Roger (2012). "Living with the H-Index? Metric Assemblages in the Contemporary Academy". *The Sociological Review, 60* (2), 355–372.

Cardozo, Karen (in press). "Academic Labor: Who Cares?". *Critical Sociology.*

Červinková, Alice and Stöckelová, Tereza (2008). *Inter/Disciplinarity in Social Sciences: Distributed Sociology and Boundary Subjects.* Paper Presented at the Conference Acting with Science, Technology and Medicine, Rotterdam.

Clegg, Sue (2013). "The Space of Academia: Privilege, Agency and the Erasure of Affect" in C. Maxwell and P. Aggleton (eds.), *Privilege, Agency and Affect: Understanding the Production and Effects of Action* (pp.71–87). Basingstoke: Palgrave Macmillan.

Code, Lorraine (1995). *Rhetorical Spaces: Essays on Gendered Locations.* New York: Routledge.

Cvetkovich, Ann (2012). *Depression: A Public Feeling.* Durham, NC: Duke University Press.

David, Miriam (2014). *Feminism, Gender and Universities: Politics, Passion and Pedagogies.* Farnham: Ashgate.

Davies, Bronwyn (2005). "The (Im)Possibility of Intellectual Work in Neoliberal Regimes". *Discourse: Studies in the Cultural Politics of Education, 26* (1), 1–14.

Davies, Bronwyn and Petersen, Eva Bendix (2005). "Neo-Liberal Discourse in the Academy: The Forestalling of (Collective) Resistance". *LATISS: Learning and Teaching in the Social Sciences, 2* (2), 77–98.

Davis, Kathy (2011). " 'I'm Just a Girl Who Can't Say No': Some Reflections on Responsibility and Resistance". *European Journal of Women's Studies, 18* (2), 115–117.

Dean, Jonathan (2010). "Feminism in the Papers: Contested Feminisms in the British Quality Press". *Feminist Media Studies, 10* (4), 391–407.

Dear, Peter (2001). "Science Studies as Epistemography" in J.A. Labinger and H.M. Collins (eds.), *The One Culture? A Conversation About Science* (pp.128–141). Chicago & London: The University of Chicago Press.

Edley, Nigel and Wetherell, Margaret (2001). "Jekyll and Hyde: Men's Constructions of Feminism and Feminists". *Feminism & Psychology, 11* (4), 439–457.

Evans, Mary (1995). "Ivory Towers: Life in the Mind" in L. Morley and V. Walsh (eds.), *Feminist Academics: Creative Agents for Change* (pp.73–85). London: Taylor & Francis.

Evans, Mary (2004). *Killing Thinking: The Death of the Universities*. London: Continuum.

Fahlgren, Siv, *et al.* (2016). "Resisting 'Overing': Teaching and Researching Gender Studies in Sweden". *Women's Studies International Forum, 54,* 119–128.

Ferguson, Roderick (2012). *The Reorder of Things: The University and Its Pedagogies of Minority Difference*. Minneapolis: University of Minnesota Press.

Franklin, Sarah (2015). "Sexism As a Means of Reproduction: Some Reflections on the Politics of Academic Practice". *New Formations, 86,* 14–33.

Gieryn, Thomas (1995). "Boundaries of Science" in S. Jasanoff, *et al.* (eds.), *Handbook of Science and Technology Studies* (2nd ed) (pp.393–443). London: Sage.

Gieryn, Thomas (1999). *Cultural Boundaries of Science: Credibility on the Line*. Chicago, IL: University of Chicago Press.

Gilbert, G. Nigel and Mulkay, Michael (1984). *Opening Pandora's Box: A Sociological Analysis of Scientists' Discourse*. Cambridge: Cambridge University Press.

Gill, Rosalind (2010). "Breaking the Silence: The Hidden Injuries of the Neoliberal University" in R. Ryan-Flood and R. Gill (eds.), *Secrecy and Silence in the Research Process: Feminist Reflections* (pp.228–244). Abingdon: Routledge.

Gill, Rosalind and Donaghue, Ngaire (2016). "Resilience, Apps and Reluctant Individualism: Technologies of Self in the Neoliberal Academy". *Women's Studies International Forum, 54,* 91–99.

Gutiérrez-Rodríguez, Encarnación (2016). "Sensing Dispossession: Women and Gender Studies Between Institutional Racism and Migration Control Policies in the Neoliberal University". *Women's Studies International Forum, 54,* 167–177.

Hackett, Edward J., *et al.* (2008). "Introduction" in E.J. Hackett, *et al.* (eds.), *The Handbook of Science and Technology Studies* (3rd ed) (pp.1–8). Cambridge, MA: MIT Press.

Harding, Sandra (1991). *Whose Science? Whose Knowledge?: Thinking from Women's Lives*. Milton Keynes: Open University.

Hark, Sabine (2016). "Contending Directions: Gender Studies in the Entrepreneurial University". *Women's Studies International Forum, 54,* 84–90.

Hemmings, Clare (2006). "The Life and Times of Academic Feminism" in K. Davis, *et al.* (eds.), *Handbook of Gender and Women's Studies* (pp.13–34). London: Sage.

Hemmings, Clare (2011). *Why Stories Matter: The Political Grammar of Feminist Theory*. Durham, NC: Duke University Press.

Henderson, Emily F. (2016). *Eventful Gender: An Ethnographic Exploration of Gender Knowledge Production at International Academic Conferences*. PhD Thesis, UCL Institute of Education.

Hey, Valerie (2001). "The Construction of Academic Time: Sub-Contracting Academic Labour in Research". *Journal of Educational Policy, 16* (1), 67–84.

Hey, Valerie (2004). "Perverse Pleasures: Identity Work and the Paradoxes of Greedy Institutions". *Journal of International Women's Studies, 5* (3), 33–43.

hooks, bell (1994). *Teaching to Transgress: Education as the Practice of Freedom*. New York: Routledge.

Hughes, Christina (2004). "Perhaps She Was Having a Bad Hair Day!: Taking Issue with Ungenerous Readings of Feminist Texts". *European Journal of Women's Studies, 11* (1), 103–109.

Husu, Liisa (2011). *Sexism, Support and Survival in Academia*. Helsinki: University of Helsinki Press.

Jenkins, Fiona (2014). "Epistemic Credibility and Women in Philosophy". *Australian Feminist Studies, 29* (80), 161–170.

Jenkins, Fiona (2015). "Gendered Hierarchies of Knowledge and the Prestige Factor: How Philosophy Survives Market Rationality" in M. Thornton (ed.), *Through a Glass Darkly: The Social Sciences Look at the Neoliberal University* (pp.49–62). Canberra: ANU Press.

Jenkins, Fiona and Keane, Helen (eds.) (2014). *Australian Feminist Studies*. Special Issue: "Gendered Excellence in the Social Sciences", *29* (80).

Kašić, Biljana (2016). " 'Unsettling' Women's Studies, Settling Neoliberal Threats in the Academia: A Feminist Gaze from Croatia". *Women's Studies International Forum, 54*, 129–137.

Lamont, Michèle (2009). *How Professors Think: Inside the Curious World of Academic Judgment*. Cambridge, MA: Harvard University Press.

Latour, Bruno and Woolgar, Steve (1986 [1979]). *Laboratory Life: The Construction of Scientific Facts*. Princeton, NJ: Princeton University Press.

Leathwood, Carole and Read, Barbara (2013). "Research Policy and Academic Performativity: Compliance, Contestation and Complicity". *Studies in Higher Education, 38* (8), 1162–1174.

Lee, Yew-Jin and Roth, Wolff-Michael (2004). "Making a Scientist: Discursive 'Doing' of Identity and Self-Presentation During Research Interviews". *Forum Qualitative Sozialforschung/Forum Qualitative Social Research, 5* (1), article 12.

Liinason, Mia (2007). "Who's the Expert? On Knowledge Seeking as Praxis: A Methodological Approach". *Graduate Journal of Social Science, 4* (2), 40–60.

Lopes, Ana and Dewan, Indra Angeli (2014). "Precarious Pedagogies? The Impact of Casual and Zero-Hour Contracts in UK Higher Education". *Journal of Feminist Scholarship* (7/8), 28–42.

Lynch, Kathleen (2010). "Carelessness: A Hidden Doxa of Higher Education". *Arts and Humanities in Higher Education, 9* (1), 54–67.

Mählck, Paula (2013). "Academic Women with Migrant Background in the Global Knowledge Economy: Bodies, Hierarchies and Resistance". *Women's Studies International Forum, 36*, 65–74.

Massey, Doreen (1994). *Space, Place and Gender*. Cambridge: Polity.

Mayer, Katja (2009). "Acting with Social Sciences and Humanities: Session Report". *EASST Review, 28* (1), 7–14.

McRobbie, Angela (2009). *The Aftermath of Feminism: Gender, Culture and Social Change*. London: Sage.

McRobbie, Angela (2016). *Women's Working Lives in the Managerial University and the Pernicious Effects of the «Normal» Academic Career*. Retrieved 10/03/2016, from http://blogs.lse.ac.uk/impactofsocialsciences/2015/09/03/womens-working-lives-in-the-managerial-university/

Mendick, Heather (2016). *Alternative Academia Network: Re-imaging Higher Education?* Retrieved 12/03/2016, from http://driftmine.org/alternative-academia-network-re-imaging-higher-education-2/

Mirowski, Philip and Sent, Esther-Mirjam (2008). "The Commercialization of Science and the Response of STS" in E.J. Hackett, *et al.* (eds.), *The Handbook of Science and Technology Studies* (3rd ed) (pp.635–689). Cambridge, MA: MIT Press.

Morley, Louise (1995). "The Micropolitics of Women's Studies: Feminism and Organizational Change in the Academy" in J. Purvis and M. Maynard (eds.), *(Hetero)sexual Politics* (pp.171–185). Washington: Taylor & Francis.

Morley, Louise (2003). *Quality and Power in Higher Education*. Buckingham: Open University Press.

Moss-Racusina, Corinne, *et al.* (2012). "Science Faculty's Subtle Gender Biases Favour Male Students". *Proceedings of the National Academy of Sciences, 109* (41), 16474–16479.

Mountz, Alison, *et al.* (2015). "For Slow Scholarship: A Feminist Politics of Resistance through Collective Action in the Neoliberal University". *ACME, 14* (4), 1235–1259.

Peça, Marta (2010). *Os Movimentos de Mulheres em Portugal: Uma Análise da Noticiabilidade na Imprensa Portuguesa*: MSc Dissertation, Universidade de Coimbra.

Pereira, Maria do Mar (2010). "Os Discursos de Género: Mudança e Continuidade nas Narrativas sobre Diferenças, Semelhanças e (Des)Igualdade entre Mulheres e Homens" in K. Wall, *et al.* (eds.), *A Vida Familiar no Masculino* (pp.225–264). Lisboa: CITE.

Pereira, Maria do Mar (2015). "Higher Education Cutbacks and the Reshaping of Epistemic Hierarchies: An Ethnographic Study of the Case of Feminist Scholarship". *Sociology, 49* (2), 287–304.

Pereira, Maria do Mar (2016). "Struggling Within and Beyond the Performative University: Articulating Activism and Work in an 'Academia Without Walls'". *Women's Studies International Forum, 54*, 100–110.

Petersen, Eva Bendix (2003). *Academic Boundary Work: The Discursive Constitution of 'Scientificity' Amongst Researchers Within the Social Sciences and Humanities*. PhD Thesis, University of Copenhagen.

Reddy, Deepa S. (2009). "Caught! The Predicaments of Ethnography in Collaboration" in J.D. Faubion and G.E. Marcus (eds.), *Fieldwork is Not What it Used to Be* (pp.89–113). Ithaca, NY: Cornell University Press.

Rose, Hilary (2001). "Life After the Science Wars?" in G. Philo and D. Miller (eds.), *Market Killing: What the Free Market Does and What Social Scientists Can Do About It* (pp.110–124). Harlow: Longman.

Roy, Srila (2010). "Spare a Thought for Those Broken and Cast Out of This Hostile Home". *Times Higher Education*, 11/03/2010, Retrieved 02/04/2016, from http://www.timeshighereducation.co.uk/410717.article

Sheridan, Susan, *et al.* (2005). "Feminism in the News" in J. Hollows and R. Moseley (eds.), *Feminism in Popular Culture* (pp.25–40). Oxford: Berg.

Sifaki, Aggeliki (2016). "Which Side Are We On? Feminist Studies in the Time of Neoliberalism or Neoliberal Feminist Studies?". *Women's Studies International Forum, 54*, 111–118.

Skeggs, Beverley (2008). "The Dirty History of Feminism and Sociology: Or the War of Conceptual Attrition". *The Sociological Review, 56* (4), 670–690.

Sparkes, Andrew C. (2007). "Embodiment, Academics, and the Audit Culture: A Story Seeking Consideration". *Qualitative Research, 7* (4), 521–550.

Strathern, Marilyn (1988). *The Gender of the Gift*. Berkeley: University of California Press.

Strathern, Marilyn (2000). "Introduction: New Accountabilities" in M. Strathern (ed.), *Audit Cultures: Anthropological Studies in Accountability, Ethics and the Academy* (pp.1–18). London: Routledge.

Swan, Elaine (2010). "States of White Ignorance, and Audit Masculinity in English Higher Education". *Social Politics, 17* (4), 477–506.

Tagore, Shaunga (2009). "A Slam on Feminism in Academia" in J. Yee (ed.), *Feminism for Real: Deconstructing the Academic Industrial Complex of Feminism* (pp.37–41). Ottawa: CCPA.

Thornton, Margaret (2013). "The Mirage of Merit". *Australian Feminist Studies, 28* (76), 127–143.

Van den Brink, Marieke (2010). *Behind the Scenes of Science: Gender Practices in the Recruitment and Selection of Professors in the Netherlands.* Amsterdam: Amsterdam University Press.

Vihlman, Maria (2009). "Tieteiden Välissä, Sukupuolitutkimuksen Kartalla" in *Elämys & Analyysi* (pp.20–22). Tampere: NaMi & University of Tampere.

Wånggren, Lena and Milatovic, Maja (2014). "Spaces of Possibility: Pedagogy and Politics in a Changing Institution" in A. Wardrop and D. Withers (eds.), *The Para-Academic Handbook* (pp.31–38). Bristol: HammerOn Press.

Wånggren, Lena, *et al.* (in press). "Feminist Work in Academia and Beyond" in R. Thwaites and A. Pressland (eds.), *Being an Early Career Feminist Academic: Global Perspectives, Experiences and Challenges.* Basingstoke: Palgrave Macmillan.

Wardrop, Alex and Withers, Deborah (eds.) (2014). *The Para-Academic Handbook.* Bristol: HammerOn Press.

Weeks, Kathi (2011). *The Problem With Work: Feminism, Marxism, Antiwork Politics, and Postwork Imaginaries.* Durham: Duke University Press.

Withers, Deborah (2013). *Dear Precariously Employed Academic Friend, I Know Your Dreams are Shattered but . . .* Retrieved 12/03/2016, from http://www.debi-rah.net/page26.htm#132130

Wunker, Erin (2015). *Dear Contract Academic Faculty.* Retrieved 12/03/2016, from http://www.hookandeye.ca/2015/02/dear-contract-academic-faculty.html

Index

1974 Revolution (Portugal) 151–2, 154

Aboim, Sofia 181, 197
Abranches, Graça 165
activism 116, 136, 172, 217
African-American Studies 131–2
age 133, 136
Ahmed, Sara 142–4, 166, 187, 208
Alatas, Syed Farid 153
Alcoff, Linda 46, 55–6
Amâncio, Lígia 74, 76, 96
Amsler, Sarah 56, 194–5
anglophone hegemony 5, 148–9, 168, 172
anthropology 9, 159, 166, 215
APEM 7, 84, 157, 190
Armengaud, Françoise 108, 158
ATHENA 30
audit culture 70–1, 185–6, 207, 212, 215, 216
austerity 4, 89, 152, 180–1, 184
Austin, John L. 143–4, 208, 213
Australia 31, 78, 204, 205

Ball, Stephen 70, 208, 214
Beleza, Teresa 157
Billig, Michael 81
black scholars 46, 55, 96, 133
Blackmore, Jill 71–2, 166, 194
Bologna Process 76–8, 89
boundary-work 8, 9, 10, 47, 52–5, 56, 57, 59–61, 63, 84–6, 97–116, 120–44, 209–11; performativity of 53–4, 142–4, 151, 213
Bourdieu, Pierre 108–9, 112, 115, 156
Braidotti, Rosi 6, 30, 33, 34, 149, 166, 168, 171
brain drain 172
Brazil 5, 145, 160, 172

Bridget Jones 204
British Psychological Society 102
Buikema, Rosemarie 70–2
Burrows, Roger 71, 196, 212
Butler, Judith 73, 74, 142, 149
Butterwick, Shauna 8, 72

Campbell, Kate 95, 114
Canada 32, 72, 152
casualisation 2, 70, 83, 212, 218
Červinková, Alice 10, 13, 202
Chen 33–4, 38, 86, 95, 149, 167
Chile 34
chilly climate 61, 84, 87, 131, 138, 188, 213
chronopolitics 150, 158, 166, 170
CIDM 76
CIEG 180, 196
cisgender 136; see also gender identity
class 11, 33, 47, 55, 106, 115, 123, 133–4, 136–7, 208
classrooms 15, 38, 100–4, 110–12, 122–4, 210
climate, epistemic; see epistemic climate
Code, Lorraine 46–7, 50–2, 54–9, 61–2, 107, 132–3, 143–4, 205
Coimbra, University of 165
colonialism 148–9, 163
conferences 11, 75, 79, 86, 97, 99–100, 106–7, 113, 120, 123–127, 149, 156, 160, 163–4, 211
Congresso Feminista 110, 116, 172
corridor talk 12, 20, 79–81, 87–8, 89, 108, 179, 202, 208, 213
Croatia 168
Crowley, Helen 31, 87
cuts to higher education funding 83, 86, 89, 181, 185, 206, 217

Cvetkovich, Ann 187–8, 193, 212
Czech Republic 89, 154, 167, 202

Davies, Bronwyn 192, 214
Davis, Kathy 15–16, 213, 215, 217
Dean, Jonathan 204
demarcation (of scientificity) 44–47
depression 184–8, 193, 212
Diacrítica 19
disability 52, 133–4, 136–7, 214
discourse 9–10, 15, 114–15, 142
Domination Masculine, La 108–9
Donaghue, Ngaire 192–3, 212

Edley, Nigel 203–4, 218
empire: British 152; Portuguese 60–61,
    152, 163, 171; see also colonialism
English (language) 17–18, 148, 185; see
    also anglophone hegemony
episteme 47, 48–9, 51, 52, 54, 61, 63
epistemic: climates 61, 69–70, 74–6,
    79–88, 112, 114, 123, 128, 131, 139,
    144–5, 165, 188, 203, 205, 209, 213;
    maps 59–61, 63, 120–132, 206,
    209–10; splitting 98, 103, 109, 113–15,
    204; threshold 97, 99–100, 104, 110,
    113–15, 218; see also epistemic status
epistemic status: definition 1, 47–8; theory
    of 47–62
epistemography 209, 211, 219
epistemology see feminist epistemology
Epstein, Steven 56–7, 129
Estado Novo 60, 63, 88, 151, 163
ethnography 7–11, 13–14, 16, 38, 50, 97,
    201, 202
Eurocentrism 47, 55
Europe 79, 151–4, 157–9, 171, 181;
    central and eastern 33, 151, 167;
    northern 151–3, 156–7, 159; southern
    151–2
European Commission 33, 181
European Research Council 181–2
European Science Foundation 197
European Union 152
Evans, Mary 14, 31, 34–5, 58, 88, 95–6,
    104, 163, 201, 204, 208
ex aequo 7, 76, 181, 191

Faces de Eva 181
Fausto-Sterling, Anne 110
FCT 76, 171, 181, 197
Felski, Rita 187–8, 195

Feminism: discourses about 203; media
    representations of 76, 204, 219; state
    163; stereotypes about 80–1, 89; see
    also feminist epistemology
feminist epistemology 2, 4, 44, 46, 50, 55,
    120–1, 130, 131, 133, 209
Feminist University (Universidade
    Feminista) 181
Ferreira, Virgínia 6, 74, 96, 191
financial crisis 152
Finland 32, 154
Foucault, Michel 4, 9–10, 19, 46, 47,
    48–50, 51, 52, 54–5, 57–9, 61, 62–3,
    109, 114, 115, 142, 166, 209
Fraiman, Susan 187–8, 195
France 5, 32, 99, 108, 152, 158

gay 80, 134–6, 145; see also lesbian
gender equality 76, 151, 163, 165, 203–4
gender identity 136–7, 170, 172
genealogy 9, 38, 53
geography 148
geopolitics 4–5, 52, 59, 148–172, 205,
    208
Germany 95, 152
Gieryn, Thomas 45, 47, 52–5, 56–9,
    59–60, 63, 73, 114, 120–1, 133, 142–4,
    148, 155–7, 171, 206
Gill, Rosalind 192–3, 212–4, 216
Gonçalves, Maria Eduarda 153, 170
Greece 78–9, 151, 171
Griffin, Gabriele 168, 171
Guardian, The 204

Haraway, Donna 2, 46, 96–7
Harding, Sandra 2, 50, 107, 209
Hark, Sabine 70, 167, 207
hegemony see anglophone hegemony; see
    west, hegemony of the
Heitor, Manuel 196
Hemmings, Clare 17, 30, 112, 167, 187,
    219
Henderson, Emily F. 13, 38, 106, 144,
    183
Henriques, Fernanda 80, 102
heteronormativity 81, 105, 123, 135
heterosexual 135
Hey, Valerie 89, 183, 201, 213, 218
history 148, 150, 160
homophobia 135; see also
    heteronormativity
humanities 6, 19, 38, 113, 127

humour 15, 61, 80–1, 89, 102–3, 105,
    111, 115, 202, 211
Hungary 89, 150

ILGA–Portugal 172
interviews 11–12
Ireland 171
ISCTE–IUL (Lisbon University Institute)
    181
Italy 3, 5, 32, 171–2

Jasser, Ghaïss 108, 158
Joaquim, Teresa 74, 84, 96, 98, 145, 162
journals 5, 11, 19, 30, 57, 70, 75, 140, 149,
    160–2, 172, 181, 190–1

Kašić, Biljana 168, 196, 208, 213
Kilomba, Grada 46

Latin America 172
Latour, Bruno 10, 132–3
Law 99–100, 157
lesbian 135, 145
LGBTQ: movement 172; rights 172;
    studies 52, 167
Liinason, Mia 115, 196, 219
Lisbon, University of 180
lusotropicalism 171
Lynch, Kathleen xii, 192, 194, 207, 216
Lyotard Jean-François 70, 73

Macedo, Ana Gabriela 19, 169
McRobbie, Angela 204, 215, 219
Magalhães, Maria José 7, 171
maps 59–61, 63, 64, 120, 148; see also
    epistemic maps
marketisation of higher education 70–4,
    76–8, 87, 205–6, 217
Masculine Domination, see Domination
    Masculine, La
Massey, Doreen 16, 150, 204
Messer-Davidow, Ellen 31, 33, 38, 39, 75,
    102
metricisation 2, 4, 71
Mignolo, Walter 150
Minho, University of 19, 191
'mode 2' 72
modern 150–72, 202, 206, 207; women as
    symbols of the 163, 167
Mohanty, Chandra 120, 150, 156, 166, 170
Monteiro, Rosa 163
mood 184–8, 192–6, 212, 214

Morley, Louise 78–9, 84, 85, 202–3
Morris, Rosalind 74

Nash, Jennifer 29, 70, 81, 134
negotiation: definition 61–2
neoliberal 4, 70, 71, 78, 183, 196, 208,
    213, 216
Netherlands, The 71
Neves, Sofia 95
Nigeria 95
Nunes, João Arriscado 151, 153, 166–7

Oliveira, João Manuel de 19, 76
Osuri, Goldie 183
Owens, Emily 29, 70, 81, 134

para-academics 218
paradox 86–8, 89, 183, 201–3, 205–7
performative academic cultures 61, 69–79,
    86–8, 114, 138, 141, 144, 153, 158,
    179–197, 201, 205–214
performativity 73–74, 142–4; see also
    boundary-work, performativity of
Pessoa, Fernando 152, 171
Petersen, Eva Bendix 10, 13, 17, 73, 192
Petö, Andrea 149–50
philosophy 46, 62, 98, 127
physics 10, 63, 132
Pickering, Andrew 96–7
Piepmeier, Alison 84–5
Pinto, Teresa 7, 39, 80, 96, 102
Poland 5, 89, 167
Portugal 1,2, 4–7, 10–11, 14, 17, 19,
    29, 35, 60–1, 63, 69, 74–89, 96, 105,
    108, 121, 123, 127, 134, 136, 140,
    145, 150–72, 179–183, 190, 195, 197,
    202–3, 205, 207, 217, 219
postcolonial scholarship 46–7, 55, 133,
    148, 150
Potter, Elizabeth 45, 58, 62
Potter, Jonathan 102–3, 107, 111–12
power 2, 55–9, 85, 149, 162, 205, 211
profitability 70–2, 76–9, 88, 138, 191,
    195, 205–7, 212, 219
psychology 102, 116, 181
publishing industry, academic 19, 148, 162

queer see LGBTQ; see sexuality

'race' 33, 46–7, 52, 55, 59, 96, 133–4,
    136–7, 153, 171, 208
racism 29, 46, 133, 142–3, 171, 208

reading 188–9
Reed, Kate 96, 104
REF 5, 87, 197, 214, 217; *see also*
    research assessment mechanisms
research assessment mechanisms 154, 180,
    196; *see also* REF
Revista de Estudos Feministas 140, 145
Rich, Adrienne 31, 120
Roque, Ricardo 154, 166
Rose, Hilary 46, 142, 210

Sachs, Judyth 71–2, 166, 194
Santos, Ana Cristina 171, 172, 181, 197
science: definition of 6, 44–64; *see also*
    demarcation (of scientificity)
Science and Technology Studies *see* STS
Scott, Joan 149
semi-periphery, academic 150–72
sexism 61, 78, 81, 86, 105, 115, 133, 135,
    183, 204, 208, 213
sexuality 59, 133–6, 145, 151
sexuality studies *see* LGBTQ studies
shame 122–3, 137, 157–8, 160, 195
Sifaki, Aggeliki 194–5
Simbürger, Elisabeth 96
Skeggs 62, 84, 87, 114, 213–14
sociology 1, 33, 38, 52–3, 80, 106, 108,
    115, 134, 145, 202
Sócrates, José 152
Sousa Santos, Boaventura de 151–2,
    159–60, 166–7
Soviet Union, former 167
space 59–60, 148, 150, 154, 157, 159
Spain 31–3, 158, 159–60, 171–2
Stanley, Liz 36, 57, 58, 59, 81, 86
Stöckelová, Tereza 149, 153, 167, 202
Strathern, Marilyn 205, 211, 215
STS 4, 6, 10, 15, 45, 52–5, 58, 61, 133,
    143, 219
Sweden 2, 11, 78–9, 89, 154, 169–70
Switzerland 152

Taiwan 33, 34, 86, 95, 149, 167
Tavares, Manuela 82–3, 172

teaching *see* classrooms
teasing 80–1, 87, 89, 105–6, 133, 135,
    180
textbooks 32, 37, 96, 115, 138–9
thinking 189
time 150, 154, 157, 159
Times, The 204
Torres, Anália 180
trade unions 217
translation 12
truth-spot (or truth-point) 156–7,
    166
Tuin, Iris Van der 70–2

UK (United Kingdom) 2, 5, 11, 29, 30, 31,
    32, 34, 38, 71, 78–9, 89, 95–6, 102,
    105, 115, 116, 145, 158–61, 163, 167,
    169–71, 183, 197, 203, 217, 219
UMAR 116, 181
United Nations 163
US (United States of America) 2, 5, 11, 30,
    31, 33, 34, 58, 73, 74, 75, 84, 87, 95,
    102, 131–2, 152, 157–61, 169–70

Vale de Almeida, Miguel 152, 171
viva, PhD 11,19, 75, 80, 85, 97, 120–1,
    129–31, 139–40, 144–5, 156

Wall, Karin 197
Weeks, Kathi 215–18
west, hegemony of the 148–50,
    167–70
Wetherell, Margaret 203–4, 218
WGFS: definition of 6–7;
    institutionalisation of 28–30,
    36–8, 158, 210, 212; individualised
    institutionalisation of 82–3; naming of
    6–7, 34–35
Whelan, Emma 10, 19, 96–7
whiteness 152–3
Wise, Sue, 170
Woolgar, Steve 10, 132–3

Yugoslavia, former 32